365 Days

to Healing,
Blessings,
and Freedom

T.D. JAKES

Devotional & Journal

365

Days

to Healing,
Blessings,
and Freedom

This title previously published as T.D. Jakes 365 Day Devotional & Journal.

Compiled by Jan Sherman

Destiny Image® Publishers, Inc.

P.O. Box 310
Shippensburg, PA 17257-0310

"Speaking to the Purposes of God for This Generation
and for the Generations to Come"

ISBN10: 0-7684-2445-3
ISBN 13: 978-0-7684-2445-4

For Worldwide Distribution
Printed in the U.S.A.

This book and all other Destiny Image, Revival Press, MercyPlace, Fresh Bread, Destiny Image Fiction, and Treasure House books are available at Christian bookstores and distributors worldwide.

2 3 4 5 6 7 8 9 10 / 10 09 08 07

For a U.S. bookstore nearest you, call
1-800-722-6774.
For more information on foreign distributors, call
717-532-3040.
Or reach us on the Internet:
www.destinyimage.com

And, behold, there was a woman which had a spirit of infirmity eighteen years, and was bowed together, and could in no wise lift up herself. And when Jesus saw her, He called her to Him, and said unto her, Woman, thou art loosed from thine infirmity. Luke 13:11-12

The Holy Spirit periodically lets us catch a glimpse of the personal testimony of one of the patients of the Divine Physician Himself. This woman's dilemma is her own, but perhaps you will find some point of relativity between her case history and your own. She could be like someone you know or have known; she could even be like you.

There are three major characters in this story. These characters are the person, the problem and the prescription. It is important to remember that for every person, there will be a problem. Even more importantly, for every problem, our God has a prescription!

Jesus' opening statement to the problem in this woman's life is not a recommendation for counseling—it is a challenging command! Often much more is involved in maintaining deliverance than just discussing past trauma. Jesus did not counsel what should have been commanded. I am not, however, against seeking the counsel of godly men. On the contrary, the Scriptures say:

> *Blessed is the man that walketh not in the counsel of the ungodly, nor standeth in the way of sinners, nor sitteth in the seat of the scornful (Psalm 1:1).*

> *Where no counsel is, the people fall: but in the multitude of counsellors there is safety (Proverbs 11:14).*

What I want to make clear is that after you have analyzed the condition, after you have understood its origin, it will still take the authority of God's Word to put the past under your feet! This woman was suffering as a result of something that attacked her 18 years earlier. I wonder if you can relate to the long-range aftereffects of past pain. This kind of trauma is as fresh to the victim today as it was the day it occurred. Although the problem may be rooted in the past, the prescription is a present word from God! The Word is the same yesterday, today and forevermore (see Heb. 13:8)! That is to say, the word you are hearing today is able to heal your yesterday!

> **Although the problem may be rooted in the past, the prescription is a present word from God!**

[Handwritten notes:]

though we understand & analyzing the origin and root cause of our problems - it still will take the authority of God's word to put (it past us - resolved.

A present word from God is needed to deal w/ pain!

But if we walk in the light, as He is in the light, we have fellowship one with another, and the blood of Jesus Christ His Son cleanseth us from all sin. 1 John 1:7

The blood is the only element in the body that reaches, affects, and fuels all other parts of the body. This rich, reddish-purple elixir flows silently through the cardiovascular system like high-powered cars moving on interstate highways. It carries the cargo of much-needed oxygen molecules and nutrients that are necessary to sustain life in every cell of the body. If the blood is restricted long enough from any member of the body, that member will internally asphyxiate, and begin to change colors. Its asphyxiated cells can quickly die—even without an external assailant—for their affliction is the result of *internal deprivation*.

Every member, every limb and organ in the human body, needs the blood. Along with its culinary duty of delivering soluble dietary contents throughout the body, our blood has the additional responsibility of functioning as a paramedic. Its white blood cells stand ready to attack adverse intruders in the form of bacteria or foreign cells, or any other foreign substance that may try to disrupt the vitality of the body. The white blood cells are the body's "militia." These cells are uniquely equipped to fight off attacking bacteria and expel it from the body—stripping it of its power and robbing it of its spoils.

> *For as we have many members in one body, and all members have not the same office: so we, being many, are one body in Christ, and every one members one of another (Romans 12:4-5).*

The physical body echoes and illustrates the power of the blood in the Church, the mystical Body of Christ. Every member of the Body of Christ—regardless of morality, maturity, or position—needs the life-giving blood of Jesus. Without the blood, we cease to have the proof of our sonship. Isn't the blood what physicians test to determine and verify who is the father of a child? Without the blood, we are only bastard sons camouflaged as real sons. Without His blood, we are pseudo-heirs trying to receive the promises reserved for the legitimate sons of God!

> Without the blood, we cease to have the proof of our sonship

To every thing there is a season, and a time to every purpose under the heaven: a time to be born, and a time to die; a time to plant, and a time to pluck up that which is planted. Ecclesiastes 3:1-2

We will always have seasons of struggles and testing. There are times when everything we attempt to do will seem to go wrong. Regardless of our prayers and consecration, adversity will come. We can't pray away God's seasons. The Lord has a purpose in not allowing us to be fruitful all the time…. When God sends the chilly winds of winter to blow on our circumstances, we must still trust Him. In spite of our dislike for the blinding winds and the icy grip of winter seasons, there is a purpose for these temporary inconveniences.

The apostle Paul calls such times "…light affliction, which is but for a moment…" (2 Cor. 4:17). I say, "This too shall pass!" Some things you are not meant to change, but to survive. So if you can't alter it, then outlive it! Be like a tree. In the frosty arms of winter the forest silently refurbishes its strength, preparing for its next season of fruitfulness. Its branches rocking in the winds, the sap and substance of the tree go underground. It is not good-bye, though; in the spring it will push its way up into the budding of a new experience. Temporary setbacks create opportunities for fresh commitment and renewal. If you were to record your accomplishments, you would notice that they were seasonal. There are seasons of sunshine as well as rain. Pleasure comes, then pain, and vice versa. Each stage has its own purpose.

One of the greatest struggles I have encountered is the temptation to make permanent decisions based on temporary circumstances. Someone once said, "Patience is a tree whose root is bitter, but its fruit is sweet." The reward of patience is reflected in gradually not having to amend your amendments. Temporary circumstances do not always require action. I have found that prayer brings us into patience. Patience results from trust. We cannot trust a God we don't talk with. Do not misunderstand me; God needs men and women who are decisive. However, every situation shouldn't get an immediate reaction. Prayer is the seasoning of good judgment. Without it, our decisions will not be palatable.

> $\mathcal{T}$emporary circum-stances do not always require action. I have found that prayer brings us into patience.

Handwritten margin notes:
Some things are not meant to be changed—but to survive

← temporary setbacks create opportunities for fresh commitment and renewal.

HOPE FOR HURTING WOMEN

For God so loved the world, that He gave His only begotten Son, that whosoever believeth in Him should not perish, but have everlasting life. John 3:16

DAY 4

Healing cannot come to a desperate person rummaging through other people's lives. One of the first things that a hurting person needs to do is break the habit of using other people as a narcotic to numb the dull aching of an inner void. The more you medicate the symptoms, the less chance you have of allowing God to heal you. The other destructive tendency that can exist with any abuse is the person must keep increasing the dosage. Avoid addictive, obsessive relationships. If you are becoming increasingly dependent upon anything other than God to create a sense of wholeness in your life, then you are abusing your relationships. Clinging to people is far different from loving them. It is not so much a statement of your love for them as it is a crying out of your need for them. Like lust, it is intensely selfish. It is taking and not giving. Love is giving. God is love. God proved His love not by His need of us, but by His giving to us....

The Scriptures plainly show that the infirmed woman who touched Jesus in the crowd had tried to lift herself. People who stand on the outside can easily criticize and assume that the infirmed woman lacks effort and fortitude. That is not always the case. Some situations in which we can find ourselves defy willpower. We feel unable to change. The Scriptures say that she "could in no wise lift up herself." That implies she had employed various means of self-ministry. Isn't it amazing how the same people who lift up countless others, often cannot lift themselves? This type of person may be a tower of faith and prayer for others, but impotent when it comes to her own limitations. That person may be the one others rely upon. Sometimes we esteem others more important than ourselves. We always become the martyr. It is wonderful to be self-sacrificing but watch out for self-disdain! If we don't apply some of the medicine that we use on others to strengthen ourselves, our patients will be healed and we will be dying.

> *If we don't apply some of the medicine that we use on others to strengthen ourselves, our patients will be healed and we will be dying.*

Elect according to the foreknowledge of God the Father, through sanctification of the Spirit, unto obedience and sprinkling of the blood of Jesus Christ: grace unto you, and peace, be multiplied. 1 Peter 1:2

We did not need the blood only for when we cried out to the Lord to come into our hearts by faith and rescue us from impending danger. On the contrary, we *still need that same blood today*. All our strength and nourishment and every promise and miracle must flow to us *through the blood*. Satan hates the blood—not only because it redeemed us, but also because it continues to give us life from day to day!

> *How much more shall the blood of Christ, who through the eternal Spirit offered Himself without spot to God, purge your conscience from dead works to serve the living God? And for this cause He is the mediator of the new testament, that by means of death, for the redemption of the transgressions that were under the first testament, they which are called might receive the promise of eternal inheritance (Hebrews 9:14-15).*

We have lost our teaching of the blood in this age of Pentecostalism (of which I am adamantly a part). We have learned about the Spirit of God, but we failed to teach believers about the blood. Consequently, we have produced a generation of believers who are empowered by the Spirit but do not feel forgiven! They are empowered, yet they are insecure. They are operating in the gifts, but living in guilt!

Oh, hear me today! The blood must be preached. Without it we have no life. No, the preaching of the blood will not weaken the Church! To the contrary, it will relieve us of a pre-paid debt. Why are we wasting the power of God on the problems of our past? *The blood has already totally destroyed the past bondages that held us down*! It was through the eternal Spirit of God that Jesus was able to offer up His blood. The Spirit always refers us back to the blood. *There can be no Pentecost where there is no Passover*!

> *All our strength and nourishment and every promise and miracle must flow to us through the blood.*

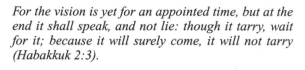
Then he answered and spake unto me, saying, This is the word of the Lord unto Zerubbabel, saying, Not by might, nor by power, but by My spirit, saith the Lord of hosts. Zechariah 4:6

For the vision is yet for an appointed time, but at the end it shall speak, and not lie: though it tarry, wait for it; because it will surely come, it will not tarry (Habakkuk 2:3).

Our struggle is in waiting for the appointment we have with destiny. Perhaps I should first point out that God is a God of order; He does everything by appointment. He has set a predetermined appointment to bring to pass His promise in our lives. An appointment is a meeting already set up. Through the many tempestuous winds that blow against our lives, God has already prepared a way of escape. Our comfort is in knowing that we have an appointment with destiny. It is the inner awareness that makes us realize that in spite of temporary circumstances, God has a present time of deliverance.

We are enveloped in peace when we know that nothing the enemy does can abort the plan of God for our lives. Greater still is the peace that comes from knowing we cannot rush God's timing. When the Lord speaks a word into our lives, it is like a seed. It takes time for a seed to sprout. God knows when we have reached the time of germination. Our confidence is in God's seed. When the promise has grown in the fertile ground of a faith-filled heart and reached the time of maturation, it will come to pass. It will be a direct result of the presence of God. It will not be by human might or power, but by the Spirit of the Lord (see Zech. 4:6). The psalmist David said, "My times are in Thy hand" (Ps. 31:15a). For me there is a sense of tranquility that comes from resting in the Lord. His appointment for us is predetermined. There is a peace that comes from knowing God has included us in His plan—even the details.

There is a peace that comes from knowing God has included us in His plan—even the details.

The Spirit of the Lord is upon Me, because He hath anointed Me to preach the gospel to the poor; He hath sent Me to heal the brokenhearted, to preach deliverance to the captives, and recovering of sight to the blind, to set at liberty them that are bruised. Luke 4:18

Many things can engender disappointment and depression. In the case of the infirmed woman who touched Jesus in the crowd, a spirit of infirmity had gripped her life. A spirit can manifest itself in many forms. For some it may be low self-esteem caused by child abuse, rape, wife abuse or divorce. I realize that these are natural problems, but they are rooted in spiritual ailments. One of the many damaging things that can affect us today is divorce, particularly among women, who often look forward to a happy relationship. Little girls grow up playing with Barbie and Ken dolls, dressing doll babies and playing house. Young girls lie in bed reading romance novels, while little boys play ball and ride bicycles in the park. Whenever a woman is indoctrinated to think success is romance and then experiences the trauma of a failed relationship, she comes to a painful awakening. Divorce is not merely separating; it is the tearing apart of what was once joined together. Whenever something is torn, it does not heal easily. But Jesus can heal a broken or torn heart!…

Approximately five out of ten marriages end in divorce. Those broken homes leave a trail of broken dreams, people and children. Only the Master can heal these victims in the times in which we live. He can treat the long-term effects of this tragedy. One of the great healing balms of the Holy Spirit is forgiveness. To forgive is to break the link between you and your past. Sadly enough, many times the person hardest to forgive is the one in the mirror. Although they rage loudly about others, people secretly blame themselves for a failed relationship. Regardless of who you hold responsible, there is no healing in blame! When you begin to realize that your past does not necessarily dictate the outcome of your future, then you can release the hurt. It is impossible to inhale new air until you exhale the old. I pray that as you continue reading, God would give the grace of releasing where you have been so you can receive what God has for you now. Exhale, then inhale; there is more for you.

> *W*henever something is torn, it does not heal easily. But Jesus can heal a broken or torn heart!

For through Him we both have access by one Spirit unto the Father. Now therefore ye are no more strangers and foreigners, but fellowcitizens with the saints, and of the household of God. Ephesians 2:18-19

There is a devilish prejudice in the Church that denies the blood to its uncomely members. If a person has a failure in an area we relate to because we have a similar weakness, we immediately praise God for the blood that cleanses us from all unrighteousness. If they are unfortunate enough to fail where we are very strong, then *we condemn them*. We tie a string around those members to mark them, and we deny them the blood.

The spirit of Cain is loose in the Church! We have spilled our brother's blood because he is different, because his skin or his sin is different from ours. Untie them right now, in the name of the Lord, and restore to them the opportunity to experience the life that only comes to the flesh through the blood. *Without the blood all flesh dies*—black, white, rich, poor, homosexual, heterosexual, drug addict, or alcoholic. Without the blood of Christ to save it and the Holy Spirit to empower it, no flesh can be saved.

But by the blood of the Lamb, any man, regardless of his failures or past sin, can come equally and unashamedly to the foot of the cross and allow the drops of Jesus' blood to invigorate the soul that sin has lacerated and destroyed. We will never experience massive revival until we allow *all sinners* to come to the fountain filled with blood, drawn from Emmanuel's veins!

Have you ever been guilty of having a condescending attitude about another person's weakness? I am ashamed to admit it, but I have. How can we dare to think we can access the soul-cleansing blood that delivers us from the cesspool of our secret sins, and then look down on another member of Christ's Body in disdain? *How can we forbid them access* to the only answer to the massive problems that consume our generation?

Healing, Blessings, and Freedom

> We tie a string around those members to mark them, and we deny them the blood.

I am God, and there is none like Me, declaring the end from the beginning, and from ancient times the things that are not yet done, saying, My counsel shall stand, and I will do all My pleasure: calling a ravenous bird from the east, the man that executeth My counsel from a far country: yea, I have spoken it, I will also bring it to pass; I have purposed it, I will also do it. Isaiah 46:9b-11

I can remember as a very small child following close behind my mother, an educator in the public school system. She was often asked to speak at luncheons and banquets....We were traveling from one of these events when I said to my mother, "Today, I travel with you and listen while you speak, but the time will come when you will travel with me and I will speak!" What was strange was this prophetic utterance came from the mouth of a then-devilish little six-year-old who, though very precocious, was nevertheless an ordinary child who would one day have a supernatural encounter with God!

I don't know how, at that early age, I knew I had an appointment with destiny, but I somehow sensed that God had a purpose for my life. I earnestly believe that everyone is predestined to accomplish certain things for the Lord. Somewhere in the recesses of your mind there should be an inner knowing that directs you toward an expected end. For me, it is this awareness that enables me to push myself up out of the bed and keep fighting for survival. You must be the kind of tenacious person who can speak to the enemy and tell him, "My life can't end without certain things coming to pass. It's not over until God says, 'It's over!'"

I don't think I really knew I would be a minister. I just felt that I would do something meaningful with my life. Twice in my childhood I spoke prophetically about things that have since come to pass. I can't say that everything I encountered in life pushed me toward my destiny. On the contrary, there were sharp contradictions as I went through my tempestuous teens. Still, I had that inner knowing, too deep to be explained. I want you to know that even if circumstances contradict purpose, purpose will always prevail! It is the opposition that clearly demonstrates to you that God is working. If the fulfillment of the prophecy was without obstruction, you would assume you had merely received serendipity. However, when all indicators say it is impossible and it still occurs, then you know God has done it again.

> *If the fulfillment of the prophecy was without obstruction, you would assume you had merely received serendipity.*

I shall not die, but live, and declare the works of the Lord. Psalm 118:17

Perhaps one of the more serious indictments against our civilization is our flagrant disregard for the welfare of our children. Child abuse, regardless of whether it is physical, sexual or emotional, is a terrible issue for an innocent mind to wrestle with. It is horrifying to think that little children who survive the peril of the streets, the public schools and the aggravated society in which we live, come home to be abused in what should be a haven. Recent statistics suggest that three in five young girls in this country have been or will be sexually assaulted. If that many are reported, I shudder to think of those that never are reported but are covered with a shroud of secrecy.

If by chance you are a pastor, please realize that these figures are actually faces in your choir, committees, etc. They reflect a growing amount of our congregational needs. Although this book [*Woman, Thou Art Loosed!*] focuses on women, many men also have been abused as children. I fear that God will judge us for our blatant disregard of this need in our messages, ministries and prayers. I even would suggest that our silence contributes to the shame and secrecy that satan attaches to these victimized persons. Whenever I think on these issues, I am reminded of what my mother used to say. I was forever coming home with a scratch or cut from schoolyard play. My mother would take the Band-Aid off, clean the wound and say, "Things that are covered don't heal well." Mother was right. Things that are covered do not heal well.

Perhaps Jesus was thinking on this order when He called the infirmed woman to come forward. It takes a lot of courage even in church today to receive ministry in sensitive areas. The Lord, though, is the kind of physician who can pour on the healing oil. Uncover your wounds in His presence and allow Him to gently heal the injuries. One woman found healing in the hem of His garment (see Mark 5:25-29). There is a balm in Gilead (see Jer. 8:22)!

Things that are covered do not heal well.

Unto Adam also and to his wife did the Lord God make coats of skins, and clothed them. Genesis 3:21

The blood of Christ is God's antidote to the plague of sin that has attacked the world and, yes, even the Body of Christ! We may have different symptoms, just as a flu virus may produce different symptoms in different people, but we all suffer from a fatal infection of sin! Sin has affected us differently according to our backgrounds and circumstances, but regardless of the symptoms, it is still the same disease. There is but one cure: the blood....

We have presented no solution to the tragedies of life that afflict our members. We have offered them no balm for the injuries that come from inner flaws and failure. Because we have offered no provision for the sons and daughters who *fall,* many of our Adams and our Eves are hiding in the bushes. Our fallen brethren hear our message, but they cannot come out to a preacher or a crowd that merely points out their nakedness and has nothing in hand to cover them. We need to offer the perfect sacrifice to the sons of God as well as to the world. Adam was God's son. He was fallen and he was foolish, but he was the son of God!

> *Which was the son of Enos, which was the son of Seth, which was the son of Adam, which was the son of God (Luke 3:38).*

The blood of Christ will even reach the falling, faltering son who hides in the bushes of our churches. He has fig leaves all around him. He is illicit and immoral. Who will walk the cool of the garden to find him? Even harder yet, who will walk the heat of the jungle to cover him? Many of us are taking the first walk to *discover the fallen*, but they have not taken the deeper walk to *cover the fallen*. How can this son stand naked and unashamed if we offer no sanctity or holiness in exchange for his failure, yet have great mercy for our own shortcomings? When God covered Adam and Eve's nakedness, *He covered what He discovered* with the bloody skins of an innocent animal, giving Himself the first sacrifice to atone for their sin.

> *Who will walk the heat of the jungle to cover him?*

And Adam knew his wife again; and she bare a son, and called his name Seth: For God, said she, hath appointed me another seed instead of Abel, whom Cain slew. Genesis 4:25

It is so important for parents to instill a sense of destiny in their children. Once they realize that they have immeasurable potential, there is no stopping them. I am not saying that they won't deviate from the path—all of us have done that. But thank God they have been given a path to deviate from....

In Genesis, the Lord promised Eve a seed. He said, "And I will put enmity between thee and the woman, and between thy seed and her seed; it shall bruise thy head, and thou shalt bruise His heel" (Gen. 3:15). When Eve produced what she may have thought to be the promised seed, there were real problems.... In the heat of rage, Cain killed his brother.... Now her eldest son was a criminal on the run, and her younger son was snuffed out in the prime of life.... She was supposed to be the mother of all living and all she had raised was a corpse and its murderer.

But God unwrapped the blanket of failure from around her and blessed her with another son. His name she called "Seth." *Seth* means "substituted."...Suddenly, as she held her new baby in her arms, she began to realize that God is sovereign. If He decrees a thing, it will surely come to pass.... Eve called her third son "Seth," for she understood that if God makes a promise to bless someone, He will find a way! Even if it means appointing a substitute, He will perform His promise.

God's purpose was not aborted when Cain killed Abel. In spite of the fact that life has its broken places, ultimately everything God has ever said will come to pass.... Satan tries to assassinate the will of God in your life. Nevertheless, He who has begun a good work in you shall perform it until the day of Jesus Christ (see Phil. 1:6). When we suffer loss like Eve did, there is a feeling of forlornness. However, you cannot allow past circumstances to abort future opportunity. If you have experienced loss in your life, I tell you that God has a way of restoring things you thought you would never see again.

> God has a way of restoring things you thought you would never see again.

Do not conform any longer to the pattern of this world, but be transformed by the renewing of your mind. Then you will be able to test and approve what God's will is— His good, pleasing and perfect will. Romans 12:2 (NIV)

Even when a victim survives, there is still a casualty. It is the death of trust. Surely you realize that little girls tend to be trusting and unsuspicious. When those who should nurture and protect them violate that trust through illicit behavior, multiple scars result. It is like programming a computer with false information; you can get out of it only what has been programmed into it. When a man tells a little girl that his perverted acts are normal, she has no reason not to believe that what she is being taught is true. She is devoted to him, allowing him to fondle her or further misappropriate his actions toward her. Usually the abuser is someone very close, with access to the child at vulnerable times. Fear is also a factor, as many children lie down with the cold taste of fear in their mouths. They believe he could and would kill them for divulging his liberties against them. Some, as the victims of rape, feel physically powerless to wrestle with the assailant.

What kind of emotions might this kind of conduct bring out in the later life of this person? I am glad you asked. It would be easy for this kind of little girl to grow into a young lady who has difficulty trusting anyone! Maybe she learns to deal with the pain inside by getting attention in illicit ways. Drug rehabilitation centers and prisons are full of adults who were abused children needing attention....

We frame our references around our own experiences. If those experiences are distorted, our ability to comprehend spiritual truths can be off center. I know that may sound very negative for someone who is in that circumstance. What do you do when you have been poorly programmed by life's events? I've got good news! You can re-program your mind through the Word of God.

> $\mathcal{Y}$ou can re-program your mind through the Word of God.

But Christ being come an high priest of good things to come, by a greater and more perfect tabernacle, not made with hands, that is to say, not of this building; neither by the blood of goats and calves, but by His own blood He entered in once into the holy place, having obtained eternal redemption for us. Hebrews 9:11-12

Before Adam could receive the covering God had provided, though, he had to disrobe himself of what he had contrived. It is in this process that many believers are trapped.... Adam stripped himself before a holy God, admitted his tragic sins, and still maintained his position as a son in the presence of God. Adam and Eve realized at that moment that *the only solution for their sin was in the perfect provision of their loving God*. That same loving God now reaches out to us *as we are*, and refashions us into what we should become!

Adam stood as I do, *in the warm skins of a freshly slain sacrifice* that made it possible for him to continue to live. It was actually no more Adam who lived; rather, he was now living the life of the innocent lamb. Just as surely as the innocent lamb had taken Adam's place in death, Adam continued to live on, wrapped in the coverings of the lamb's life! Can you understand more clearly what Paul means when he says, "accepted in the beloved"? (See Ephesians 1:6.) If Adam were seen out from under the covering of those bloody skins, he could not be accepted. But because of the shedding of innocent blood, there was remission of sin for him!

We hear no further mention of blame or guilt concerning the first family as they walked away from the worst moment in the history of humanity. Why? They were wrapped and protected in the provision of God. We can find no more arguments, fault-finding, or condemnation in Scripture. I have not read where Adam blamed Eve anymore. Neither did Eve judge Adam, for they both realized that *had it not been for the blood*, neither would have been there.

We too need to have this knowledge—regardless of the differences in our specific flaws; regardless of whom we would want to blame or belittle. If the blood had failed to reach the liar, then he would be as lost as the child molester! The symptoms are different, but the disease and its prognosis are the same. The disease is sin, the wage or prognosis is death, and the antidote prescribed is the blood and the blood alone. Never forget the blood, for without it we have no good news at all!

> *Never forget the blood, for without it we have no good news at all!*

If a man die, shall he live again? all the days of my appointed time will I wait, till my change come. Job 14:14

We come into this world fully cognizant of the fact that we have a limited amount of time. We don't live here for very long before we are confronted with the cold realities of death…. Yet what disturbs me most is not the quantity of life, but the quality of life. Simply stated, when death comes to push me through its window from time into eternity, I want to feel as though I accomplished something worthwhile. I want to feel that my life made some positive statement….

It would be terrible to look back over your life and see that the many times you thought your request was denied was actually only delayed. Life will always present broken places, places of struggle and conflict. If you have a divine purpose and life has put you on hold, hang on! Stay on the line until life gets back to you. If you believe as I do, then it's worth the wait to receive your answer from the Lord.

> *I waited patiently for the Lord; and He inclined unto me, and heard my cry. He brought me up also out of an horrible pit, out of the miry clay, and set my feet upon a rock, and established my goings. And He hath put a new song in my mouth, even praise unto our God: many shall see it, and fear, and shall trust in the Lord (Psalm 40:1-3).*

The real test of faith is in facing the silence of being on hold. Those are the suspended times of indecision. Have you ever faced those times when your life seemed stagnant? Have you felt you were on the verge of something phenomenal, that you were waiting for that particular breakthrough that seemed to be taunting you by making you wait? All of us have faced days that seemed as though God had forgotten us. These are the moments that feel like eternity. These silent coaches take your patience into strenuous calisthenics. Patience gets a workout when God's answer is no answer. In other words, God's answer is not always yes or no; sometimes He says, "Not now!"

> God's answer is not always yes or no; sometimes He says, "Not now!"

Sanctify them through Thy truth: Thy word is truth. John 17:17

You can have a complete metamorphosis through the Word of God. It has been my experience as a pastor who does extensive counseling in my own ministry and abroad, that many abused people, women in particular, tend to flock to legalistic churches who see God primarily as a disciplinarian. Many times the concept of fatherhood for them is a harsh code of ethics. This type of domineering ministry may appeal to those who are performance-oriented. I understand that morality is important in Christianity; however, there is a great deal of difference between morality and legalism. It is important that God not be misrepresented. He is a balanced God, not an extremist....

The glory of God is manifested only when there is a balance between grace and truth. Religion doesn't transform. Legalism doesn't transform. For the person who feels dirty, harsh rules could create a sense of self-righteousness. God doesn't have to punish you to heal you. Jesus has already prayed for you....

Believe the Word of God and be free. Jesus our Lord was a great emancipator of the oppressed. It does not matter whether someone has been oppressed socially, sexually or racially; our Lord is an eliminator of distinctions....

That is to say, God is no respecter of persons. He tears down barriers that would promote prejudice and separation in the Body of Christ. Yet it is important also to note that while there is no distinction in the manner in which we receive any of those groups, there should be an appreciation for the uniqueness of the groups' individuality. There is a racial, social and sexual uniqueness that we should not only accept, but also appreciate. It is cultural rape to teach other cultures or races that the only way to worship God is the way another race or culture does.

> God doesn't have to punish you to heal you. Jesus has already prayed for you.

But God commendeth His love toward us, in that, while we were yet sinners, Christ died for us. Romans 5:8

I can't help but wonder what would happen if we would ever love like Jesus loves…. As we peel away layer by layer, as we become more comfortable with our God and our own humanity, we become increasingly transparent. We are surprised to find that there are not nearly as many significant differences between us as we were led to believe.

Perhaps we can learn how to be as open about our failures as we are about our successes. Without that kind of honesty, we create a false image that causes others to needlessly struggle. When others hear our one-sided testimony of successes with no failure, they become discouraged…. They feel that they don't qualify to receive what God has done for us because we have falsified the records and failed to tell the truth!

Adam found himself stripped of his fig leaves. He stood naked before his wife and his God. Those are two important areas. We must wrestle to achieve a level of honesty that will keep us from being estranged from the ones we are connected to. We have to love and be loved by someone to the degree that we can say, *This is who I am, and it is all that I am. Love me and be patient with me. There is no telling what I will become, but today this is who I am.*

When you find someone who can see your flaws and your underdeveloped character, *and love you in spite of it all*, you are blessed. If the only way you can love me is after I have perfected my imperfections, then you really don't love me. As I progress I will always wonder, "Do you love me for who I am?"

Many marriages seem to pass the test as long as both parties are perfect in the major areas. But when one party becomes defective in one of those major areas, the relationship is often destroyed. God was too wise to wait until you perfected the defective. He loved you while you were unlovable so you would never have to hide in the bushes again! He has loved you with an everlasting love!

> **He loved you while you were unlovable so you would never have to hide in the bushes again!**

Wait on the Lord: be of good courage, and He shall strengthen thine heart: wait, I say, on the Lord.
Psalm 27:14

It is God's timing that we must learn. He synchronizes His answers to accomplish His purpose. Recently, while traveling on a major American airline, we were told that the plane could not land at its scheduled time. Evidently the air traffic controller instructed that we should wait in the air. What a strange place to have to wait—in the air! I have often felt like that aircraft suspended in the air when God says, "Wait!" Then the captain spoke into the PA system. He said, "We are going to assume a holding pattern until further instructions come from the tower." After some time, a few rather intoxicated passengers began to question the traffic controller's decision. Perhaps we were all concerned. It's just that some had their concern lubricated with several stiff shots of rum!

The anxious looks and acidic remarks that came from the crowd subsided as the stewardess quickly eased people's fears. She informed several worried passengers that the planes always carry enough fuel to withstand the demands of these kinds of delays. There was a calm assurance on the faces of the attendants. I would have to attribute it to the fact that they had prepared for a delay. I began to wonder if we as the children of God shouldn't be better prepared for those times in our lives when God speaks from His throne, "Assume a holding pattern until further notice." The question is not always, "Do you have enough faith to receive?" Sometimes it is this: "Do you have enough faith to assume a holding pattern and wait for the fulfillment of the promise?"

You feel a deep sense of contentment when you know God has not forgotten you. I will never forget the time I went through a tremendous struggle. I thought it was an emergency. I thought I had to have an answer right then. I learned that God isn't easily spooked by what I call an emergency.

> Do you have enough faith to assume a holding pattern and wait for the fulfillment of the promise?

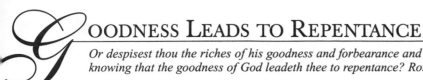
Or despisest thou the riches of his goodness and forbearance and longsuffering; not knowing that the goodness of God leadeth thee to repentance? Romans 2:4

It sounds mushy, and to the religious zealot it may sound too loose and simplistic, but we need to remember that *it is the goodness of God that leads to repentance* (see Rom. 2:4). Repentance doesn't come because of the scare tactics and threats of raging ministers who need mercy themselves. Repentance comes because of the unfailing love of a perfect God, a God who cares for the cracked vases that others would have discarded. It is His great love that causes a decision to be made in the heart: *I must live for Him!*

There is no way that you can see Him stand with you when all others forsake you, and not want to please Him! There is no way you can weather a storm in His loving arms and not say, "I am Yours, O Lord. Such as I have I give to You." One gaze into His holiness will bring the sinner crashing to the floor on bended knees, confessing and forsaking, wrestling and controlling every issue that would have engulfed him before his wandering eye affixed itself on the manifold graces of God!

In other words, God is too good for us to experience His love and then be contented to abuse that love. *Accepting the rejected is not the weakness of the gospel; it is its strength!...*

As we hold out our arms do, they will come—the halt and the lame, the deaf and dumb. They will need much of the Word and much time before their marriages cease to tremble and their self-images improve. They will have flashbacks and relapses, and require intensive care. Yet we swing wide the doors of ministry and admit, at the risk of being blatantly naked, that *most of our doctors have at one time been patients*, and that many of them are still being treated. Still we say, "Come," for we are not the medicine—it is Christ who is the cure!

To the overlooked and the castaway, to the downtrodden and the wayfaring, we cry, "Come into this shelter; come out of the cold. If nowhere else, and by no one else, you are *accepted in the beloved!*"

> **God cares for the cracked vases that others would have discarded.**

There is neither Jew nor Greek [racial], *there is neither bond nor free* [social], *there is neither male nor female* [sexual]: *for ye are all one in Christ Jesus. Galatians 3:28*

Unity should not come at the expense of uniqueness of expression. We should also tolerate variance in social classes. It is wonderful to teach prosperity as long as it is understood that the Church is not an elite organization for spiritual yuppies only, one that excludes other social classes.

If uniqueness is to be appreciated racially and socially, it is certainly to be appreciated sexually. Male and female are one in Christ. Yet they are unique and that uniqueness is not to be tampered with. Let the male be masculine and the female be feminine! It is a sin for a man to misrepresent himself by conducting himself as a woman. I am not merely speaking of homosexuality. I am also talking about men who are feminine in their mannerisms. Many of these men may not be homosexual in their behavior, but the Bible says that they must be healed of feminine mannerisms, or vice versa. It is equally sad to see a masculine woman. Nevertheless, God wants them healed, not hated!

> *Know ye not that the unrighteous shall not inherit the kingdom of God? Be not deceived: neither fornicators, nor idolaters, nor adulterers, nor effeminate, nor abusers of themselves with mankind...* (1 Corinthians 6:9).

Strong's #3120 "*malakos* (mal-ak-os'); of uncertain affinity; soft, i.e. fine (clothing); figuratively, a catamite:—effeminate, soft" (*Strong's Exhaustive Concordance of the Bible*, Hendrickson Publishers, n.d.).

I realize that these behavioral disorders are areas that require healing and prayer. My point is simply that unity does not negate uniqueness. God is saying, "I don't want men to lose their masculine uniqueness." This is true racially, socially and sexually. God can appreciate our differences and still create unity. It is like a conductor who can orchestrate extremely different instruments into producing a harmonious, unified sound. Together we produce a sound of harmony that expresses the multifaceted character of God.

> God can appreciate our differences and still create unity.... Together we produce a sound of harmony that expresses the multifaceted character of God.

Work out your own salvation with fear and trembling. For it is God which worketh in you both to will and to do of His good pleasure. Philippians 2:12b-13

God is too good for us to experience His love and then be contented to abuse that love. *Accepting the rejected is not the weakness of the gospel; it is its strength*! No, we cannot shelter hardened criminals who are content to live as outlaws from the Word of the Lord. But there is a great deal of difference between the cold callousness of a rebellious heart and the deeply troubled heart of a transforming Christian whose whispered prayer is, "God, save me from myself." It is to the distraught heart that seeks so desperately for a place of refuge that we extend soft hands and tender words....

How can we then define the Church, with its rising divorce rate and afflicted leadership? Doesn't the Church need to bathe itself in its own message? Yes, it does. But then who said the Church would not? This "dippity-doo, a little dab will do you" mentality that we preach is not scriptural at all. We need treatment every day. We have strengths and struggles. We have conflicts and conquests, conquerings and challenges. We are not a finished product. Why have we boxed ourselves in and lifted ourselves up as the epitome of sanctity? Beneath our stained glass windows and padded pews lie broken hearts and torn families, those who chose to wait in the aisle of His presence rather than die in the stables of our wretchedness!

We have no right to be blessed, in ourselves. We are neither worthy nor deserving of it. Yet He has blessed us "in spite of us." Our testimony must change. Away with the polished brass words from silver-spooned lips that suggest anonymity from failure and fear. If we tell the truth (and we seldom do), it was the *blood* that brought us here. Beneath the streaming tears of a grateful heart, through our trembling lips must emerge the birthing thoughts that Christ has done it all, and that we have nothing to boast in but His precious blood—and His blood alone!

$\mathcal{W}$e are not a finished product.

For He knoweth our frame; He remembereth that we are dust. Psalm 103:14

Once while struggling in my heart to understand why God had not more readily answered one of my requests, I stumbled upon a word that brought streams into my desert.

> *But God remembered Noah and all the wild animals and the livestock that were with him in the ark, and He sent a wind over the earth, and the waters receded (Genesis 8:1 NIV).*

The first four words were all I needed. I still quote them from time to time. When you realize that God knows where you are and that He will get back to you in time—what peace, what joy! Before Noah ran out of resources and provisions, God remembered him! The Lord knows where you are and He knows how much you have left in reserve. Just before you run out, God will send the wind to blow back the waters of impossibility and provide for you.

I can't begin to describe the real ammunition I received out of those four powerful words: *But God remembered Noah*! I too need ministry to keep my attitude from falling while I wait on the manifestation of the promise of God. Sometimes very simplistic reminders that God is still sovereign bring great joy to the heart of someone who is in a holding pattern. The comforting Spirit of God calms my fears every time He reminds me that God doesn't forget.

When working with people, we often must remind them that we are still there. They seem to readily forget who you are or what you did. God doesn't! Don't confuse your relationship with Him with your relationship with people. God says, through Paul, that it is unrighteous to forget. God simply doesn't forget. He has excellent records.

> *For God is not unrighteous to forget your work and labour of love, which ye have showed toward His name, in that ye have ministered to the saints, and do minister (Hebrews 6:10).*

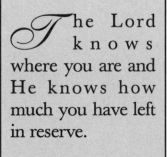

The Lord knows where you are and He knows how much you have left in reserve.

And being found in fashion as a man, He humbled Himself, and became obedient unto death, even the death of the cross. Philippians 2:8

To fully understand the precious effect of Jesus' blood, we must take a look back at Calvary's bloody banks. As the eclipsed sun tucked itself behind the trembling ground, a ground still wet with the cascading blood of a loving Savior, Jesus' love was so awesome that it could only be depicted by the morbidity of His dying. Allow this country preacher, this West Virginia hillbilly, a final glimpse at the only hope his soul has of Heaven. Brush a tear from a face full of thanksgiving and look at His bruised, mutilated, and lacerated body. Look at the 33-year-old body that could have been the object of some loving lady's desire. The body that was filled with such youth and potential now hangs from the cross like a slab of unused meat. From His beaten back to His ripped torso, we see a wounded knight without armor. His garments lie crumbled on the ground, the object of the desires of His villainous guards who now gamble up their leisure moments, waiting on the death angel to flap his wings in the face of the Savior.

Ignore the ice-cream social pictures of modern artists who portray a sunning Savior, basking in divine light before an alabaster sky as He gazes listlessly and lovingly out at a dying world. Ignore their imagery of a prince clad in some magical loincloth that seems, even in the pictures, to be somehow superimposed on the body of this spiritual celebrity. When you look at this icon of grace, remove your religious glasses and you will see a sweat-drenched, trembling, bleeding offering. That crucifixion was a debauchery and degradation so horrible that it embarrassed the sun into hiding its face and made the ground tremble at the nervous sight of the King of glory. He hung dying as if He were the bastard son of Mary, not the King that He was—dying like a thief in the night! His body, twisted and mangled, was held to a tree and suspended by nails as if some Marquis de Sade-type sadist had relished torturing the innocent.

> From his beaten back to His ripped torso, we see a wounded knight without armor.

Submit yourselves, then, to God. Resist the devil, and he will flee from you. James 4:7 (NIV)

Let us discuss some aspects of the uniqueness of the woman. By nature a woman is a receiver. She is not physically designed to be a giver. Her sexual and emotional fulfillment becomes somewhat dependent on the giving of her male counterpart (in regard to intimate relationships). There is a certain vulnerability that is a part of being a receiver. In regard to reproduction (sexual relationships), the man is the contributing factor, and the woman is the receiver.

What is true of the natural is true of the spiritual. Men tend to act out of what they perceive to be facts, while women tend to react out of their emotions. If your actions and moods are not a reaction to the probing of the Holy Spirit, then you are reacting to the subtle taunting of the enemy. He is trying to produce his destructive fruit in your home, heart, and even in your relationships. Receiver, be careful what you receive! Moods and attitudes that satan would offer, you need to resist. Tell the enemy, "This is not me, and I don't receive it." It is his job to offer it and your job to resist it. If you do your job, all will go well....

Don't allow the enemy to plug into you and violate you through his subtle seductions. He is a giver and he is looking for a receiver. You must discern his influence if you are going to rebuke him. Anything that comes, any mood that is not in agreement with God's Word, is satan trying to plug into the earthly realm through your life. He wants you to believe you cannot change. He loves prisons and chains!

> *Eve could have put the devil out!*

And killed the Prince of life, whom God hath raised from the dead; whereof we are witnesses. Acts 3:15

And they stripped Him, and put on Him a scarlet robe. And when they had platted a crown of thorns, they put it upon His head, and a reed in His right hand: and they bowed the knee before Him, and mocked Him, saying, Hail, King of the Jews! And they spit upon Him, and took the reed, and smote Him on the head. And after that they had mocked Him, they took the robe off from Him, and put His own raiment on Him, and led Him away to crucify Him. And as they came out, they found a man of Cyrene, Simon by name: him they compelled to bear His cross. And when they were come unto a place called Golgotha, that is to say, a place of a skull, they gave Him vinegar to drink mingled with gall: and when He had tasted thereof, He would not drink. And they crucified Him, and parted His garments, casting lots: that it might be fulfilled which was spoken by the prophet, They parted My garments among them, and upon My vesture did they cast lots. And sitting down they watched Him there (Matthew 27:28-36).

To me, Jesus Christ is the Prince of Peace. But to them, He was the entertainment for the evening. *They stripped Him completely and totally.* They humiliated Him by placing a robe upon His nude body and a crown upon His weary head, and then they amused themselves with Him. When they could do no more, they stripped Him of the robe and put His own clothes upon Him and led Him away to the cross. At the cross, Jesus again was stripped of His own clothes like the innocent animal in the Book of Genesis was stripped of its coat of skin.

Likewise, *Jesus was made bare that I might be covered.* Climbing naked upon the cross, He lay nailed to a tree! They then parted His garments among themselves and watched Him, *naked and not ashamed*! They watched until grace grew weary and mercifully draped a curtain over the sun, allowing darkness to veil Him from the watchful eyes of unconcerned hearts. These are the eyes of coldhearted men, men whose eyes are still darkened today lest they behold the wonder of His glory. That is why they can't quite see what we see when we look at Calvary!

> *T*hey then parted His garments among themselves and watched Him, *naked and not ashamed*!

For I know the thoughts that I think toward you, saith the Lord, thoughts of peace, and not of evil, to give you an expected end. Jeremiah 29:11

God's records are so complete that the hairs on your head are numbered (see Matt. 10:30). They are not just counted. Counted would mean He simply knows how many. No, they are numbered, meaning He knows which hair is in your comb! You know He has chronological records of your hair strands. Then you should know He has your family, your tithes, and your faithfulness in His view. How much more would God watch over you, if He already watches the numerical order of your hair? No wonder David declares, "What is man, that Thou art mindful of him?" (Ps. 8:4a) My friend, God's mind is full of you. Even in those moments of absolute stagnation in your life, He is working an expected end for your good (see Jer. 29:11).

When Noah had been held up long enough to accomplish what was necessary for his good, God sent the wind. There is a wind that comes from the Presence of God. It blows back the hindrances and dries the ground beneath your feet. The wind of the Holy Spirit often comes as a sign to you from the control tower. You have been cleared for a landing! Whenever the breath of the Almighty breathes a fresh anointing on you, it is a divine indication of a supernatural deliverance.

Regardless of the obstacle in your life, there is a wind from God that can bring you out. Let the wind of the Lord blow down every spirit of fear and heaviness that would cause you to give up on what God has promised you. The description of the Holy Spirit says He is as "a rushing mighty wind" (Acts 2:2). For every mighty problem in your life, there is a mighty rushing wind! Now, a normal wind can be blocked out. If you close the door and lock the windows, the wind just passes over without changing the building. But if the wind is a mighty rushing wind, it will blow down the door and break in the windows. There is a gusty wind from the Lord that is too strong to be controlled. It will blow back the Red Sea. It will roll back the Jordan River. It will blow dry the wet, marshy, flooded lands as in the days of Noah. God's wind is still ultra-effective against every current event in your life.

> *Even in those moments of absolute stagnation in your life, He is working an expected end for your good.*

Neither give place to the devil. Ephesians 4:27

It is not enough to reject the enemy's plan. You must nurture the Word of the Lord. You need to draw the promise of God and the vision for the future to your breast. It is a natural law that anything not fed will die. Whatever you have drawn to the breast is what is growing in your life. Breast-feeding holds several advantages for what you feed: (a) It hears your heart beat; (b) it is warmed by your closeness; (c) it draws nourishment from you. Caution: Be sure you are nurturing what you want to grow and starving what you want to die.

As you read this, you may feel that life is passing you by. You often experience success in one area and gross defeat in others. You need a burning desire for the future, the kind of desire that overcomes past fear and inhibitions. You will remain chained to your past and all the secrets therein until you decide: Enough is enough! I am telling you that when your desire for the future peaks, you can break out of prison. I challenge you to sit down and write 30 things you would like to do with your life and scratch them off, one by one, as you accomplish them. There is no way you can plan for the future and dwell in the past at the same time. I feel an earthquake coming into your prison! It is midnight—the turning point of days! It is your time for a change. Praise God and escape out of the dungeons of your past.

> *And at midnight Paul and Silas prayed, and sang praises unto God: and the prisoners heard them. And suddenly there was a great earthquake, so that the foundations of the prison were shaken: and immediately all the doors were opened, and every one's bands were loosed (Acts 16:25-26).*

Praise God and escape out of the dungeons of your past.

Who His own self bare our sins in His own body on the tree, that we, being dead to sins, should live unto righteousness: by whose stripes ye were healed. 1 Peter 2:24

The Savior's head is pricked with the thorns of every issue that would ever rest on my mind. His hands are nailed through for every vile thing I have ever used mine to do. His feet are nailed to the tree for every illicit, immoral place you and I have ever walked in! Sweat and blood race down His tortured frame. His oozing, gaping wounds are tormented by the abrasive bark of that old rugged cross, and are assaulted by the salty sweat of a dying man. In spite of His pain and abuse, in spite of His torment and His nudity, He was still preaching as they watched Him dying—*naked and not ashamed*!

Oh preacher, you say you've been through some things and that you've been hurt—still you must not stop preaching. Even though you have been stripped and others have beheld your nakedness, there are still some who will hear your words. Some dying thief will relate to you—if you can preach through your nudity and minister through your pain. Someone will relate to you and be saved because you stayed at your post and did what you were called to do!

Yes, the tormentors unveiled Him as if they were unmasking a painting. His nailed hands were denied the privilege of hiding Himself. He was exposed. So what about the issue of the loincloth? Where did this loincloth come from? Why is it painted on most of the pictures I see of the cross? Isn't that what hinders us now? Are we, the Body of Christ, hiding beneath a loincloth that has stifled our testimony and blocked our ability to be transparent, even with one another? There is seemingly some secret order whereby *we have not been allowed to share our struggles as well as our successes*. Our ministers are dying of loneliness because they feel obligated to maintain some false image of perfection in order to be serviceable in our society. We have no one to laugh with, no one to cry with, and no one who will sit down and share a sandwich with us. Beneath the loincloth of human expectation and excessive demands, many men and women are bleeding to death!

> *A*re we, the Body of Christ, hiding beneath a loincloth that has stifled our testimony and blocked our ability to be transparent, even with one another?

For we have not an high priest which cannot be touched with the feeling of our infirmities; but was in all points tempted like as we are, yet without sin. Hebrews 4:15

Have you ever noticed how hard it is to communicate with people who will not give you their attention? Pain will not continue to rehearse itself in the life of a preoccupied, distracted person. Distracted people almost seem weird. They do not respond! Every woman has something she wishes she could forget. There is a principle to learn here. Forgetting isn't a memory lapse; it is a memory release! Like carbon dioxide the body can no longer use, exhale it and let it go out of your spirit.

> *Brethren, I count not myself to have apprehended: but this one thing I do, forgetting those things which are behind, and reaching forth unto those things which are before, I press toward the mark for the prize of the high calling of God in Christ Jesus. Let us therefore, as many as be perfect, be thus minded: and if in any thing ye be otherwise minded, God shall reveal even this unto you (Philippians 3:13-15).*

Jesus set the infirmed woman of Luke 13 free. She was able to stand upright. The crippling condition of her infirmity was removed by the God who cares, sees and calls the infirmity to the dispensary of healing and deliverance. You can call upon Him even in the middle of the night. Like a 24-hour medical center, you can reach Him at anytime. He is touched by the feeling of your infirmity....

In the name of our High Priest, Jesus Christ, I curse the infirmity that has bowed the backs of God's women. I pray that, as we share together out of the Word of God, the Holy Spirit would roll you into the recovery room where you can fully realize that the trauma is over. I am excited to say that God never loosed anybody that He wasn't going to use mightily. May God reveal healing and purpose as we continue to seek Him.

$\mathscr{F}$orgetting isn't a memory lapse; it is a memory release!

The Lord hath made bare His holy arm in the eyes of all the nations; and all the ends of the earth shall see the salvation of our God. Isaiah 52:10

Why is a loincloth painted on most of the pictures I see of the cross?…

The tragedy is the fact that the loincloth represents all those things that are *humanly imposed upon us*, things that God does not require! The loincloth, regardless of how appropriate, moral, or sanctimonious it might seem, only exists in the minds of the artists who, in turn, painted what *they thought* we could stand to see. The Bible, on the other hand, says, "The Lord hath made bare His holy arm…" (Isa. 52:10)!

I resent the loincloth because it is almost prophetic of what the Church, the mystical Body of Christ, has done today. We have hidden our humanity beneath the man-made cloths of religiosity. *We have covered up what God has made bare!* Now we have to face secular news reporters who are trying to expose what should have been uncovered from the beginning. We are not God! We are men—men made of clay who have the power of God. We should apologize for ever trying to pass ourselves off as anything more. *We need no loincloth; the Body of Christ was meant to be naked and not ashamed.* Like the physical body of Christ, we have been camouflaged beneath religious loincloths. Like Adam's fig leaves, our loincloth is our attempt to cover what only God can cover.

Was the body of Christ covered? Yes, but not with any man-made material. The body of Christ was meant to be covered with nothing but the blood of Christ. Anything else is vain and ineffective. The cascading blood that flowed from His gaping wounds was the dressing of the Lord. His provision for our nudity was His blood. He knew that the death angel would soon pass by, and loincloths do not impress him. But that angel said, "When I see the blood, I will pass over you."

I hope you have only one defense when it is your turn to go on trial. Do not submit a loincloth for evidence; it is inadmissible. But my wounded, hurting, healing, helping, giving and needing friend, when they try your case (and they surely will), open your mouth, clear your throat, and plead, *No additives; the blood alone!*

> We have covered up what God has made bare!

But the scripture hath concluded all under sin, that the promise by faith of Jesus Christ might be given to them that believe. Galatians 3:22

Many Christians experienced the new birth early in their childhood. It is beneficial to have the advantage of Christian ethics. I'm not sure what it would have been like to have been raised in the church and been insulated from worldliness and sin. Sometimes I envy those who have been able to live victoriously all of their lives. Most of us have not had that kind of life. My concern is the many persons who have lost their sensitivity for others and who suffer from spiritual arrogance. Jesus condemned the Pharisees for their spiritual arrogance, yet many times that self-righteous spirit creeps into the Church.

There are those who define holiness as what one wears or what a person eats. For years churches displayed the name "holiness" because they monitored a person's outward appearance. They weren't truly looking at character. Often they were carried away with whether someone should wear makeup or jewelry when thousands of people were destroying themselves on drugs and prostitution. Priorities were confused. Unchurched people who came to church had no idea why the minister would emphasize outward apparel when people were bleeding inside.

The fact is, we were all born in sin and shaped in iniquity. We have no true badge of righteousness that we can wear on the outside. God concluded all are in sin so He might save us from ourselves (see Gal. 3:22). It wasn't the act of sin, but the state of sin, that brought us into condemnation. We were born in sin, equally and individually shaped in iniquity, and not one race or sociological group has escaped the fact that we are Adam's sinful heritage.

We have no true badge of righteousness that we can wear on the outside.

For a just man falleth seven times, and riseth up again: but the wicked shall fall into mischief.
Proverbs 24:16

Sometimes Christians become frustrated and withdraw from activity on the basis of personal struggles. They think it's all over, but God says not so! The best is yet to come. The Lord doesn't like pity parties, and those who have them are shocked to find that although He is invited, He seldom attends. Many morbid mourners will come to sit with you as you weep over your dear departed dreams. But if you want the Lord to come, you mustn't tell Him that you aren't planning to get up.

If you ever get around people who have accomplished much, they will tell you that those accomplishments didn't come without price. Generally that cost is much more expensive than you normally want to pay. Still, the cost of total transformation means different things to different people. When you arrive at your destination, don't be surprised that some people will assume everything you achieved came without price. The real price of success lies within the need to persevere. The trophy is never given to someone who does not complete the task. Setbacks are just setups for God to show what He is able to do. Funerals are for people who have accepted the thought that everything is over. Don't do that; instead tell the enemy, "I am not dead yet."…

The whole theme of Christianity is one of rising again. However, you can't rise until you fall. Now that doesn't mean you should fall into sin. It means you should allow the resurrecting power of the Holy Ghost to operate in your life regardless of whether you have fallen into sin, discouragement, apathy, or fear. There are obstacles that can trip you as you escalate toward productivity. But it doesn't matter what tripped you; it matters that you rise up. People who never experience these things generally are people who don't do anything. There is a certain safety in being dormant. Nothing is won, but nothing is lost. I would rather walk on the water with Jesus. I would rather nearly drown and have to be saved than play it safe and never experience the miraculous.

Tell the enemy, "I am not dead yet."

To the praise of the glory of His grace, wherein He hath made us accepted in the beloved. Ephesians 1:6

I remember, in my early days as a new Christian, that *I tried to become what I thought all the other Christians were.* I didn't understand that my goal should have been to achieve God's purpose for my life. I was young and so impressionable. Secretly suffering from low self-esteem, I thought that the Christians around me had mastered a level of holiness that seemed to evade me. I groaned in the night; I cried out to God to create in me a robotlike piety that would satisfy what I thought was required of me. I deeply admired those virtuous "faith heroes" whose flowery testimonies loftily hung around the ceiling like steam gathering above a shower. They seemed so changed, so sure, and so stable! I admired their standards and their purity, and I earnestly prayed, *Make me better, Lord!*

I don't think I have changed that prayer, but I have changed the *motivation* behind it. Suddenly, I began to realize that God knew me and loved me as I was, although I had never been taught about perfect love. I had always been surrounded by a love that was based upon performance. So I thought God's love was doled out according to a merit system. If I did well today, God loved me. However, if I failed, He did not love me. What a roller-coaster ride! I didn't know from moment to moment whether I was accepted in the beloved, or not!

I viewed my friends as paragons, or ultimate examples of what I should be, and I attacked my carnality with brutality. I didn't realize that everything that is born has to grow and develop to maturity. I was expecting an immediate, powerful, all-inclusive metamorphosis that would transform me into a new creature of perfection. Granted, I had never realized this goal, but I was also sure it was possible, and that this perfect creature must be much better than I. Surely God was waiting on him to come forth so He could *really* love me.

> *I* thought God's love was doled out according to a merit system. If I did well today, God loved me.

For all have sinned, and come short of the glory of God.
Romans 3:23

No one person needs any more of the blood of Jesus than the other. Jesus died once and for all. Humanity must come to God on equal terms, each individual totally helpless to earn his or her way to Him. When we come to Him with this attitude, He raises us up by the blood of Christ. He doesn't raise us up because we do good things. He raises us up because we have faith in the finished work on the cross.

Many in the Church were striving for holiness. What we were striving to perfect had already fallen and will only be restored at the second coming of the Lord. We were trying to perfect flesh. Flesh is in enmity against God, whether we paint it or not.

The Church frequently has, and still does, major on the minors. When that begins to happen, it is a sign that the Church has lost touch with the world and with the inspiration of the Lord. It is no longer reaching out to the lost. A church that focuses on the external has lost its passion for souls. When we come into that position, we have attained a pseudo-holiness. It's a false sanctity.

What is holiness? To understand it, we must first separate the pseudo from the genuine because, when you come into a church, it is possible to walk away feeling like a second-class citizen. Many start going overboard trying to be a super spiritual person in order to compensate for an embarrassing past. You can't earn deliverance. You have to just receive it by faith. Christ is the only righteousness that God will accept. If outward sanctity had impressed God, Christ would have endorsed the Pharisees.

> *Humanity must come to God on equal terms, each individual totally helpless to earn his or her way to Him.*

And He said unto me, My grace is sufficient for thee: for My strength is made perfect in weakness. Most gladly therefore will I rather glory in my infirmities, that the power of Christ may rest upon me. 2 Corinthians 12:9

When the AIDS epidemic hit this country, pandemonium erupted. Terror caused many people, Christians as well as non-Christians, to react out of ignorance and intimidation. The media continually presented the sickness as it attacked many individuals in highly visible positions. In listening to the discussions on TV and elsewhere, the primary concern didn't seem to be for the victim. People were whispering, wanting to know how it was contracted. I told the church I pastor that it was absolutely absurd to concern themselves with how anybody contracted AIDS. The issue is that they have it, and what are we going to do to help? It is not as though the disease is any less vicious to someone whom we approve of or exonerate. It has the same effect. Many are the methods by which we can contract it, but somewhere there will be but one cure.

In that same sense, regardless of what causes us to fall, what matters is that we get up! The enemy wants to lull us into a state of acceptance whereby we consider ourselves unable to alter the circumstances that limit us. However, the just man is successful because he continues to get up. The Holy Spirit challenges us to stand in the midst of contrary winds, and if we stumble to our knees, to grasp the hand of God's grace and arise.

If we intend to accomplish anything, we must react to adversity like yeast. Once yeast is thoroughly stirred into the dough, it cannot be detected. Although it is invisible, it is highly effective. When the heat is on, it will rise. The warmer the circumstance, the greater the reaction. Likewise, God sets us in warm, uncomfortable places so we can rise. Consider Israel in Egypt. The more the enemy afflicted them, the more the Israelites grew. Sometimes the worst times in our lives do more to strengthen us than all our mountaintop experiences. The power of God reacts to struggle and stress. Isn't that what God meant when He told Paul, "…My strength is made perfect in weakness" (2 Cor. 12:9a)?

> *Sometimes the worst times in our lives do more to strengthen us than all our mountaintop experiences.*

All scripture is given by inspiration of God, and is profitable for doctrine, for reproof, for correction, for instruction in righteousness: that the man of God may be perfect, thoroughly furnished unto all good works. 2 Timothy 3:16-17

Why did God bring this miraculous new creature so easily into the lives of some people when it seemed so far removed from others (like me)? I didn't realize that the "new man" starts out as a child, a child that has to grow into the mature character and nature of the Lord. No one shared with me that they had experienced struggles before they obtained victories. No one told me that wars come before success.

I was saved, but I was miserable. My misery deepened as I tried to measure up to others and answer all the concerns that plagued my heart. I was in a desperate search before anyone else realized that I wasn't always on the mountaintop like those around me seemed to be. I felt ashamed. My heart cried out, *What must I do to be perfected in the Lord?*

It is a tormenting experience for us to try to accomplish *through ourselves* what only God and maturity can accomplish in time. No matter how much my young son wants to wear my clothes, he cannot wear them today because he isn't old enough or developed enough to wear them. Yet, *there is absolutely nothing wrong with him.* He is as big as he should be for his age. Sometimes we are expected to be further along than we should be for the age we are in God!

It is important for us to let God mature us—without our self-help efforts to impress others with a false sense of piety. That kind of do-it-yourself righteousness and religion keeps us from being naked before God and from being comfortable with our own level of growth. Yes, I want to be all that God wants me to be. But while I am developing at the rate He has chosen, I will certainly thank Him for His rich grace and bountiful mercy along the way. This is the divine mercy that lets us mature naturally.

> *D*o-it-yourself righteousness and religion keep us from being naked before God.

And He said unto me, My grace is sufficient for thee: for My strength is made perfect in weakness. 2 Corinthians 12:9

There is a sanctity of your spirit that comes through the blood of the Lord Jesus Christ and sanctifies the innermost part of your being. Certainly, once you get cleaned up in your spirit, it will be reflected in your character and conduct. You won't be like Mary the mother of Jesus and dress like Mary Magdalene did before she met the Master. The Spirit of the Lord will give you boundaries. On the other hand, people must be loosed from the chains of guilt and condemnation. Many women in particular have been bound by manipulative messages that specialize in control and dominance.

The Church must open its doors and allow people who have a past to enter in. What often happens is they're spending years in the back pew trying to pay through obeisance for something in the past. Congregations often are unwilling to release reformed women. Remember, the same blood that cleanses the man can restore the woman also.

The Bible never camouflaged the weaknesses of the people God used. God used David. God used Abraham. We must divorce our embarrassment about wounded people. Yes, we've got wounded people. Yes, we've got hurting people. Sometimes they break the boundaries and they become lascivious and out of control and we have to readmit them into the hospital and allow them to be treated again. That's what the Church is designed to do. The Church is a hospital for wounded souls.

> The Bible never camouflaged the weaknesses of the people God used.

Not only so, but we also rejoice in our sufferings, because we know that suffering produces perseverance; perseverance, character; and character, hope. Romans 5:3-4 (NIV)

Several years ago a young man walked up to me and said, "I am getting ready to pioneer a church. Do you have any advice for me?" In fact, he asked, "If you could sum up in one word what it takes to be effective in ministry, what would that word be?" I thought about it a moment, then responded, "Relentless!" You must be a person who is relentless—always abounding in the work of the Lord. If you give up easily, there is no need for you to attempt to accomplish much for God. *Relentless* is a word I use to describe people who will not take no for an answer! They try things one way, and if that doesn't work, they try it another way. But they don't give up. You who are about to break beneath the stress of intense struggles, be relentless! Do not quit!

A terrible thing happens to people who give up too easily. It is called *regret*. It is the nagging, gnawing feeling that says, "If I had tried harder, I could have succeeded." When counseling married couples, I always encourage them to be sure they have done everything within their power to build a successful marriage. It is terrible to lie down at night thinking, "I wonder what would have happened if I had tried this or that." Granted, we all experience some degree of failure. That is how we learn and grow. If a baby had to learn how to walk without falling, he would never learn. A baby learns as much from falling on his bottom as he does from his first wobbly steps. The problem isn't failure; it is when we fail and question if it was our lack of commitment that allowed us to forfeit an opportunity to turn the test into a triumph! We can never be sure of the answer unless we rally our talents, muster our courage, and focus our strength to achieve a goal. If we don't have the passion to be relentless, then we should leave it alone.

> *I*f we don't have the passion to be relentless, then we should leave it alone.

EARTHEN VESSELS

But we have this treasure in earthen vessels, that the excellency of the power may be of God, and not of us. 2 Corinthians 4:7

Many Christians struggle to produce a *premature change* when God-ordained change can only be accomplished according to His time. We cannot expect to change the flesh. It will not respond to therapy. God intends for us to grow spiritually while we live in our vile, corrupt flesh. It is His will that our treasure be displayed in a cabinet of putrid, unregenerated flesh—openly displaying the strange dichotomy between the temporal and the eternal.

It is amazing that God would put so much in so little. The true wonder of His glory is painted on the dark canvas of our old personhood. What a glorious backdrop our weakness makes for His strength! This backdrop is absolutely crucial. "Paul's thorn," the glaring symbol of human weakness contrasted with God's greatness, was given as a humbling reminder to the great apostle to insure him against arrogance and pride (see 2 Cor. 12:7).

Paul wanted the thorn removed, but God wanted it "endured." Many times we, like Paul, *ask God to remove what He wants us to endure.* There is a great deal of power released through the friction of the holy graces of God grating against the dry, gritty surface of human incapacities and limitations. We sharpen our testimonies whenever we press His glory against our struggles. Although Paul sought diligently for the removal of his thorn, the reality is that Paul's thorn was as much in God's plan for the apostle's life as any other trial, victory, or accomplishment in ministry....

The problem is that while we are changed in our spirit by the new birth, our old corruptible body and fleshly desires are not. They are Spirit-controlled, but not Spirit-destroyed! The Holy Spirit is living with us in a stinking clay pot—a putrid, decaying, clay-covered, vile body. Its stench is so bad that we must continually wash and perfume it just to endure living there ourselves. Yet God Himself, the epitome of purity, has forsaken the rich, robust pavilions of His holy domain to live in a failing, decaying, deteriorating, collapsing, and corroding shell.

> The Holy Spirit is living with us in a stinking clay pot....

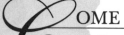

[Jesus said] *"Come unto Me, all ye that labor and are heavy laden, and I will give you rest."*
Matthew 11:28

The staff in a hospital understand that periodically people get sick and they need a place to recover. Now, I'm not condoning the sin. I'm just explaining that it's a reality. Many of those in Scripture were unholy. The only holy man out of all of the characters in the Bible is Jesus Christ, the righteousness of God.

We have all wrestled with something, though it may not always be the same challenge. My struggle may not be yours. If I'm wrestling with something that's not a problem to you, you do not have the responsibility for judging me when all the while you are wrestling with something equally as incriminating....

Thank God He calls women with a past. He reaches out and says, "Get up! You can come to Me." Regardless of what a person has done, or what kind of abuse one has suffered, He still calls. We may think our secret is worse than anyone else's. Rest assured that He knows all about it, and still draws us with an immutable call.

No matter how difficult life seems, people with a past need to make their way to Jesus. Regardless of the obstacles within and without, they must reach Him. You may have a baby out of wedlock cradled in your arms, but keep pressing on. You may have been abused and molested and never able to talk to anyone about it, but don't cease reaching out for Him. You don't have to tell everyone your entire history. Just know that He calls, on purpose, women with a past. He knows your history, but He called you anyway.

> He knows your history, but He called you anyway.

Even so ye, forasmuch as ye are zealous of spiritual gifts, seek that ye may excel to the edifying of the church. 1 Corinthians 14:12

You would be surprised to know how many people there are who never focus on a goal. They do several things haphazardly without examining how forceful they can be when they totally commit themselves to a cause. The difference between the masterful and the mediocre is often a focused effort. On the other hand, mediocrity is masterful to persons of limited resources and abilities. So in reality, true success is relative to ability. What is a miraculous occurrence for one person can be nothing of consequence to another. A person's goal must be set on the basis of his ability to cultivate talents and his agility in provoking a change. I often wonder how far my best work is in front of me. I am convinced that I have not fully developed my giftings. But, I am committed to the cause of being. "Being what?" you ask. I am committed to being all that I was intended and predestined to be for the Lord, for my family, and for myself. How about you—have you decided to roll up your sleeves and go to work? Remember, effort is the bridge between mediocrity and masterful accomplishment!

Multiple talents can also be a source of confusion. People who are effective at only one thing have little to decide. At this point let me distinguish between talent and purpose. You may have within you a multiplicity of talent. But if the Holy Spirit gives no direction in that area, it will not be effective. Are you called to the area in which you feel talented? On the other hand, consider this verse: "And we know that all things work together for good to them that love God, to them who are the called according to His purpose" (Rom. 8:28). So then you are called according to His purpose and not your talents. You should have a sense of purpose in your ministry and not just talent.

> You should have a sense of purpose in your ministry and not just talent.

In whom all the building fitly framed together groweth unto an holy temple in the Lord: in whom ye also are builded together for an habitation of God through the Spirit. Ephesians 2:21-22

Within our decaying shells, we constantly peel away, by faith, the lusts and jealousies that adorn the walls of our hearts. If the angels were to stroll through the earth with the Creator and ask, "Which house is Yours?" He would pass by all the mansions and cathedrals, all the temples and castles. Unashamedly, He would point at you and me and say, "That house is Mine!" Imagine the shock and disdain of the heavenly host to think that the God whose face they fan with their wings would choose to live in such a shack and shanty! We know where our greatest conflict lies. We who blunder and stumble in our humanity, we who stagger through our frail existence—we continually wrestle with the knowledge that *our God has put so much in so little!*

Yes, it is true: Despite all our washing and painting, all our grooming and exercising, this old house is still falling apart! We train it and teach it. We buy books and tapes, and we desperately try to convince it to at least think differently. But like a squeaky hinge on a swollen door, the results of our efforts, at best, come slowly. There is no doubt that we have been saved, and *there is no doubt that the house is haunted.* The Holy Ghost Himself resides beneath this sagging roof. (Although the tenant is prestigious, the accommodations are still substandard.)

This divine occupation is not an act of a desperate guest who, having no place else to stay, chose this impoverished site as a temporary place to "ride out" the storm of some deplorable situation. No, God Himself has—of His own free will and predetermined purpose—put us in the embarrassing situation of entertaining a Guest whose lofty stature so far exceeds us that we hardly know how to serve Him!

> *Although the tenant is prestigious, the accommodations are still substandard.*

FROM TEST TO TESTIMONY

As for me, I will call upon God; and the Lord shall save me. Evening, and morning, and at noon, will I pray, and cry aloud: and He shall hear my voice. He hath delivered my soul in peace from the battle that was against me: for there were many with me. Psalm 55:16-18

And, behold, there was a woman which had a spirit of infirmity eighteen years, and was bowed together, and could in no wise lift up herself. And when Jesus saw her, He called her to Him, and said unto her, Woman, thou art loosed from thine infirmity. And He laid His hands on her: and immediately she was made straight, and glorified God (Luke 13:11-13).

Jesus' actions were massively different from ours. He focused on hurting people. Every time He saw a hurting person, He reached out and ministered to their need. Once when He was preaching, He looked through the crowd and saw a man with a withered hand. He immediately healed him (see Mark 3:1-5). He sat with the prostitutes and the winebibbers, not the upper echelon of His community. Jesus surrounded Himself with broken, bleeding, dirty people. He called a woman who was crippled and bent over (see Luke 13:11-13). She had come to church and sat in the synagogue for years and years and nobody had helped that woman until Jesus saw her. He called her to the forefront.

At first when I thought about His calling her, I thought, "How rude to call her." Why didn't He speak the word and heal her in her seat? Perhaps God wants to see us moving toward Him. We need to invest in our own deliverance. We will bring a testimony out of a test. I also believe that someone else there had problems. When we can see someone else overcoming a handicap, it helps us to overcome.

We can't know how long it took her to get up to the front. Handicapped people don't move as fast as others do. As believers, we often don't grow as fast as other people grow because we've been suffering for a long time. We are incapacitated. Often what is simple for one person is extremely difficult for another. Jesus challenged this woman's limitations. He called her anyway.

We need to invest in our own deliverance.

But I keep under my body, and bring it into subjection: lest that by any means, when I have preached to others, I myself should be a castaway. 1 Corinthians 9:27

The very best of us camouflage the very worst in us with religious colloquialisms that reduce Christianity to more of an act than an attitude. Even the most pious among us—while in the quiet booth of some confessional or kneeling in solitude at the edge of our beds—must murmur our confession before God: *We have earnestly pursued a place in You that we have not attained.*

Our struggle continues to feed the ravenous appetite of our holy Guest, whose divine hunger requires us to perpetually feed Him a sacrificial life. He daily consumes, and continually requires, that which we alone know God wants from us. Paul battled to bring into submission the hidden things in his life that could bring destruction. Perhaps they were putrid thoughts, or vain imaginations, or pride; but whatever they were, he declared war on them if they resisted change. He says, in essence, that as he waits for the change, he keeps his body in chains, beating back the forces of evil.

This is the struggle of the same man who wrote the majority of the New Testament! With a testimony like this, I pay very little attention to those among us who feel obligated to impress us with the ludicrous idea that they have already attained what is meant to be a lifelong pursuit. The renewal of the old man is a daily exercise of the heart. It progressively strengthens the character day by day, not overnight!

I remember some of those wonderful gospel songs that we used to sing that said, "I looked at my hands and my hands looked new, I looked at my feet and they did too…." Those are wonderful lyrics, but they are completely erroneous. They sounded exciting, but they were tragically misleading. If you want to know the truth, if you had a bunion on your foot *before* you got saved, and you were to take your shoes off and check it *after* you got saved, it would still be holding on!

> The renewal of the old man is a daily exercise of the heart.

For He has rescued us from the dominion of darkness and brought us into the kingdom of the Son He loves. Colossians 1:13 (NIV)

God will give you a miracle. He'll do it powerfully and publicly. Many will say, "Is this the same woman that was bent over and wounded in the church?" Perhaps some will think, "Is this the same woman who had one foot in the church and the other in an affair?"

Many of the people who were a part of the ministry of Jesus' earthly life were people with colorful pasts. Some had indeed always looked for the Messiah to come. Others were involved in things that were immoral and inappropriate.

A good example is Matthew. He was a man who worked in an extremely distasteful profession. He was a tax collector. Few people like tax collectors still today. Their reputation was even worse at that time in history. Matthew collected taxes for the Roman empire. He had to have been considered a traitor by those who were faithful Jews. Romans were their oppressors. How could he have forsaken his heritage and joined the Romans?

Tax collectors did more than simply receive taxes for the benefit of the government. They were frequently little better than common extortioners. They had to collect a certain amount for Rome, but anything they could collect above that set figure was considered the collector's commission. Therefore they frequently claimed excessive taxes. Often they acted like common thieves.

Regardless of his past, Jesus called Matthew to be a disciple. Later he served as a great apostle and wrote one of the books of the New Testament. Much of the history and greatness of Jesus would be lost to us were it not for Jesus calling Matthew, a man with a past. We must maintain a strong line of demarcation between a person's past and present.

These were the people Jesus wanted to reach. He was criticized for being around questionable characters. Everywhere He went the oppressed and the rejected followed Him. They knew that He offered mercy and forgiveness.

> *We must maintain a strong line of demarcation between a person's past and present.*

Who hath saved us, and called us with an holy calling, not according to our works, but according to His own purpose and grace, which was given us in Christ Jesus before the world began. 2 Timothy 1:9

If you are only talented, you may feel comfortable taking your talents into a secular arena. Talent, like justice, is blind; it will seek all opportunities the same. But when you are cognizant of divine purpose, there are some things you will not do because they would defeat the purpose of God in your life! For instance, if it is your purpose to bless the Body of Christ in song or ministry, though you may be talented enough to aspire to some secular platform of excellence, if you are cognizant of your purpose, you will do what you are called to do. Being called according to purpose enables you to focus on the development of your talent as it relates to your purpose!

Whenever we bring our efforts into alignment with His purpose, we automatically are blessed. Second Timothy 2:4-5 says, "No man that warreth entangleth himself with the affairs of this life; that he may please him who hath chosen him to be a soldier. And if a man also strive for masteries, yet is he not crowned, except he strive lawfully." In order to strive lawfully, our efforts must be tailored after the pattern of divine purpose. Everyone is already blessed. We often spend hours in prayer trying to convince God that He should bless what we are trying to accomplish. What we need to do is spend hours in prayer for God to reveal His purpose. When we do what God has ordained to be done, we are blessed because God's plan is already blessed.

Perhaps you have known times of frustration. Most of us at one time or another have found ourselves wrestling to birth an idea that was conceived in the womb of the human mind as opposed to the divine. For myself, I learned that God will not be manipulated. If He said it, that settles it. No amount of praying through parched lips and tear-stained eyes will cause God to avert what He knows is best for you.

> Whenever we bring our efforts into alignment with His purpose, we automatically are blessed.

Now we know that if the earthly tent we live in is destroyed, we have a building from God, an eternal house in heaven, not built by human hands.... Now it is God who has... given us the Spirit as a deposit, guaranteeing what is to come. 2 Corinthians 5:1-5 (NIV)

So the bad news is that the old house is still a death trap; it's still infested with rodents. A legion of thoughts and pesky memories crawl around in our heads like roaches that come out in the night and boldly parade around the house. Add to this pestilence an occasional groaning in the dungeon, and you will have a picturesque view of the inner workings of a Christian! That should not negate our joy, though; it merely confesses our struggles.

What do I mean by "groaning"? The occasional groaning you hear is not demonic. Rather, it is a painful groan that pierces our nights like the whelping cry of a wounded animal. We have not been taught about the crying of the Spirit, but I tell you that the Holy Spirit can be grieved. He has the capacity and ability to groan within us until His groaning emerges as conviction in the heart of the humble. Yes, it is bad news, but the Guest we entertain desires more for us than what we have in us! He enjoys neither the house nor the clothing we offer Him. He just suffers it like a lover suffers adversity to be in the company of the one he loves.

The good news is that the bad news won't last long! Jesus said, "...every city or house divided against itself shall not stand" (Matt. 12:25). Ever since we were saved, there has been a division in the house. Eventually the old house will have to yield to the new one! Yes, we are constantly renovating through the Word of God, but the truth is that God will eventually *recycle* what you and I have been trying to *renovate*! It is then that the groaning of the regenerated spirit within us will transform into sheer glory!

> *Eventually the old house will have to yield to the new one!*

For I delight in the law of God after the inward man: but I see another law in my members, warring against the law of my mind, and bringing me into captivity to the law of sin which is in my members. O wretched man that I am! who shall deliver me from the body of this death? Romans 7:22-24

Christianity means conflict. At the least, if it doesn't mean conflict, it certainly creates conflict! The question is, why are we so silent? Why do we seldom hear anyone say that "living holy" isn't natural? *It isn't natural—it is spiritual!* Unless we walk consistently in the Spirit, living holy is difficult. No, it is impossible! It isn't natural to "do good to them that hate you" (Matt. 5:44). You don't see one dog steal another one's bone and then see the betrayed dog wag his tail in happiness! No, forgiveness isn't natural.

Without God it cannot be done! Being a Christian means that one part of you is constantly wanting to do the right thing while the other part of you is desperately campaigning for you to walk in your old habits. We often talk about how God saved us from sin. I agree. I am grateful for the terribly wicked things that He saved me from. Because I was saved, I didn't commit those wicked sins, but I would have had He not set up a protest in my heart! He brought my trembling soul to His bleeding side and cleansed my very imaginations, intentions, and ambitions! Yes, the Christian life is a life of conflict, and I thank God that He groans and protests my sinful behavior. It is because He challenges my proclivities that growth begins!

> *Now there was long war between the house of Saul and the house of David: but David waxed stronger and stronger, and the house of Saul waxed weaker and weaker (2 Samuel 3:1).*

Transformation is a process! It takes faith and patience to see the results that bring out the true nature of Christ in any of us. It is when we strip away the facade of the superficial and ask God to bring about the supernatural that we experience the real power of God. God wants to transport us from the superficial to the supernatural!

> The Christian life is a life of conflict.

Stand fast therefore in the liberty wherewith Christ hath made us free, and be not entangled again with the yoke of bondage. Galatians 5:1

People with a past have always been able to come to Jesus. He makes them into something wonderful and marvelous. It is said that Mary Magdalene was a prostitute. Christ was moved with compassion for even this base kind of human existence. He never used a prostitute for sex, but He certainly loved them into the Kingdom of God.

> *And it came to pass, as Jesus sat at meat in the house, behold, many publicans and sinners came and sat down with Him and His disciples. And when the Pharisees saw it, they said unto His disciples, Why eateth your Master with publicans and sinners? But when Jesus heard that, He said unto them, They that be whole need not a physician, but they that are sick (Matthew 9:10-12).*

When Christ was teaching in the temple courts, there were those who tried to trap Him in His words. They knew that His ministry appealed to the masses of lowly people. They thought that if they could get Him to say some condemning things, the people wouldn't follow Him anymore....

The blood of Jesus is efficacious, cleansing the woman who feels unclean. How can we reject what He has cleansed and made whole? Just as He said to the woman then, He proclaims today, "Neither do I condemn thee: go and sin no more." How can the Church do any less?

The chains that bind are often from events that we have no control over. The woman who is abused is not responsible for the horrible events that happened in her past. Other times the chains are there because we have willfully lived lives that bring bondage and pain. Regardless of the source, Jesus comes to set us free. He is unleashing the women of His Church. He forgives, heals and restores. Women can find the potential of their future because of His wonderful power operating in their lives.

> Regardless of the sou.rce, Jesus comes to set us free. He is unleashing the women of His Church.

O Lord, how many are my foes! How many rise up against me! Many are saying of me, "God will not deliver him." Selah. But You are a shield around me, O Lord; You bestow glory on me and lift up my head. To the Lord I cry aloud, and He answers me from His holy hill. Selah.
Psalm 3:1-4 (NIV)

David declares that it is the Lord who sustains you in the perilous times of inner struggle and warfare. It is the precious peace of God that eases your tension when you are trying to make decisions in the face of criticism and cynicism. When you realize that some people do not want you to be successful, the pressure mounts drastically. Many have said, "God will not deliver him." However, many saying it still doesn't make it true. I believe that the safest place in the whole world is in the will of God. If you align your plan with His purpose, success is imminent! On the other hand, if I have not been as successful as I would like to be, then seeking the purpose of God inevitably enriches my resources and makes the impossible attainable....

I remember when my wife and I were raising two children (now we have four). Times were tough and money was scarce. I am not the kind of husband who doesn't care about the provisions of the Lord in his house. So many were the nights that I languished over the needs in our home. Tossing and turning, praying and worrying—I wasn't sure we were going to survive the struggle. During these times satan always shows you images of yourself and your children wrapped up in dirty quilts, nestled under a bridge with a burning 55-gallon drum as the only source of heat. He is such a sadist. I was nearly frazzled with stress trying to raise the standard of our living.

I prayed, or more accurately, I complained to God. I explained to Him how I was living closer to Him than I had ever lived and yet we were suffering with utility bills and lack of groceries. I wondered, "Where are You, Lord!" I was a preacher and a pastor. All the other men of God seemed to have abundance, yet I was in need...If the storm comes and I know I am in the will of God, then little else matters.

If you align your plan with His purpose, success is imminent!

Have mercy upon me, O God, according to Thy lovingkindness: according unto the multitude of Thy tender mercies blot out my transgressions.... Against Thee, Thee only, have I sinned, and done this evil in Thy sight: that Thou mightest be justified when Thou speakest, and be clear when Thou judgest. Psalm 51:1-4

Saul was anointed by God to be king. He was more moral than David in that he didn't struggle in some of the areas that plagued David. His weakness wasn't outward; it was inward. Saul looked like a king, whereas David looked like an underage juvenile delinquent who should have been home taking care of the flocks. But David wasn't in the palace; he was out there with the men, fighting the giants and bringing about change. Saul's armor shined in the noonday sun. David had no armor. He fought naked, free from the entanglements of trying to be impressive. He was not ashamed. Even his weapon looked substandard; it was just an old, ragged, shepherd's slingshot.

Although David's weapon was outwardly substandard, it was nevertheless lethal; it led to the destruction of the giant. We can never destroy our enemy with the superficial armor of a pious king. We don't need the superficial. We need the supernatural! David's naked, transparent demeanor was so translucent that he often seems extremely vulnerable. He seems almost naive at times. When he worships, he does it with holy abandonment. When he lusts, he does it to obsessive dimensions. You would almost think he was unfit, except that when he repents, there is something so powerful in his prayer that even his most adamant critic must admire his openness with God!

Hide Thy face from my sins, and blot out all mine iniquities. Create in me a clean heart, O God; and renew a right spirit within me. Cast me not away from Thy presence; and take not Thy Holy Spirit from me. Restore unto me the joy of Thy salvation; and uphold me with Thy free spirit. Then will I teach transgressors Thy ways; and sinners shall be converted unto Thee. Deliver me from bloodguiltiness, O God, Thou God of my salvation: and my tongue shall sing aloud of Thy righteousness (Psalm 51:9-14).

> We don't need the superficial. We need the supernatural!

And the scribes and Pharisees brought unto Him a woman taken in adultery; and when they had set her in the midst, they say unto Him, Master, this woman was taken in adultery, in the very act.... So when they continued asking Him, He lifted up Himself, and said unto them, He that is without sin among you, let him first cast a stone at her. John 8:3-7

Clearly Jesus saw the foolish religious pride in their hearts. He was not condoning the sin of adultery. He simply understood the need to meet people where they were and minister to their need. He saw the pride in the Pharisees and ministered correction to that pride. He saw the wounded woman and ministered forgiveness. Justice demanded that she be stoned to death. Mercy threw the case out of court.

Have you ever wondered where the man was who had been committing adultery with this woman? She had been caught in the very act. Surely they knew who the man was. There still seems to be a double standard today when it comes to sexual sin. Often we look down on a woman because of her past but overlook who she is now. Jesus, however, knew the power of a second chance.

> *When Jesus had lifted up Himself, and saw none but the woman, He said unto her, Woman, where are those thine accusers? hath no man condemned thee? She said, No man, Lord. And Jesus said unto her, Neither do I condemn thee: go, and sin no more (John 8:10-11).*

There are those today who are very much like this woman. They have come into the Church. Perhaps they have made strong commitments to Christ and have the very Spirit of God living within them. Yet they walk as cripples. They have been stoned and ridiculed. They may not be physically broken and bowed over, but they are wounded within. Somehow the Church must find room to throw off condemnation and give life and healing.

> Somehow the Church must find room to throw off condemnation and give life and healing.

DECEIT AND DISOBEDIENCE

And Samuel said, Hath the Lord as great delight in burnt offerings and sacrifices, as in obeying the voice of the Lord? Behold, to obey is better than sacrifice, and to hearken than the fat of rams.... And Saul said unto Samuel, I have sinned: for I have transgressed the commandment of the Lord, and thy words: because I feared the people, and obeyed their voice. I Samuel 15:22-24

What a sharp contrast there is between David and King Saul, whose stately demeanor and pompous gait didn't stop him from being an incredible deceiver. Even when he was face-to-face with Samuel the prophet, Saul lied at a time he should have repented! The problem with Saul and people like him is that they are more interested in their *image* than they are concerned about being immaculate in their hearts.

While Saul stood arrayed in his kingly attire, boasting of his conquest over an enemy king and lying about his real struggles, the heathen king whom Saul had been commanded to kill was still alive. The sheep that he had been ordered to destroy were still bleating in the valley. God did not destroy Saul for not killing what he should have killed; that wasn't the biggest problem. God can work with weakness; in fact, His strength is made perfect in our human weakness (see 2 Cor. 12:9). The central problem was that Saul's *deceitfulness* had become a breach too wide to bridge. David might have been weak, and struggled with moral issues, but at least *he was naked before God*!

> *And Saul said, They have brought them from the Amalekites: for the people spared the best of the sheep and of the oxen, to sacrifice unto the Lord thy God; and the rest we have utterly destroyed. Then Samuel said unto Saul, Stay, and I will tell thee what the Lord hath said to me this night.... And the Lord sent thee on a journey, and said, Go and utterly destroy the sinners the Amalekites, and fight against them until they be consumed. Wherefore then didst thou not obey the voice of the Lord, but didst fly upon the spoil, and didst evil in the sight of the Lord? And Saul said unto Samuel, Yea, I have obeyed the voice of the Lord, and have gone the way which the Lord sent me, and have brought Agag the king of Amalek, and have utterly destroyed the Amalekites. But the people took of the spoil, sheep and oxen, the chief of the things which should have been utterly destroyed, to sacrifice unto the Lord thy God in Gilgal (1 Samuel 15:15-16,18-21).*

> They are more interested in their *image* than they are concerned about being immaculate in their hearts.

As one whom his mother comforteth, so will I comfort you; and ye shall be comforted in Jerusalem.
Isaiah 66:13

I remember when our car broke down. It didn't have too far to break down because it already was at death's door. The only way to fix that car was to commit the body to the ground and give the engine to the Lord. At the time, though, I needed to get uptown to ask the electric company not to cut off the only utility I had left. I caught the bus to town. I walked into the office prepared to beg, but not prepared to pay. I pleaded with the young lady; I promised her money. Nothing seemed to move her, and she cut it off anyway. I was crushed. I had been laid off my job, and my church was so poor it couldn't even pay attention. I was in trouble. I walked out of the utility office and burst into tears. I don't mean the quiet leaking of the tear ducts, either. I mean a deluge of sobbing, heaving, quaking, and wailing. I looked like an insane person walking down the street. I was at the end of my rope.

To this melodramatic outburst God said absolutely nothing. He waited until I had gained some slight level of composure and then spoke. I will never forget the sweet sound of His voice beneath the broken breathing of my fearful frustration. He said, in the rich tones of a clarinet-type voice, "I will not suffer thy foot to be moved!" That was all He said, but it was how He said it that caused worship to flush the pain out of my heart. It was as if He were saying, "Who do you think that I am? I will not suffer thy foot to be moved. Don't you understand that I love you?" I shall never forget as long as I live the holy hush and the peace of His promise that came into my spirit. Suddenly the light, the gas, and the money didn't matter. What mattered was I knew I was not alone. He sat down beside me and we rode home smiling in each other's face. It was the Lord and I.

What mattered was I knew I was not alone.

BE HONEST WITH GOD

He that worketh deceit shall not dwell within my house: he that telleth lies shall not tarry in my sight. Psalm 101:7

Saul was anointed by God to be king. He had a terrible character flaw, that of deceit…. Even when he was face-to-face with Samuel the prophet, Saul lied at a time he should have repented! (See First Samuel 15:15-24)…Saul represents that part of all of us that must be overthrown. It is *the leadership of Saul in us* that must be renounced if we are to go beyond the superficial and fulfill our destiny in the supernatural. God knows who we are. He can deliver us from ourselves, but we must be honest enough to say, *This is all You have to work with, God. What can You do with what I have presented?* Misrepresentation will not be tolerated! There must be an open confession that enables God's grace to be allocated to your need.

Now hear this, you who would allow the spirit of Saul to reign in your life: The house of Saul represents those fleshly areas that we war against. These are areas that hide in religious clothes but do not worship God in honesty—not perfection, just honesty. Saul was perhaps "more moral" than David, but David was by far "more honest." Consequently, the house of Saul grew weaker and weaker and the house of David grew stronger and stronger!

There is a gradual and perpetual transference of authority as we walk with God. We move from the Saul-like rule of superficial religion to a Davidic anointing based on honesty and transparency. Like a chick pecking through its shell, we press through our concerns and over other people's opinions, and break into the light to know God in a more definitive way!

"My little children, of whom I travail in birth again until Christ be formed in you" (Gal. 4:19). Only God knows the process it will take for the Christ who saved you to be formed in you. He is taking each of us to that place where the child begins to bear a greater resemblance to his Father.

Be assured that this only occurs at the end of travailing prayer and openness of heart, as we confess and forsake every trace of Saul's rule in our lives.

> There must be an open confession that enables God's grace to be allocated to your need.

The chosen people had become a great empire. Israel was at its zenith under the leadership of a godly king named David. There can be no argument that David frequently allowed his passions to lead him into moral failure. However, he was a man who recognized his failures and repented. He was a man who sought God's heart.

Although David longed to follow God, some of his passions and lust were inherited by his children. Maybe they learned negative things from their father's failures. That is a tendency we must resist. We ought not repeat the failure of our fathers. We are most vulnerable, however, to our father's weaknesses.

> *And it came to pass after this, that Absalom the son of David had a fair sister, whose name was Tamar; and Amnon the son of David loved her. And Amnon was so vexed, that he fell sick for his sister Tamar; for she was a virgin. ...He took hold of her, and said unto her, Come lie with me, my sister. And she answered him, Nay, my brother, do not force me; for no such thing ought to be done in Israel: do not thou this folly. And I, whither shall I cause my shame to go? and as for thee, thou shalt be as one of the fools in Israel. Now therefore, I pray thee, speak unto the king; for he will not withhold me from thee. Howbeit he would not hearken unto her voice: but, being stronger than she, forced her, and lay with her (2 Samuel 13:1-2,11-14).*

The name *Tamar* means "palm tree." Tamar is a survivor. She stands in summer and spring. She even faces fall with leaves when other trees lose theirs. She still stands. When the cold blight of winter stands up in her face, she withstands the chilly winds and remains green throughout the winter. Tamar is a survivor. You are a survivor. Through hard times God has granted you the tenacity to endure stresses and strains.

> Through hard times God has granted you the tenacity to endure stresses and strains.

He delivered me from my strong enemy, and from them which hated me: for they were too strong for me. They prevented me in the day of my calamity: but the Lord was my stay. He brought me forth also into a large place; He delivered me, because He delighted in me. Psalm 18:17-19

There is a deep-seated need in all of us to sense purpose—even out of calamity. Out of this thirst for meaning is born the simplistic yet crucial prayer, *"Why?"*...

Many times, we want to know and understand. It is part of our superior creative ability. It separates us from lower forms of life that tend to accept events as they come. There is within us this insatiable need to understand. On the other hand, we seem to draw some degree of solace from our very quest to know why. No matter how painful the quest, we will still search through the rubbish of broken dreams, broken promises, and twisted childhood issues looking for clues.

We ambitiously pursue these clues because we believe there is a reward for the discovery. This emotional autopsy often takes us through the bowels of human attitudes and dysfunctional behavior. We don't have to necessarily erase the cause of our pain; we mainly just want to find some reason or justification for the pain and discomfort.

> *And Jacob was left alone; and there wrestled a man with him until the breaking of the day (Genesis 32:24).*

Like Jacob, all of us know what it means to be left alone. Whether through death, desertion, or even disagreement, we have all been left alone at times. We are sometimes disillusioned when we find out how easily people will leave us. Generally they leave us when we think that we *need them*....

This may be difficult, but it is all part of God's "scholastic-achievement program" for strong believers. He is determined to strip us of our strong tendency to be dependent on others, thereby teaching us self-reliance and God-reliance. Thus the struggle truly begins not when men surround us, but rather when they forsake us. It is then that we begin to discover our own identity and self-worth!

It is unrealistic to expect no pain when there is disappointment or rejection. No matter how spiritual we may be, when covenants are broken and trust is betrayed, even the most stoic person will wince at the pain!

> *It is all part of God's "scholastic-achievement program" for strong believers.*

I remember so well the early struggles that my wife and I had to maintain our family, finances, and overall well-being while building a ministry. I was working a secular job that God wanted me to leave for full-time ministry. Full-time ministry—what a joke! I was scarcely asked to preach anywhere that offered more than a few pound cakes, a couple jars of jelly, and if I was lucky, enough gas money to get home. My hotel generally would be the back room of some dear elderly church mother who charmingly entertained me as best she could with what she had. It was there, around old coal stoves in tiny churches that never even considered buying a microphone, that I learned how to preach. Often I would preach until sweaty and tired, to rows of empty pews with two or three people who decorated the otherwise empty church like earrings placed on the head of a bald doll.

Finally I said yes to full-time ministry. I did it not because I wanted it, but because the company I worked for went out of business and I was forced out of my comfort zone into the land of faith. What a frightening experience it was to find myself without. "Without what?" you ask. I was without everything you could think of: without a job and then a car. Later I was without utilities and often without food. I scraped around doing odd jobs trying to feed two children and a wife without looking like life wasn't working. I thought God had forgotten me. I even preached in suits that shined. They shined not because they were in style, but because they were worn, pressed with an iron, and eventually washed in the washing machine because cleaners were out of the question. I am not ashamed to tell you—in fact I am proud to tell you—that I experienced more about God in those desperate days of struggle as I answered the charges of satan with the perseverance of prayer.

> *I* experienced more about God in those desperate days of struggle as I answered the charges of satan with the perseverance of prayer.

I know that the Lord will maintain the cause of the afflicted, and the right of the poor.
Psalm 140:12

It's hard for me as a man to fully understand how horrible rape is for women. I can sympathize, but the violation is incomprehensible. I don't feel as vulnerable to being raped as a woman would. However, I have come to realize that rape is another creature inflicting his will on someone without her permission. It is more than just the act of sex. It is someone victimizing you. There are all kinds of rape—emotional, spiritual and physical. There are many ways to be victimized. Abuse is abnormal use. It is terrible to misuse or abuse anyone.

Many women feel guilty about things they had no control over. They feel guilty about being victimized. Often their original intention was to help another, but in the process they are damaged. Tamar was the king's daughter. She was a virgin. She was a "good girl." She didn't do anything immoral. It is amazing that her own brother would be so filled with desire that he would go to such lengths to destroy his sister. He thought he was in love. It wasn't love. It was lust. He craved her so intensely that he lost his appetite for food. He was visibly distorted with passion. Love is a giving force, while lust is a selfish compulsion centralized on gratification.

> *So Amnon lay down, and made himself sick: and when the king was come to see him, Amnon said unto the king, I pray thee, let Tamar my sister come, and make me a couple of cakes in my sight.... And Tamar took the cakes which she had made, and brought them into the chamber to Amnon her brother. And when she had brought them unto him to eat, he took hold of her... (2 Samuel 13:6,10-11).*

It is frightening to think about the nights that he plotted and conjured her destruction. The intensity of his passion for her was awesome. So much so, that even his father and cousin recognized that something had altered his behavior. He was filled with lustful passion for her.

> **Love is a giving force, while lust is a selfish compulsion centralized on gratification.**

Therefore we do not lose heart. Though outwardly we are wasting away, yet inwardly we are being renewed day by day. For our light and momentary troubles are achieving for us an eternal glory that far outweighs them all. 2 Corinthians 4:16-17 (NIV)

We went through a phase once when we thought real faith meant having no feelings. Now I believe that life without feelings is like a riverbed without water. The water is what makes the river a place of activity and life. You don't want to destroy the water, but you do need to control it. Feelings that are out of control are like the floodwaters of a river. The gushing currents of boisterous waters over their banks can bring death and destruction. They must be held at bay by restrictions and limitations. Although we don't want to be controlled by feelings, we must have access to our emotions. We need to allow ourselves the pleasure and pain of life.

Emotional pain is to the spirit what physical pain is to the body. Pain warns us that something is out of order and may require attention. Pain warns us that something in our body is not healed. In the same way, when pain fills our heart, we know that we have an area where healing or restoration is needed. We dare not ignore these signals, and neither dare we let them control us.

Above all, we need to allow the Spirit of God to counsel us and guide us through the challenges of realignment when upheavals occur in our lives. Even the finest limousine requires a regular schedule of tune-ups or realignments. Minor adjustments increase performance and productivity.

It is important to understand the difference between minor and major adjustments. The removal of a person from our lives is painful, but it is not a major adjustment. Whether you realize it or not, people are being born and dying every day. They are coming and going, marrying and divorcing, falling in love and falling out of love. You can survive the loss of people, *but you can't survive without God*! He is the force that allows you to overcome when people have taken you under. His grace enables you to overcome!

> We need to allow ourselves the pleasure and pain of life.

Thou hast caused men to ride over our heads; we went through fire and through water: but Thou broughtest us out into a wealthy place. Psalm 66:12

Then Satan answered the Lord, and said, Doth Job fear God for nought? Hast not Thou made an hedge about him, and about his house, and about all that he hath on every side? Thou hast blessed the work of his hands, and his substance is increased in the land. But put forth Thine hand now, and touch all that he hath, and he will curse Thee to Thy face (Job 1:9-11).

Satan cannot dispute your serving God, but he challenges our reason for serving Him. He says it is for the prominence and protection that God provides. He further insinuates that if things weren't going so well, we would not praise God so fervently. The devil is a liar! In each of our lives, in one way or another, we will face times when we must answer satan's charges and prove that even in the storm, He is still God!

Those early times of challenge sorely tried all that was in me. My pride, my self-esteem, and my self-confidence teetered like a child learning to ride a bicycle. My greatest fear was that it would never end. I feared that, like a person stuck in an elevator, I would spend the rest of my life between floors—neither here nor there in an intermediate stage of transition. I felt like a shoulder out of joint and in pain.

I learned, however, that if you can remember your beginnings and still reach toward your goals, God will bless you with things without fear of those items becoming idols in your life. Oddly, there is a glory in the agonizing of early years that people who didn't have to struggle seem not to possess. There is a strange sense of competence that comes from being born in the flames of struggle. How wildly exuberant are the first steps of the child who earlier was mobile only through crawling on his hands and knees.

> There is a strange sense of competence that comes from being born in the flames of struggle.

Deliver the poor and needy: rid them out of the hand of the wicked. Psalm 82:4

And when she had brought them unto him to eat, he took hold of her....but, being stronger than she, forced her, and lay with her (2 Samuel 13:11,14).

Amnon draws a picture for us of how badly the enemy wants to violate God's children. He is planning and plotting your destruction. He has watched you with wanton eyes. He has great passion and perseverance. Jesus told Peter, "Satan hath desired to have you, that he may sift you as wheat: but I have prayed for thee…" (Luke 22:31-32). Satan lusts after God's children. He wants you. He craves for you with an animalistic passion. He awaits an opportunity for attack. In addition, he loves to use people to fulfill the same kinds of lust upon one another.

Desire is a motivating force. It can make you do things you never thought yourself capable of doing. Lust can make a man break his commitment to himself. It will cause people to reach after things they never thought they would reach for.

Like Peter, you may have gone through some horrible times, but Jesus intercedes on your behalf. No matter the struggles women have faced, confidence is found in the ministry of our High Priest. He prays for you. Faith comes when you recognize that you can't help yourself. Only trust in Christ can bring you through. Many have suffered mightily, but Christ gives the strength to overcome the attacks of satan and human, selfish lust.

Often the residual effects of being abused linger for many years. Some never find deliverance because they never allow Christ to come into the dark places of their life. Jesus has promised to set you free from every curse of the past. If you have suffered abuse, please know that He will bring you complete healing. He wants the whole person well—in body, emotions and spirit. He will deliver you from all the residue of your past. Perhaps the incident is over but the crippling is still there. He also will deal with the crippling that's left in your life.

> *If you have suffered abuse, please know that He will bring you complete healing.*

$\mathscr{S}$URVIVAL PRODUCES PEACE

Consider it pure joy, my brothers, whenever you face trials of many kinds, because you know that the testing of your faith develops perseverance. James 1:2-3 (NIV)

Like a child who has fallen from his bicycle needs to find a place out of the view of his peers where he can honestly say, "Ouch! That hurt more than I showed in front of other people," we too need a private place of honesty. We need to be honest with ourselves. We need a place where we can sit down, reflect, and mourn. However, we must be careful not to mourn over the past longer than necessary. After the funeral, there is always a burial. The burial separates the survivor from the deceased, and it is as far as we can go. So you must come to a place of separation and decide to live on.

> *And the Lord said unto Samuel, How long wilt thou mourn for Saul, seeing I have rejected him from reigning over Israel? fill thine horn with oil, and go, I will send thee to Jesse the Bethlehemite: for I have provided Me a king among his sons (1 Samuel 16:1).*

In spite of the pain and distaste of adversity, it is impossible not to notice that *each adverse event leaves sweet nectar behind*, which, in turn, can produce its own rich honey in the character of the survivor. It is this bittersweet honey that allows us to enrich the lives of others through our experiences and testimonies. There is absolutely no substitute for the syrupy nectar of human experiences. It is these experiences that season the future relationships God has in store for us.

Unfortunately, many people leave their situation bitter and not better. Be careful to bring the richness of the experience to the hurting, not the unresolved bitterness. This kind of bitterness is a sign that the healing process in you is not over and, therefore, is not ready to be shared. When we have gone through the full cycle of survival, the situations and experiences in our lives will produce no pain, only peace.

> $\mathscr{E}$*ach adverse event leaves sweet nectar behind,* **which, in turn, can produce its own rich honey in the character of the survivor.**

Therefore thus saith the Lord God, Behold, I lay in Zion for a foundation a stone, a tried stone, a precious corner stone, a sure foundation: he that believeth shall not make haste. Isaiah 28:16

According to the grace of God which is given unto me, as a wise masterbuilder, I have laid the foundation, and another buildeth thereon. But let every man take heed how he buildeth thereupon (1 Corinthians 3:10).

Why do so many people try to convey the image that they have always been on top? The truth is most people have struggled to attain whatever they have. They just try to convince everyone that they have always had it. I, for one, am far more impressed with the wealth of a person's character who doesn't use his success to intimidate others. The real, rich inner stability that comes from gradual success is far more lasting and beneficial than the temperamental theatrics of spiritual yuppies who have never learned their own vulnerabilities. We must not take ourselves too seriously. I believe that God grooms us for greatness in the stockades of struggle....

I have found God to be a builder of men. When He builds, He emphasizes the foundation. A foundation, once it is laid, is neither visible nor attractive, but nevertheless still quite necessary. When God begins to establish the foundation, He does it in the feeble, frail beginnings of our lives. Paul describes himself as a wise master builder. Actually, God is the Master Builder. He knows what kind of beginning we need and He lays His foundation in the struggles of our formative years.

The concern over the future coupled with the fear of failure brings us to the posture of prayer. I don't think I completely realized how severe my early years of ministry were because I saw them through the tinted glasses of grace. I had been gifted with the grace to endure. Often we don't realize how severe our beginnings were until we are out or about to come out of them. Then the grace lifts and we behold the utter devastating truth about what we just came through.

> God is the Master Builder.... He lays His foundation in the struggles of our formative years.

And this I pray, that your love may abound still more and more in knowledge and all discernment. Philippians 1:9 (NKJ)

One of the things that makes many women particularly vulnerable to different types of abuse and manipulation is their maternal instinct. Wicked men frequently capitalize on this tendency in order to have their way with women. Mothers like to take care of little helpless babies. It seems that the more helpless a man acts, the more maternal you become. Women instinctively are nurturers, reaching out to needy people in order to nurture, love and provide inner strength. All too often, these healthy desires are taken advantage of by those who would fulfill their own lusts. The gift of discernment must operate in your life. There are many wonderful men. But I must warn you against someone like David's son Amnon. He is dangerous.

And Tamar took the cakes which she had made, and brought them into the chamber to Amnon her brother. And when she had brought them unto him to eat, he took hold of her, and said unto her, Come lie with me, my sister. And she answered him, Nay, my brother, do not force me; for no such thing ought to be done in Israel: do not thou this folly...Howbeit he would not hearken unto her voice: but, being stronger than she, forced her, and lay with her (2 Samuel 13:10-12,14).

The number of cases of violence within relationships and marriages is growing at an alarming rate. The incidence of date rape is reaching epidemic proportions. The fastest growing form of murder today is within relationships. Husbands and wives and girlfriends and boyfriends are killing one another. Often women have taken to murder in order to escape the constant violence of an abusive husband. It is important that you do not allow loneliness to coerce you into Amnon's bed.

Another form of abuse is more subtle. There are those men who often coerce women into a sexual relationship by claiming that they love them. Deception is emotional rape! It is a terrible feeling to be used by someone. Looking for love in all the wrong places leads to a feeling of abuse. A deceiver may continually promise that he will leave his wife for his lover. This woman holds on to that hope, but it never seems to come true. He makes every kind of excuse possible for taking advantage of her, and she, because of her vulnerability, follows blindly along until the relationship has gone so far that she is trapped.

> *All too often,* healthy desires are taken advantage of by those who would fulfill their own lusts.

And He arose, and rebuked the wind, and said unto the sea, Peace, be still. And the wind ceased, and there was a great calm. Mark 4:39

Have you allowed God to stand in the bow of your ship and speak peace to the thing that once terrified you? We can only benefit from resolved issues. The great tragedy is that most of us keep our pain active. Consequently, our power is never activated because our past remains unresolved. If we want to see God's power come from the pain of an experience, we must allow the process of healing to take us far beyond bitterness into a resolution that releases us from the prison and sets us free.

God's healing process makes us free to taste life again, free to trust again, and free to live without the restrictive force of threatening fears. Someone may say, "I don't want to trust again." That is only because you are not healed. To never trust again is to live on the pinnacle of a tower. You are safe from life's threatening grasp, but you are so detached from life that you soon lose consciousness of people, places, dates, and events. You become locked into a time warp. You always talk about the past *because you stopped living years ago*. Listen to your speech. You discuss the past as if it were the present because *the past has stolen the present* right out of your hand! In the name of Jesus, get it back!

Celebration is in order. Yes, it is time to celebrate—regardless of whether you've lost a marriage, a partnership, or a personal friend. Celebration is in order because you were split from your Siamese twin and you are not dead. You are still alive!…Are you ready to live, or do you still need to subject all your friends to a history class? Will you continue your incessant raging and blubbering about that which no one can change—the past?…

I am only trying to jump-start your heart and put you back into the presence of a real experience, far from the dank, dark valley of regret and remorse. It is easy to unconsciously live in an euphoric, almost historical mirage that causes current opportunities to evade you.

> *Y*ou discuss the past as if it were the present because *the past has stolen the present* right out of your hand!

And I, brethren, could not speak unto you as unto spiritual, but as unto carnal, even as unto babes in Christ. 1 Corinthians 3:1

When I was very small, my family had a tradition we observed every Sunday breakfast. Every Sunday morning my mother would go into the kitchen while we were still asleep and begin making homemade waffles for breakfast. These were real waffles. I don't remember all the ingredients she had in them, but I do remember that this particular recipe required beating the egg whites and then folding them into the waffle batter....

When I would rise, clad in a pair of worn pajamas and scuffy shoes, the smell of waffles would fill the room with the kind of aroma that made you float out of the bed. I can still see that old waffle iron. It was round and had an old cord that was thick and striped. On the top of the shiny round lid was a thermostat that showed how hot the waffles were. My mother never needed it because the waffle would begin to steam and hiss. It would push that lid up as if the waffle had been sleeping too and decided to rise. There was no doubt in anybody's mind that they were done. They smelled like Hallelujah and they looked like glory to God—if you know what I mean. They took a long time to prepare, but these waffles took your mouth to the butter-filled streams of heaven. Breakfast on Sunday morning was a religious experience.

The other day I tasted some of these modern carbon-copy, freezer burned, cardboard-clad waffles. My taste buds recoiled. Those things should be arrested for impersonating a waffle. I am convinced that most of the following generations will never know the soft, succulent experience of sticking a clean fork into the butter-filled, syrup-drenched, angel-light waffles that I grew up on. These instant waffles that leap out of a toaster like Houdini have about all the tender texture of rawhide. My point is, I am afraid that too many Christians pop off the altar like these cardboard waffles. They are overnight wonders. They are 24-hour pastors with a Bible they haven't read and a briefcase more valuable than the sermons in it!

> Too many Christians pop off the altar like these cardboard waffles.

...For the Lord hath comforted His people, and will have mercy upon His afflicted. Isaiah 49:13

Men who have sex with women without being committed to them are just as guilty of abuse as a rapist. A woman may have given her body to such a man, but she did so because of certain expectations. When someone uses another person for sex by misleading them, it is the same as physical rape. The abuse is more subtle, but it amounts to the same thing. Both the abuser and the victim are riding into a blazing inferno. Anything can happen when a victim has had enough.

Some women suffer from low self-esteem. They are victims and they don't even know it. Perhaps every time something goes wrong, you think it's your fault. It is not your fault if you are being abused in this way; it is your fault if you don't allow God's Word to arrest sin and weakness in your life. It is time to let go of every ungodly relationship. Do it now!

> So Tamar went to her brother Amnon's house; and he was laid down. And she took flour, and kneaded it, and made cakes in his sight, and did bake the cakes. And she took a pan, and poured them out before him; but he refused to eat. And Amnon said, Have out all men from me. And they went out every man from him. And Amnon said unto Tamar, Bring the meat into the chamber, that I may eat of thine hand. And Tamar took the cakes which she had made, and brought them into the chamber to Amnon her brother...but, being stronger than she, forced her, and lay with her (2 Samuel 13:8-10,14b).

When Tamar came into that ancient Israeli bedroom, her brother took advantage of her maternal instincts. He told her that he needed help. He sought her sympathy. Once she gave in to his requests for help, he violently raped her. Although the circumstances be different, the same thing is happening today.

The kind of violent act that Amnon performed that night was more than an offense against a young lady. He offended God and society by committing incest. There are those who attend church who are incestuous. It still happens today, but God is saying that enough is enough!

> Allow God's Word to arrest sin and weakness in your life.

RE YOU ALONE?

Be still, and know that I am God: I will be exalted among the heathen, I will be exalted in the earth. Psalm 46:10

DAY 69

All too often, our thoughts and conversations reveal that we wrestle with characters who have moved on and events that don't really matter. The people who surround us are kept on hold while we invest massive amounts of attention to areas of the past that are dead and possess no ability to reward. It is like slow dancing alone, or singing harmony when there is no melody. There is something missing that causes our presentation to lose its luster. Stop the music! Your partner is gone and you are waiting by yourself!

I think that the greatest of all depressions comes when we live and gather our successes just to prove something *to someone who isn't even looking*. The problem is we can't really appreciate our successes because they are done *by us* but not *for us*. They are done in the name of a person, place, or thing that has moved on, leaving us trapped in a time warp, wondering why we are not fulfilled by our job, ministry, or good fortune.

God did most of His work on creation with no one around to applaud His accomplishments. So He praised Himself. He said, "It was good!" Have you stopped to appreciate what God has allowed you to accomplish, or have you been too busy trying to make an impression on someone? No one paints for the blind or sings for the deaf. Their level of appreciation is hindered by their physical limitations. Although they may be fine connoisseurs in some other arena, they will never appreciate what they can't detect.

Let's clap and cheer for the people whose absence teaches us the gift of being alone. Somewhere beyond loneliness there is contentment, and contentment is born out of necessity. It springs up in the hum of the heart that lives in an empty house, and in the smirk and smile that comes on the face of a person who has amused himself with his own thoughts.

> Somewhere beyond loneliness there is contentment, and contentment is born out of necessity.

But, beloved, be not ignorant of this one thing, that one day is with the Lord as a thousand years, and a thousand years as one day. 2 Peter 3:8

I know this sounds old-fashioned, but I believe anything worth doing is worth doing well. God Himself takes His time developing us. No instant success will do. He wants to put the quality in before the name goes out. A small beginning is just the prelude to a tremendous crescendo at the finale! Many of God's masterpieces were developed in small obscure circumstances. Moses, the messiah of the Old Testament sent to the lost sheep of Israel, was trained in leadership while shoveling sheep dung on the backside of the desert. There was no fancy finishing school for this boy. Granted, his discipline was developed in the royal courts of Pharaoh's house, but his disposition was shaped through a failure in his life and a desert kingdom with no one to lead but flies, gnats, and sheep. Who would have thought, looking at Moses' church of goat deacons and gnats for choir members, that he later would lead the greatest movement in the history of Old Testament theology?

Who would have guessed that old impotent Abraham, whose sun had gone down and force gone out, would finally father a nation—in fact, a nationality? One moment he is sitting on the edge of the bed with an embarrassed look on his face and the next moment he is fathering children even after Sarah's death. You can't tell what's in you by looking at you. God is establishing patience, character, and concentration in the school of "nothing seems to be happening." Take the class and get the course credit; it's working for your good.

Many misunderstand the prophecies of the Lord and so feel discontentment and despair. Just because God promises to move in your life and anoints you to do a particular function doesn't mean that your foundation will be immediately built.

> God is establishing patience, character, and concentration in the school of "nothing seems to be happening."

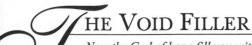

Now the God of hope fill you with all joy and peace in believing, that ye may abound in hope, through the power of the Holy Ghost. Romans 15:13

Some have been abused, misused and victimized. Some played a part in their own demise. There are those who live in fear and pain because of the immoral relationships that took place in the home. If you know this kind of pain, the Lord wants to heal you. Those who have a desperate need for male attention, have usually come from a situation where there has been an absence of positive male role models in the home. Perhaps you didn't get enough nurturing as a girl. Therefore, it becomes easy to compromise and do anything to find male acceptance and love.

The Lord is calling the hurting to Him. He will fill that void in your life. He wants to be that heavenly Father who will mend your heart with a positive role model. Through the Spirit, He wants to hold and nurture you. Millions have longed for a positive hug and nurturing embrace from fathers without ever receiving what they longed for. There is a way to fill that emptiness inside. It is through a relationship with God.

Men, God is healing us so we can recognize that a woman who is not our wife is to be treated as our sister. Women must learn that they can have a platonic relationship with men. A brotherly and sisterly love does not include sexual intimacy. It does not include self-gratification.

There is a place in the heart of most women for an intimate and yet platonic relationship. Big brothers tend to protect their little sisters. They tend to watch for traps that may be placed in the sisters' way. Abused women have confused ideas abut relationships, and may not understand a healthy platonic relationship with the opposite sex. This confusion comes from the past. One lady said that she could never trust a man who didn't sleep with her. Actually, she had a long history of victimization that led to her poor view of relationships.

> There is a way to fill that emptiness inside. It is through a relationship with God.

In whom also we have obtained an inheritance, being predestinated according to the purpose of Him who worketh all things after the counsel of His own will. Ephesians 1:11

Have you reached that place in life where you enjoy your own company? Have you taken the time to enjoy your own personhood? Have you massaged lotion into your own skin, or set the dinner table for yourself? Drive yourself to the mall and spend an afternoon picking out a gift for yourself. These self-affirming ministries can never be given to you by someone else. When other people give it, it reflects their opinion about you. When they leave, you may feel worthless and insignificant. But when you speak comfort and blessings to yourself, it reflects your own opinion about yourself. The best scenario is to enjoy both kinds of affirmation.

There are reasons to give yourself a standing ovation. The first is the fact that your steps are carefully observed and arranged by God Himself. They are designed to achieve a special purpose in your life. He brings people in and out of your life, yet you are blessed going in and going out (see Deut. 28:6). That is to say, your blessing has not and never will be predicated upon the action of another. The Bible says, "If God be for us, who can be against us?" (Rom. 8:31b) So you must rejoice because you are in step with the beat of Heaven and the purposes of God.

Second, you ought to rejoice because you are pursuing a goal that defies human manipulation. Your blessing rests in accomplishing the will of God. Jesus went to Samaria in John 4 to minister to a hostile, religiously indifferent woman who initially had little appreciation for Him. Yet, He was nourished even by her defensive demeanor because He clearly understood that His purpose for being there was greater than the need of any one woman. Her comments lost their meaning when He weighed them against His purpose. He knew that her struggle to understand and affirm Him was of little consequence because He had a mission, yet He knew she was a part of the plan. He wasn't there to pass the time away. He was there to provoke destiny!

> You ought to rejoice because you are pursuing a goal that defies human manipulation.

Until we all reach unity in the faith and in the knowledge of the Son of God and become mature, attaining to the whole measure of the fullness of Christ.
Ephesians 4:13 (NIV)

Many misunderstand the prophecies of the Lord and so feel discontentment and despair. Just because God promises to move in your life and anoints you to do a particular function doesn't mean that your foundation will be immediately built. Directly after David was anointed to lead Israel, he was sent back into the field to feed the sheep. Joseph received a dream from the Lord that showed him ruling and reigning over his brothers, but in the next event his brothers stripped him, beat him, and tossed him in a hole. Can you imagine what the devil said to Joseph while he nursed his scrapes and bruises in the dark hole of small beginnings?

Swallowed up with bruises and scars, he listened to the sound of depression sweeping through his throbbing head that beat like the congo drums of an African warrior. Satan's laugh filled the dark channels of the hole with his evil hysteria. "So you were going to reign, were you? I thought the dream said you were in charge," the enemy taunted. Satan didn't understand that all great prophecies start out small. Like chestnuts in the hand of a child, those same chestnuts will one day be large enough to hold a child like the one who once held them. God has not changed His mind. His methods may seem crude, but His purpose is to provide wonderful success. Don't die in the hole! God hasn't changed His mind. He is a Master Builder and He spends extra time laying a great foundation.

When the first man Adam was created, he was created full grown. He had no childhood, no small things. He was just immediately a man. But when it was time for the last man Adam, God didn't create Him full grown. No, He took His time and laid a foundation. He was born a child and laid in a manger. The Manager of the universe was laid in a manger. "For unto us a child is born, unto us a son is given…" (Isa. 9:6). The Bible says that He grew in favor with God and man (see Luke 2:52). Not too fast, but He grew. Please allow yourself time to grow.

> *When it was time for the last man Adam, God didn't create Him full grown.*

Let your light so shine before men, that they may see your good works, and glorify your Father which is in heaven. Matthew 5:16

It is wonderful to have a plan, but that means nothing if you have no power to perform the plan and accomplish the purpose. God sends people in and out of your life to exercise your faith and develop your character. When they are gone, they leave you with the enriched reality that your God is with you to deliver you wherever you go! Moses died and left Joshua in charge, but God told him, "As I was with Moses, so I will be with thee" (Josh. 1:5). Joshua never would have learned that while Moses was there. You learn this kind of thing when "Moses" is gone. Power is developed in the absence of human assistance. Then we can test the limits of our resourcefulness and the magnitude of the favor of God.

As we go further, you may want to reevaluate who your real friends are. You see more clearly that the people who treated you the worst were actually preparing you for the best. They stripped from you the cumbersome weights and entanglements that hindered the birth of inner resilience. Yes, such friends leave us feeling naked and even vulnerable, but it is through those feelings that we begin to adapt and see our survival instincts peak. There is within the most timid person—beneath that soft, flaccid demeanor—a God-given strength that supercedes any weakness he appeared to have. The Bible puts it this way: "I can do all things through Christ which strengtheneth me" (Phil. 4:13)!

Greater still is the fact that we gain great direction through *rejection*. Rejection helps us focus on new horizons without the hindrances of wondering, "What if?"

Power is developed in the absence of human assistance.

WOMAN, THOU ART LOVED

DAY 75

By this shall all men know that ye are My disciples, if ye have love one to another.
John 13:35

Society often places a woman's worth on her sexual appeal. Nothing is further from the truth. Self-esteem cannot be earned by performance in bed. Society suggests that the only thing men want is sex. Although the male sex drive is very strong, all men are not like David's son Amnon who raped his sister Tamar (see 2 Sam. 13:1-21). Men, in general, are not the enemy. We cannot use Amnon as a basis to evaluate all men. Do not allow an Amnon experience to taint your future. Draw a line of demarcation and say to yourself, "That was then and this is now!"

The Song of Solomon shows a progression of the relationship between the author and his wife. First she was his sister, then she became his bride. He also wrote of protecting a little sister. There are many new converts in the Church who are to be treated as little sisters. Solomon says, "enclose her with boards of cedar" (Song of Sol. 8:9). The Church is God's cedar chest!

God's people are to nurture and protect one another. It makes no difference how tempestuous our past life has been. Even in the face of abuse, God still cares. Allow Him the privilege of doing what Absalom did for Tamar. He took her in. "He that dwelleth in the secret place of the most High shall abide under the shadow of the Almighty" (Ps. 91:1). Tamar lay outside Amnon's door—a fragmented, bruised rose petal. Her dreams were shattered. Her confidence was violated. Her virginity was desecrated. But Absalom took her into his domain. Did you know that God has intensive care? He will take you in His arms. That love of God is flowing into broken lives all over the country. Don't believe for one moment that no one cares; God cares and the Church is learning to become a conduit of that concern. At last, we are in the school of love.

> At last, we are in the school of love.

For even Christ did not please Himself; but as it is written, "The reproaches of those who reproached You fell on Me." Romans 15:3 (NKJ)

Buried deep within the broken heart is a vital need to *release and resolve*. Although we feel pain when we fail at any task, there is a sweet resolve that delivers us from the cold clutches of uncertainty. If we had not been through some degree of rejection, we would have never been selected by God. *Do you realize that God chooses people that others reject?!* From a rejected son like David to a nearly murdered son like Joseph, God gathers the castaways of men and recycles them for Kingdom building.

What frustration exists in the lives of people who want to be used of God, but who cannot endure rejection from men. I admit I haven't always possessed the personality profile that calloused me and offered some protection from the backlash of public opinion. This ability to endure is similar to having a taste for steak tartare—it must be acquired! If you want to be tenacious, you must be able to walk in the light of God's selection rather than dwell in the darkness of people's rejection. These critics are usually just a part of God's purpose in your life.

Focus is everything in ministry. If your attention is distracted by the constant thirst of other people, or if you are always trying to win people over, you will never be able to minister to the Lord—not if you are trying to win people. It seems almost as though He orchestrates your rejections to keep you from idolatry. We can easily make idols out of other people. However, God is too wise to build a house that is divided against itself. Against this rough canvas of rejection and the pain it produces, God paints the greatest sunrise the world has ever seen!

Healing, Blessings, and Freedom

God gathers the cast-aways of men and recycles them for Kingdom building.

DON'T OUTGROW YOUR FOUNDATION

I will liken him unto a wise man, which built his house upon a rock: And the rain descended, and the floods came, and the winds blew, and beat upon that house; and it fell not: for it was founded upon a rock.... and the winds blew, and beat upon that house; and it fell: and great was the fall of it. Matthew 7:24b-27

Once I was praying for the Lord to move mightily in my ministry. I had asked, fasted, and prayed. I had probably begged a little and foamed at the mouth too, but none of it hurried the plan of God in my life. After many days of absolute silence, He finally sent me a little answer. The Lord answered my prayer by saying, "You are concerned about building a ministry, but I am concerned about building a man." He concluded by mentioning this warning, which has echoed in my ears all of my life. He said, "Woe unto the man whose ministry becomes bigger than he is!" Since then I have concerned myself with praying for the minister and not for the ministry. I realized that if the house outgrows the foundation, gradually the foundation will crack, the walls will collapse, and great will be the fall of it!

No matter what you are trying to build, whether it is a business, a ministry, or a relationship, give it time to grow. Some of the best friendships start out gradually. Some of the strongest Christians once desperately needed prayer for their weaknesses. I am still amazed at who I am becoming as I put my life daily into His hands. He is changing me. He's not finished. There is so much more that needs to be done. Every day I see more immaturity in me. But, what a sharp contrast I am now to what I was.

Humility is a necessity when you know that every accomplishment had to be the result of the wise Master Builder who knows when to do what. He knew when I needed friends. He knew when I needed to sit silently in the night, wrap my arms around my limitations, and whisper a soft request for help into the abyss of my pain. He is the One who rolls back the clouds on the storms and orders the rain to stop. Oh, how I trust Him more dearly and more nearly than I have ever trusted Him before. He is too wise to make a mistake!

> If the house outgrows the foundation, gradually the foundation will crack, the walls will collapse, and great will be the fall of it!

Jesus saith unto them, Did ye never read in the scriptures, The stone which the builders rejected, the same is become the head of the corner: this is the Lord's doing, and it is marvellous in our eyes? Matthew 21:42

Jesus concluded that the rejections of men He experienced were the doings of the Lord! As Joseph so aptly put it, "…Ye thought evil against me; but God meant it unto good" (Gen. 50:20a). The Lord orchestrates what the enemy does and makes it accomplish His purpose in your life. This is the Lord's doing! How many times have "evil" things happened in your life that later you realized were necessary? If I hadn't faced trials like these, I know that I wouldn't have been ready for the blessings I now enjoy.

In the hands of God, even our most painful circumstances become marvelous in our eyes! When we see how perfectly God has constructed His plan, we can laugh in the face of failure. However, *rejection is only marvelous in the eyes of someone whose heart has wholly trusted in the Lord!* Have you wholly trusted in the Lord, or are you grieving over something that someone has done—as though you have no God to direct it and no grace to correct it?

This is an important question because it challenges the perspectives you have chosen to take for your life. The statement, "It is marvelous in our eyes" simply means that from our perspective, the worst things look good! That is what you need faith to do! Faith is not needed just to remove problems; it is also needed to *endure* problems that seem immovable. Rest assured that even if God didn't move it, He is able! If your able God chose to stand passively by and watch someone come whose actions left you in pain, you still must trust in His sovereign grace and immutable character. He works for your good. Someone wrote a song that said, "If life hands you a lemon, just make lemonade." That's cute, but the truth is, if you walk with God, He will do the squeezing and the mixing that turns lemons into lemonade!

> The Lord orchestrates what the enemy does and makes it accomplish His purpose in your life.

Bear ye one another's burdens, and so fulfil the law of Christ. Galatians 6:2

Love embraces the totality of the other person. It is impossible to completely and effectively love someone without being included in that other person's history. Our history has made us who we are. The images, scars and victories that we live with have shaped us into the people we have become. We will never know who a person is until we understand where they have been.

The secret of being transformed from a vulnerable victim to a victorious, loving person is found in the ability to open your past to someone responsible enough to share your weaknesses and pains. You don't have to keep reliving it. You can release it.

There can be no better first step toward deliverance than to find a Christian counselor or pastor and come out of hiding. Of course, some care should be taken. No one is expected to air their personal life to everyone or even everywhere. However, if you seek God's guidance and the help of confident leadership, you will find someone who can help you work through the pain and suffering of being a victim. The Church is a body. No one operates independent of another. We are all in this walk together, and therefore can build one another up and carry some of the load with which our sisters are burdened.

Tamar was victimized brutally, yet she survived. There is hope for victims. There is no need to feel weak when one has Jesus Christ. His power is enough to bring about the kinds of changes that will set you free. He is calling, through the work of the Holy Spirit, for you to be set free.

> You will find someone who can help you work through the pain and suffering of being a victim.

Normally, anytime there is a crash, there is an injury. If one person collides with another, they generally damage everything associated with them. In the same way, a crashing relationship affects everyone associated with it, whether it is in a corporate office, a ministry, or a family. That jarring and shaking does varying degrees of damage to everyone involved. Whether we like to admit it or not, we are affected by the actions of others to various degrees. The amount of the effect, though, depends on the nature of the relationship.

What is important is the fact that we don't have to die in the crashes and collisions of life. We must learn to live life with a seat belt in place, even though it is annoying to wear. Similarly, we need spiritual and emotional seat belts as well. We don't need the kind that harness us in and make us live like a mannequin; rather, we need the kind that are invisible, but greatly appreciated in a crash.

Inner assurance is the seat belt that stops you from going through the roof when you are rejected. It is inner assurance that holds you in place. It is the assurance that God is in control and that what He has determined no one can disallow! If He said He was going to bless you, then disregard the mess and believe a God who cannot lie. The rubbish can be cleared and the bruises can be healed. Just be sure that when the smoke clears, you are still standing. You are too important to the purpose of God to be destroyed by a situation that is only meant to give you character and direction. No matter how painful, devastated, or disappointed you may feel, you are still here. Praise God, for He will use the cornerstone developed through rejections and failed relationships to perfect what He has prepared!

Lift your voice above the screaming sirens and alarms of men whose hearts have panicked! Lift your eyes above the billowing smoke and spiraling emotions. Pull yourself up—it could have killed you, but it didn't. Announce to yourself, "I am alive. I can laugh. I can cry, and by God's grace, I can survive!"

> We must learn to live life with a seat belt in place, even though it is annoying to wear.

Not that I speak in respect of want: for I have learned, in whatsoever state I am, therewith to be content. I know both how to be abased, and I know how to abound: every where and in all things I am instructed both to be full and to be hungry, both to abound and to suffer need. Philippians 4:11-12

If you are praying, "Lord, make me bigger," you are probably miserable, although prayerful. Did you know you can be prayerful and still be miserable? Anytime you use prayer to change God, who is perfect, instead of using prayer to change yourself, you are miserable. Stop manipulating God! Stop trying to learn something you can say to God to make Him do what He knows you are not ready to endure or receive. Instead, try praying this: "Lord, make me better." I admit that better is harder to measure and not as noticeable to the eye. But better will overcome bigger every time....

The real, rich inner stability that comes from gradual success is far more lasting and beneficial than the temperamental theatrics of spiritual yuppies who have never learned their own vulnerabilities. We must not take ourselves too seriously. I believe that God grooms us for greatness in the stockades of struggle....

What a joy it is to be at peace with who you are and where you are in your life. How restful it is to not try and beat the clock with friends or try to prove anything to foes. You will never change their minds anyway, so change your own. I want to be better—to have a better character, better confidence, and a better attitude! The desire to be bigger will not allow you to rest, relax, or enjoy your blessing. The desire to be better, however, will afford you a barefoot stroll down a deserted beach. You can sit in the sand, throw shells into the water, and shiver when the tide rushes up too high. Sing into the wind a song out of tune. It may not harmonize, but it will be full of therapy. There are probably many things you didn't get done and so much you have left to do. But isn't it nice to sigh, relax, and just thank God for the things—the little, tiny, small things—that you know He brought you through. Thank God for small things.

> The desire to be bigger will not allow you to rest, relax, or enjoy your blessing.

Hear counsel, and receive instruction, that thou mayest be wise in thy latter end. Proverbs 19:20

This morning when I rose, the land was still asleep. I watched the miracle of beginnings from the veranda of my hotel. The waves of the sea wandered listlessly in and dashed themselves on empty beaches where the sand smiled at the peacefulness of the breaking day. Like the initial sounds of an orchestra warming up for a concerto, the sea gulls cried and screeched out their opening solos. The wind watched, occasionally brushing past the palm trees spreading their leaves like the fan of a distinguished lady. Far to the east the sun creeped up on stage as if it was trying to arrive without disturbing anyone. It peeked up over the ocean like the eye of a child around a corner as he stealthily plays peek-a-boo.

If I had not stayed perched on my window's edge, I would have misjudged the day. I would have thought that the morning or perhaps the bustling sun-drenched afternoon was the most beautiful part of the day. I would have thought the sound of laughing, hysterically happy children running into or away from the ocean would, without contention, have won the award for the best part of the day. But just before I turned in my ballot and cast my vote in the poll, the wisdom of the evening slipped up on the stage. The early morning entertainment and the bustling sounds of the afternoon had distracted me. Now I looked over in the distance as the sun began its descent. I noticed that the crescendo of the concert is always reserved for the closing. How had I not noticed that the sun had changed her sundress to an evening gown, full of color and grandeur. The grace of a closing day is far greater than the uncertainty of morning. The next time you get a chance to notice a sun burst into its neon rainbow and curtsy before setting in the west, you will scratch out your early scribbling and recast your vote; for the most beautiful part of the day, in fact the most beautiful part of a woman's life, is at the setting of the sun.

> For the most beautiful part of the day, in fact the most beautiful part of a woman's life, is at the setting of the sun.

For you know that we dealt with each of you as a father deals with his own children, encouraging, comforting and urging you to live lives worthy of God, who calls you into His kingdom and glory. 1 Thessalonians 2:11-12 (NIV)

We often face discouragement in this world. Many have never had anyone who believed in them. Even after achieving some level of success in one area or another, many have not had anyone to point out their potential. Isn't it amazing how we can see so much potential in others, yet find it difficult to unlock our own hidden treasure? Highly motivated people are not exempt from needing someone to underline their strengths and weaknesses. It is impossible to perceive how much stronger we might be if we had had stronger nurturing. Nurturing is the investment necessary to stimulate the potential that we possess. Without nurturing, inner strengths may remain dormant. Therefore it is crucial to our development that there be some degree of nurturing the intrinsic resources we possess.

There is a difference in the emotional makeup of a child who has had a substantial deposit of affection and affirmation. Great affirmation occurs when someone invests into our personhood. I believe that people are the greatest investments in the world. A wonderful bond exists between the person who invests and the one in whom the investment is made. This bond evolves from the heart of anyone who recognizes the investment was made before the person accomplished the goal. Anyone will invest in a sure success, but aren't we grateful when someone supports us when we were somewhat of a risk?

Although it is true that fire will not destroy gold, it is important to note that fire purifies the gold. When God gets ready to polish His gold, He uses fiery trials. Unfortunately, nothing brings luster to your character and commitment to your heart like opposition does. The finished product is a result of the fiery process. Whenever you see someone shining with the kind of brilliancy that enables God to look down and see Himself, you are looking at someone who has been through the furnace of affliction.

> **N**urturing is the investment necessary to stimulate the potential that we possess.

To every thing there is a season, and a time to every purpose under the heaven. Ecclesiastes 3:1

I write this with my mother in mind. Her hair has changed colors before my eyes. Like afterthoughts of an artist, lines have been etched upon her brow. Her arms are much weaker now and her gait much slower; but she is somehow warmer at life's winter age than she was in the summer days. All of life's tragedy has been wrestled to the mat and still she stands to attest to the authenticity of her goals, dreams and ambitions. What is wrong with hanging around the stage to collect an encore from a grateful audience whose lives have been touched by the beauty of your song? Just because the glare of summer doesn't beat upon your face doesn't mean that there is nothing left for you to do. Whose presence will stand as a witness that God will see you through? Who will care to catch a glimpse of your children run their race or catch them when they fall beneath the weight of their day? God never extends days beyond purpose. My daughters are in their springtime, my wife is in the middle of summer, and my mother is walking through autumn to step into winter. Together they form a chord of womanhood—three different notes creating a harmonious blend. To the reader, I would suggest: Enjoy every note.

> *While the earth remaineth, seedtime and harvest, and cold and heat, and summer and winter, and day and night shall not cease (Genesis 8:22).*

Our culture has celebrated youth to such a degree that we have isolated the elderly. The Hollywood mentality accentuates the dynamics of youth as though each season of life didn't have its own beauty. Anyone who observes nature will tell you that all seasons have their own advantages and disadvantages.

> Anyone who observes nature will tell you that all seasons have their own advantages and disadvantages.

NOWHERE TO HIDE

Am I a God at hand, saith the Lord, and not a God afar off? Can any hide himself in secret places that I shall not see him? saith the Lord. Do not I fill heaven and earth? saith the Lord. Jeremiah 23:23-24

There is no tiptoeing around the presence of God with pristine daintiness—as if we could tiptoe softly enough not to awaken a God who never sleeps nor slumbers. We shuffle in His presence like children who were instructed not to disturb their Father, although God isn't sleepy and He doesn't have to go to work. He is alive and awake, and He is well. We blare like trumpets announcing our successes, but we whisper our failures through parched lips in the shadows of our relationship with Him. We dare not air our inconsistencies with arrogance because we know we are so underdeveloped and dependent upon Him for everything we need.

His holiness is our objective; we have aspired to acquire it for years, but none have attained it. Surely there is some qualitative relationship that we imperfect sons can master in the presence of our Holy Father! I, for one, need a Father whose wrinkled-up eyes can see beyond my broken places and know the longing of my heart.

It is the nature of a fallen man to hide from God. If you will remember, Adam also hid from God. How ridiculous it is for us to think that we can hide from Him! His intelligence supercedes our frail ability to be deceptive. Adam confessed (after he was cornered by his Father), "I heard Thy voice in the garden, and I was afraid, because I was naked; and I hid myself" (Gen. 3:10). Do you see what the first man did? He hid himself. No wonder we are lost. We have hidden ourselves....

When a man hides himself from God, he loses himself. What good is it to know where everything else is, if we cannot find ourselves? Our loss causes a desperation that produces sin and separation. Like the prodigal son in chapter 15 of Luke, in our desperation we need to come to ourselves and come out from under the bushes where we have hidden ourselves. We need to become transparent in the presence of the Lord.

It is the nature of a fallen man to hide from God.

Now she that is a widow indeed, and desolate, trusteth in God, and continueth in supplications and prayers night and day. 1 Timothy 5:5

And she said unto them, Call me not Naomi, call me Mara: for the Almighty hath dealt very bitterly with me. I went out full, and the Lord hath brought me home again empty: why then call ye me Naomi, seeing the Lord hath testified against me, and the Almighty hath afflicted me? (Ruth 1:20-21)

It is important that we teach women to prepare for the winter. I believe age can be stressful for women in a way that it isn't for men—only because we have not historically recognized women at other stages in their lives. Equally disturbing is the fact that statisticians tell us women tend to live longer, more productive lives than their male counterparts. It is not their longevity of life that is disturbing; it is the fact that many times, because of an early death of their spouse, they have no sense of companionship.

The Bible admonishes us to minister to the widows. Little instruction is given in regard to the care of aged men. We need to invest some effort in encouraging older women. They have a need for more than just provision of natural substance. Many women spend their lives building their identity around their role rather than around their person. When the role changes, they feel somewhat displaced. Because being a good mother is a self-sacrificing job, when those demands have subsided, many women feel like Naomi. Her name meant "my joy." But after losing her children and husband she said, "Change my name to 'Mara'." *Mara* means "bitterness." Don't allow changing times to change who you are. It is dangerous to lose your identity in your circumstances. Circumstances change and when they do, the older woman can feel empty and unfulfilled. In spite of Naomi's bout with depression, God still had much for her to contribute. So just because the demands have changed, that doesn't mean your life is over. Redefine your purpose, gather your assets and keep on living and giving. As long as you can maintain a sense of worth, you can resist the "Mara" mentality.

> Redefine your purpose, gather your assets and keep on living and giving.

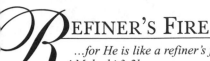

REFINER'S FIRE

...for He is like a refiner's fire, and like fullers' soap.
Malachi 3:2b

Let me warn you: God places His prize possessions in the fire. The precious vessels that He draws the most brilliant glory from often are exposed to the melting pot of distress. The bad news is, even those who live godly lives will suffer persecution. The good news is, you might be in the fire, but God controls the thermostat! He knows how hot it needs to be to accomplish His purpose in your life. I don't know anyone I would rather trust with the thermostat than the God of all grace.

Every test has degrees. Some people have experienced similar distresses, but to varying degrees. God knows the temperature that will burn away the impurities from His purpose. It is sad to have to admit this, but many times we release the ungodliness from our lives only as we experience the dread chastisement of a faithful God who is committed to bringing about change. How often He has had to fan the flames around me to produce the effects that He wanted in my life. In short, God is serious about producing the change in our lives that will glorify Him.

> *I indeed baptize you with water unto repentance: but He that cometh after me is mightier than I, whose shoes I am not worthy to bear: He shall baptize you with the Holy Ghost, and with fire: whose fan is in His hand, and He will thoroughly purge His floor, and gather His wheat into the garner; but He will burn up the chaff with unquenchable fire (Matthew 3:11-12).*

His hand has fanned the flames that were needed to teach patience, prayer, and many other invaluable lessons. We need His corrections. We don't enjoy them, but we need them. Without the correction of the Lord, we continue in our own way. What a joy to know that He cares enough to straighten out the jagged places in our lives. It is His fatherly corrections that confirm us as legitimate sons and not illegitimate ones. He affirms my position in Him by correcting and chastening me.

> *You might be in the fire, but God controls the thermostat!*

Trust in the Lord with all thine heart; and lean not unto thine own understanding. In all thy ways acknowledge Him, and He shall direct thy paths. Proverbs 3:5-6

And Elimelech Naomi's husband died; and she was left, and her two sons. And they took them wives of the women of Moab; the name of the one was Orpah, and the name of the other Ruth: and they dwelled there about ten years. And Mahlon and Chilion died also both of them; and the woman was left of her two sons and her husband (Ruth 1:3-5).

Naomi was a collection of tragedies. She had weathered many storms.

And she said unto them, Call me not Naomi, call me Mara: for the Almighty hath dealt very bitterly with me. I went out full, and the Lord hath brought me home again empty: why then call ye me Naomi, seeing the Lord hath testified against me, and the Almighty hath afflicted me? (Ruth 1:20-21)

Discouragement comes when people feel they have seen it all and most of it was really terrible! No matter what age you are, you have never seen it all. There are no graduations from the school of life other than death. No one knows how God will end His book, but He does tend to save the best for last. Israel didn't recognize Jesus because they were so used to seeing what they had already seen. God had sent dozens of prophets, and when He finally sends a king, they failed to recognize Him. It is dangerous to assume that what you will see out of life will be similar to what you saw before. God has the strangest way of restoring purpose to your life. For Naomi, it was through a relationship she tried to dissuade. It is dangerous to keep sending people away. The very one you are trying to send away may have the key to restoring purpose and fulfillment to your life.

And Ruth said, Entreat me not to leave thee, or to return from following after thee: for whither thou goest, I will go; and where thou lodgest, I will lodge: thy people shall be my people, and thy God my God (Ruth 1:16).

God has the strangest way of restoring purpose to your life.

Let us therefore come boldly unto the throne of grace, that we may obtain mercy, and find grace to help in time of need. Hebrews 4:16

I heard Thy voice in the garden, and I was afraid, because I was naked; and I hid myself (Genesis 3:10).

Adam's meager attempt at morality caused him to sew together a few leaves in a figgy little apron that was dying even while he was sewing it. Why would a lost man cover himself with leaves? Adam said, "I was afraid." Fear separated this son from his Father; fear caused him to conspire to deceive his only Solution. This fear was not reverence. It was desperation.

If Adam had only run *toward* instead of *away* from God, he could have been delivered! Why then do we continue to present a *God who cannot be approached* to a dying world? Many in the Christian family are still uncomfortable with their heavenly Father. Some Christians do not feel accepted in the beloved. They feel that their relationship with God is meritorious, but they are intimidated because of His holiness. I admit that His holiness all the more exposes our flawed, soiled personhood. Yet His grace allows us to approach Him—though we are not worthy—through the bloody skins soaked with Christ's blood.

We are properly draped and dressed to come into the presence of a Holy God only because His accepted Son, Jesus Christ, has wrapped us in His own identity. Like Adam, we are draped by a bloody sacrifice that has made it possible for us to approach our Father and live.

Neither is there any creature that is not manifest in His sight: but all things are naked and opened unto the eyes of Him with whom we have to do (Hebrews 4:13).

It is futile to hide from our Father. It is His intelligence (often referred to as His omniscience) that exposes us! We cannot alter His ability to see, so we need to develop enough security to be comfortable with His intelligence. Who else knows you like God does? If you hide from His perfect love, you will never be able to enjoy a relationship with your heavenly Father and be comfortable enough to sit in His lap.

> **Why do we continue to present a *God who cannot be approached* to a dying world?**

GOD-BONDS

That is, that I may be comforted together with you by the mutual faith both of you and me. Romans 1:12

Day 90

And Elimelech Naomi's husband died; and she was left, and her two sons. And they took them wives of the women of Moab; the name of the one was Orpah, and the name of the other Ruth: and they dwelled there about ten years. And Mahlon and Chilion died also both of them; and the woman was left of her two sons and her husband (Ruth 1:3-5).

Ruth was Naomi's daughter-in-law. Naomi thought their only connection was her now dead son. Many times we, who have been very family-oriented, do not understand friendships. When family circumstances change, we lapse into isolation because we know nothing of other relationships.

A man that hath friends must show himself friendly: and there is a friend that sticketh closer than a brother (Proverbs 18:24).

There are bonds that are stronger than blood. They are God-bonds! When God brings someone into our life, He is the bonding agent. Ruth said, "Your God shall be my God." God wanted Naomi to see the splendor of winter relationships, the joy of passing the baton of her wisdom and strength to someone worthy of her attention. Let God choose such a person for us because too often we choose on the basis of fleshly ties and not godly ties. I have noticed in the Scriptures that the strongest female relationships tend to be exemplified between older and younger women. I am certainly not suggesting that such will always be the case....

Ruth would have died in Moab, probably marrying some heathenistic idolator if it were not for the wisdom of Naomi, an older, more seasoned woman. Naomi knew how to provide guidance without manipulation—a strength many women at that stage of life do not have. Ruth was, of course, one of the great-grandparents in the lineage of Jesus Christ. She had greatness in her that God used Naomi to cultivate. Perhaps Naomi would have been called Mara and perhaps she would have ended up dying in bitterness instead of touching lives if it had not been for Ruth.

> When God brings someone into our life, He is the bonding agent.

Verily, verily, I say unto you, Except a corn of wheat fall into the ground and die, it abideth alone: but if it die, it bringeth forth much fruit. John 12:24

But if ye be without chastisement, whereof all are partakers, then are ye bastards, and not sons (Hebrews 12:8).

Strong's #G3541 "*nothos* (noth'os); of uncertain affinity; a spurious or illegitimate son:—bastard."

It is impossible to discuss the value of investing in people and not find ourselves worshiping God—what a perfect picture of investment. God is the major stockholder. No matter who He later uses to enhance our characters, we need to remember the magnitude of God's investment in our lives. The greatest primary investment He made was the inflated, unthinkable price of redemption that He paid. No one else would have bought us at that price. He paid the ultimate price when He died for our sins. What He did on the cross was worship. According to *Nelson's Bible Dictionary*, the word *worship*, literally translated, means "to express the worth of an object." Normally the lesser worships the greater, but this time, the greater worshiped the lesser. What an investment!

Explore with me the concept that God has an investment in our lives. First of all, no one invests without the expectation of gain. What would a perfect God have to gain from investing in an imperfect man? The apostle Paul wrote, "But we have this treasure in earthen vessels, that the excellency of the power may be of God, and not of us" (2 Cor. 4:7). Thus, according to Scripture, we possess treasure. However, the excellency of what we have is not of us, but of God. The treasure is "of" God. That implies that this treasure originates from God. It is accumulated in us and then presented back to Him. No farmer plants a field in the ground because he wants more earth. No, his expectation is in the seed that he planted. The ground is just the environment for the planted seed. The seed is the farmer's investment. The harvest is his return, or more accurately, his inheritance as the outer encasement of the seed dies in the ground. Harvest cost the seed its life.

> **Harvest cost the seed its life.**

Likewise, teach the older women to be reverent in the way they live, not to be slanderers or addicted to much wine, but to teach what is good. Then they can train the younger women to love their husbands and children.
Titus 2:3-4 (NIV)

Elisabeth, the wife of the priest Zacharias, is the biblical synonym for the modern pastor's wife. She was a winter woman with a summer experience. She was pregnant with a promise. In spite of her declining years, she was fulfilling more destiny then than she had in her youth. She is biblical proof that God blesses us in His own time and on His own terms. She is also in seclusion. Perhaps it was the attitude of the community. Many times when an older woman is still vibrant and productive it can cause jealousy and intimidation. Perhaps it was the silent stillness in her womb which some believe she experienced. Whatever the reason, she was a recluse for six months until she heard a knock at the door. If you have isolated yourself from others, regardless of the reason, I pray you will hear the knocking of the Lord. He will give you the garment of praise to clothe the spirit of heaviness (see Isa. 61:3).

When Elisabeth lifted her still-creaking body, which seemed almost anchored down to the chair, and drug her enlarged torso to the door, she saw a young girl, a picture of herself in days gone by, standing there. Opening that door changed her life forever. As you open the door to new relationships and remove the chain from your own fears, God will overwhelm you with new splendor. Mary, the future mother of our Savior and Lord, Elisabeth's young cousin, was at the door. The salutation of this young woman, the exposure to her experience, made the baby in Elisabeth's womb leap and Elisabeth was filled with the Holy Ghost. God will jump-start your heart! He doesn't mean for you to go sit in a chair and die! *In Jesus' name, get up and answer the door!* People probably wondered why these women were so close who were so different, but it was a God-bond!

> As you open the door to new relationships and remove the chain from your own fears, God will overwhelm you with new splendor.

$\mathcal{I}$T TAKES TRUST

He that dwelleth in the secret place of the most High shall abide under the shadow of the Almighty. I will say of the Lord, He is my refuge and my fortress: my God; in Him will I trust. Psalm 91:1-2

The basis of any relationship must be trust. Trusting God with your successes isn't really a challenge. The real test of trust is to be able to share your secrets, your inner failures and fears. A mutual enhancement comes into a relationship where there is intimacy based on honesty.

Jesus told the woman at the well, a woman whose flaws and failures He had supernaturally revealed, "…true worshippers shall worship the Father in spirit and in truth: for the Father seeketh such [real people, flawed people like the woman at the well] to worship Him. God is a Spirit: and they that worship Him must worship Him in spirit and in truth" (John 4:23-24).

We have nothing to fear, for our honesty with the Father doesn't reveal anything to Him that He doesn't already know! His intellect is so keen that He doesn't have to wait for you to make a mistake. He knows of your failure before you fail. His knowledge is all-inclusive, spanning the gaps between times and incidents. He knows our thoughts even as we unconsciously gather them together to make sense in our own mind!

> *The Lord knoweth the thoughts of man, that they are vanity (Psalm 94:11).*

Once we know this, all our attempts at silence and secrecy seem juvenile and ridiculous. He is "the all-seeing One," and He knows perfectly and completely what is in man. When we pray, and more importantly, when we commune with God, we must have the kind of confidence and assurance that neither requires nor allows deceit. Although my Father abhors my sin, He loves me. His love is incomprehensible, primarily because there is nothing with which we can compare it! What we must do is accept the riches of His grace and stand in the shade of His loving arms.

$\mathcal{T}$he real test of trust is to be able to share your secrets, your inner failures and fears.

For I will restore health unto thee, and I will heal thee of thy wounds, saith the Lord. Jeremiah 30:17a

It takes patience to overcome the effects of years of use and abuse. If you are not committed to getting back what you once had, you could easily decide that the process is impossible. Nevertheless, I assure you it is not impossible. David, the psalmist, declares, "He restoreth my soul" (Ps. 23:3). The term *restoreth* is a process. Only God knows what it takes to remove the build-up that may be existing in your life. But He specializes in restoring and renewing the human heart....

After her husband and two sons had died, Naomi almost changed her name to Mara. She felt that God had dealt very bitterly with her. It is dangerous to be prejudiced against God. Prejudice is to pre-judge. People, even believers, have often prejudged God. However, He isn't finished yet. Before it was over, everyone agreed that the hand of the Lord was upon Naomi. Therefore, you are not off course. Trust Him to see you through days that may be different from the ones you encountered earlier. You are being challenged with the silent struggles of winter. I believe the most painful experience is to look backward and have to stare into the cold face of regret. Most people have thought, "I wonder how things would have been had I not made this decision or that one." To realize that you have been the victim and the assailant in your own life may be difficult to accept—especially since most of those dilemmas are birthed through the womb of your own decisions. Admittedly, there are those who inadvertently crashed into circumstances that stripped them, wounded them and left them feeling like the victim on the Jericho road! No matter which case best describes your current situation, first pause and thank God that, like Naomi, in spite of the tragedies of youth, it is a miracle that you survived the solemn chill of former days. Your presence should be a praise. Look over your shoulder and see what could have been. Has God dealt with you bitterly? I think not.

> *I* believe the most painful experience is to look backward and have to stare into the cold face of regret.

But He knoweth the way that I take: when He hath tried me, I shall come forth as gold. Job 23:10

We are fertile ground—broken by troubles, enriched by failures, and watered with tears. Yet undeniably there is a deposit within us. This deposit is valuable enough to place us on satan's hit list. In writing to the Ephesian church, Paul prayed that "the eyes of your understanding being enlightened…" (Eph. 1:18). One of the things he wanted the people to know is the riches of His inheritance in the saints! Paul challenged them to become progressively aware of the enormity of His inheritance in us, not our inheritance in Him. We spend most of our time talking about what we want from God. The real issue is what He wants from us. It is the Lord who has the greatest investment. We are the parched, dry ground from which Christ springs. Believe me, God is serious about His investment!

To the enemy the Lord says, "Touch not Mine anointed, and do My prophets no harm" (1 Chron. 16:22). God will fight to protect the investment He has placed in your life. What a comfort it is to know that the Lord has a vested interest in my deliverance. He has more than just concern for me. God has begun the necessary process of cultivating what He has invested in my life. Have you ever stopped to think that it was God's divine purpose that kept you afloat when others capsized beneath the load of life? Look at Job; he knew that God had an investment in his life that no season of distress could eradicate.

Remember the story of the three Hebrew boys in the fiery furnace? When the wicked king placed them in the fire, he thought the fire would burn them. He didn't know that when you belong to God, the fire only burns the ties that bind you. People have said that God took the heat out of the furnace. That is not true. Consider the soldiers who threw the Hebrews into the fire—they were burned to death at the door! There was plenty of heat in the furnace. God, however, controls the boundaries. Have you ever gone through a dilemma that should have scorched every area of your life and yet you survived the pressure? Then you ought to know that He is Lord over the fire!

> *The fire only burns the ties that bind you.*

Therefore the redeemed of the Lord shall return, and come with singing unto Zion; and everlasting joy shall be upon their head: they shall obtain gladness and joy; and sorrow and mourning shall flee away. Isaiah 51:11

Anyone can recognize Him in the sunshine, but in the storm His disciples thought He was a ghost (see Matt. 14:26). There is one thing every Naomi can rely upon as she gathers wood for winter days and wraps quilts around weak, willowy legs: God is a restorer. That is to say, as you sit by the fire sipping coffee, rehearsing your own thoughts, playing old reruns from the scenes in your life—some things He will explain and others He will heal. Restoration doesn't mean all the lost people who left you will return. Neither Naomi's husband nor her sons were resurrected. It is just that God gives purpose back to the years that had question marks. How many times have you been able to look back and say, "If I hadn't gone through that, I wouldn't have known or received this." Simply said, "He'll make it up to you." He restores the effects of the years of turmoil. People who heard Naomi running through the house with rollers in her hair complaining that God had dealt bitterly, should have waited with their noses pressed against the window pane as God masterfully brought peace into her arms. If you wait by the window, you will hear the soft hum of an old woman nodding with her grandchild clutched in her arms. Perhaps she is too proud to tell you that she charged God foolishly, but the smile on her leathery face and the calmness of her rest says, "He doeth all things well" (see Mark 7:37).

And I will restore to you the years that the locust hath eaten, the cankerworm, and the caterpillar, and the palmerworm, my great army which I sent among you. And ye shall eat in plenty, and be satisfied, and praise the name of the Lord your God, that hath dealt wondrously with you: and My people shall never be ashamed (Joel 2:25-26).

He'll make it up to you.

Likewise the Spirit also helpeth our infirmities: for we know not what we should pray for as we ought: but the Spirit itself maketh intercession for us with groanings which cannot be uttered. Romans 8:26

What creates a feeling of wholeness in the heart of the believer is the awareness that while God's standards do not change, neither does His compassion. One thing we search for at every level of our relationships is "to be understood." When I am properly understood, I don't always have to express and explain. *Thank You, Lord, for not asking me to explain what I oft can scarcely express!*

We quickly grow weary when we are around anyone who demands that we constantly qualify our statements and explain our intent. We want to be near those who comprehend the subtle expressions of affection, intimacy, and need—a touch, a brief hug, a sigh emitted in the stillness of a moment. Communication cannot be typed or taught; it must be understood. At this level there is a communication so intense that those who understand it can clearly speak it, even through closed lips. As with lovers staring at each other across a crowded and smoke-filled room, words seem so unnecessary when there is understanding. It is with this kind of understanding that God clearly perceives and understands our every need.

I believe that when the Scriptures declare that men "ought always to pray, and not to faint" (Luke 18:1), that they are speaking of living in a state of open communication with God, not necessarily jabbering at Him nonstop for hours. Many people say, "I am going to pray for a certain amount of time." They ramble on in prayer for hours on their knees, and they end up watching the clock while they utter mindless rhetoric, trying to get in the specified amount of time in prayer.

Let me ask you, would you want someone to talk to you like that? True friends can drive down a road and lapse in and out of conversation, deeply enjoying each other's company—all without any obligation to maintain a steady rhythm of rhetoric. Their communication is just an awareness of the presence of someone they know and understand. We don't need to labor to create what is already there. I am glad my Savior knows what my speech and my silence suggest. I need not labor to create what we already share in the secret place of our hearts!

> Communication cannot be typed or taught; it must be understood.

Inasmuch as ye have done it unto one of the least of these My brethren, ye have done it unto Me.
Matthew 25:40b

Naomi lost her husband and both sons (see Ruth 1). She becomes a picture of a woman in a winter season of life. There is something every Naomi can rely on during their winter. The Lord will be known as: the nourisher. This may be a difficult role for you who have clutched babies and men alike to the warm breast of your sensitivity. You, who have been the source for others to be strengthened, may find it difficult to know what to do with this role reversal. The nourisher must learn to be nourished. Many women pray more earnestly as intercessors for others than for themselves. That is wonderful, but there ought to be a time that you desire certain things for yourself. Our God is El Shaddai, "the breasted one" (from Gen. 17:1). He gives strength to the feeble and warmth to the cold. There is great comfort in His arms. Like children, even adults can snuggle into His everlasting arms and hear the heartbeat of a loving God who says, "And ye shall eat in plenty, and be satisfied, and praise the name of your God…" (Joel 2:26).

Expect God in all His varied forms. He is a master of disguise, a guiding star in the night, a lily left growing in the valley, or an answered prayer sent on the breath of an angel. Angels are the butlers of Heaven; they open doors. He sends angels to minister to His own. Have you ever seen an angel? They aren't always dressed in white with dramatically arched wings. Sometimes they are so ordinary that they can be overlooked. Ruth was an angel that Naomi almost sent away. God can use anyone as a channel of nourishment. Regardless of the channel, He is still the source.

> *Do not forget to entertain strangers, for by so doing some people have entertained angels without knowing it (Hebrews 13:2 NIV).*

Ruth was an angel that Naomi almost sent away.

When thou passest through the waters, I will be with thee; and through the rivers, they shall not overflow thee: when thou walkest through the fire, thou shalt not be burned; neither shall the flame kindle upon thee. Isaiah 43:2

It has been suggested that if you walk in the Spirit, you won't have to contend with the fire. Real faith doesn't mean you won't go through the fire. Real faith simply means that when you pass through the fire, He will be with you.... The presence of the Lord can turn a burning inferno into a walk in the park! The Bible says a fourth person was in the fire, and so the three Hebrews were able to walk around unharmed in it (see Dan. 3).

King Nebuchadnezzar was astonished when he saw them overcome what had destroyed other men. I cannot guarantee that you will not face terrifying situations if you believe God. I can declare that if you face them with Christ's presence, the effects of the circumstance will be drastically altered. It is quite popular to suggest that faith prohibits trouble. But when I read about these young Hebrew men, I realize that if you believe God, you can walk in what other men burn in. Seldom will anyone fully appreciate the fire you have walked through, but be assured that God knows the fiery path to accomplishment. He can heal the blistered feet of the traveler.

When John was on the isle of Patmos, he was limited to a cave but free in his spirit (see Rev. 1). Remember, satan may work feverishly to limit the ministry and reputation of God's vessel, but he can never confine the anointing and the call on your life. In fact, John's predicament on Patmos proves that negative circumstances reveal Christ, not veil Him. While in the dank, dismal, dark caves of persecution, surrounded by the sounds of other abused prisoners, John caught a vision. In his newfound image of Christ, he describes the crisp clarity of a revelation given in the midst of chaos. A crisis can clear your perceptions as you behold His face, looking for answers that will not be found in the confines of the situation.

> God knows the fiery path to accomplishment.

And in the sixth month the angel Gabriel was sent from God unto a city of Galilee, named Nazareth, to a virgin espoused to a man whose name was Joseph, of the house of David; and the virgin's name was Mary. Luke 1:26-27

And Abraham rose up early in the morning, and took bread, and a bottle of water, and gave it unto Hagar, putting it on her shoulder, and the child, and sent her away: and she departed, and wandered in the wilderness of Beersheba. And the water was spent in the bottle, and she cast the child under one of the shrubs. And she went, and sat her down over against him a good way off, as it were a bowshot: for she said, Let me not see the death of the child. And she sat over against him, and lift up her voice, and wept. And God heard the voice of the lad; and the angel of God called to Hagar out of heaven, and said unto her, What aileth thee, Hagar? fear not; for God hath heard the voice of the lad where he is. Arise, lift up the lad, and hold him in thine hand; for I will make him a great nation (Genesis 21:14-18).

When Hagar was lost in the wilderness of depression and wrestling exasperation, God sent an angel. When the labor-ridden mother of Samson was mundane and barren, God sent an angel. When young Mary was wandering listlessly through life, God sent an angel. When the grief-stricken Mary Magdalene came stumbling down to the tomb, God sent an angel. For every woman in crises, there is an angel! For every lonely night and forgotten mother, there is an angel. For every lost young girl wandering the concrete jungle of an inner city, there is an angel. My sister, set your coffee down, take the blanket off your legs, and stand up on your feet! Hast thou not known, hast thou not heard? For every woman facing winter, *there is an angel*!

Are not all angels ministering spirits sent to serve those who will inherit salvation? (Hebrews 1:14 NIV)

Through faith also Sarah herself received strength to conceive seed, and was delivered of a child when she was past age, because she judged Him faithful who had promised (Hebrews 11:11).

For every lonely night and forgotten mother, there is an angel.

Neither is there any creature that is not manifest in His sight: but all things are naked and opened unto the eyes of Him with whom we have to do. Hebrews 4:13

We are called to live in a state of openhearted communication with the Lord. Yes, we feel vulnerable when we realize that our hearts are completely exposed before God. Yet every one of us desperately needs to have *someone* who is able to help us, *someone* who is able to understand the issues that are etched on the tablets of our heart!

Since we already feel exposed when we realize that there is not one thought we have entertained that God has not seen and heard, then *there is no need for a sanctimonious misrepresentation of who we are!* We no longer need to live under the strain of continual camouflage. Neither flagrant nor flamboyant, we are *naked before Him* in the same sense that a man sprawls naked on the operating table before a surgeon. The man is neither boastful nor embarrassed, for he understands that his exposed condition is a necessity of their relationship. Whether the doctor finds good or evil, what is there is there, and the man's comfort lies in the conviction that the surgeon possesses the wherewithal to restore order to any area that may be in disarray.

Blessed are the pure in heart: for they shall see God (Matthew 5:8).

The purity that attracts the presence of God comes from allowing Him to perpetually flush away the corrosion that threatens to block the abundant arterial flow of His grace and mercy toward us. In short, we need to show Him what is clogging or hindering His flow of life to us so He can clean us and keep us acceptable before Him in love.

The Greek word *katheros* is used here to express "purity." It is from this word that we have the English derivative "catharize," which describes medical processes used to cleanse, flush, or release fluids from the body. God is continually sending a deluge of His cleansing grace into the hearts of His children, *but He can't clean or purify what we hide in the secret corners of our hearts and minds.*

> **W**e feel vulnerable when we realize that our hearts are completely exposed before God.

Being confident of this very thing, that He which hath begun a good work in you will perform it until the day of Jesus Christ. Philippians 1:6

I think it would be remiss of me not to share, before moving on, the miracles of winter. In the summer, all was well with Sarah. At that time she knew little about Jehovah, her husband's God. She basically knew she was in love with a wonderful man. She was the luckiest woman in Ur. An incredibly beautiful woman already, she wore her love like a striking woman wears a flattering dress. The air smelled like honeysuckle and the wind called her name. Then her husband spoke to her about moving. Where, she didn't know, and crazy as it may sound to those who have forgotten the excitement of summer, she really didn't care. She ran into the tent and began to pack. Sometimes it's good to get away from relatives and friends. Starting over would be fun!

Soon the giddy exuberance of summer started to ebb as she began wrestling with the harsh realities of following a dreamer. Abraham had not done what he said; he carried a few of their relatives with them. "I am sure he had a good reason," she thought. What was really troubling her wasn't the strife between the relatives or the fighting herdsmen, it was the absence of a child. By now she was sure she was barren. She felt like she had cheated Abraham out of an important part of life. Someone had said she would have a baby. Sarah laughed, "If I am going to get a miracle, God had better hurry." I want to warn you against setting your own watch. God's time is not your time. He may not come when you want Him to, but He is right on time. Twice it is mentioned that Sarah laughed. The first time she laughed at God; in the winter time she laughed with God. The first time she laughed at the impossibility of God's promise. After she had gone through life's experiences, she learned that God is faithful to perform His word.

> *I want to warn you against setting your own watch. God's time is not your time.*

When thou passest through the waters, I will be with thee; and through the rivers, they shall not overflow thee: when thou walkest through the fire, thou shalt not be burned; neither shall the flame kindle upon thee. Isaiah 43:2

John wrote that he heard the thunderous voice of the Lord. In the process of seeking the voice, he encountered seven golden candlesticks. The candlesticks are later revealed as the Church. We need men and women who hear the voice of God before they see the work of God. What good will it do us to polish the candelabra and light the candles if there is no voice of God to cause men to turn aside and see?

When the voice of God led to the presence of Christ, John collapsed in the presence of the Lord. A deluge flooded the cave as Christ opened His mouth; His voice sounded as the noise of many waters. John said that many waters were in His voice, but the fire was on His feet. Effective communication is always transmitted from the base of burned feet. John said Jesus' feet looked as if they had been in the fire. What a comfort to the indicted character of this Pentecost preacher to find that the feet of his Consoler had been through the fire. Dearly beloved, hear me today: Your Deliverer has feet that have been burned. He knows what it feels like to be in the fire.

Thank God for the smoldering feet of our Lord that run swiftly to meet His children in need. But still the question remains, "Is there any preventive protection that will at least aid the victim who struggles in the throes of a fiery test?" If you are in a fiery trial, be advised that it is your faith that is on trial. If you are to overcome the dilemma, it will not be by your feelings, but by your faith. First John 5:4 says, "For whatsoever is born of God overcometh the world: and this is the victory that overcometh the world, even our faith." Yes, it is the shield of faith that quenches the fiery darts of the devil (see Eph. 6:16). The term *quench* means "to extinguish." Are there any fires brewing that you would like to extinguish? Your faith will do the job. If faith doesn't deliver you from it, then it will surely deliver you through it.

> *Your Deliverer has feet that have been burned. He knows what it feels like to be in the fire.*

Now no chastening for the present seemeth to be joyous, but grievous: nevertheless afterward it yieldeth the peaceable fruit of righteousness unto them which are exercised thereby.... lest that which is lame be turned out of the way; but let it rather be healed. Hebrews 12:11-13

THE FIRST LAUGH

Abraham and Sarah were already old and well advanced in years, and Sarah was past the age of childbearing. So Sarah laughed to herself as she thought, "After I am worn out and my master is old, will I now have this pleasure?" Then the Lord said to Abraham, "Why did Sarah laugh and say, 'Will I really have a child, now that I am old?' Is anything too hard for the Lord? I will return to you at the appointed time next year and Sarah will have a son" (Genesis 18:11-14 NIV).

THE LAST LAUGH

Sarah became pregnant and bore a son to Abraham in his old age, at the very time God had promised him. Abraham gave the name Isaac to the son Sarah bore him. When his son Isaac was eight days old, Abraham circumcised him, as God commanded him. Abraham was a hundred years old when his son Isaac was born to him. Sarah said, "God has brought me laughter, and everyone who hears about this will laugh with me." And she added, "Who would have said to Abraham that Sarah would nurse children? Yet I have borne him a son in his old age" (Genesis 21:2-7 NIV).

Listen carefully at what I am about to say. It is relevant to you. I am not so much concerned with the eighteenth chapter of Genesis where she laughs in unbelief. Nor am I focusing my attention on the twenty-first chapter where she laughs with "the joy of the Lord." I want to discuss with you the events that led to the miracles of her winter. Often we share our personal testimony. We tell where we started and even where we ultimately arrived, without sharing the process or the sequence of events that led to our deliverance. Then our listeners feel defeated because they named it and claimed it and still didn't attain it! We didn't tell them about the awful trying of our faith that preceded our coming forth as pure gold. Today, however, we will share the whole truth and nothing but the truth! Amen.

> **We will share the whole truth and nothing but the truth!**

Healing, Blessings, and Freedom

WHITER THAN SNOW

Come now, and let us reason together, saith the Lord: though your sins be as scarlet, they shall be as white as snow; though they be red like crimson, they shall be as wool. Isaiah 1:18

The hymnist wrote a powerful verse when he penned:

"Lord Jesus, I long to be perfectly whole.
I want Thee forever to live in my soul.
Break down every idol, cast out every foe.
Now wash me and I shall be whiter than snow"
("Whiter Than Snow," James Nicholson, 1872).

I can still remember the great joy that flooded my soul when Christ came into my heart. I was walking on air for weeks. It was, and in fact, still is exciting to me to know that my many deplorable sins have been rinsed from my records by the efficacious blood of the Lamb! I shouted and praised the Lord with an abandonment as if it were the last time I would have to praise the Lord.

Upon reflection, I came to understand that the slate had been cleansed at Calvary, but the *mind* is being renewed from day to day. As images came from time to time with flashbacks of things that haunted the attic of my mind like ghosts unexorcised, I began to seek the Lord *who saved me* for *the grace to keep me*. It was then that I began to realize the great truth that the blood of Christ doesn't just reach backwards into the bleakness of my past debauchery—it also has the power to cover my ongoing struggles!

I hadn't known then that Jesus paid it all! The blood of Christ covers my past, present, and future struggles, not so I could run through my inheritance like the prodigal son (if that were possible), but so I might have a comfort as I lie on the table of His grace. I must relax in this comfort and assurance and allow the tools of day-to-day tests and struggles to skillfully implant into my heart and mind a clearer reflection of His divine nature in me.

> The blood of Christ covers my past, present, and future struggles....

The fear of the Lord tendeth to life: and he that hath it shall abide satisfied; he shall not be visited with evil. Proverbs 19:23

And the Lord appeared unto him in the plains of Mamre: and he sat in the tent door in the heat of the day... And he said, I will certainly return unto thee according to the time of life; and, lo, Sarah thy wife shall have a son... (Genesis 18:1,10a).

Sarah became pregnant and bore a son to Abraham in his old age, at the very time God had promised him (Genesis 21:2 NIV).

In between these powerful moments in the life of one of God's finest examples of wives, everything in her was tested. I believe that her love for Abram gave her the courage to leave home, but her love for God brought forth the promised seed. Careful now, I am not saying that her love for God replaced her love for her husband; I am merely saying that it complemented the other to the highest level. After all, what good is it to appreciate what God gave us if we do not appreciate the God who gave it to us? If age should do nothing else, it should help us put things in proper perspective. There is nothing like time to show us that we have misplaced priorities.

In summer, she followed Abram out of their country and away from their kindred. As the seasons of life changed, she takes another pilgrimage into what could have been a great tragedy. Abraham, her beloved husband, leads his wife into Gerar. As I am a man and a leader myself, I dare not be too hard on him. Anyone can make a poor decision. The decision to go to Gerar I could defend, even though *Gerar* means "halting place." I have made decisions that brought me to a halting place in my life. What's reprehensible is that Abraham, Sarah's protector and covering, when afraid for his own safety, lied about her identity (Gen. 20). You never know who people are until you witness them under pressure. Now, I am not being sanctimonious about Abraham's flagrant disregard for truth. But it was a life-threatening lie.

> There is nothing like time to show us that we have misplaced priorities.

From that time on Jesus began to explain to His disciples that He must go to Jerusalem and suffer many things at the hands of the elders, chief priests and teachers of the law, and that He must be killed and on the third day be raised to life....
Matthew 16:21-23 (NIV)

The fanaticism of some faith theology has intimidated many Christians from faith concepts as they relate to the promises of God. Yet faith is such a key issue for the Christian that the people of the early Church were simply called believers in recognition of their great faith. One thing we need to do is understand the distinctions of faith. Faith cannot alter purpose; it only acts as an agent to assist in fulfilling the predetermined purpose of God. If God's plan requires that we suffer certain opposition in order to accomplish His purpose, then faith becomes the vehicle that enables us to persevere and delivers us through the test. On the other hand, the enemy afflicts the believer in an attempt to abort the purpose of God. Faith is a night watchman sent to guard the purpose of God. It will deliver us out of the hand of the enemy—the enemy being anything that hinders the purpose of God in our lives.

Hebrews chapter 11 discusses at length the definition of faith. It then shares the deeds of faith in verses 32-35a and finally it discusses the perseverance of faith in verses 35b-39. There are distinctions of faith as well. In Hebrews 11:32-35a, the teaching has placed an intensified kind of emphasis on the distinct faith that escapes peril and overcomes obstacles.

> *Quenched the violence of fire, escaped the edge of the sword, out of weakness were made strong, waxed valiant in fight, turned to flight the armies of the aliens (Hebrews 11:34).*

However, in the verses that end the chapter, almost as if they were footnotes, the writer deals with the distinctions of another kind of faith. In his closing remarks, he shares that there were some other believers whose faith was exemplified *through* suffering and not *from* suffering.

> *Faith cannot alter purpose; it only acts as an agent to assist in fulfilling the predetermined purpose of God.*

And others had trial of cruel mockings and scourgings, yea, moreover of bonds and imprisonment: they were stoned, they were sawn asunder, were tempted, were slain with the sword: they wandered about in sheepskins and goatskins; being destitute, afflicted, tormented (Hebrews 11:36-37).

Wherefore let him that thinketh he standeth take heed lest he fall. There hath no temptation taken you but such as is common to man: but God is faithful, who will not suffer you to be tempted above that ye are able; but will with the temptation also make a way to escape, that ye may be able to bear it. 1 Corinthians 10:12-13

Have you ever known someone upon whom you had cast the weight of your confidence, only to have your trust defrauded in a moment of self-gratification and indulgence? Someone who has a selfish need can jeopardize all that you have.

And Abraham journeyed from thence toward the south country, and dwelled between Kadesh and Shur, and sojourned in Gerar. And Abraham said of Sarah his wife, She is my sister: and Abimelech king of Gerar sent, and took Sarah (Genesis 20:1-2).

Abraham's infamous lie jeopardized the safety of his wife. King Abimelech was a heathen king. He was used to getting whatever he wanted. His reputation for debauchery preceded him to the degree that Abraham, the father of faith, feared for his life. Rather than risk himself, he told the king that his lovely wife was really his sister. Abraham knew that such a statement would cause Sarah to have to fulfill the torrid desires of a heathenist. Sarah now finds herself being bathed and perfumed to be offered up as an offering of lust for the passions of the king. Imagine the icy grip of fear clutching the first lady of faith. Imagine her shock to realize that under real stress, a person can never be sure what another individual will do to secure his own well-being. Her Abraham failed her. But God did not!

But God came to Abimelech in a dream by night, and said to him, Behold, thou art but a dead man, for the woman which thou hast taken; for she is a man's wife...And Abimelech took sheep, and oxen, and menservants, and womenservants, and gave them unto Abraham, and restored him Sarah his wife (Genesis 20:3,14).

Maybe there is someone in your life who selfishly threw you into a tempestuous situation. Take courage! Just because satan has set a snare doesn't mean you can't escape. The God we serve is able. His word to you is, "*Woman, thou art loosed.*"

> *Just because satan has set a snare doesn't mean you can't escape.*

And He raised us up with Christ and gave us a seat with Him in the heavens. He did this for those in Christ Jesus so that for all future time He could show the very great riches of His grace by being kind to us in Christ Jesus. Ephesians 2:6-7 (NCV)

Now, amidst the joy that I still possess, I have a growing appreciation for the peace that comes from knowing I am His child. I am His—even when I feel like a mess, even when I am embarrassed to openly discuss my frailties and flaws, for *His grace is sufficient for me*. I thank Him for the peace He has given to every believer who matures into a trust-filled relationship with Jesus Christ. My initial surgery may be completed, but daily I remain under His intensive care as He monitors my progressions and occasional digressions. I wouldn't trust my future with anybody but Him. What about you?

Dear friend, you will never worship God correctly if you live in the shadows, wrestling with unconfessed sin. Whatever you do, there is an ever-increasing need for you to find *a place of comfort* in the presence of the Lord. It is possible to escape my presence, but not His. He is ever present, waiting on you to stand before Him and be healed.

Open relationships with other people can never be attained until you first drop the towel and stand naked before God. If you cannot trust Him, then all hope is lost. When Mary, the sinner, came and washed Jesus' feet with her tears, some mocked Jesus and discredited Him, insinuating that He lacked the discernment to know she was a woman with a questionable past (see Luke 7:39). The sad truth is they had been with Jesus and still didn't know His heart. They had heard His commandments but not His heart. It wasn't that Jesus didn't know the hands that washed His feet had done wrong. It wasn't that He didn't know the hair that dried Him had been let down before. It was that He didn't care!

> *I* wouldn't trust my future with anybody but Him.

The Lord is at hand. Be careful for nothing; but in every thing by prayer and supplication with thanksgiving let your requests be made known unto God. Philippians 4:5b-6

Abraham's faith had always been the star of the Old Testament, but not that day. It's amazing how faith will come up in your heart at a crisis.

And Abraham journeyed from thence toward the south country, and dwelled between Kadesh and Shur, and sojourned in Gerar. And Abraham said of Sarah his wife, She is my sister: and Abimelech king of Gerar sent, and took Sarah (Genesis 20:1-2).

Consider Sarah. She is facing the anxious footsteps of her rapist. She knows it will not be long until she will be abused. Like a frightened rabbit crouched in a corner, she realizes Abraham will not rescue her. I don't know what she prayed, but I know she cried out to the only One she had left! Maybe she said, "God of Abraham, I need you to be my God too. Save me from this pending fate." Or maybe she just cried, "O God! Have mercy on me!" Whatever she said, God heard her. He will hear you as well. You don't have time to be angry or bitter. You've just got enough time to pray. Call out to Him. He is your God too!

So Abraham prayed unto God: and God healed Abimelech, and his wife, and his maidservants; and they bare children. For the Lord had fast closed up all the wombs of the house of Abimelech, because of Sarah Abraham's wife (Genesis 20:17-18).

God shut up all the wombs in the king's household. He spoke up for Sarah when no one else would. He threatened the king and revealed the truth. "She is Abraham's wife," declared God! He stopped the footsteps of danger! Very few men understand a woman's terror of being raped or sexually assaulted. I can only imagine the tears that ran down her face when she heard the door open. Her would-be rapist comes in, falls to the floor and begins to cry out, "He touched me!" Did you know that the heart of the king is in His hand and He turneth it as He will (see Prov. 21:1)?

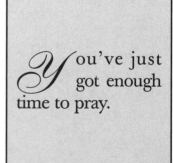

You've just got enough time to pray.

Yea doubtless, and I count all things but loss for the excellency of the knowledge of Christ Jesus my Lord: for whom I have suffered the loss of all things, and do count them but dung, that I may win Christ... that I may know Him... Philippians 3:8-10

Christianity's foundation is not built upon elite mansions, stocks and bonds, or sports cars and cruise-control living. All these things are wonderful if God chooses to bless you with them. However, to make finances the symbol of faith is ridiculous. The Church is built on the backs of men who withstood discomfort for a cause. These men were not the end but the means whereby God was glorified. Some of them exhibited their faith through their shadows' healing people. Still others exhibited their faith by bleeding to death beneath piles of stone. They also had a brand of faith that seemed to ease the effects, though it didn't alter the cause.

I am crucified with Christ: nevertheless I live; yet not I, but Christ liveth in me: and the life which I now live in the flesh I live by the faith of the Son of God, who loved me, and gave Himself for me (Galatians 2:20).

There are times in our lives when God will take us from one realm of faith to another. There are multiplicities of fiery trials, but thank God that for every trial there is a faith that enables us. Christ is the Author and the Finisher of our faith (see Heb. 12:2). He knows what kind of heat to place upon us to produce the faith needed in the situation. Remember, when we present our bodies as living sacrifices, He is the God who answers by fire. The good news lies in the fact that when our faith collapses beneath the weight of unbelievable circumstances, He gives us His faith to continue on....

As the fire of persecution forces us to make deeper levels of commitment, it is so important that our faith be renewed to match our level of commitment. There is a place in God where the fire consumes every other desire but to know the Lord in the power of His resurrection. At this level all other pursuits tarnish and seem worthless in comparison. Perhaps this is what Paul really pressed toward, that place of total surrender. Certainly that is the place I reach toward, which often escapes my grasp, but never my view. Like a child standing on his toes, I reach after a place too high to be touched. I conclude by saying my hands are extended, but my feet are on fire!

> **A**ll other pursuits tarnish and seem worthless in comparison.

It is a good thing to give thanks unto the Lord, and to sing praises unto Thy name, O most High: to show forth Thy lovingkindness in the morning, and Thy faithfulness every night. Psalm 92:1-2

And Abraham journeyed from thence toward the south country, and dwelled between Kadesh and Shur, and sojourned in Gerar. And Abraham said of Sarah his wife, She is my sister: and Abimelech king of Gerar sent, and took Sarah....And Abimelech took sheep, and oxen, and menservants, and womenservants, and gave them unto Abraham, and restored him Sarah his wife (Genesis 20:1-2,14).

When Sarah came out of Gerar, she knew something about life, about people, and most of all, about God. She didn't lose her relationship with Abraham, as we will soon see. But she did learn something that all of us must learn too. She learned the faithfulness of God. I am convinced that the things that worry us would not, if we knew the faithfulness of God. Have you ever spent the night in a Gerar situation? If you have, you know the Lord in a way you could never know Him otherwise. He cares for you! Look over your past and remember His faithfulness. Look at your future and trust Him now!

Right after this nightmare experience, the Bible says in Genesis 21:1-2, "And the Lord visited Sarah as He had said, and the Lord did unto Sarah as He had spoken. For Sarah conceived, and bare Abraham a son in his old age, at the set time of which God had spoken to him." It wasn't Abraham's visit to the tent that left that woman filled with the promise of God. Without God he could do nothing. Always remember that man may be the instrument, but God is the life source. It was God who visited Sarah. Now Sarah knew God like she had never known Him. Some things you can learn about God only in the winter. Sarah won a spot in the hallmark of faith. When Hebrews chapter 11 lists the patriarchs and their awesome faith, this winter woman's name is included. Abraham is mentioned for the kind of faith that would leave home and look for a city whose builder and maker is God (v. 10). But when it comes to discussing the kind of faith that caused an old woman's barren womb to conceive, it was Sarah's faith that did it. She didn't take faith classes. She just went through her winter clutching the warm hand of a loving God who would not fail. So when you hear Sarah laughing the last time, she is laughing with God. She is holding her baby to her now wrinkled breast. She understands the miracles that come only to winter women.

> *L*ook over your past and remember His faithfulness.

For He hath regarded the low estate of His handmaiden: for, behold, from henceforth all generations shall call me blessed. Luke 1:48

I believe it is important that women get healed and released in their spirits. I'm excited about what God is doing. I believe that God will move freshly in the lives of women in an even greater way.

God knows how to take a mess and turn it into a miracle. If you're in a mess, don't be too upset about it because God specializes in fixing messes. God is saying some definite things about women being set free and delivered to fulfill their purpose in the Kingdom.

Let's look at the infirm woman of the Gospel of Luke, chapter 13:

> *And He laid His hands on her: and immediately she was made straight, and glorified God. And the ruler of the synagogue answered with indignation, because that Jesus had healed on the sabbath day...The Lord then answered him, and said, Thou hypocrite, doth not each one of you on the sabbath loose his ox or his ass from the stall, and lead him away to watering? And ought not this woman, being a daughter of Abraham, whom Satan hath bound, lo, these eighteen years, be loosed from this bond on the sabbath day? And when He had said these things, all His adversaries were ashamed: and all the people rejoiced for all the glorious things that were done by Him (Luke 13:13-17).*

When the Lord gets through working on you, all your adversaries will be ashamed. All your accusers will be ashamed of themselves. All the people who contributed to your sense of low self-esteem will be ashamed when God gets through unleashing you. You won't have to prove anything. God will prove it. He will do it in your life. When He gets through showing that you've done the right thing and come to the right place, they will drop their heads and be ashamed.

We have already shown how this woman was so bound by satan for 18 years that she could not even straighten herself up. She had a past that tormented her, but Jesus set her free. He unleashed her potential that satan had bound up.

> **God knows how to take a mess and turn it into a miracle.**

Not that we are sufficient of ourselves to think any thing as of ourselves; but our sufficiency is of God; who also hath made us able ministers of the new testament.... 2 Corinthians 3:5-6

Tinkling gently in the night, a child's mobile turns in the stillness. It is, to the gentle bundle of love beneath it, a million miles away. Wrapped in clean crisp sheets below the mobile is a mystery of creation. Stardust is sprinkled in the eyes of the child wandering in and out of sleep. Baby's soft gurgle blends with the occasional tinkling sounds of its overhead entertainment. Time has hidden the future of the baby deeply within the tiny hands that someday will be different things to different people. "Who is this child?" the parents ponder. "When we are old, who will this child be? What is the level of contribution we have given to this world?" All these questions are raised in the stillness of the night. Time listens quietly, patting its foot, but still offers no answer.

We toddle through childhood, from tricycles to training wheels, racing into the maze of adolescence. Too old to be a child, yet too childlike to be an adult, we often feel lost in space. The haunting question dulls with time, but still hums beneath the mind of the mature. "Who am I?" We have a deep need to find some answer for that question. A friend once told me that the best way to hold someone's attention in a conversation is to talk about that person! We are very interested in ourselves. Many of us come to know the Lord because we desperately need to know ourselves. Does that seem strange? It isn't, really. If we have a problem with an appliance, we always refer to the owner's manual. In our case it's the Bible. When repairs are needed, we go to the Manufacturer. Psalm 100 says, "It is He that hath made us, and not we ourselves" (Ps. 100:3b).

When repairs are needed, we go to the Manufacturer.

But I am poor and needy; yet the Lord thinketh upon me: Thou art my help and my deliverer; make no tarrying, O my God. Psalm 40:17

Many women in the Church have not really seen Christ as the answer to their dilemma. They go to church, they love the Lord, they want to go to Heaven when they die, but they still do not see Christ as the solution to their problem. Often we try to separate our personal life from our spiritual life. Many see Jesus as a way to Heaven and the solution to spiritual problems, but they fail to see that He is the solution to all of life's problems.

Can you imagine how hard life was for the infirmed woman who was bowed over? (See Luke 13.) She had to struggle, because of her problem, to come to Jesus. Few of us are crippled in the same way. However, we all face crippling limitations. We can be bowed over financially. We can be bowed over emotionally. We can be bowed over where we have no self-esteem. He wants to see us struggling toward Him. Jesus could have walked to this woman, but He chose not to. He wants to see us struggle toward Him.

He wants you to want Him enough to overcome obstacles and to push in His direction. He doesn't want to just throw things at you that you don't have a real conviction to receive. When you see a humped-over person crawling through the crowd, know that that person really wants help. That kind of desire is what it takes to change your life. Jesus is the answer.

I may seek help by going from one person to another, but only He is the answer. I may be sick in my body, but He is the answer. If my son is dead, or insane on drugs, and I need Him to resurrect my child, He is the answer. If I am having family problems with my brother who is in trouble, He's the answer. It doesn't matter what the problem is, He is the answer.

It doesn't matter what the problem is, He is the answer.

What time I am afraid, I will trust in thee. Psalm 56:3

Fear is as lethal to us as paralysis of the brain. It makes our thoughts become arthritic and our memory sluggish. It is the kind of feeling that can make a graceful person stumble up the stairs in a crowd. You know what I mean—the thing that makes the articulate stutter and the rhythmic become spastic. Like an oversized growth, fear soon becomes impossible to camouflage. Telltale signs like trembling knees or quivering lips betray fear even in the most disciplined person.

From the football field to the ski slope, fear has a visa or entrance that allows it to access the most discriminating crowd. It is not prejudiced, nor is it socially conscious. It can attack the impoverished or the aristocratic....

To me, there is no fear like the fear of the innocent....I can remember moments as a child when I thought my heart had turned into an African tom-tom that was being beaten by an insane musician whose determined beating would soon break through my chest like the bursting of a flood-engorged dam.

Even now I can only speculate how long it took for fear to give way to normalcy, or for the distant rumble of a racing heart to recede into the steadiness of practical thinking and rationality. I can't estimate time because fear traps time and holds it hostage in a prison of icy anxiety. Eventually, though, like the thawing of icicles on the roof of an aged and sagging house, my heart would gradually melt into a steady and less pronounced beat.

I confess that maturity has chased away many of the ghosts and goblins of my youthful closet of fear. Nevertheless, there are still those occasional moments when reason gives way to the fanciful imagination of the fearful little boy in me, who peeks his head out of my now fully developed frame like a turtle sticks his head out of its shell with caution and precision.

Fear is as lethal to us as paralysis of the brain.

And besought Him that they might only touch the hem of His garment: and as many as touched were made perfectly whole. Matthew 14:36

And He laid His hands on her: and immediately she was made straight, and glorified God (Luke 13:13).

Jesus touched the infirmed woman. There's a place in God where the Lord will touch you and provide intimacy in your life when you're not getting it from other places. You must be open to His touch. If you can't receive from Him, you may find yourself like the woman at the well, who sought physical gratification (see John 4:18). If you seek only the physical when you really need intimacy, what you end up getting is simply sex. Sex is a poor substitute for intimacy. It's nice with intimacy, but when it is substituted for intimacy, it's frustrating.

Jesus knew this woman. He was the only one who truly knew her. He touched her and healed her. He unleashed her potential that had been bound for 18 years. You can accomplish everything once you have been called to Jesus. From that moment on you become invincible.

However, most likely your words have hindered you. Often we are snared by the words in our own mouth. The enemy would love to destroy you with your own words. Satan has turned your back against you. He will use your strength against you. Many of you have beat yourself down with the power of your own words. You have twisted your own back. The enemy worked you against yourself until you saw yourself as crippled. Reverse his plan. If you had enough force to bend yourself, you've got enough force to straighten yourself back up again.

The Lord told this woman the truth about herself. He told her that she was loosed and set free. He saw the truth despite what everyone else saw. She was important.

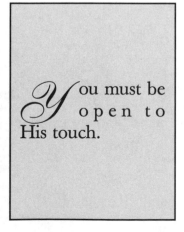

*Y*ou must be open to His touch.

And the Gentiles shall see thy righteousness, and all kings thy glory: and thou shalt be called by a new name, which the mouth of the Lord shall name. Isaiah 62:2

Jacob was his mother's darling. It was probably she who had given him his name. He was what we would call a "momma's boy."…Jacob had learned how to be very manipulative and tricky. It was only when his trickery brought him to a dead end that he began to struggle with God for an answer.

Jacob, whose name meant "supplanter" or "trickster," literally "con man," was left alone with God. God cannot accomplish anything with us until we are left alone with Him. There, in the isolation of our internal strife, God begins the process of transforming disgrace into grace. It only took a midnight rendezvous and an encounter with a God he couldn't "out slick" to bring Jacob's leg to a limp and his fist to a hand clasped in prayer. "I won't let You go till You bless me," he cries. God then tells him what he really needs to know. He tells Jacob that he is not who he thinks he is. In fact, he is really Israel, a prince. (See Genesis 32:24-30.) My friend, when we, like Jacob, seek to know God, He will inevitably show us our real identity. The greatest riches Jacob would ever receive were given while he was alone with the Father. It was simply the Father's telling him his name!

Imagine how shocking it was for this almost dysfunctional person to find that he was not who he thought he was. Here everyone had been calling him something that he really wasn't. All of his life they had called him a trickster. They called him that morning, noon, and night. When they called him to dinner, they would say, "Hey, Jacob, come and eat," which meant, "Hey, trickster, come and eat." Jacob simply acted out what everyone had said he was. But with the grip of a desperate man he caught the horns of the altar of prayer and prayed until the Father gave him his real identity. He said to Jacob, "Your name is Israel, and as a prince you have wrestled with God" (see Gen. 32:28). You could be a prince and not really know it. My friend, if no one else knows who you are, God knows. If you pray, the Father will give you a name.

You could be a prince and not really know it.

The Lord is my light and my salvation; whom shall I fear? the Lord is the strength of my life; of whom shall I be afraid? When the wicked, even mine enemies and my foes, came upon me to eat up my flesh, they stumbled and fell.... Psalm 27:1-3

The religious critics didn't like what Jesus had done. His power showed how powerless their religion was. They accused Him of breaking the law by performing a miracle on the Sabbath day. Christ acknowledged their hypocrisy by addressing a common occurrence in the area. They all valued their livestock, He said. Then He reminded them that they would loose their ass on the Sabbath so that it could get a drink. Surely this woman was more valuable than any animal. She could be loosed from her pain and sickness regardless of the day.

Sometimes pain can become too familiar. Ungodly relationships often become familiar. Change doesn't come easily. Habits and patterns are hard to break. Sometimes we maintain these relationships because we fear change. However, when we see our value the way Jesus sees us, we muster the courage to break away.

He is your defense. He will defend you before your critics. Now is the time for you to focus on receiving the miraculous and getting the water that you could not get before. He is loosing you to water. You haven't been drinking for 18 years, but now you can get a drink. With Jesus, you can do it.

Have you been a beast of burden? Some of you have been a pack horse for many years. People have dumped on you. You've had to grit your teeth. You've never been allowed to develop without stress and weights, not just because of the circumstances, but because of how deeply things affect you. Our God, however, is a liberator.

> *N*ow is the time for you to focus on receiving the miraculous and getting the water that you could not get before.

My little children, of whom I travail in birth again until Christ be formed in you. Galatians 4:19

Thank God that He understands the hidden part within each of us. He understands the child in us, and He speaks to our blanket-clutching, thumb-sucking infantile need. In spite of our growth, income, education, or notoriety, He still speaks to the childhood issues of the aging heart. This is the ministry that only a Father can give.

Have you ever noticed that you are never a grown-up to the ones who birthed you? They completely disregard the gray hairs, crowfeet, and bulging, blossoming waistlines of abundant life. No matter how many children call you "Dad" or "Mom," to your parents you are still just a child yourself. They seem to think you have slipped into the closet to put on grown-up clothes and are really just playing a game. They must believe that somewhere beneath the receding hairline there is still a child, hiding in the darkness of adulthood. The worst part about it is (keep this quiet), I think they are right!

The Lord looks beyond our facade and sees the trembling places in our lives. He knows our innermost needs. No matter how spiritually mature we try to appear, He is still aware that lurking in the shadows is a discarded candy wrapper from the childish desire we just prayed off last night—the lingering evidence of some little temper or temptation that only the Father can see hiding within His supposedly "all grown-up" little child.

It is He alone whom we must trust to see the very worst in us, yet still think the very best of us. It is simply the love of a Father. It is the unfailing love of a Father whose son should have been old enough to receive his inheritance without acting like a child, without wandering off into failure and stumbling down the mine shaft of lasciviousness. Nevertheless, the Father's love throws a party for the prodigal and prepares a feast for the foolish. Comprehend with childhood faith the love of the Father we have in God!

> God understands the child in us, and He speaks to our blanket-clutching, thumb-sucking infantile need.

Now the Lord had said unto Abram, Get thee out of thy country, and from thy kindred, and from thy father's house, unto a land that I will show thee: and I will make of thee a great nation, and I will bless thee, and make thy name great; and thou shalt be a blessing.... Genesis 12:1-3

You must reach the point where it is the Lord whom you desire. Singleness of heart will bring about deliverance. Perhaps you have spent all your time and effort trying to prove yourself to someone who is gone. Maybe an old lover left you with scars. The person may be dead and buried, but you are still trying to win his approval.

In this case, you are dedicated to worthless tasks. You are committed to things, unattainable goals, that will not satisfy. Christ must be your ambition.

Luke 13:13b reads, "And immediately she was made straight, and glorified God." Christ dealt with 18 years of torment in an instant. One moment with Jesus, and immediately she was well. For some things you don't have time to recover gradually. The moment you get the truth, you are loosed. Immediately she recovered.

Once you realize that you have been unleashed, you will feel a sudden change. When you come to Jesus, He will motivate you. You will see that other woman in you. You need to blossom and bring her forth.

Notice the sixteenth verse of Luke 13. "And ought not this woman, being a daughter of Abraham, whom Satan hath bound, lo, these eighteen years, be loosed from this bond on the sabbath day?" He called her, "a daughter of Abraham." She may have been bent over, but she was still Abraham's daughter. Don't let your condition negate your position.

She was unleashed because of who her father was. It had little to do with who she was. The Bible doesn't even mention her name. We will never know who she was until we reach Heaven. Although we don't know who she was, we know whose she was. She was a daughter of Abraham.

$\mathcal{D}$on't let your condition negate your position.

Set your affection on things above, not on things on the earth. For ye are dead, and your life is hid with Christ in God. Colossians 3:2-3

Becoming a Christian is not like becoming a Muslim, however. You don't have to change your name in order to be in the Church. I want you to understand that the new birth is not a change on your birth certificate; it is a change in your heart. When you are in the presence of God, He will remove the stench of your old character and give you a new one. In this sense we have a name change as it pertains to our character. This is not a work of man, or a typist on a birth certificate. This is a work of the *Holy Spirit*. In the Bible names were generally significant to the birth, as in Isaac, whose name meant "laughter." His mother broke into fits of laughter when she saw what God had done for her in the winter season of her life. On other occasions names were prophetic. The name *Jesus* is prophetic. It means "salvation." Jesus was born to save His people from their sins. In a few cases, the names were relative both to origin and prophecy. A keen example is that of Moses, whose name meant "drawn out." He was originally drawn out of the water by Pharaoh's daughter, but prophetically called of God to draw his people out of Egypt.

Understand then that a name is important. It tells something about your origin or your destiny. You don't want just anyone to name you. No one should want just anyone to prophesy over him without knowing whether or not that person is right. Words have power! Many of God's people are walking under the stigma of their old nature's name. That wretched feeling associated with what others called you or thought about you can limit you as you reach for greatness. However, it is not what others think that matters. You want to be sure, even if you are left alone and no one knows but you, to know who the Father says you are. Knowing your new name is for your own edification. When the enemy gets out his list and starts naming your past, tell him, "Haven't you heard? The person you knew died! I am not who he was and I am certainly not what he did!"

> The new birth is not a change on your birth certificate; it is a change in your heart.

FAITH IN ACTION

We give thanks to God always for you all, making mention of you in our prayers; remembering without ceasing your work of faith, and labor of love, and patience of hope in our Lord Jesus Christ, in the sight of God and our Father. 1 Thessalonians 1:2-3

Faith is an equal opportunity business. There is no discrimination in it. Faith will work for you. When you approach God, don't worry about the fact that you are a woman. Never become discouraged on that basis when it comes to seeking Him. You will only get as much from God as you can believe Him for.

You won't be able to convince Him, seduce Him, break Him down, or trick Him. God will not move because you cry and act melancholy. Now, you may move me like that. Certainly that works with men, but not with God. God only accepts faith, not just feminine rhetoric, not hysteria—just plain old faith in God.

He wants you to believe Him. He wants you to personalize the truth that you can do all things through Him (see Phil. 4:13). He is trying to teach you so when the time for a real miracle does come, you'll have some faith to draw from. God wants you to understand that if you can believe Him, you can go from defeat to victory and from poverty to prosperity!

Faith is more than a fact—faith is an action. Don't tell me you believe when your actions do not correspond with your conviction. If your actions don't change, you might still think you are tied. When you finally understand that you are loose, you will start behaving as if you were set free.

When you are loose, you can go anywhere. If I had one end of a rope around my neck, I would only be able to walk the length of the rope. Once I am unleashed from that rope, I can walk as far as I want. You are whole; you are loose. You can go anywhere.

> Faith is more than a fact—faith is an action.

He shall feed His flock like a shepherd: He shall gather the lambs with His arm, and carry them in His bosom, and shall gently lead those that are with young. Isaiah 40:11

When the disciples asked Jesus to teach them to pray, the first thing He taught them was to acknowledge the *fatherhood* of God. When we say "Our Father," we acknowledge His fatherhood and declare our sonship. Sonship is the basis for our relationship with Him as it relates to the privilege of belonging to His divine family…So knowing your father helps you understand your own identity as a son or daughter. Greater still is the need to know not only *who* my father is, but *how he feels about me.*

It is not good to deny a child the right to feel his father's love. In divorce cases, some women use the children to punish their ex-husbands. Because of her broken covenant with the child's father, the mother may deny him the right to see his child. This is not good for the child!…

> *Philip saith unto Him, Lord, show us the Father, and it sufficeth us (John 14:8).*

Philip didn't know who the Father was, but he longed to see Him. I can still remember what it was like to fall asleep watching television and have my father pick up my listless, sleep-ridden frame from the couch and carry me up the stairs to bed. I would wake up to the faint smell of his "Old Spice" cologne and feel his strong arms around me, carrying me as if I weighed nothing at all. I never felt as safe and protected as I did in the arms of my father—that is, until he died and I was forced to seek refuge in the arms of my heavenly Father.

What a relief to learn that God can carry the load even better than my natural father could, and that He will never leave me nor forsake me! Perhaps it was this holy refuge that inspired the hymnist to pen the hymn, "What a fellowship, what a joy divine. Leaning on the everlasting arms" ("Leaning On the Everlasting Arms," Elisha A. Hoffman, 1887).

> What a relief to learn that God can carry the load even better than any natural father could.

Now faith is the substance of things hoped for, the evidence of things not seen. For by it the elders obtained a good report. Hebrews 11:1-2

Hebrews chapter 11 is a faith "hall of fame." It lists great people of God who believed Him and accomplished great exploits. Abraham is given tremendous attention in this chapter. He is revered by millions as the father of faith. He is the first man in history to believe God to the point where it was counted as righteousness. He was saved by faith. Jesus said that the infirm woman was a daughter of Abraham. She was worthy. She had merit because she was Abraham's descendant and had faith.

There are two contrasting women mentioned in the faith "hall of fame." Sarah, Abraham's wife, is listed. Rahab, the Jericho prostitute, is listed as well. A married woman and a whore made it to the hall of fame. A good clean godly woman and a whore made it into the book. I understand how Sarah was included, but how in the world did this prostitute get to be honored? She was listed because God does not honor morality. He honors faith. That was the one thing they had in common; nothing else.

The Bible doesn't talk about Rahab having a husband. She had the whole city. Sarah stayed in the tent and knit socks. She moved wherever her husband went and took care of him. There was no similarity in their life styles, just in their faith. God saw something in Sarah that He also saw in Rahab. Do not accept the excuse that because you have lived like a Rahab you can't have the faith experience.

> God does not honor morality. He honors faith.

Even though you have ten thousand guardians in Christ, you do not have many fathers, for in Christ Jesus I became your father through the gospel. 1 Corinthians 4:15 (NIV)

We must know the difference between guardians and fathers. Paul said that he became their father through the gospel. For myself, I grew up in a church that had what we called "church mothers." These old saintly women prayed with fire and corrected us with the zeal of lightning. As awesome as they were, what were missing in the church were fathers. I don't necessarily mean men who carried the title of father, but men who spoke into the lives of other men with the unfeigned love of a father. We cannot take a nation of women and produce a nation of men. Everything basically reproduces after its own kind. Although that phrase in Genesis 1 refers to the creation, it has a larger application in terms of spiritual reproduction. Have you ever noticed that churches with a lot of men draw more men? Men do not always feel comfortable in a setting where there are no other men.

Many young men come into the church bleeding over their relationships—or lack of relationships—with their fathers. It is important that they be sired by pastors who can lay hands on them and affirm them by giving back to them their identity and self-esteem. Boys are nurtured by their mothers, but they receive their identity and definition of masculinity from their fathers! Thank God for the mothers in the Church—but where are our fathers? We have raised a generation of young men who couldn't find their natural fathers and now they struggle with their spiritual fathers. It is difficult to develop healthy spiritual authority in the heart of a man who hasn't seen healthy male relationships. Such men tend to be overly sensitive or rebellious, quickly associating authority with abuse as that may be their only past experience. To you men, whether younger or older, who still wrestle with these issues, allow the hand of your heavenly Father to heal the abuse and neglect of your earthly fathers. God is so wise that He will give you a spiritual father to fill the voids in your life. Trust Him!

> *Allow the hand of your heavenly Father to heal the abuse and neglect of your earthly fathers.*

Looking unto Jesus the author and finisher of our faith; who for the joy that was set before Him endured the cross, despising the shame, and is set down at the right hand of the throne of God. Hebrews 12:2

God wants you to believe Him. Make a decision and stand on it. Rahab decided to take a stand on the side of God's people. She hid the spies. She made the decision based on her faith. She took action. Faith is a fact and faith is an action. She took action because she believed God would deliver her when Jericho fell to the Israelites.

Sarah received strength to carry and deliver a child when she was well past childbearing age. She took action because she judged Him faithful who had promised.

> *Through faith also Sarah herself received strength to conceive seed, and was delivered of a child when she was past age, because she judged Him faithful who had promised (Hebrews 11:11).*

She went through the birth process and delivered a child not because of her circumstance, but because of her faith. She believed God.

God wants your faith to be developed. Regardless of your position and your past, God raises people up equally. Faith is an equal opportunity business. No matter how many mistakes you have made, it is still faith that God honors. You see, you may have blown it, but God is in the business of restoring broken lives. You may have been like Rahab, but if you can believe God, He will save your house. You know, He didn't save only her. He saved her entire household. All the other homes in Jericho were destroyed. The only house God saved in the city was the house where the prostitute lived.

You would have thought He would have saved some nice little lady's house. Perhaps He would have saved some cottage housing an old woman, or a little widow's house, with petunias growing on the sidewalk. No, God saved the whore's house. Was it because He wanted it? No, He wanted the faith. That is what moves God.

> *Faith is an equal opportunity business.*

That Christ may dwell in your hearts by faith; that ye, being rooted and grounded in love, may be able to comprehend with all saints what is the breadth, and length, and depth, and height; and to know the love of Christ, which passeth knowledge, that ye might be filled with all the fulness of God.
Ephesians 3:17-19

The Hebrew term for "fear" in the verse above is *yir'ah*, according to *Strong's Exhaustive Concordance of the Bible*. It means a moral fear, or reverence. So what attitude should we have toward our heavenly Father? The Bible declares that we should have a strong degree of reverence for Him. But a distinction must be made here: there is a great deal of difference between fear and reverence.

The term *reverence* means to respect or revere; but the term *fear* carries with it a certain connotation of terror and intimidation. That kind of fear is not a healthy attitude for a child of God to have about his heavenly Father. The term rendered "fear" in Job 28:28 could be better translated as "respect." Fear will drive man away from God like it drove Adam to hide in the bushes at the sound of the voice of his only Deliverer. Adam said, "I heard Thy voice in the garden, and I was afraid…" (Gen. 3:10). That is not the reaction a loving father wants from his children. I don't want my children to scatter and hide like mice when I approach! I may not always agree with what they have done, but I will always love who they are.…Oh friend, He may not approve of your conduct, but He still loves you! In fact, when you come to understand this fact, it will help you improve your conduct.

Or despisest thou the riches of His goodness and forbearance and longsuffering; not knowing that the goodness of God leadeth thee to repentance? (Romans 2:4)

If this text is true (and it is), then we must tell of God's goodness to those who need to repent.…I believe that we must assume the ministry of reconciliation and cause men to be reconciled back to their God.…I am convinced that the very people who need healing the most have been driven away from the only Healer they will ever find in this world.

> *He may not approve of your conduct, but He still loves you!*

Now the just shall live by faith: but if any man draw back, my soul shall have no pleasure in him. Hebrews 10:38

If you believe that your background will keep you from moving forward with God, then you don't understand the value of faith. The thing God is asking from you is faith. Some may live good, clean, separated lives; maybe you are proud of how holy you are. He still honors only faith.

If you want to grasp the things of God, you will not be able to purely because of your life style, but because of your conviction. God gave healing to some folks who weren't even saved. They were sinners. Perhaps some of them never did get saved, but they got healed because they believed Him. The thing that moves God is faith. If you believe Him, He will move in your life according to your faith and not to your experience.

> And the city shall be accursed, even it, and all that are therein, to the Lord: only Rahab the harlot shall live, she and all that are with her in the house, because she hid the messengers that we sent.... And they burnt the city with fire, and all that was therein: only the silver, and the gold, and the vessels of brass and of iron, they put into the treasury of the house of the Lord. And Joshua saved Rahab the harlot alive, and her father's household, and all that she had; and she dwelleth in Israel even unto this day; because she hid the messengers, which Joshua sent to spy out Jericho (Joshua 6:17,24-25).

There was something in Rahab's house that God called valuable. Faith was there. God protected her from the fire.

He also saved her things. When the fire was over, Rahab was the richest woman in the city. She was the only woman left in town that owned property. So He will save your finances. You must simply believe Him.

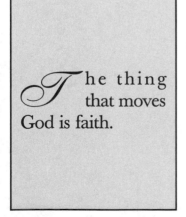

The thing that moves God is faith.

And they journeyed from Bethel; and there was but a little way to come to Ephrath: and Rachel travailed, and she had hard labor.... And it came to pass, as her soul was in departing, (for she died) that she called his name Benoni: but his father called him Benjamin. Genesis 35:16-18

Jacob, now Israel, becomes a picture of an incapacitated leader who, through his struggles, has come to a point of resting in the presence of the Lord and his God-given identity. God's grace is so good at piloting those of us who walk through life on limping limbs. But now Israel has seasoned and matured. He has produced many strong sons. One son is yet in the loins of the love of his life, Rachel, who is in the final stages of pregnancy. Her husband is desperately trying to get her to Ephrath by wagon....Before they could reach their destination, Rachel goes into gut-wrenching contractions and out in the desert she births a son. However, this scene is clouded by death who, hovering like a buzzard, stealthily creeps around the bed. Just before death claims another victim, Rachel looks at her baby and names him *Benoni*, which means "son of my sorrow." She closes her eyes in one final contraction, but this one is not for the baby. It is for the mother, and like a puff of smoke in the night, she is gone.

A weeping midwife holds the stained infant in her arms. He is all that remains of Rachel. Now Jacob limps up into the wagon. Finding his lovely wife gone and his son born, his emotions are scrambled like eggs in a pan. "What is, uh, what is his name?" he asks. The midwife's trembling voice responds, "She said he was Benoni, son of my sorrow." Jacob's eyes turn deeply within. Perhaps he remembers what a wrong name can do to a child. Whatever the reflection, he speaks with the wisdom that is born only out of personal experience. "He shall not be called Benoni, son of my sorrow. He shall be called Benjamin, son of my right hand. He is my strength, not my sorrow!" he declares. Guess whose name prevailed, Benjamin; you are who your father says you are.

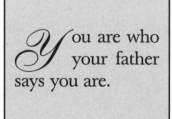

You are who your father says you are.

Wherefore come out from among them, and be ye separate, saith the Lord, and touch not the unclean thing; and I will receive you, and will be a Father unto you, and ye shall be My sons and daughters, saith the Lord Almighty.
2 Corinthians 6:17

There were a group of sisters in the Old Testament who proved that God was interested in what happens to women.

Then came the daughters of Zelophehad, the son of Hepher, the son of Gilead, the son of Machir, the son of Manasseh, of the families of Manasseh, the son of Joseph: and these are the names of his daughters; Mahlah, Noah, and Hoglah, and Milcah, and Tirzah. And they stood before Moses, and before Eleazar the priest, and before the princes and all the congregation, by the door of the tabernacle of the congregation, saying, Our father died in the wilderness, and he was not in the company of them that gathered themselves together against the Lord in the company of Korah; but died in his own sin, and had no sons (Numbers 27:1-3).

There were a group of women who were left alone. There were no men left in the family. Their father had wealth, but he had no sons. Prior to this time, women were not allowed to own property or to have an inheritance except through their husbands. Only men could own property.

They continued with their appeal. "Why should the name of our father be done away from among his family, because he hath no son? Give unto us therefore a possession among the brethren of our father" (Num. 27:4).

They appealed to Moses for help on the basis of who their father was. They stated their case and looked to him as God's authority. They couldn't understand why they should not have some of their father's wealth simply because they were born female. Their uncles would have received all their father's wealth. They would have been poor and homeless, receiving only leftovers from others. However, these women were daughters of Abraham. If you want the enemy to release you, remind him whose daughter you are.

> *I*f you want the enemy to release you, remind him whose daughter you are.

Wherefore God also hath highly exalted Him, and given Him a name which is above every name: that at the name of Jesus every knee should bow, of things in heaven, and things in earth, and things under the earth. Philippians 2:9-10

And whatsoever ye do in word or deed, do all in the name of the Lord Jesus, giving thanks to God and the Father by Him (Colossians 3:17).

In the name of Jesus you must break the spell of every name that would attach itself to you. If your heavenly Father didn't give you that name, then it isn't right. You are who He says you are. Rest in the identity that He places upon you. No one knew any better than Jacob/Israel the power of a name change! Remember, it was in his Father's presence that he discovered he was not a trickster, but a prince! When you believe on the covenant name of Jesus, you break the strength of every other name that would attach itself to your identity. In the early Church, entire cities were delivered from satanic attack in that name. Even today, drug addicts, lesbians, pimps, and every other name is subject to the name of the Lord. His name is strong enough to break the bondage of any other name that would attach itself to your life.

A good name is a very precious possession. It is often more lucrative than financial prosperity. If your name is associated with wealth, ministry, scandal, etc., then your name soon becomes synonymous with whatever it is most often associated. If I were to mention certain names, you would immediately think of Hollywood, wealth, or perhaps a certain university. Or I could refer to other names that would immediately conjure up images of mobs, murders, adultery, or deceit.…The names of some people are damaged because of past failures and indiscretions. Still others wrestle with the stains of rumors and the disgraceful, damaging, defamation of character. Whether or not a rumor is true does not matter; people prefer excitement and speculation.…The dilemma in which many people find themselves ensnared can be put like this: "How can I reverse the image or stigma that has been placed upon my name?".…

Whether you have acquired an infamous name through being a victim or a villain, I have good news. If you are wrestling with the curse and stigma of public opinion, if people have categorized you for so long that you have accepted your origin for your prophecy—I still have good news for you. You don't have to stay the way you are.

> Your name soon becomes synonymous with whatever it is most often associated.

GOD IS NO RESPECTER OF PERSONS

And it came to pass, that, as Jesus sat at meat in his house, many publicans and sinners sat also together with Jesus and His disciples: for there were many, and they followed Him. And...the scribes and Pharisees...said...How is it that he eateth and drinketh with publicans and sinners? Mark 2:15-16

Then came the daughters of Zelophehad, the son of Hepher, the son of Gilead, the son of Machir, the son of Manasseh, of the families of Manasseh, the son of Joseph: and these are the names of his daughters; Mahlah, Noah, and Hoglah, and Milcah, and Tirzah. And they stood before Moses, and before Eleazar the priest, and before the princes and all the congregation, by the door of the tabernacle of the congregation, saying, Our father died in the wilderness, and he was not in the company of them that gathered themselves together against the Lord in the company of Korah; but died in his own sin, and had no sons (Numbers 27:1-3).

No one would have listened to them if they had not initiated a meeting to plead their case. Perhaps you who have struggled need to call a meeting. Get in touch with people in power and demand what you want, or you will not get it. Speak for yourself. They could not understand why they were being discriminated against because of their gender.

One of the reasons Zelophehad's daughters could make a proper case for themselves was they were right. It was time to teach God's people that women have value. Abraham's daughters have worth. They didn't wait for a man to defend them; they took action in faith. God saw faith in those women.

And Moses brought their cause before the Lord. And the Lord spake unto Moses, saying, The daughters of Zelophehad speak right: thou shalt surely give them a possession of an inheritance among their father's brethren; and thou shalt cause the inheritance of their father to pass unto them (Numbers 27:5-7).

God is no respecter of persons. Faith is based on equal opportunity.

Moses didn't know what to do, so he asked God. The women were vindicated. If they had failed, surely they would have been scorned by all the good people of Israel who would have never challenged Moses in such a way. Instead they received the wealth of their father. God is no respecter of persons. Faith is based on equal opportunity.

And God shall wipe away all tears from their eyes; and there shall be no more death, neither sorrow, nor crying, neither shall there be any more pain: for the former things are passed away. And He that sat upon the throne said, Behold, I make all things new. Revelation 21:4-5

If you are wrestling with the curse and stigma of public opinion, if people have categorized you for so long that you have accepted your origin for your prophecy—I still have good news for you. You don't have to stay the way you are. The Potter wants to put you back together again. Do you believe that God is a God of second chances? If you do, I want to unite my faith with yours, because I believe He gives second chances.

This good news is that God changes names. Throughout the Scriptures He took men like Abram, the exalted father, and transformed his image and character into Abraham, the father of many nations. Jacob, the supplanter, became Israel, the prince. A name is an expression of character; it means no more than the character behind it. Now, I don't want everyone to run to the courthouse and change his name. However, I do want you to realize that there is a place in your walk with God—a place of discipleship—whereby God radically changes your character. With that change He can erase the stigma of your past and give you, as it were, a fresh name in your community—but most importantly, in your heart. You see, my friend, when you were wandering in search of yourself like the prodigal son, God knew who you really were all the time. When you finally came to yourself, He was there. I recommend you get on your knees and wrestle with Him in prayer until you can arise knowing what He knows. Rise up from prayer knowing who you really are in the Spirit and in the Kingdom.

Many of you are like Hananiah, Mishael, and Azariah. If you don't know them, perhaps you'll recognize them by the heathen names Nebuchadnezzar gave them: Shadrach, "command of Aku," Meshach, "pagan name," and Abednego, "servant of Nego." These names expressed worship to heathen gods, as defined by *Nelson's Bible Dictionary*. Their real names, however, were Hananiah, "Jehovah is gracious," Mishael, "who is like God," and Azariah, "Jehovah has helped." When the wicked king threw them into the fiery furnace, the names God called them prevailed!

> Do you believe that God is a God of second chances?

The eyes of your understanding being enlightened; that ye may know what is the hope of His calling, and what the riches of the glory of His inheritance in the saints.
Ephesians 1:18

Like the infirm woman Jesus healed in Luke 13, you are a daughter of Abraham if you have faith. You want the inheritance of your father to pass on to you. Why should you sit there and be in need when your Father has left you everything? Your Father is rich, and He left everything to you. However, you will not get your inheritance until you ask for it. Demand what you father left you. That degree has your name on it. That promotion has your name on it. That financial breakthrough has your name on it.

There is no need to sit around waiting on someone else to get you what is yours. Nobody else is coming. The One who needed to come has already come. Jesus said, "I am come that they might have life, and that they might have it more abundantly" (John 10:10b). That is all you need.

The power to get wealth is in your tongue. You shall have whatever you say. If you keep sitting around murmuring, groaning and complaining, you use your tongue against yourself. Your speech has got you bent over and crippled. You may be destroying yourself with your words.

Open your mouth and speak something good about yourself so you can stand up on your feet. You used your mouth against yourself. Then you spoke against all the other women around you because you treated them like you treated yourself. Open your mouth now and begin to speak deliverance and power. You are not defeated. You are Abraham's daughter.

When you start speaking correctly, God will give you what you say. You say you want it. Jesus said, "And all things, whatsoever ye shall ask in prayer, believing, ye shall receive" (Matt. 21:22). God willed you something. Your Father left you an inheritance. If God would bless the sons of Abraham, surely He would bless the daughters of Abraham.

> There is no need to sit around waiting on someone else to get you what is yours.

I Am Come in My Father's Name

I am come in My Father's name, and ye receive Me not: if another shall come in his own name, him ye will receive. John 5:43

There is nothing quite like trouble to bring out your true identity. Aren't you glad that you are not limited to public opinion? God's opinion will always prevail. Those three Hebrews came out of the furnace without a trace of smoke. That old king tried to change the name on the package, but he couldn't change the contents of the heart! Can you imagine those boys shouting when they came out? One would say, "Who is like God?" Another would lift his hands and say, "Jehovah is gracious!" The other would smell his clothes, touch his hair, and shout, "Jehovah has helped!"

If you have agonized on bended knees, praying at the altar to know the purpose and will of God for your life, and His answer doesn't line up with your circumstances, then call it what God calls it! The doctor might call it cancer, but if God calls it healed, then call it what God calls it. The word of the Lord often stands alone. It has no attorney and it needs no witness. It can stand on its own merit. Whatever He says, you are! If you are to fight the challenge of this age, then shake the enemy's names and insults off your shoulder. Look the enemy in the eye without guilt or timidity and declare:

"I have not come clothed in the vesture of my past. Nor will I use the opinions of this world for my defense. No, I am far wiser through the things I have suffered. Therefore I have come in my Father's name. He has anointed my head, counseled my fears, and taught me who I am. I am covered by His anointing, comforted by His presence, and kept by His auspicious grace. Today, as never before, I stand in the identity He has given me and renounce every memory of who I was yesterday. I was called for such a time as this, and I have come in my Father's name!"

> If you are to fight the challenge of this age, then shake the enemy's names and insults off your shoulder.

Young men likewise exhort to be sober minded. In all things showing thyself a pattern of good works: in doctrine showing uncorruptness, gravity, sincerity. Titus 2:6-7

God will give you whatever you ask for (see John 14:13). God will give you a business. God will give you a dream. He will make you the head and not the tail (see Deut. 28:13). God's power brings all things up under your feet. Believe him for your household. God will deliver. You don't need a sugar daddy. You have the Jehovah-jireh, the best provider this world has ever known.

"For ye are all the children of God by faith in Christ Jesus" (Gal. 3:26). Women are just as much children of God as men are. Everything that God will do for a man, He will do for a woman. You are not disadvantaged. You can get an inheritance like any man. Generally men don't cry about being single—they simply get on with life and stay busy. There is no reason a woman can't be complete in God without a husband.

If you choose to get married, you should get married for the right reasons. Don't give in to a desperate spirit that forces you to put up with someone less than what you would want. You could become stuck with someone immature and bear three little boys. Then you would have four little boys. That is no way to live. You need someone who has some shoulders and backbone.

You need to marry someone who will hold you, help you, strengthen you, build you up, and be with you when the storms of life are raging. If you want a cute man, buy a photograph. If you want some help, marry a godly man.

For as many of you as have been baptized into Christ have put on Christ. There is neither Jew nor Greek, there is neither bond nor free, there is neither male nor female: for ye are all one in Christ Jesus (Galatians 3:27-28).

> If you want a cute man, buy a photograph. If you want some help, marry a godly man.

But ye are a chosen generation, a royal priesthood, an holy nation, a peculiar people; that ye should show forth the praises of Him who hath called you out of darkness into His marvellous light: which in time past were not a people, but are now the people of God: which had not obtained mercy, but now have obtained mercy. 1 Peter 2:9-10

Those ancient Israelite women, the daughters of Zelophehad, thought it was a disgrace for them to be starving when they considered who their father was.

And Moses brought their cause before the Lord. And the Lord spake unto Moses, saying, The daughters of Zelophehad speak right: thou shalt surely give them a possession of an inheritance among their father's brethren; and thou shalt cause the inheritance of their father to pass unto them (Numbers 27:5-7).

Rahab was a harlot until she found faith.

By faith the harlot Rahab perished not with them that believed not, when she had received the spies with peace (Hebrews 11:31).

Once she had faith, she no longer turned to her old profession. The infirmed woman in Luke 13 was bowed over until Jesus touched her. Once He touched her, she stood up. You have put on Christ. There is no reason to be bent over after His touch. You can walk with respect even when you have past failures. It's not what people say about you that makes you different. It is what you say about yourself, and what your God has said about you, that really matters.

Just because someone calls you a tramp doesn't mean you have to act like one. Rahab walked with respect. You will find her name mentioned in the lineage of Jesus Christ. She went from being a prostitute to being one of the great-grandmothers of our Lord and Savior Jesus Christ. You can't help where you've been, but you can help where you're going.

God is not concerned about race. He is not concerned about your being Black. You may think, " My people came over on a boat and picked cotton on a plantation." It doesn't make any difference. The answer isn't to be White. Real spiritual advantage does not come from the color of your skin. It's not the color of your skin that will bring deliverance and help from God; it's the contents of your heart.

> *Real spiritual advantage does not come from the color of your skin.*

Therefore being justified by faith, we have peace with God through our Lord Jesus Christ: by whom also we have access by faith into this grace wherein we stand, and rejoice in hope of the glory of God. Romans 5:1-2

Some of us have particular problems based on where we came from. We've got to deal with it. God says there is neither Greek nor Jew. There is no such thing as a Black church. There is no such thing as a White church. It's only one Church, purchased by the blood of the Lamb. We are all one in Christ Jesus.

You may have been born with a silver spoon in your mouth too, but it doesn't make any difference. In the Kingdom of God, social status doesn't mean anything. Rahab can be mentioned right next to Sarah because if you believe, God will bless. Faith is the only thing in this world where there is true equal opportunity. Everyone can come to Jesus.

"There is neither male nor female" (Gal. 3:28). God doesn't look at your gender. He looks at your heart. He doesn't look at morality and good works. He looks at the faith that lives within. God is looking in your heart. You are spirit, and spirits are sexless. That's why angels don't have sexes; they simply are ministering spirits. Don't think of angels in terms of gender. They can manifest themselves as men, but angels are really ministering spirits. All people are one in Christ Jesus.

Christ saw the worth of the infirm woman of Luke 13 because she was a daughter of Abraham. She had faith. He will unleash you also from the pain you have struggled with and the frustrations that have plagued you. Faith is truly equal opportunity. If you will but dare to believe that you are a daughter of Abraham, you will find the power to stand up straight and be unleashed. The potential that has been bound will then truly be set free.

> **I**f you will but dare to believe that you are a daughter of Abraham, you will find the power to stand up straight and be unleashed.

Lo, children are an heritage of the Lord: and the fruit of the womb is his reward. As arrows are in the hand of a mighty man; so are children of the youth. Happy is the man that hath his quiver full of them: they shall not be ashamed, but they shall speak with the enemies in the gate. Psalm 127:3-5

The birth of a child is still the greatest miracle I have ever seen. Standing in the sterile white environment of a hospital maternity ward with the smell of disinfectant strong on my hands like a strange new cologne, they just handed me my link into the future, my ambassador to the next generation. Blinking, winking, squirming little slice of love, wrapped in a blanket and forever fastened to my heart—we had just had a baby! To me a piece of Heaven had been pushed through the womb of our consummated love. Children are living epistles that should stand as evidence to the future that the past made some level of contribution.

The psalmist David wrote a brief note that is as loud as an atomic bomb. It speaks to the heart of men about their attitude toward their offspring. This was David, the man whose indiscretion with Bathsheba had produced a love child. Though inappropriately conceived, the baby was loved nonetheless. David is the man who lay upon the ground in sackcloth and ashes praying feverishly for mercy as his child squirmed in the icy hands of death. Somewhere in a tent the cold silence slowly grew. The squirming stopped, the crying stilled; the baby has gone into eternal rest. If anybody knows the value of children, it is those who just left theirs in the ground. "As arrows are in the hand of a mighty man; so are children of the youth," says King David whose arrow they lowered in the ground.

Why did he compare children to arrows? Maybe it was for their potential to be propelled into the future. Perhaps it was for the intrinsic gold mine that lies in the heart of every child who is shot through the womb. Maybe he was trying to tell us that children go where we, their parents, aim them. Could it be that we, as parents, must be responsible enough to place them in the kind of bow that will accelerate their success and emotional well-being? How happy I am to have a quiver full of arrows.

> *P*arents must be responsible enough to place their children in the kind of bow that will accelerate their success and emotional well-being.

Be careful in your life and in your teaching. If you continue to live and teach rightly, you will save both yourself and those who listen to you. 1 Timothy 4:16 (NCV)

I will never forget in the early years of my pastoring, a particular church....This handful of members initially was the right number for inviting the whole church to almost anyone's house for dinner. That...was about all I could handle and, at the tender era of my early twenties, more than I could lead. I learned how to pray in those days of struggle and I gained a humility that prepared me for the things God would later do in my life. I remember certain situations that arose during that time which were all I could handle....

Once a young lady, who had been attending my church, came to me in tears. She had been brutally raped by several young men. She was just a teenager. I was wounded to hear of this adversity that had left her feeling filthy, vile, and used. I was full of compassion, but not wisdom. I really didn't know what to say to her; I could only share her pain and pray for her future. She told me that the hospital gave her what they call a morning-after pill to stop the possibility of her being pregnant as a result of this tragedy. I later learned that this pill is designed to kill any possibility of pregnancy after rape. I scarcely knew how to counsel her, I was so afraid of saying the wrong thing. I realized that she could not undo what had been done. None of us could.

I mentioned her because I wish there was a spiritual morning-after pill we could get to kill the unwanted spiritual embryos left behind from our previous associations with dead things. Since we have succeeded in destroying our relationships with the past, let's deal with all those side effects that resulted from our previous infidelities. There can be progeny born in us from our relationships with the past; they must be sought out and destroyed. These offsprings of another time when we were less spiritually mature cannot be allowed to exist in us.

> There can be progeny born in us from our relationships with the past; they must be sought out and destroyed.

Let them melt away as waters which run continually: when he bendeth his bow to shoot his arrows.... Psalm 58:7

If someone must be hurt, if it ever becomes necessary to bear pains, weather strong winds, or withstand trials or opposition, let it be adults and not children. Whatever happens, happens. I can accept the fate before me. I was my father's arrow and my mother's heart. My father is dead, but his arrows are yet soaring in the wind. You will never know him; he is gone. However, my brother, my sister, and I are flying, soaring, scientific proof that he was, and through us, continues to be. So don't worry about me; I am an arrow shot. If I don't succeed, I have had the greatest riches known to man. I have had an opportunity to test the limits of my destiny. Whether preferred or rejected, let the record show: I am here. Oh, God, let me hit my target! But if I miss and plummet to the ground, then at least I can say, "I have been shot!"

It is for the arrows of this generation that we must pray—they who are being aimed at the streets and drugs and perversion. Not all of them, but some of them have been broken in the quiver! I write to every empty-eyed child I have ever seen sit at my desk with tears and trembling lips struggling to tell the unmentionable secret. I write to the trembling voice of every caller who spoke into a telephone a secret they could not keep and could not tell. I write to every husband who holds a woman every night, a child lost in space, a rosebud crushed before you met her, a broken arrow shaking in the quiver. I write to every lady who hides behind silk dresses and leather purses a terrible secret that makeup can't seem to cover and long showers will not wash. Some people call them abused children. Some call them victimized. Some call them statistics. But I call them broken arrows.

> *Oh, God, let me hit my target! But if I miss and plummet to the ground, then at least I can say, "I have been shot!"*

For His anger endureth but a moment; in His favor is life: weeping may endure for a night, but joy cometh in the morning. Psalm 30:5

Jealousy is the child of low self-esteem. Then there is always little tiny suicide wrapped in a blanket hiding in the shadows, born in the heart of a person who has been lying in bed with despair or guilt. Then there are people who habitually lie because fantasy seems more exciting than reality. Promiscuity, the child of a twisted need, has an insatiable appetite like that of greed's, which devours all whom it can touch. For all this, you weep through the night. But David said that if we could hold out, joy comes in the morning (see Ps. 30:5). The bad news is, everybody has had a bad night at one time or another. The good news is there will be a morning after. Allow the joy of the morning light to push away any unwanted partners, curses, or fears that stop you from achieving your goal.

So let the hungry mouth of failure's offspring meet the dry breast of a Christian who has determined to overcome the past. In order for these embryos of destruction to survive, they must be fed. They feed on the fears and insecurities of people who haven't declared their liberty. Like a horseleech, they are always sucking the life, the excitement, and the exuberance out of precious moments. The parent is dead; you have laid him to rest, but if not destroyed, the residue of early traumas will attach itself to your successes and abort your missions and goals. It nurses itself in your thought life, feeding off your inner struggles and inhibitions.

Once you realize that you are the source from which it draws its milk, you regain control. Put that baby on a fast! Feed what you want to live and starve what you want to die! Anything you refuse to feed will eventually die. You could literally starve and dehydrate those crying, screaming childhood fears into silence, security, and successful encounters. It's your milk—it's your mind! Why not think positively until every negative thing that is a result of dead issues turns blue and releases its grip on your home and your destiny? It's your mind. You've got the power!

> The good news is there will be a morning after.

The Spirit of God has made me, and the breath of the Almighty gives me life. Job 33:4 (NKJ)

"Someone tell me how to rinse the feeling of fingers off my mind?" This is the cry of little children all over this country. This is the cry of worried minds clutching dolls, riding bicycles—little girls and even little boys sitting on school buses who got more for Christmas than they could ever show and tell. The Church must realize that the adult problems we are fighting to correct are often rooted in the ashes of childhood experiences....

In the ministry, there is a different prerequisite for effectiveness than what the textbooks alone can provide. It is not a medicine compiled by a pharmacist that is needed for the patients lying on the tables of my heart. We don't need medicine; we need miracles. I always laugh at the carnal mind that picks up books like this to critique the approach of the prophet. They weigh the words of divine wisdom against the data they have studied. Many have more faith in a textbook written by a person whose eyes may be clouded by their own secrets, than to rely upon the word of a God who knows the end from the beginning. Whatever the psychologist learned, he read it in a book, heard it in a lecture, or discovered it in an experiment. I appreciate the many who have been helped through these precious hearts. Yet I know that, at best, we are practicing an uncertain method on people as we ramble through the closets of a troubled person's mind. We need divine intervention!

If there is something minor wrong with my car, like a radiator hose needing replaced or a tire changed, I can take it almost anywhere. But if I suspect there is serious trouble with it, I always take it to the dealer. The manufacturer knows his product better than the average mechanic. So like the dealership, ministers may work with, but need not be intimidated by, the sciences of the mind! God is not practicing. He is accomplished. I want to share God-given, biblical answers to troubling questions as we deal with the highly sensitive areas of sexually abused children.

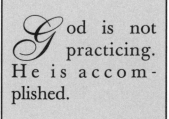

God is not practicing. He is accomplished.

For as he thinketh in his heart, so is he. Proverbs 23:7a

Be careful for nothing; but in every thing by prayer and supplication with thanksgiving let your requests be made known unto God. And the peace of God, which passeth all understanding, shall keep your hearts and minds through Christ Jesus. Finally, brethren, whatsoever things are true, whatsoever things are honest, whatsoever things are just, whatsoever things are pure, whatsoever things are lovely, whatsoever things are of good report; if there be any virtue, and if there be any praise, think on these things (Philippians 4:6-8).

In this final summation of Pauline wisdom is some wonderful food for thought. In verse 6 he admonished the Philippians that prayer would produce the offspring of verse 7, which is peace. This is not just any peace, however; it is the peace of God that stands guard over the spirits and hearts of man like a night watchman keeping us from hysteria in a crisis. The apostle Paul swelled to a theological crescendo in verse 8 as he began to teach thought modification. He taught that if we exercise the discipline of thought modification, we can produce internal or intrinsic excellence. The phrase, "if there be any virtue," suggests that if there is to be any intrinsic excellence, we must modify our thoughts to think on the things he mentioned first.

Strong's #G703 "*arete* (ar-et'-ay); from the same as 730; properly, manliness (valor), i.e. excellence (intrinsic or attributed):—praise, virtue."

Don't be mystified by the term *virtue*. It refers to intrinsic excellence. That means people who are filled with excellence achieve that excellence by the thoughts they have about themselves and about the world around them. Thoughts are powerful. They feed the seeds of greatness that are in the womb of our minds. They also can nurse the negative insecurities that limit us and exempt us from greatness. There is a virtue that comes from tranquil, peaceful thoughts that build positive character in the heart. As a rule, people who are cynical and vicious tend to be unsuccessful. If they are successful, they don't really feel their success because their cynicism robs from them the sweet taste of reward.

> *Thoughts are powerful. They feed the seeds of greatness that are in the womb of our minds.*

He hath made His wonderful works to be remembered: the Lord is gracious and full of compassion. Psalm 111:4

I earnestly believe that where there is no compassion, there can be no lasting change. As long as Christian leadership secretly jeers and sneers at the perversion that comes into the Church, there will be no healing. Perversion is the offspring of abuse! As long as we crush what is already broken by our own prejudices and phobias, there will be no healing. The enemy robs us of our healing power by robbing us of our concern.

Compassion is the mother of miracles! When the storm had troubled the waters and Peter thought he would die, he didn't challenge Christ's power; he challenged His compassion. He went into the back of the ship and said, "Carest Thou not that we perish?" (Mark 4:38) He understood that if there is no real compassion, then there can be no miracle. Until we, as priests, are touched with the feelings of our parishioners' illnesses rather than just turned off by their symptoms, they will not be healed. To every husband who wants to see his wife healed, to every mother who has a little girl with a woman's problem: The power to heal is in the power to care. If you are a broken arrow, please allow someone into the storm. I know you usually do not allow anyone to come to your aid. I realize a breach of trust may have left you leery of everyone, but the walls you built to protect you have also imprisoned you. The Lord wants to loose you out of the dungeon of fear. He does care. We care. No one would take hours away from themselves and from their family praying for you, preaching to you, or even writing this to you if they didn't care. *Rise and be healed in the name of Jesus.*

> There there is no compassion, there can be no lasting change.

How precious also are Thy thoughts unto me, O God! how great is the sum of them! Psalm 139:17

Thoughts are powerful. They feed the seeds of greatness that are in the womb of our minds. They also can nurse the negative insecurities that limit us and exempt us from greatness. There is a virtue that comes from tranquil, peaceful thoughts that build positive character in the heart. As a rule, people who are cynical and vicious tend to be unsuccessful. If they are successful, they don't really feel their success because their cynicism robs from them the sweet taste of reward.

Thoughts are secrets hidden behind quick smiles and professional veneers. They are a private world that others cannot invade. None of us would be comfortable at having all our thoughts played aloud for the whole world to hear. Yet our thoughts can accurately forecast approaching success or failure. No one can hear God think, but we can feel the effects of His thoughts toward us. Like sprouts emerging from enriched soil, our words and eventually our actions push through the fertilized fields of our innermost thoughts. Like our Creator we deeply affect others by our thoughts toward them.

> *For I know the thoughts that I think toward you, saith the Lord, thoughts of peace, and not of evil, to give you an expected end (Jeremiah 29:11).*

Stinking thinking is like the stench that came from the tomb of Lazarus. It is a result of interaction with dead things. Once the body is removed, however, the odor will eventually dissipate. There is a great need to clear the air in our minds because when the odor is left to cling, it can make the mind just as unpleasant as if the dead object was still there. I believe that's what makes preaching so powerful—it comes down and arrests the lingering odors and offspring of past experiences and removes them like old cobwebs from the sanctuary of our inner beings.

> **No one can hear God think, but we can feel the effects of His thoughts toward us.**

The Lord upholdeth all that fall, and raiseth up all those that be bowed down. Psalm 145:14

But when He saw the multitudes, He was moved with compassion on them, because they fainted, and were scattered abroad, as sheep having no shepherd (Matthew 9:36).

And Jesus went forth, and saw a great multitude, and was moved with compassion toward them, and He healed their sick (Matthew 14:14).

Then the lord of that servant was moved with compassion, and loosed him, and forgave him the debt (Matthew 18:27).

And Jesus, moved with compassion, put forth His hand, and touched him, and saith unto him, I will; be thou clean (Mark 1:41).

And Jesus, when He came out, saw much people, and was moved with compassion toward them, because they were as sheep not having a shepherd: and He began to teach them many things (Mark 6:34).

Preceding miracle after miracle, compassion provoked power. We can build all the churches we want. We can decorate them with fine tapestry and ornate artifacts, but if people cannot find a loving voice within our hallowed walls, they will pass through unaltered by our clichés and religious rhetoric. We can no longer ostracize the victim and let the assailant escape! Every time you see some insecure, vulnerable, intimidated adult who has unnatural fear in her eyes, low self-esteem or an apologetic posture, she is saying, "Carest thou not that I perish?" Every time you see a bra-less woman in men's jeans, choosing to act like a man rather than to sleep with one; every time you see a handsome young man who could have been someone's father, walking like someone's mother—you may be looking child abuse in the face. If you think it's ugly, you're right. If you think it's wrong, you're right again. If you think it can't be healed, you're dead wrong! If you look closely into these eyes I've so feebly tried to describe, you will sense that something in this person is weak, hurt, maimed or disturbed, but fixable.

We can no longer ostracize the victim and let the assailant escape!

But by the grace of God I am what I am: and His grace which was bestowed upon me was not in vain; but I labored more abundantly than they all: yet not I, but the grace of God which was with me. 1 Corinthians 15:10

Some years ago I was birthing my ministry in terms of evangelism....It was not at all uncommon for me to drive for hours into some rural, secluded "backwoods" area to minister to a handful of people who were often financially, and in some cases mentally, deprived! God teaches men character in the most deplorable of classrooms. So He had me in school. I thought I was traveling to minister to the people, but in actuality God was taking me through a series of hurdles and obstacles in order to strengthen my legs for the sprints ahead.

It was while on one of these pilgrimages...I stayed in a room that had a bed so bowed it looked like a musical instrument. The entire house was infested with flies...I can remember being horrified at the filth and slime that existed in the bathroom, and lying in my bed at night praying for the grace not to run....

I encountered some children who came over to talk to me. I noticed immediately that most of them were either physically or mentally abnormal. These abnormalities ranged in severity from slurred speech to missing fingers and dwarfed limbs....One little boy came over and whispered in my ear. He said, "That little boy turning somersaults is my cousin-brother." It seemed that the little boy was the product of some hot summer night when need had overruled common sense and the little boy's mother had slept with her own brother and produced a mutated offspring that halted around as a testimony to their impropriety.

Suddenly I began to understand that these children were the result of inordinate affections and incestuous relationships....This plight is unnecessary; it could have been avoided. So are the children of the mind: the crippled need we sometimes have to receive the accolades of men; the twisted, angry tears that flood cold pillows in the night because we are left holding the offspring of yesterday's mistakes in our arms. Like a young girl left saddled with a child she can hardly rear, we wonder what we could have been if one thing or another had not happened.

> We wonder what we could have been if one thing or another had not happened.

He healeth the broken in heart, and bindeth up their wounds. Psalm 147:3

Splintered, broken arrows come in all colors and forms. Some are black, some white; some are rich, some poor. One thing about pain, though: It isn't prejudiced. Often camouflaged behind the walls of otherwise successful lives, people wrestle with secret pain. We must not narrow the scope of our ministries. Many people bear no outward signs of trauma as dramatic as I have described. Yet there are tragedies severe enough to have destroyed their lives had God not held them together. To God be the glory. He is a magnificent Healer!

Each person who has been through these adversities has her own story. Some have been blessed by not having to experience any such circumstance. Let the strong bear the infirmities of the weak. God can greatly use you to restore wholeness to others who walk in varying degrees of brokenness. After all, every car accident doesn't have the same assessment of damage. Many people have sustained injury without submitting to the ineffective narcotics of sinful and often perverted life styles. But to those who have fallen prey to satan's snares, we teach righteousness while still loving the unrighteous. Most of us have had some degree of cracking, tearing or damage. The fact that we have persevered is a testimony to all who understand themselves to be broken arrows....

Anything, whether an injured animal or a hospital patient, if it is hurt, is unhappy. We cannot get a wounded lion to jump through hoops! Hurting children as well as hurting adults can carry the unpleasant aroma of bitterness. In spite of the challenge, it is foolish to give up on your own....

Even if you were exposed to grown-up situations when you were a child, God can reverse what you've been through. He'll let the grown-up person experience the joy of being a child in the presence of God!

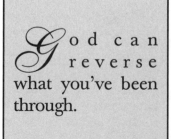

$\mathcal{G}$od can reverse what you've been through.

(For the weapons of our warfare are not carnal, but mighty through God to the pulling down of strong holds;) casting down imaginations, and every high thing that exalteth itself against the knowledge of God, and bringing into captivity every thought to the obedience of Christ. 2 Corinthians 10:4-5

There is a difference, however, between natural children and the crippled ones that haunt the recesses of our minds. There is a difference between psychological and biological offspring. To abort a biological child is wrong. To abort psychological offspring is deliverance....Every remaining psychological embryo that ties us to a dead issue can be and must be aborted!

You don't have to leave some grossly deformed generation of problems that beget more problems! God has given you power over the enemy! This power is not rejoicing power, to sing or preach. It's not power over people and external dilemmas. He has given you the power to abort the seeds of failure. Abortion is a strong term, but effective in this case. Pull down the strongholds. Pull down those things that have taken a strong hold in your life. If you don't pull them down, they will refuse to relinquish their grip. It will take an act of your will and God's power to stop the spiritual unborn from manifesting in your life. God will not do it without you—but He will do it through you....

These thoughts, wounds, and emotional oddities are self-exalting. They establish themselves as god in your life. They endeavor to control or manipulate you. These progeny of lesser days want to crown themselves as indications of your destiny. How can you afford to submit your future to the discretion of your past? The greatest freedom you have is the freedom to change your mind. Enthroned in the recesses of your mind may be some antichrist that would desire to keep you connected to what you have forsaken. Cast it down! The Bible says to repent. Repentance is when the mind decides to organize a mutiny and overthrow the government that controlled it in the past. As long as these other things reign in your life, Christ's seat is taken because these thoughts and feelings of the past are sitting on the throne. If they are on the throne, then Christ is on the cross. Put Christ on the throne and your past on the cross.

> $\mathcal{P}$ull down those things that have taken a strong hold in your life.

Then were there brought unto Him little children, that He should put His hands on them, and pray: and the disciples rebuked them. Matthew 19:13

It is interesting to me that just before this took place the Lord was ministering on the subject of divorce and adultery. When He brought up that subject, someone brought the children to Him so He could touch them. Broken homes often produce broken children. These little ones are often caught in the cross fire of angry parents. It reminds me of a newscast report on the Gulf War. It was a listing of the many young men who were accidentally killed by their own military—killed, however innocently, in the confusion of the battle. The newscaster used a term I had not heard before. He called it "friendly fire." I thought, *What is friendly about bleeding to death with your face buried in the hot sun of a strange country? I mean, it doesn't help much when I am dead!* Many children are wounded in the friendly fire of angry parents.

Who were these nameless persons who had the insight and the wisdom to bring the children to the Master? They brought the children to Him that He might touch them. What a strange interruption to a discourse on adultery and divorce. Here are these little children dragging dirty blankets and blank gazes into the presence of a God who is dealing with grown-up problems. He takes time from His busy schedule not so much to counsel them, but just to touch them. That's all it takes. I salute all the wonderful people who work with children. Whether through children's church or public school, you have a very high calling. Don't forget to touch their little lives with a word of hope and a smile of encouragement. It may be the only one some will receive. You are the builders of our future. Be careful, for you may be building a house that we will have to live in!

*B*e careful, for you may be building a house that we will have to live in!

This people have I formed for Myself; they shall show forth My praise. Isaiah 43:21

In the special moments when thankful hearts and hands lifted in praise come into corporate levels of expression with memories of what could have happened had God not intervened, we find our real ministry. Above all titles and professions, every Christian is called to be a worshiper. We are a royal priesthood that might have become extinct had the mercy of the Lord not arrested the villainous horrors of the enemy. Calloused hands are raised in praise—hands that tell a story of struggle, whether spiritual or natural....Who could better thank the Lord than the oppressed who were delivered by the might of a loving God whose love is tempered with the necessary ability to provoke change.

> *By Him therefore let us offer the sacrifice of praise to God continually, that is, the fruit of our lips giving thanks to His name (Hebrews 13:15).*

If we are a priesthood, and we are, then we need an offering. There are many New Testament offerings that we can offer unto the Lord. As an induction into the office of the priest, we offered up our dead issues to a living Christ who quickened the pain and turned it into power! The intensity of our praise is born out of the ever-freshness of our memories, not so much of our past, but of His mercies toward us. The issue then is not whether we remember, but how we choose to remember what we've been through. He is able to take the sting out of the memory and still leave the sweet taste of victory intact. When that happens, we are enriched by our struggles, not limited.

Woe be to the priest who tries to have a fresh worship experience while constantly reliving the dead issues of the past. In that case the memories become an obstacle around your neck. Lift up your head and be blessed in the presence of the Lord. Nothing is nearly as important as ministering to the Lord. What would it matter for all the voices in the earth to harmoniously explode into accolades of appreciation commending you for your contributions, if God disagreed?

> **Above all titles and professions, every Christian is called to be a worshiper.**

And they brought young children to Him, that He should touch them: and His disciples rebuked those that brought them. But when Jesus saw it, He was much displeased, and said unto them, Suffer the little children to come unto Me, and forbid them not: for of such is the kingdom of God.... Mark 10:13-16

What is wrong with these disciples that they became angry at some nameless person who aimed these little arrows at the only answer they might ever have gotten to see? Who told them they were too busy to heal their own children? Jesus stopped teaching on the cause of divorce and marital abuse to touch the victim, to minister to the effect of the abuse. He told them to suffer the little children to come. Suffer the suffering to come! It is hard to work with hurting people, but the time has come for us to suffer the suffering to come....So they brought the "ouch" to the Band-Aid, and He stopped His message for His mission. Imagine tiny hands outstretched, little faces upturned, perching like sparrows on His knee. They came to get a touch, but He always gives us more than we expected. He held them with His loving arms. He touched with His sensitive hands. But most of all, He blessed them with His compassionate heart!

I am concerned that we maintain our compassion. How can we be in the presence of a loving God and then not love little ones? When Jesus blessed the children, He challenged the adults to become as children. Oh, to be a child again, to allow ourselves the kind of relationship with God that we may have missed as a child. Sometimes we need to allow the Lord to adjust the damaged places of our past. I am glad to say that God provides arms that allow grown children to climb up like children and be nurtured through the tragedies of early days. Isn't it nice to toddle into the presence of God and let Him hold you in His arms? In God, we can become children again. Salvation is God giving us a chance to start over again. He will not abuse the children that come to Him. Through praise, I approach Him like a toddler on unskillful legs. In worship, I kiss His face and am held by the caress of His anointing. He has no ulterior motive, for His caress is safe and wholesome. It is so important that we learn how to worship and adore Him. There is no better way to climb into His arms.

> *In God, we can become children again.*

GIVE YOUR HEART A BATH

And such were some of you: but ye are washed, but ye are sanctified, but ye are justified in the name of the Lord Jesus, and by the Spirit of our God. 1 Corinthians 6:11

If we would reach new levels in worship, then we wouldn't be able to touch dead things! Instead they become obstacles that hinder us from deeper experiences in the Lord. In the early Church, the disciples experienced awesome displays of power that we don't seem to experience to the same degree. Few of us are walking in enough light to cast the kind of shadow that causes others to be healed.... What is wrong? We have become a nation of priests who spend too much time touching the dead and not enough washing our hearts with pure water!

> *He that toucheth the dead body of any man shall be unclean seven days. He shall purify himself with it on the third day, and on the seventh day he shall be clean: but if he purify not himself the third day, then the seventh day he shall not be clean. Whosoever toucheth the dead body of any man that is dead, and purifieth not himself, defileth the tabernacle of the Lord; and that soul shall be cut off from Israel: because the water of separation was not sprinkled upon him, he shall be unclean; his uncleanness is yet upon him (Numbers 19:11-13).*

Give your heart a bath. Submerge it deeply into the purity of God's Word and scrub away the remaining debris of deathly ills and concerns. These may be stopping you from participating in the greatest move of God that this generation will ever see! A clouded heart cannot move into the realm of faith. It takes clarity to flow in divine authority. Satan knows that pureness of heart is necessary to see God, to see the will of God, and to see the Word of God. You see, God's will is revealed in His Word. As for the Word, "...the Word was with God, and the Word was God" (John 1:1). These distresses and stresses are spiritual cholesterol! They will stop the heart from being able to see God.

> *Submerge it deeply into the purity of God's Word and scrub away the remaining debris of deathly ills and concerns.*

Because thou shalt forget thy misery, and remember it as waters that pass away: and thine age shall be clearer than the noonday; thou shalt shine forth, thou shalt be as the morning. And thou shalt be secure, because there is hope; yea, thou shalt dig about thee, and thou shalt take thy rest in safety.... Job 11:16-19

It is inconceivable to the injured that the injury can be forgotten. However, as I mentioned in the first chapter, to forget isn't to develop amnesia. It is to reach a place where the misery is pulled from the memory as a stinger pulled out of an insect bite. Once the stinger is gone, healing is inevitable. This passage points out so eloquently that the memory is as "waters that pass away." Stand in a stream with waters around your ankles. The waters that pass by you at that moment, you will never see again. So it is with the misery that has challenged your life: Let it go, let it pass away. The brilliance of morning is in sharp contrast to the darkness of night; simply stated, it was night, but now it is day. Perhaps David understood the aftereffects of traumatic deliverance when he said, "Weeping may endure for a night, but joy cometh in the morning" (Ps. 30:5b).

There is such a security that comes when we are safe in the arms of God. It is when we become secure in our relationship with God that we begin to allow the past to fall from us as a garment. We remember it, but choose not to wear it! I am convinced that resting in the relationship that we have with God heals us from the feelings of vulnerability. It is a shame that many Christians have not yet rested in the promise of God. Everyone needs reassurance. Little girls as well as grown women need that sense of security. In the process of creating Eve, the mother of all living, His timing was crucial. In fact, God did not unveil her until everything she needed was provided. From establishment to relationship, all things were in order. Innately the woman tends to need stability. She wants no sudden changes that disrupt or compromise her security.

> *It is when we become secure in our relationship with God that we begin to allow the past to fall from us as a garment.*

And though after my skin worms destroy this body, yet in my flesh shall I see God: whom I shall see for myself, and mine eyes shall behold, and not another; though my reins be consumed within me. Job 19:26-27

If the priest, the worshiper, has so many unresolved issues on his heart, how can he see God? If he cannot see his God, his worship becomes routine and superficial. I can't help but wonder how much more we all would see of God if we would remove life's little buildups that clog the arteries of our hearts and not allow us to see the glory of God. These are the obstacles that keep us seeking the wisdom of men rather than the wisdom of God! These are the obstacles that make us feel insecure while we wait for an answer. These are the obstacles that keep many well-meaning Christians needing prayer rather than giving prayer. In short, let's clean out our hearts and we will hear, worship, and experience God in a new dimension. Clean out every thought that hinders the peace and power of God.

> *Blessed are the pure in heart: for they shall see God (Matthew 5:8).*

This Scripture clearly draws a line of prerequisites necessary to see God in His fullest sense. He is often described as the invisible God (see Col. 1:15). God's invisibility doesn't refer to an inability to be seen as much as it does to your inability to behold Him. To the blind all things are invisible. How can I see this God who cannot be detected in my vision's periphery? Jesus taught that a pure heart could see God. No wonder David cried out, "Create in me a clean heart..." (Ps. 51:10). The term used in Matthew 5:8 for pure comes from the Greek word *katharos*, which means "to clean out," much like a laxative. That may be funny, but it's true. Jesus is saying to give your heart a laxative when you've heard too much or seen too much. Don't carry around what God wants discarded. Give your heart a laxative and get rid of "every weight, and the sin which doth so easily beset us" (Heb. 12:1)! What God wants to unveil to you is worth the cleaning up to see.

$\mathcal{W}$hat God wants to unveil to you is worth the cleaning up to see.

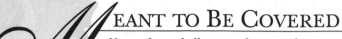

MEANT TO BE COVERED

None of you shall approach to any that is near of kin to him, to uncover their nakedness: I am the Lord. Leviticus 18:6

DAY 158

Eve was meant to be covered and originally Adam was her covering, to nurture and protect her. My sister, you were made to be covered even as a child. If someone "uncovered" you, there is a feeling of being violated. Even when these feelings are suppressed, and they often are, they are still powerful. I think it is interesting that when the Bible talks about incest, it uses the word *uncover*. Sexual abuse violates the covering of the family and the responsible persons whom we looked to for guidance. This stripping away of right relation leaves us exposed to the infinite reality of corrupt, lustful imaginations. Like fruit peeled too soon, it is damaging to uncover what God had wanted to remain protected! Who among us can repeel a banana once it has been peeled? The Bible says, "With men it is impossible, but not with God: for with God all things are possible" (Mark 10:27).

To molest a child is to uncover them. It leaves them feeling unprotected. Do you realize that one of the things the blood of Jesus Christ does is cover us? Like Noah's sons who covered their father's nakedness, the blood of Jesus will cover the uncovered. He will not allow you to spend the rest of your life exposed and violated. In Ezekiel, He speaks a message to the nation of Israel with an illustration of an abused woman. He speaks about how, as a child, this little girl was not cared for properly. But the Lord passed by her and salted, swaddled and cared for her as a baby. He says the baby would have bled to death if He hadn't stopped the bleeding. Did you know that God can stop the bleeding of an abused child? Even as you grow older, He still watches out for you! He will cover your nakedness.

> The blood of Jesus will cover the uncovered.

If any man's work shall be burned, he shall suffer loss: but he himself shall be saved; yet so as by fire. 1 Corinthians 3:15

I often build a fire on those cold wintry nights in West Virginia. Gathering the wood is a small price to pay once the logs have been ignited and that warm, engulfing glow of hot fire begins to reach out from the stove and fill the room with the soothing sound of crackling wood and the slight aroma of fresh fire. On those nights, when the day has taken its toll, I stare into the fire and watch it dance gleefully across the wood like children skipping on a hillside. Bursting up into the air, these occasional eruptions of sparks are nature's answer to fireworks, each group of sparks exploding into neon rainbows of splendor. It is a feast to weary eyes that need to be distracted into a lull of tranquillity.

While gazing deep into the fire you will notice that the sparks leave the burning log as hot as the fire itself. They swirl into the chimney with an angry ascension into the dark chambers above. But these flickering lights are soon extinguished by no other force than the aftereffects of being separated from their source. I thought, still staring silently into the glowing embers of the next fiery production, "How many Christians explode into the brilliancy of worship and praise, but are soon dark and cold, losing their first fire." Stay in the fire, my friend, where the other embers can share their heat with you and keep you ablaze! It is the fire of God that will assist you in burning up the offspring, the oddities, and the obstacles of yesteryear.

Perhaps that is what happened in the fiery furnace with the Hebrew boys. Yes, there was a fire; I'm not denying that. But the fire was on assignment. It could burn only what was an obstacle hindering those who refused to worship idols from worshiping God. I don't know what they said as they walked around in the flames, observed by the king but preserved by the Lord! Perhaps they were saying what I feel compelled to share with you. Simply stated, some people He saves from the fire; praise God for them. But all too often God saves most of us by the fire!

> $\mathcal{B}$ut all too often God saves most of us by the fire!

Because God wanted to make the unchanging nature of His purpose very clear to the heirs of what was promised, He confirmed it with an oath. God did this so that, by two unchangeable things in which it is impossible for God to lie, we who have fled to take hold of the hope offered to us may be greatly encouraged. Hebrews 6:17-18 (NIV)

Then I passed by and saw you kicking about in your blood, and as you lay there in your blood I said to you, "Live!" I made you grow like a plant of the field. You grew up and developed and became the most beautiful of jewels. Your breasts were formed and your hair grew, you who were naked and bare. Later I passed by, and when I looked at you and saw that you were old enough for love, I spread the corner of My garment over you and covered your nakedness. I gave you My solemn oath and entered into a covenant with you, declares the Sovereign Lord, and you became Mine. I bathed you with water and washed the blood from you and put ointments on you. I clothed you with an embroidered dress and put leather sandals on you. I dressed you in fine linen and covered you with costly garments (Ezekiel 16:6-10 NIV).

Reach out and embrace the fact that God has been watching over you all of your life. My sister, He covers you, He clothes you, and He blesses you! Rejoice in Him in spite of the broken places. God's grace is sufficient for your needs and your scars. He will anoint you with oil. The anointing of the Lord be upon you now! May it bathe, heal and strengthen you as never before.

For the hurting, God has intensive care. There will be a time in your life when God nurtures you through crisis situations. You may not even realize how many times God has intervened to relieve the tensions and stresses of day-to-day living. Every now and then He does us a favor. Yes, a favor, something we didn't earn or can't even explain, except as the loving hand of God. He knows when the load is overwhelming. Many times He moves (it seems to us) just in the nick of time.

The Bible instructs the men to dwell with women according to knowledge (see 1 Pet. 3:7). It will pay every husband to understand that many, many women do not deal easily with such stress as unpaid bills and financial disorder. A feeling of security is a plus, especially in reference to the home. That same principle is important when it comes to your relationship with God. He is constantly reassuring us that we might have a consolation and a hope for the soul, the mind and emotions, steadfast and unmovable. He gives us security and assurance.

> *Y*ou may not even realize how many times God has intervened to relieve the tensions and stresses of day-to-day living.

Whom God hath set forth to be a propitiation through faith in His blood, to declare His righteousness for the remission of sins that are past, through the forbearance of God. Romans 3:25

The Bible instructs the men to dwell with women according to knowledge (see 1 Pet. 3:7). It will pay every husband to understand that many, many women do not deal easily with such stress as unpaid bills and financial disorder. A feeling of security is a plus, especially in reference to the home. That same principle is important when it comes to your relationship with God. He is constantly reassuring us that we might have a consolation and a hope for the soul, the mind and emotions, steadfast and unmovable. He gives us security and assurance....

"Also thou shalt lie down, and none shall make thee afraid" (Job 11:19a), is the word of God to you. God wants to bring you to a place of rest, where there is no pacing the floor, no glaring at those with whom you are involved, through frightened eyes. Like a frightened animal backed into a corner, we can become fearful and angry because we don't feel safe. Christ says, "Woman, thou art loosed!"

There is no torment like inner torment. How can you run from yourself? No matter what you achieve in life, if the clanging, rattling chains of old ghosts are not laid to rest, you will not have any real sense of peace and inner joy. God says, "None shall make thee afraid." A perfect love casts out fear (see 1 John 4:18)! It is a miserable feeling to spend your life in fear. Many grown women live in a fear that resulted from broken arrow experiences. This kind of fear can manifest itself in jealousy, depression and many other distresses. As you allow the past to pass over you as waters moving in the sea, you will begin to live and rest in a new assurance. God loves you so much that He is even concerned about your rest. Take authority over every flashback and every dream that keeps you linked to the past. Even as we share together here, the peace of God will do a new thing in your life. I encourage you to claim Job 11:16-19 as yours.

> As you allow the past to pass over you as waters moving in the sea, you will begin to live and rest in a new assurance.

And they shall be Mine, saith the Lord of hosts, in that day when I make up My jewels; and I will spare them, as a man spareth his own son that serveth him. Malachi 3:17

I was raised in the rich, robust Appalachian mountains of West Virginia where the plush greenery accentuates the majestic peaks of the rugged mountainous terrain....

If you know much about the Appalachian mountains, you know they were the backyard for many, many Indians in days gone by. There are many large, man-made hills, which the Indians called mounds, that served as cemeteries for the more affluent members of the tribes. During my childhood, occasionally either my classmates or myself would find old Indian memorabilia in the rocks and creek beds in the hills. The most common thing to find would be discarded arrowheads carved to a point and beaten flat. Perhaps an Indian brave from the pages of history had thrown away the arrow, assuming he had gotten out of it all the possible use he could. Though worthless to him, it was priceless to us as we retrieved it from its hiding place and saved it in a safe and sacred place. I believe that God gathers discarded children who, like arrows, have been thrown away from the quiver of vain and ruthless people. If children are like arrows in the quiver of a mighty man, then broken arrows who are thrown away by that man belong to God, who is forever finding treasure in the discarded refuse of our confused society....

Please, Holy Spirit, translate these meager words into a deluge of cleansing and renewal. I pray that you who have been marred would allow the reconstructive hand of the Potter to mend the broken places in your lives. Amidst affairs and struggles, needs and incidents, may the peace and calmness of knowing God cause the birth of fresh dreams. But most of all, may it lay to rest old fears.

Healing, Blessings, and Freedom

> If children are like arrows in the quiver of a mighty man, then broken arrows who are thrown away by that man belong to God, who is forever finding treasure in the discarded refuse of our confused society.

Some friends play at friendship but a true friend sticks closer than one's nearest kin.
Proverbs 18:24 (NRSV)

Friendship is the last remaining sign of our fleeting childhood dreams. It is the final symptom of our youth that lingers around the shadows of our adult mind. It reminds us of the sweet taste of a *chosen love*. Different from family love, which is not chosen but accepted, this love develops like moss on the slippery edges of a creek. It emerges without warning. There is no date to remember. It just gradually grows until one day an acquaintance has graduated into a friend. Love is the graduation diploma, whether discussed or hinted.

It is real and powerful, sweet and bitter. It is fanciful, idealistic, and iridescent enough to shine in the chilly night of an aloof world that has somehow lost the ability to interpret or appreciate the value of a friend. Only occasionally in the course of a lifetime do we meet the kind of friend that is more than an acquaintance. This kind of kindred spirit feels as warm and fitting as an old house shoe, with its personalized contours impressed upon soft fabric for the benefit of weary feet.

The tragedy is that we all yearn for, but seldom acquire, true trust and covenant. The truth is that *real relationship is hard work*. Let no man deceive you; contouring the heart to beat with another requires extensive whittling to trim away the self-centeredness with which many of us have enveloped ourselves. It is like riding the bus. If you are going to have company riding with you, you must be willing to scoot over and rearrange to accommodate another person and the many parcels that he brings. Your actions in doing this express the importance of the other person.

Every relationship undergoes adjustments. The reason one relationship becomes more valuable than others is found in its ability to survive circumstances and endure realignments. We never know the magnitude of a relationship's strength until it is tested by some threatening force. There must be a strong adhesive that can withstand the pressure and not be weakened by outside forces.

> The truth is that *real relationship is hard work.*

But as many as received Him, to them gave He power to become the sons of God, even to them that believe on His name. John 1:12

I pray that we as Christians never lose our conviction that God does change lives. We must protect this message. Our God enables us to make the radical changes necessary for fulfilling our purposes and responsibilities. Like the caterpillar that eats and sleeps its way into change, the process occurs gradually, but nonetheless powerfully. Many people who will rock this world are sleeping in the cocoon of obscurity, waiting for their change to come. The Scriptures declare, "...it is high time to awake out of sleep: for now is our salvation nearer than when we believed" (Rom. 13:11).

A memory of my twin sons playing on the floor when they were children tailors the continuity of John 1:12 for me. They were playing with a truck, contributing all the sounds of grinding gears and roaring engines. I didn't pay much attention as I began unwinding from the day's stresses and challenges. Distractedly, I glanced down at the floor and noticed that the boys were now running an airplane down an imaginary runway. I asked, "What happened to the truck you were playing with?" They explained, "Daddy, this is a transformer!" I then inquired, "What is a transformer?" Their answer brought me into the Presence of the Lord. They said, "It can be transformed from what it was before into whatever we want it to be!"

Suddenly I realized that God had made the first transformer! He created man from dust. He created him in such a way that, if need be, He could pull a woman out of him without ever having to reach back into the dust. Out of one creative act God transformed the man into a marriage. Then He transformed the marriage into a family, the family into a society, etc. God never had to reach into the ground again because the power to transform was intrinsically placed into man. All types of potential were locked into our spirits before birth. For the Christian, transformation at its optimum is the outworking of the internal. God placed certain things in us that must come out. We house the prophetic power of God. Every word of our personal prophetic destiny is inside us. He has ordained us to be!

> *Suddenly I realized that God had made the first transformer!*

Remove from me reproach and contempt; for I have kept Thy testimonies. Psalm 119:22

A mnon was wicked. He brutally raped his sister Tamar (see 2 Sam. 13:1-21). He destroyed her destiny and her future. He slashed her self-esteem. He spoiled her integrity. He broke her femininity like a twig under his feet. He assassinated her character. She went into his room a virgin with a future. When it was over, she was a bleeding, trembling, crying mass of pain.

That is one of the saddest stories in the Bible. It also reveals what people can do to one another if left alone without God. For when Amnon and Tamar were left alone, he assassinated her. The body survived, but her femininity was destroyed. She felt as though she would never be the woman that she would have been had it not happened.

Have you ever had anything happen to you that changed you forever? Somehow, you were like a palm tree and you survived. Yet you knew you would never be the same. Perhaps you have spent every day since then bowed over. You could in no wise lift up yourself. You shout. You sing. You skip. But when no one is looking, when the crowd is gone and the lights are out, you are still that trembling, crying, bleeding mass of pain that is abused, bowed, bent backward, and crippled.

Maybe you are in the Church, but you are in trouble. People move all around you, and you laugh, even entertain them. You are fun to be around. But they don't know. You can't seem to talk about what happened in your life.

The Bible says Tamar was in trouble. The worst part about it is, after Amnon had abused her, he didn't even want her. He had messed up her life and spoiled what she was proud of. He assassinated her future and damaged her prospects. He destroyed her integrity and self-esteem. He had changed her countenance forever. Afterward, he did not even want her. Tamar said, "What you're doing to me now is worse than what you did to me at first." She said, "Raping me was horrible, but not wanting me is worse" (see 2 Sam. 13:16). When women feel unwanted, it destroys their sense of esteem and value.

> *W*hen women feel unwanted, it destroys their sense of esteem and value.

A friend loveth at all times, and a brother is born for adversity. Proverbs 17:17

Part of what we want from relationships is to know that *you won't leave*, regardless of what is encountered—even if you discover my worst imperfection and I disclose my deepest scars! Isn't the real question, "Can I be transparent with you, and be assured that my nudity has not altered your commitment to be my friend?" I know that someone reading this chapter has given up on friendship, with its many expenses and desertions. If you will not believe me, then believe the Word of God. It is possible to attain real abiding friendship.

Even natural blood ties don't always wear as well as heart ties. The Bible says there is a kind of friend that "sticketh closer than a brother" (Prov. 18:24b). What a tremendous statement. This is why we must not allow our friendships to be easily uprooted—not only in our individual lives, but also collectively as the Body of Christ. Too often we have thrown away good people who did a bad thing. The tragedy is in the fact that we usually forget all the good a friend has done and dwell only on the one bad thing he did to damage us. Have you ever done something like that? The deeper question is this: Are you throwing away the whole car over a bad battery? Is there any possibility of repair? No way, huh? Then how does God ever love you? If He ever forgave you of your debts *as you forgave your debtors*, could you stand?

The obvious friend is the one who stands by you, honoring and affirming you. The obvious friend affirms your marriage and family. You cannot be a friend and not uphold the institution of marriage and family. A true friend should desire to see me prosper in my marriage, in my finances, and in my health and spirituality. If these virtues are present in the relationship, then we can easily climb over the hurdles of personal imperfection and, generally, are mature enough to support what supports us. We, in turn, transmit through fleeting smiles, handshakes, hugs and warm exchanges of mutual affection, our celebration of friendship and appreciation.

> The obvious friend is the one who stands by you, honoring and affirming you.

Before I formed thee in the belly I knew thee; and before thou camest forth out of the womb I sanctified thee, and I ordained thee a prophet unto the nations. Jeremiah 1:5

Only when we are weary from trying to unlock our own resources do we come to the Lord, receive Him, and allow Him to release in us the power to become whatever we need to be. Actually, isn't that what we want to know—our purpose? Then we can use the power to become who we really are. Life has chiseled many of us into mere fragments of who we were meant to be. To all who receive Him, Christ gives the power to slip out of who they were forced into being so they can transform into the individual they each were created to be.

Salvation as it relates to destiny is the God-given power to become what God has eternally decreed you were before. "Before what?" you ask; before the foundation of the world. What Christians so often refer to as grace truly is God's divine enablement to accomplish predestined purpose. When the Lord says to Paul, "My grace is sufficient for thee…" (2 Cor. 12:9), He is simply stating that His power is not intimidated by your circumstances. You are empowered by God to reach and accomplish goals that transcend human limitations! It is important that each and every vessel God uses realize that they were able to accomplish what others could not only because God gave them the grace to do so. Problems are not really problems to a person who has the grace to serve in a particular area.

How many times have people walked up to me and said, "I don't see how you can stand this or that." If God has given us the grace to operate in a certain situation, those things do not affect us as they would someone else who does not have the grace to function in that area. Therefore, it is important that we not imitate other people. Assuming that we may be equally talented, we still may not be equally graced. Remember, God always empowers whomever He employs. Ultimately, we must realize that the excellency of our gifts are of God and not of us. He doesn't need nearly as much of our contributions as we think He does. So it is God who works out the internal destinies of men. He gives us the power to become who we are eternally and internally.

> *He gives us the power to become who we are eternally and internally.*

So don't be afraid; you are worth more than many sparrows. Matthew 10:31 (NIV)

Some of you have gone through divorces, tragedies and adulterous relationships, and you've been left feeling unwanted. You can't shout over that sort of thing. You can't leap over that kind of wall. It injures something about you that changes how you relate to everyone else for the rest of your life. Amnon didn't even want Tamar afterwards. She pleaded with him, "Don't throw me away." She was fighting for the last strands of her femininity. Amnon called a servant and said, "Throw her out." The Bible says he hated her with a greater intensity than that with which he had loved her before (see 2 Sam. 13:15).

God knows that the Amnon in your life really does not love you. He's out to abuse you. The servant picked Tamar up, opened the door and threw that victimized woman out. She lay on the ground outside the door with nowhere to go. He told the servant, "Lock the door."

What do you do when you are trapped in a transitory state, neither in nor out? You're left lying at the door, torn up and disturbed, trembling and intimidated. The Bible says she cried. What do you do when you don't know what to do? Filled with regrets, pains, nightmare experiences, seemingly unable to find relief...unable to rise above it, she stayed on the ground. She cried.

She had a coat, a cape of many colors. It was a sign of her virginity and of her future. She was going to give it to her husband one day. She sat there and ripped it up. She was saying, "I have no future. It wasn't just that he took my body. He took my future. He took my esteem and value away."

> You've been left feeling unwanted. You can't shout over that sort of thing.

Two are better than one; because they have a good reward for their labor. For if they fall, the one will lift up his fellow: but woe to him that is alone when he falleth; for he hath not another to help him up. Ecclesiastes 4:9-10

What we all need is *the unique gift of acceptance*. Most of us fear the bitter taste of rejection, but perhaps worse than rejection is the naked pain that attacks an exposed heart when a relationship is challenged by some struggle.

Suppose I share my heart, my innermost thoughts, with someone who betrays me, and I am wounded again? The distress of betrayal can become a wall that insulates us, but it also isolates us from those around us. Yes, I must admit that there are good reasons for being protective and careful. I also admit that love is always a risk. Yet I still suggest that *the risk is worth the reward*! What a privilege to have savored the contemplations of idle moments with the tender eyes of someone whose glistening expression invites you like the glowing embers of a crackling fire.

Communication becomes needless between people who need no audible speech. Their speech is the quick glance and the soft pat on a shoulder. Their communication is a concerned glance when all is not well with you. If you have ever sunken down into the rich lather of a real covenant relationship, then you are wealthy.

This relationship is the wealth that causes street people to smile in the rain and laugh in the snow. They have no coats to warm them; their only flame is the friendship of someone who relates to the plight of daily living. In this regard, many wealthy people are impoverished. They have things, but they lack camaraderie. The greatest blessings are often void of expense, yet they provide memories that enrich the credibility of life's dreary existence.

> *You say, "I am rich; I have acquired wealth and do not need a thing." But you do not realize that you are wretched, pitiful, poor, blind and naked (Revelation 3:17 NIV).*

What we all need is the unique gift of acceptance.

And the Lord said unto Moses, Gather unto Me seventy men of the elders of Israel, whom thou knowest to be the elders of the people, and officers over them; and bring them unto the tabernacle of the congregation, that they may stand there with thee. Numbers 11:16

Wherefore, my beloved, as ye have always obeyed, not as in my presence only, but now much more in my absence, work out your own salvation with fear and trembling. For it is God which worketh in you both to will and to do of His good pleasure (Philippians 2:12-13).

Today in the Body of Christ a great deal of emphasis is placed on the process of mentoring. The concept of mentoring is both scriptural and effective; however, as we often do, many of us have gone to extremes. Instead of teaching young men to pursue God, the ultimate Rabbi, they are running amuck looking for a man to pour into them. All men are not mentored as Joshua was—under the firm hand of a strong leader. Some, like Moses, are prepared by the workings of the manifold wisdom of God. This latter group receive mentoring through the carefully orchestrated circumstances that God ordains to accomplish an end result. Regardless of which describes your ascent to greatness, it is still God who "worketh in you both to will and to do." When you understand this, you appreciate the men or the methods God used, but ultimately praise the God whose masterful ability to conduct has crescendoed in the finished product of a man or woman of God....

In keeping with this mentoring concept, let's consider Moses' instructions when asked to consecrate elders in Israel. I found it interesting that God told Moses to gather unto him men whom he knew were elders. God says, "I want you to separate men to be elders who are elders." You can only ordain a man to be what he already is. The insight we need to succeed is the discernment of who is among us. Woe unto the man who is placed into what he is not. Moses was to bring these men into a full circle. In other words, they were to be led into what they already were. Perhaps this will further clarify my point: When the prodigal son was in the "hog pen," it was said, "And when he came to himself..." (Luke 15:17). We are fulfilled only when we are led into being who we were predestined to be. Real success is coming to ourselves.

*R*eal success is coming to ourselves.

Since thou wast precious in My sight, thou hast been honorable, and I have loved thee: therefore will I give men for thee, and people for thy life. Isaiah 43:4

Many of you have been physically or emotionally raped and robbed. You survived, but you left a substantial degree of self-esteem in Amnon's bed. Have you lost the road map that directs you back to where you were before?

There's a call out in the Spirit for hurting women. The Lord says, "I want you." No matter how many men like Amnon have told you, "I don't want you," God says, "I want you. I've seen you bent over. I've seen the aftereffects of what happened to you. I've seen you at your worst moment. I still want you." God has not changed His mind. God loves with an everlasting love.

When Jesus encountered the infirm woman of Luke 13, He called out to her. There may have been many fine women present that day, but the Lord didn't call them forward. He reached around all of them and found that crippled woman in the back. He called forth the wounded, hurting woman with a past. He issued the Spirit's call to those who had their value and self-esteem destroyed by the intrusion of vicious circumstances.

The infirm woman must have thought, "He wants me. He wants *me*. I'm frayed and torn, but He wants me. I have been through trouble. I have been through this trauma, but He wants me." Perhaps she thought no one would ever want her again, but Jesus wanted her. He had a plan.

She may have known that it would take a while for her life to be completely put back together. She had many things to overcome. She was handicapped. She was probably filled with insecurities. Yet Jesus still called her forth for His touch.

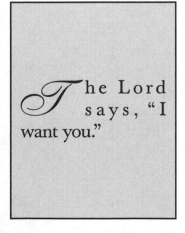

The Lord says, "I want you."

A COMMON BOND

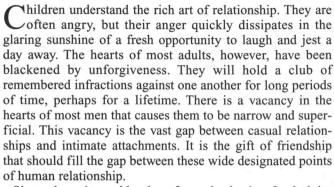

And let us consider one another to provoke unto love and to good works. Hebrews 10:24

$\mathcal{D}$AY 172

Children understand the rich art of relationship. They are often angry, but their anger quickly dissipates in the glaring sunshine of a fresh opportunity to laugh and jest a day away. The hearts of most adults, however, have been blackened by unforgiveness. They will hold a club of remembered infractions against one another for long periods of time, perhaps for a lifetime. There is a vacancy in the hearts of most men that causes them to be narrow and superficial. This vacancy is the vast gap between casual relationships and intimate attachments. It is the gift of friendship that should fill the gap between these wide designated points of human relationship.

Since there is no blood to form the basis of relativity between friends, the bond must exist through some other mode of reality. A commonality is needed to anchor the relationship of two individuals against the chilly winds of passing observers, whose suspicious minds activate and attempt to terminate any of your relationships. They are not accustomed to relationships outside of the junglelike, carnivorous stalkings of one another as prey. However, this bond may exist in an area that outsiders would never understand, but thank God their confusion doesn't dilute the intensity of admiration that exists between true friends.

Many people are surrounded by crowds of business people, coworkers, and even family members—yet they are alone. Disenchanted with life, they become professional actors on the stage of life. They do not allow anyone to get close, fearing to risk the pain and bleeding of a disappointed heart. Whether they be battered wives or distraught husbands, some among us have given up—not daring to be transparent with anyone for any reason. These have decided to present a fictitious, fragmented appearance among us that never solidifies or really alters us in any way!

I must admit there is no shield for broken hearts that will protect us from the flaws of those whom we dare to befriend. At best, there will be times of trembling need and emotional debates, *yet we need to make the investment* and even face the risk of depletion rather than live in a glass bubble all our lives!

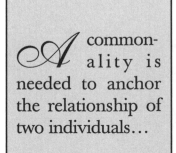

A common-ality is needed to anchor the relationship of two individuals…

GRACE TO CHANGE

God exalted Him to His own right hand as Prince and Savior that He might give repentance and forgiveness of sins to Israel. Acts 5:31 (NIV)

The thing that gives a man power to arise above his circumstances is his coming to himself. You feel fulfilled when you achieve a sense of belonging through your job, family, or ministry. Have you ever met anyone who left you with a feeling of familiarity—almost as if you had known the person? A sense of bonding comes out of similarities. Likewise, there are certain jobs or ministries that feel comfortable, even if they are tasks you have never done before. If you are discerning, you can feel a sense of belonging in certain situations. However, weary are the legs of a traveler who cannot find his way home. Spiritual wanderings plague the lives of many people who wrestle with discontentment. May God grant you success in finding your way to a sense of wholeness and completion.

Change is a gift from God. It is given to the person who finds himself too far removed from what he feels destiny has ordained for him. There is nothing wrong with being wrong—but there is something wrong with not making the necessary adjustments to get things right! Even within the Christian community, some do not believe in God's ability to change the human heart. This unbelief in God's ability to change causes people to judge others on the basis of their past. Dead issues are periodically revived in the mouths of gossips. Still, the Lord progressively regenerates the mind of His children. Don't assume that real change occurs without struggle and prayer. However, change can be achieved....

The Bible calls change *repentance*. Repentance is God's gift to a struggling heart who wants to find himself. The Lord wants to bring you to a place of safety and shelter. Without the Holy Spirit's help you can search and search and still not find repentance. The Lord will show the place of repentance only to those who hunger and thirst after righteousness. One moment with the Spirit of God can lead you into a place of renewal that, on your own, you would not find or enjoy. I believe it was this kind of grace that made John Newton record, "It was grace that taught my heart to fear and grace my fears relieved. How precious did that grace appear the hour I first believed" ("Amazing Grace," early American melody). When God gives you the grace to make changes that you know you couldn't do with your own strength, it becomes precious to you.

> **God gives you the grace to make changes that you know you couldn't do with your own strength.**

And let us consider one another to provoke unto love and to good works. Hebrews 10:24

I know that betrayal can be painful. It is hard to receive disloyalty from hands and hearts you trusted. The fear of a "Judas" has caused many preachers, leaders, as well as the general masses to avoid the attack. Now if you understand anything about God, then you know that *God can give direction out of rejection.* It was Judas' ministry that brought Christ to the cross! Although this betrayal was painful, it was an essential part of His destiny.

It is important to understand destiny as it relates to relationships. God is too wise to have His plans aborted by the petty acts of men. We have to rely on God's divine administration as we become involved with people. Their access to our future is limited by the shield of divine purpose that God Himself has placed on our lives!

> *I hate double-minded men, but I love Your law. You are my refuge and my shield; I have put my hope in Your word (Psalm 119:113-114 NIV).*

The extent of damage that mortal men can do to the upright is limited by the purposes of God. What a privilege it is to know that and understand it in your heart. It destroys the constant paranoia that restricts many of us from exploring possible friendships and covenant relationships. Let me be very clear, though; the possibility of getting hurt in a relationship is always present. Any time you make an investment, there is the possibility of a loss. But there is a difference between being hurt and being altered or destroyed.

You belong to God, and He watches over you every day. He monitors your affairs, and acts as your protection. Sometimes He opens doors (we always get excited about God opening doors). But the same God who opens doors also closes doors. I am, perhaps, more grateful for the doors He has closed in my life than I am for the ones He has opened. Had I been allowed to enter some of the doors He closed, I would surely have been destroyed! God doesn't intend for every relationship to flourish. There are some human cliques and social groups in which He doesn't want you to be included!

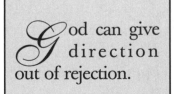

God can give direction out of rejection.

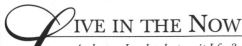

And now, Lord, what wait I for? my hope is in Thee. Psalm 39:7

And, behold, there was a woman which had a spirit of infirmity eighteen years, and was bowed together, and could in no wise lift up herself. And when Jesus saw her, He called her to Him, and said unto her, Woman, thou art loosed from thine infirmity. And He laid His hands on her: and immediately she was made straight, and glorified God (Luke 13:11-13).

If you can identify with the feelings of this infirm woman, then know that He's waiting on you and that He wants you. He sees your struggling and He knows all about your pain. He knows what happened to you 18 years ago or 10 years ago or even last week. With patience He waits for you, as the father waited for the prodigal son. Jesus says to the hurting and crippled, "I want you enough to wait for you to hobble your way back home."

Now God says, "I'm going to deliver you and heal you. Now I'm going to renew you and release you. I'm going to tell you who you really are. Now I'm ready to reveal to you why you had to go through what you did to become what you shall become." He says, "Now I'm going to tell you a secret, something between you and I no one else knows. Amnon didn't know. Your boyfriend didn't know, your first husband didn't know. I'll tell you something that your father, uncle, brother or whoever abused you had no knowledge of. Just realize that you are the daughter of a king. Your Father is the King."

When the infirmed woman came to Jesus, He proclaimed her freedom. Now she stands erect for the first time in 18 years. When you come to Jesus, He will cause you to stand in His strength. You will know how important you are to Him. Part of your recovery is to learn how to stand up and live in the "now" of life instead of the "then" of yesterday. That was then but this is now.

> *P*art of your recovery is to learn how to stand up and live in the "now" of life instead of the "then" of yesterday.

I will instruct thee and teach thee in the way which thou shalt go: I will guide thee with mine eye. Be ye not as the horse, or as the mule, which have no understanding: whose mouth must be held in with bit and bridle, lest they come near unto thee. Psalm 32:8-9

And to the angel of the church in Philadelphia write; These things saith He that is holy, He that is true, He that hath the key of David, He that openeth, and no man shutteth; and shutteth, and no man openeth (Revelation 3:7).

The letter to the Philadelphia church, the church of brotherly love, basically ends with the words, "I am the One who closes doors." The art to surviving painful moments is living in the "yes" zone. We need to learn to respond to God with a yes when the doors are open, and a yes when they are closed. Our prayer must be:

I trust Your decisions, Lord; and I know that if this relationship is good for me, You will allow it to continue. I know that if the door is closed, then it is also for my good. So I say "yes" to You as I go into this relationship. I appreciate brotherly love, and I still say "yes" if You close the door.

This is the epitome of a trust that is seldom achieved, but is to be greatly sought after. In so doing, you will be able to savor the gift of companionship without the fear of reprisal!

If God allows a relationship to continue, and some negative, painful betrayals come from it, you must realize that He will only allow what ultimately works *for your good*. Sometimes such a betrayal ushers you into the next level of consecration, a level you could never reach on your own. For that we give thanks! What a privilege to live in the assurance that God is in control of you, and of everyone whom He allows to get behind "the shield" of His purposes for your life! He intimately knows every person whom He cherishes enough to call His child. Any good parent tries to ensure that his or her children are surrounded by positive influences. The unique thing about God's parenting is that He sometimes uses a negative to bring about a positive.

> We need to learn to respond to God with a *yes* when the doors are open, and a *yes* when they are closed.

For ye know how that afterward, when he would have inherited the blessing, he was rejected: for he found no place of repentance, though he sought it carefully with tears. Hebrews 12:17

Brother Esau sought for the place of repentance and could not secure it. To be transformed is to be changed. If you are not moving into your divine purpose, you desperately need to repent....If God wants you to change, it is because He wants you to be prepared for what He desires to do next in your life. Get ready; the best is yet to come.

For whom He did foreknow, He also did predestinate to be conformed to the image of His Son, that He might be the firstborn among many brethren (Romans 8:29).

And be not conformed to this world: but be ye transformed by the renewing of your mind, that ye may prove what is that good, and acceptable, and perfect, will of God (Romans 12:2).

...The word *conformed* in Romans 8:29 is *summorphoo* (James Strong, *The Exhaustive Concordance of the Bible* [Peabody, MA: Hendrickson Publishers, n.d.], #G4832), which means "to be fashioned like or shaped into the image or the picture" of—in this case—Christ...Christ is the first-born of a huge family of siblings who all bear a striking resemblance to their Father. The shaping of a will, however, requires a visit to the garden of Gethsemane. *Gethsemane* literally means "oil press" (Strong's #G1068). God presses the oil of His anointing out of your life through adversity. When you forsake your will in order to be shaped into a clearer picture of Christ, you will see little drops of oil coming out in your walk and work for God....

In Romans 12:2 we are instructed not to be conformed to this world. Literally, it says we are not to be conformed to the same pattern of this world....We are to avoid using those standards as a pattern for our progress. On a deeper level God is saying, "Do not use the same pattern of the world to measure success or to establish character and values." The term *world* in Greek is *aion* (Strong's #G165), which refers to ages. Together these words tell us, "Do not allow the pattern of the times you are in to become the pattern that shapes your inward person."

> God presses the oil of His anointing out of your life through adversity.

I waited patiently for the Lord; and He inclined unto me, and heard my cry. He brought me up also out of an horrible pit, out of the miry clay, and set my feet upon a rock, and established my goings.
Psalm 40:1-2

I proclaim to the abused: There is a healing going into your spirit right now. I speak life to you. I speak deliverance to you. I speak restoration to you. All in the mighty name of Jesus, in the invincible, all-powerful, everlasting name of Jesus. I proclaim victory to you. You will recover the loss you suffered at the hands of your abuser. You will get back every stolen item. He will heal that broken twig. He will rebuild your self-esteem, your self-respect, and your integrity.

All you need do is allow His power and anointing to touch the hurting places. He will take care of the secrets. He touches the places where you've been assassinated. He knows the woman you would have been, the woman you should have been, the woman you could have been. God is healing and restoring her in you as you call out to Him.

The enemy wanted to change your destiny through a series of events, but God will restore you to wholeness as if the events had never happened. The triumphant woman locked inside shall come forth to where she belongs. He's delivering her. He's releasing her. He's restoring her. He's building her back. He's bringing her out. He's delivering by the power of His Spirit. "Not by might, nor by power, but by My spirit, saith the Lord of hosts" (Zech. 4:6).

The anointing of the living God is reaching out to you. He calls you forth to set you free. When you reach out to Him and allow the Holy Spirit to have His way, His anointing is present to deliver you. Demons will tremble. He wants to keep you at the door, but never let you enter. He wants to keep you down. Now his power is broken in your life.

> God will restore you to wholeness as if the events had never happened.

And we know that all things work together for good to them that love God, to them who are the called according to His purpose. Romans 8:28

If no good can come out of a relationship or situation, then God will not allow it. This knowledge sets us free from internal struggle and allows us to be transparent.

> *Every good gift and every perfect gift is from above, and cometh down from the Father of lights, with whom is no variableness, neither shadow of turning (James 1:17).*

If you don't understand the sovereignty of God, then all is lost. There must be an inner awareness within your heart, a deep knowledge that God *is in control* and that *He is able to reverse the adverse*. When we believe in His sovereignty, we can overcome every humanly induced trial because we realize that they are divinely permitted and supernaturally orchestrated. He orchestrates them in such a way that the things that could have paralyzed us only motivate us.

God delights in bestowing His abundant grace upon us so we can live with men *without fear*. In Christ, we come to the table of human relationships feeling like we are standing before a great "smorgasbord" or buffet table. There will be some relationships whose "taste" we prefer over others, but the richness of life is in the opportunity to explore the options. What a dull plate we would face if everything on it was duplicated without distinction. God creates different types of people, and all are His handiwork.

Even in the most harmonious of relationships there are injuries and adversity. If you live in a cocoon, you will miss all the different levels of love God has for you. God allows different people to come into your life to accomplish His purposes. Your friends are ultimately the ones who will help you become all that God wants you to be in Him. When you consider it in that light, you have many friends—some of them expressed friends, and some implied friends.

> **G**od is in control and that He is able to reverse the adverse...

To be made new in the attitude of your minds. Ephesians 4:23 (NIV)

I can almost hear someone saying, "How do you respond to the preexisting circumstances and conditions that have greatly affected you?" Or, "I am already shaped into something less than what God would want me to be because of the times in which I live or the circumstances in which I grew up." I am glad you asked these things. You see, every aspect of your being that has already been conformed to this age must be transformed! The prefix *trans* implies movement, as in the words *transport, translate, transact, transition,* etc. In this light, *transform* would imply moving the form. On a deeper level it means moving from one form into another, as in the tadpole that is transformed into the frog and the caterpillar into the butterfly. No matter what has disfigured you, in God is the power to be transformed.

Many individuals in the Body of Christ are persevering without progressing. They wrestle with areas that have been conformed to the world instead of transformed. This is particularly true of we Pentecostals who often emphasize the gifts of the Spirit and exciting services. It is imperative that, while we keep our mode of expression, we understand that transformation doesn't come from inspiration! Many times preachers sit down after ministering a very inspiring sermon feeling that they accomplished more than they actually did. Transformation takes place in the mind.

The Bible teaches that we are to be renewed by the transforming of our minds (see Rom. 12:2; Eph. 4:23). Only the Holy Spirit knows how to renew the mind. The struggle we have inside us is with our self-perception. Generally our perception of ourselves is affected by those around us. Our early opinion of ourselves is deeply affected by the opinions of the authoritative figures in our formative years. If our parents tend to neglect or ignore us, it tears at our self-worth. Eventually, though, we mature to the degree where we can walk in the light of our own self-image, without its being diluted by the contributions of others.

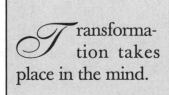

*T*ransformation takes place in the mind.

To appoint unto them that mourn in Zion, to give unto them beauty for ashes, the oil of joy for mourning, the garment of praise for the spirit of heaviness; that they might be called trees of righteousness, the planting of the Lord, that He might be glorified. Isaiah 61:3

Then Amnon hated her exceedingly; so that the hatred wherewith he hated her was greater than the love wherewith he had loved her. And Amnon said unto her, Arise, be gone....And Absalom her brother said unto her, Hath Amnon thy brother been with thee? but hold now thy peace, my sister: he is thy brother; regard not this thing. So Tamar remained desolate in her brother Absalom's house (2 Samuel 13:15,20).

Tamar knew the feeling of desertion. She understood that she was cast out. However, the Bible explains that Absalom came and said, "I'm going to take you in." You too may have been lying at the door. Perhaps you didn't have anywhere to go. You may have been half in and half out. You were broken and demented and disturbed. But God sent Absalom to restore his sister.

In this instance, Absalom depicts the purpose of real ministry. Thank God for the Church. It's the place where you can come broken and disgusted, and be healed, delivered and set free in the name of Jesus.

Jesus said, "The Spirit of the Lord is upon Me, because He hath anointed Me to preach the gospel to the poor; He hath sent Me to heal the brokenhearted, to preach deliverance to the captives, and recovering of sight to the blind, to set at liberty them that are bruised" (Luke 4:18).

You may have thought that you would never rejoice again. God declares that you can have freedom in Him—now! The joy that He brings can be restored to your soul. He identifies with your pain and suffering. He knows what it is like to suffer abuse at the hands of others. Yet He proclaims joy and strength. He will give you the garment of praise instead of the spirit of heaviness (see Isa. 61:3).

> **He will give you the garment of praise instead of the spirit of heaviness.**

The Lord is on my side; I will not fear: what can man do unto me? Psalm 118:6

God has used certain "friends" and their negativity to accomplish His will for our lives. Now, because our ultimate goal is to please Him, we must widen our definition of friendship *to include the betrayer* if his betrayal ushered us into the next step of God's plan for our lives.

> *And forthwith he came to Jesus, and said, Hail, master; and kissed Him. And Jesus said unto him, Friend, **wherefore art thou come?** Then came they, and laid hands on Jesus, and took Him. And, behold, one of them which were with Jesus stretched out his hand, and drew his sword, and struck a servant of the high priest's, and smote off his ear. Then said Jesus unto him, Put up again thy sword into his place: for all they that take the sword shall perish with the sword. Thinkest thou that I cannot now pray to My Father, and He shall presently give Me more than twelve legions of angels? But how then shall the scriptures be fulfilled, that thus it must be? (Matthew 26:49-54)*

I understand that in its narrow sense, a friend is one who has good intentions. However, because of the sovereignty of God, I have come to realize that there are some who were actually instrumental in my blessing, although they never really embraced or affirmed me as a person! They played a crucial part in my well-being. These kinds of "friends" are the "Judas sector" that exists in the life of every child of God.

Every child of God not only has, but also *desperately needs*, a "Judas" to carry out certain aspects of divine providence in his life! In the passage quoted above, Judas was more of a friend than Peter! Although Peter was certainly more amiable and admirable, Judas was the one God selected to usher in the next step of the process. Peter's love was almost a deterrent to the purpose of God. Sometimes your friends are the ones who can cause you the most pain. They wound you and betray you, but through their betrayal God's will can be executed in your life.

> *E*very child of God not only has, but also *desperately needs*, a "Judas" to carry out certain aspects of divine providence in his life!

For we are His workmanship, created in Christ Jesus unto good works, which God hath before ordained that we should walk in them. Ephesians 2:9b

When we experience the new birth, we again go back to the formative years of being deeply impressionable. It's important to be discerning in who we allow to influence us in the early years. Whenever we become intimate with someone, the first thing we should want to know is, "Who do you say that I am?" Our basic need is to be understood by the inner circle of people with whom we walk. However, we must be ready to abort negative, destructive information that doesn't bring us into an accelerated awareness of inner realities and strengths. Jesus was able to ask Peter, "Who do you say that I am?" because He already knew the answer! (See Matthew 16:15.) To ask someone to define you without first knowing the answer within yourself is dangerous. When we ask that kind of question, without an inner awareness, we open the door for manipulation. In short, Jesus knew who He was.

The Lord wants to help you realize who you are and what you are graced to do. When you understand that He is the only One who really knows you, then you pursue Him with fierceness and determination. Pursue Him! Listen to what Paul shares at the meeting on Mars' Hill.

> *And hath made of one blood all nations of men for to dwell on all the face of the earth, and hath determined the times before appointed, and the bounds of their habitation; that they should seek the Lord, if haply they might feel after Him, and find Him, though He be not far from every one of us: for in Him we live, and move, and have our being; as certain also of your own poets have said, For we are also His offspring (Acts 17:26-28).*

The basic message of this passage is that God has set the bounds on our habitations. He knows who we are and how we are to attain. This knowledge, locked up in the counsel of God's omniscience, is the basis of our pursuit, and it is the release of that knowledge that brings immediate transformation. He knows the hope or the goal of our calling. He is not far removed from us; He reveals Himself to people who seek Him. The finders are the seekers. The door is opened only to the knockers and the gifts are given to the askers! (See Luke 11:9.) Initiation is our responsibility. Whosoever hungers and thirsts shall be filled. Remember, in every crisis He is never far from the seeker!

> To ask someone to define you without first knowing the answer within yourself is dangerous.

And He hath put a new song in my mouth, even praise unto our God: many shall see it, and fear, and shall trust in the Lord. Psalm 40:3

Once you have called out to Him, you can lift up your hands in praise. No matter what you have suffered, you can hold up your head. Regardless of who has hurt you, hold up your head! Forget how many times you've been married. Put aside those who mistreated you. You may have been a lesbian. You may have been a crack addict. It doesn't matter who you were. You may have even been molested. You can't change where you have been, but you can change where you are going.

> *Lift up your heads, O ye gates; even lift them up, ye everlasting doors; and the King of glory shall come in. Who is this King of glory? The Lord of hosts, He is the King of glory. Selah (Psalm 24:9-10).*

He will restore to you that which the cankerworm and the locust ate up (see Joel 2:25). He said, "I'm going to give it back to you." Maybe you wrestle with guilt. You've been hearing babies crying in your spirit. You feel so dirty. You've had abortions. You've been misused and abused. The devil keeps bringing up to you your failures of the past.

> *Come now, and let us reason together, saith the Lord: though your sins be as scarlet, they shall be as white as snow; though they be red like crimson, they shall be as wool (Isaiah 1:18).*

All my life I have had a tremendous compassion for hurting people. When other people would put their foot on them, I always tended to have a ministry of mercy. Perhaps it is because I've had my own pain. When you have suffered, it makes you able to relate to other people's pain. The Lord settled me in a ministry that just tends to cater to hurting people. Sometimes when I minister, I find myself fighting back tears. Sometimes I can hear the cries of anguished people in the crowd.

> Once you have called out to Him, you can lift up your hands in praise.

What shall we then say to these things? If God be for us, who can be against us?
Romans 8:31

Judas was no mistake. He was handpicked and selected. His role was crucial to the death and resurrection of Christ. No one helped Christ reach His goal like Judas. If God allowed certain types of people to come into our lives, they would hinder us from His divine purpose. "Thank You, Lord, for my mysterious friends whose venomous assault led me to lean on You more explicitly than I would have, had they not tried to destroy me!" This is the prayer of the seasoned heart that has been exercised by the tragedies of life. It has reduced and controlled the fatty feelings and emotions that cause us to always seek those whose actions tickle our ears.

We all want to be surrounded by a friend like John, whose loving head lay firmly on Jesus' breast. We may long for the protective instincts of a friend like Peter, who stood ready to attack every negative force that would come against Jesus. In his misdirected love, Peter even withstood Jesus to His face over His determination to die for mankind. But the truth of the matter is, Jesus could have accomplished His goal without Peter, James, or John; but *without Judas He would never have reached the hope of His calling*!

Leave my Judas alone. I need him in my life. He is my mysterious friend, the one who aids me without even knowing it. When you encounter a Judas in your life, remember that it is his actions that carry out the purpose of God in your life! Look back over your life and understand that it is persecution that strengthens you. It is the struggles and the trauma we face that help us persevere.

Thank God for your friends and family and their support, but remember that it is often your relationship with that mysterious friend of malice and strife, weakness and defective behavior, that becomes the catalyst for greatness in your life! It is much easier to forgive the actions of men when you know the purposes of God! Not only should we refuse to fear their actions—we should release them.

> *When you encounter a Judas in your life, remember that it is his actions that carry out the purpose of God in your life!*

That He might sanctify and cleanse it with the washing of water by the word. Ephesians 5:26

Transforming truths are brought forth through the birth canal of our diligence in seeking His face. It is while you are in His presence that He utters omniscient insights into your individual purpose and course. Jesus told a woman who had been wrestling with a crippling condition for 18 years that she was not really bound—that in fact she was loosed! Immediately she was transformed by the renewing of her mind.

> *And, behold, there was a woman which had a spirit of infirmity eighteen years, and was bowed together, and could in no wise lift up herself. And when Jesus saw her, He called her to Him, and said unto her, Woman, thou art loosed from thine infirmity. And He laid His hands on her: and immediately she was made straight, and glorified God (Luke 13:11-13).*

It is no wonder David said, "In Thy presence is fullness of joy" (Ps. 16:11b). The answer is in the Presence—the Presence of God, not man! There is a renewing word that will change your mind about your circumstance. Just when the enemy thinks he has you, transform before his very eyes!

No matter who left his impression upon you, God's Word prevails! The obstacles of past scars can be overcome by present truths. Your deliverance will not start in your circumstances; it will always evolve out of your mentality. As the Word of God waxes greater, the will of men becomes weaker. Paul said in Ephesians 5:26 that Jesus cleanses by the "washing of water by the word." So turn the faucet on high and ease your mind down into the sudsy warm water of profound truth. Gently wash away every limitation and residue of past obstacles and gradually, luxuriously, transform into the refreshed, renewed person you were created to become. Whenever someone tells you what you can't do or be, or what you can't get or attain, then tell them, "I can do all things through Christ who strengthens me" (see Phil. 4:13).

> So turn the faucet on high and ease your mind down into the sudsy warm water of profound truth.

...for by faith ye stand. 2 Corinthians 1:24

You're a survivor. You should celebrate your survival. Instead of agonizing over your tragedies, you should celebrate your victory and thank God you made it. I charge you to step over your adversity and walk into the newness. It is like stepping from a storm into the sunshine. Just step into it now.

God has blessed me with two little boys and two little daughters. As a father, I have found that I have a ministry of hugs. When something happens, and I really can't fix it, I just hug them. I can't change how other people treated them. I can't change what happened at school. I can't make the teacher like them. I can't take away the insults. But I can hug them!

I believe the best nurses are the ones who have been patients. They have compassion on the victim. If anyone understands the plight of women, it ought to be women. The Church needs to develop a ministry of hugs. The touch of the Master sets us free. The touch of a fellow pilgrim lets us know we are not alone in our plight.

The Holy Spirit is calling for the broken, infirm women to come to Jesus. He will restore and deliver. How do we come to Jesus? We come to His Body, the Church. It is in the Church that we can hear the Word of God. The Church gives us strength and nourishment. The Church is to be the place where we share our burdens and allow others to help us with them. The Spirit calls; the burdened need only heed the call.

There are three tenses of faith! When Lazarus died, Martha, his sister, said, "Lord, if You would have been here, my brother would not have died." This is historical faith. Its view is digressive. Then when Jesus said, "Lazarus will live again," his sister replied, "I know he will live in the resurrection." This is futuristic faith. It is progressive. Martha says, "But *even now* You have the power to raise him up again." (See John 11:21-27.) I feel like Martha. Even now, after all you've been through, God has the power to raise you up again! This is the present tense of faith. Walk into your newness even now.

> *Even now, after all you've been through, God has the power to raise you up again!*

It is good for me that I have been afflicted; that I might learn Thy statutes. Psalm 119:71

What happens when friendship takes an unusual form? Did you know that God, our ultimate Friend, sometimes manipulates the actions of our enemies to cause them to work as friends in order to accomplish His will in our lives? *God can bless you through the worst of relationships!* That is why we must learn how to accept even the relationships that seem to be painful or negative. The time, effort, and pain we invest in them is not wasted because *God knows how to make adversity feed destiny into your life!*

In short, the bleeding trail of broken hearts and wounded relationships ultimately leads us to the richness of God's purpose in us. Periodically each of us will hear a knock on the door. It is the knock of our old friend Judas, whose cold kiss and calloused heart usher us into the will of God. To be sure, these betrayals call bloody tears to our eyes and nail us to a cold cross. Nevertheless, the sweet kiss of betrayal can never abort the precious promises of God in our life! The challenge is to sit at the table with Judas on one side and John on the other, and to treat one no differently from the other, even though we are distinctly aware of each one's identity and agenda. If you have been betrayed or wounded by someone you brought too close, please forgive them. They really were a blessing. You will only be better when you cease to be bitter!

I cannot stop your hurts from coming; neither can I promise that everyone who sits at the table with you is loyal. But I can suggest that the sufferings of success give us direction and build character within us. Finally, as you find the grace to reevaluate your enemies and realize that many of them were friends in disguise, I can only place a warm hand of solace on your sobbing shoulders and wipe the gentle rain of soft tears from your eyes. As God heals what hurt you have, I want to whisper gently in your ears, "Betrayal is only sweetened when it is accompanied by survival. Live on, my friend, live on!"

> *B*etrayal is only sweetened when it is accompanied by survival.

The Lord possessed me in the beginning of His way, before His works of old....Then I was by Him, as one brought up with Him: and I was daily His delight, rejoicing always before Him. Proverbs 8:22,30

The streaming fount of holy blood that flows from the gaping wounds of my loving Savior has draped my wretchedness in His holiness. He has covered me like Boaz covered Ruth. He has covered me just like the dripping blood of lambs covered the aged doorposts and lintels of the Hebrew slaves in Egypt on the night of the passover.

His blood also has covered me like a warm blanket on a cold wintry night. I found my past nestled beneath His omnipresent banner of love and concern, taking the chill out of my life and removing the stiffness from my heart. When I had no one to snuggle close to, He became my eternal companion—always seeking out what is best for me and bringing before me great and mighty things.

I confess that I often used to resist loneliness. I filled my life with work and with people who meant me no good at all. At that time, I would rather have filled my life with noise than run the risk of total silence. How foolish of me not to note the difference between being *alone* and being *lonely*.

Have you ever wearied of people? Of course we love the people around us and we enjoy their company, but there comes a time in life that all the fillers we add to avoid emptiness leave us feeling more empty than emptiness could ever be. There is nothing more hollow than empty words and lofty clichés that have no real meaning or compassion in them. They roll listlessly from the mouths of people whose conversations are designed to entertain, but have no capacity to edify.

> *How foolish of me not to note the difference between being alone and being lonely.*

When I was a child, I spoke as a child, I understood as a child, I thought as a child; but when I became a man, I put away childish things. For now we see in a mirror, dimly, but then face to face. Now I know in part, but then I shall know just as I also am known. 1 Corinthians 13:11-12 (NKJ)

Attitudes affect the way we live our lives. A good attitude can bring success. A poor attitude can bring destruction. An attitude results from perspective. I'm sure you understand what perspective is. Everyone seems to have a different perspective. It comes from the way we look at life, and the way we look at life is often determined by our history.

The events of the past can cause us to have an outlook or perspective on life that is less than God's perspective. The little girl who was abused learns to defend herself by not trusting men. This attitude of defensiveness often stretches into adulthood. If we have protected ourselves a certain way in the past with some measure of success, then it is natural to continue that pattern throughout life. Unfortunately, we often need to learn how to look past our perspective and change our attitudes.

And, behold, there was a woman which had a spirit of infirmity eighteen years, and was bowed together, and could in no wise lift up herself. And when Jesus saw her, He called her to Him, and said unto her, Woman, thou art loosed from thine infirmity. And He laid His hands on her: and immediately she was made straight, and glorified God (Luke 13:11-13).

The infirm woman whom Jesus healed was made completely well by His touch. She couldn't help herself no matter how hard she tried, but Jesus unleashed her. He lifted a heavy burden from her shoulders and set her free.

We often need to learn how to look past our perspective and change our attitudes.

Now also when I am old and greyheaded, O God, forsake me not; until I have showed Thy strength unto this generation, and Thy power to every one that is to come. Psalm 71:18

I recently had the privilege of entertaining my 90-year-old grandmother, whose robust frame and bountiful body has deteriorated to just a mere shadow of its former presence. The arms that were once filled with strength, that once trembled violently while churning butter deep in the state of Mississippi, were now hollow and frail....

Grandmother's eyes held within them the burning embers of a fire, embers buried deep beneath the ashes of her experiences. I realized when I looked at her now foreign frame that, beneath her willowy arms and straggling gait, she still possessed more flame in her winter than most people muster in the heat of summer!

I remembered her strong voice with that piercing edge that had once warned us to shut that raggedy screen door she had. I remembered her standing on her old screened-in porch, which was supported by a patchwork of bricks and blocks laced together interchangeably as a foundation to her old farmhouse....She would wave at us to come in from the field where we played much more than we worked, to receive her fried chicken and biscuits, baptized in sorghum molasses.

This was the Trojan-like woman who had worked her way through college doing laundry, studying in the wee hours of the night. This was the Mississippi matron who had reached high and hit hard, who captured a teaching degree in the middle of her life and went from canning butter beans to educating children. Now she had come to the setting of the sun.

I could see that sun burning behind her leathery skin and glazed eyes. It seemed that age had somehow smothered her need to talk, and she would lapse into long periods of silence that left me clamoring foolishly through asinine conversations. Whenever I asked her if she was all right, she would respond affirmatively and assure me that she was greatly enjoying my company. Then she would flee into the counsel of her own thoughts and come out at intervals to play with me, with some humorous statement that would remind me of her earlier years.

> She still possessed more flame in her winter than most people muster in the heat of summer!

Behold, I go forward, but He is not there; and backward, but I cannot perceive Him: on the left hand, where He doth work, but I cannot behold Him; He hideth Himself on the right hand, that I cannot see Him. Job 23:8-9

There are times when it is difficult to understand God's methods. There are moments when discerning His will is a frustrating endeavor. Perhaps we have these moments because we haven't been given all the information we need to ascertain His ways as well as His acts. Many times we learn more in retrospect than we do while in the thick of the struggle. I can look over my shoulder at my past and see that the hand of the Lord has been on me all my life. Yet there were times when I felt completely alone and afraid. Even Jesus once cried out, "Eli, Eli, lama sabachthani? that is to say, My God, My God, why hast Thou forsaken Me?" (Matt. 27:46b) Suspended on the cross with a bloody, beaten body, He was questioning the acts of God—but He never questioned His relationship with Him. Jesus says in essence, "I don't understand why, but You are still *My God*!"

I'm sure we have all felt our faith weighed down by a severe struggle that left us wondering what in the world God was doing. I can hardly believe that anyone who seriously walks with God has never felt like a child whose tiny toddling legs couldn't keep up with the strong stride of his parent. Sometimes I've thought, "Daddy, don't walk so fast." We can't see as well or move as quickly. It takes time to develop spiritual dexterity. To remain calm in crises and faithful in frightening times is easier said than done. Generally we see the workings of God when we look back, but while in the throes of the rumbling winds of life, we are often in search of the Lord.

Perhaps we are at our best when we are searching for Him; we have no independence, just raw need. There's no dawdling around with things that have no help or healing. Those are the times we know are jobs for God. If He doesn't help us, we will die.

> *Perhaps we are at our best when we are searching for Him; we have no independence, just raw need.*

The lamp of the Lord searches the spirit of a man; it searches out his inmost being.
Proverbs 20:27 (NIV)

I recently spent time with my 90-year-old grandmother, whose robust frame and bountiful body has deteriorated to just a mere shadow of its former presence.... It seemed that age had somehow smothered her need to talk, and she would lapse into long periods of silence that left me clamoring foolishly through asinine conversations....

As I pondered her different behavior and her silent, Indian-like demeanor, I realized that her silence was not boredom. It was, first of all, the mark of someone who has learned how to be *alone*. It reflected the hours she had spent sitting in a rocking chair, entertaining herself with her own thoughts, and reconciling old accounts that brought the past into balance before the books were presented to the Master Himself. My grandmother had prepared her heart for the God who audits our thoughts in the chambers of His own wisdom, and rewards us according to what He finds hidden within us. She had entered into the state where things that seemed so important when you are young and full of days now seem trivial and unimportant. She was at peace, with the kind of peace that comes from a firm faith and deep resolution....

I savored her friendship and love like a dry-mouthed traveler savors a cool glass of water on a hot, blistering day....

I am rewarded with a friendly reminder from a loving God who speaks through the glazed eyes of an aged relative, telling me to relax and enjoy life. It was there that I made two commitments in my own mind, as my grandmother smiled and gazed out of a window as if she were looking at Heaven itself. I committed to a renewed faith and trust in the ableness of God. The other commitment I made may seem strange, but I promised to spend more time with myself, to warm myself at the fire of my own thoughts and smile with the contentments of the riches contained therein.

> *I* promised to spend more time with myself, to warm myself at the fire of my own thoughts and smile with the contentments of the riches contained therein.

You were taught, with regard to your former way of life, to put off your old self, which is being corrupted by its deceitful desires; to be made new in the attitude of your minds; and to put on the new self, created to be like God in true righteousness and holiness. Ephesians 4:22-24 (NIV)

Today, many of us have things we need to be separated from or burdens we need lifted. We will not function effectively until those things are lifted off of us. We can function to a certain point under a load, but we can't function as effectively as we would if the thing was lifted off of us. Perhaps some of you right now have things that are burdening you down.

You need to commend yourselves for having the strength to function under pressure. Unfortunately, we often bear the weight of it alone, since we don't feel free to tell anyone about our struggles. So whatever strides you have made, be they large or small, you have made them against the current.

It is God's intention that we be set free from the loads we carry. Many people live in codependent relationships. Others are anesthetized to their problems because they have had them so long. Perhaps you have become so accustomed to having a problem that even when you get a chance to be delivered, you find it hard to let it go. Problems can become like a security blanket.

> *And He was teaching in one of the synagogues on the sabbath. And, behold, there was a woman which had a spirit of infirmity eighteen years, and was bowed together, and could in no wise lift up herself. And when Jesus saw her, He called her to Him, and said unto her, Woman, thou art loosed from thine infirmity. And He laid His hands on her: and immediately she was made straight, and glorified God (Luke 13:10-13).*

Jesus took away this woman's excuse. He said, "Woman, thou art loosed from thine infirmity." The moment He said that, it required something of her that she hadn't had to deal with before. For 18 years she could excuse herself because she was handicapped. The moment He told her the problem was gone, she had no excuse.

Before you get out of trouble, you need to straighten out your attitude. Until your attitude is corrected, you can't be corrected.

> **B**efore you get out of trouble, you need to straighten out your attitude.

HEALING OF THE MIND

Finally, brethren, whatsoever things are true, whatsoever things are honest, whatsoever things are just, whatsoever things are pure, whatsoever things are lovely, whatsoever things are of good report; if there be any virtue, and if there be any praise, think on these things. Philippians 4:8

We must understand that modern medicine can heal many afflictions of the body, and can even treat the tumors that sometimes attach themselves to the brain, but only God Himself can heal the mind. Do you know that many times your *thoughts* need to be healed? Your thoughts are often the product of damaged emotions, traumatic events, and vicious opinions forced upon you by the bodacious personalities of domineering people who continually feel it necessary to express their opinions about you.

One of the great challenges of our walk with God is to resist the temptation to allow what happened in the past determine who we are today. We each must begin to understand and declare: "I am not what happened yesterday. I *endured* what happened. I *survived* what happened, but *I am not what happened* yesterday!"

Many people are plagued all their lives by memories of failed marriages, broken promises, and personal calamities.... These negative impressions, armed with memories and flashback "movies," strengthen themselves by rehearsing past failures and wounds over and over again. It is somehow like bad television reruns—we don't even enjoy watching them, yet we find ourselves transfixed to the screen....

In the same sense, you must remind yourself that you don't have to watch the "movie" in your mind if you are not enjoying what is being played. That's right—hit the remote control. You *do have control* over your thoughts. The Bible teaches us that if we are going to be healed in our own mind, then we must occasionally reprogram ourselves to "think on better thoughts."

You must choose what you are going to meditate upon. Choose carefully, though, for *you will ultimately become whatever it is you meditate upon*. The enemy knows this, so when he wants to destroy your morality, he doesn't start with an act; he starts with a thought. A thought is a seed that, if not aborted, will produce offspring somewhere in your life.

> *I endured* what happened. *I survived* what happened, but *I am not what happened* yesterday!

As the hart panteth after the water brooks, so panteth my soul after Thee, O God. My soul thirsteth for God, for the living God: when shall I come and appear before God? My tears have been my meat day and night, while they continually say unto me, Where is thy God? When I remember these things, I pour out my soul in me: for I had gone with the multitude, I went with them to the house of God, with the voice of joy and praise, with a multitude that kept holyday. Psalm 42:1-4

The search for God is an "equal opportunity" experience for all Christians. Regardless of how successful you may be, you will always have times when you just need to find Him. Consecration is the Siamese twin of sanctification. They are born together and are connected. You can't be consecrated to without being sanctified from. Sanctification sets you apart from distractions, and consecration takes that separated person and quenches his thirst in the presence of the Lord! …

The search for God is a primary step into worship. We never search for anything we don't value. The very fact that we search for Him indicates that He has become essential to us. There are millions of people who seem to live their lives without noticing that something is missing. They seemingly sense no real void. Our separating ourselves from these ranks and saying, "God, I need You," is a form of worship. The word *worship* stems from the term *worth-ship*. It expresses the worth of an object. The kind of intensity that causes an individual to pursue the invisible in spite of all the visible distractions is a result of need. If we didn't need Him desperately, we could easily be satisfied with carnal things.

God instructs us to seek Him, but not as though He were hiding from us. He is not a child playing hide-and-go-seek. He isn't crouched behind trees giggling while we suffer. The request to seek Him is as much for our benefit as His. When we seek Him, we make a conscious decision that is necessary for bringing us into the realm of the spiritual. The pursuit of God is rewarding in the development of the seeker's character. Some levels of blessings are never received unless they are diligently sought. It is this seeking after God that often propels Him to perform. If that were not true, the woman with the issue of blood would never have been healed. Her conscious decision to seek the impossible released the invisible virtue of God.

> *God instructs us to seek Him, but not as though He were hiding from us.*

Let the words of my mouth, and the meditation of my heart, be acceptable in Thy sight, O Lord, my strength, and my redeemer. Psalm 19:14

Satan plants seeds in the form of thoughts. These evil seeds aren't yours just because they come to mind; they become yours when you allow those thoughts to move in and rearrange furniture! An evil thought will rearrange your goals, your dreams, and your ambitions (that is a *very powerful* house guest). A thought left to ramble in your mind will attach itself to an incident in your past. It will begin to feed on that incident and grow like a tick that attaches itself to your body while you walk through a forest. That thing isn't a part of your body, but it begins by attaching itself to the body and then drains strength from it.

These evil thoughts impede progress and destroy morals. They are as dangerous as the act of sin itself. Thoughts are previews of coming attractions. That is why Jesus gave us some strong teachings about lust. He knew that if an evil thought is not aborted, if it is savored long enough, it will be acted upon!…

You must quickly cast down an evil thought. "Push the remote control" before it drains away your commitment to excellence and leaves you crying in the valley of regret. The real temptation to entertain thoughts is in the privacy of the mind. Who will know what you really think? You can smile at people and never disclose your innermost thoughts.

I always laugh when I see people act as though they have conquered the battle with the mind. I've asked people in my services, "Which of you would be comfortable with having everything that comes to mind played on a television screen for all of your Christian friends to watch? Or which of you would like to have all our thoughts through the week played over the loudspeaker at church next Sunday?" I'm sure I don't have to tell you, they all put their hands down. Our mind is a private battleground that can easily become a secret place for contamination, lust, fear, low self-esteem, and God only knows what else!

> Thoughts are previews of coming attractions.

Therefore, since Christ suffered in His body, arm yourselves also with the same attitude, because he who has suffered in his body is done with sin. As a result, he does not live the rest of his earthly life for evil human desires, but rather for the will of God. 1 Peter 4:1-2 (NIV)

Why should we put up all the ramps and rails for the handicapped if we can heal them? You want everyone to make an allowance for your problem, but your problem needs to make an allowance for God and to humble itself to the point where you don't need special help. I'm not referring to physical handicaps; I'm addressing the emotional baggage that keeps us from total health. You cannot expect the whole human race to move over because you had a bad childhood. They will not do it. So you will end up in depression and frustration, and even confusion. You may have trouble with relationships because people don't accommodate your hang-up.

One woman I pastored was extremely obnoxious. It troubled me deeply, so I took the matter to God in prayer. The Lord allowed me to meet her husband. When I saw how nasty he talked to her, I understood why, when she reached down into her reservoir, all she had was hostility. That's all she had taken in. You cannot give out something that you haven't taken in.

Christ wants to separate you from the source of your bitterness until it no longer gives you the kind of attitude that makes you a carrier of pain. Your attitude affects your situation—your attitude, not other people's attitude about you. Your attitude will give you life or death.

> You cannot give out something that you haven't taken in.

Healing, Blessings, and Freedom

Thou knowest my downsitting and mine uprising, Thou understandest my thought afar off. Psalm 139:2

When we clean our homes we tend to focus our efforts first on what people will see rather than on what they will not see. Only the most ardent of housekeepers spends as much time scrubbing the basement steps as she does the foyer or the living room. We emphasize what will be inspected.

Can you imagine how much clutter we allow to fester in our minds, simply because no one sits in our heads sipping tea and examining the thoughts and imaginations of our hearts? If no one knows what we think, why shouldn't we allow our minds to collect scum and clutter without any regard to cleaning and renewing the mind? There are several reasons not to do that, but I will give only three.

First, a certain *Someone does know what we think.* Second, we need to continually purge our thoughts because *we become what we think.* Third, we need to renew our minds daily in God's presence, for I believe that *as we hear the thoughts of God, His thinking becomes increasingly contagious.* Let's deal with the first of these three.

God sits in the living quarters of the minds of men and beholds their thoughts. He knows our thoughts afar off (see Ps. 139:2). If we are serious about entertaining His presence, we cannot lie to Him—He sees us from the inside out. We must be honest and admit to Him:

This is what I am being tempted with…I cannot hide from You. I am naked before You. All my thoughts are played on the screen before You. I want to clean up this mess so You can replace it with a greater revelation and a stronger direction for my life. I praise You for loving me, in spite of all You know about me. Forgive me for condemning and judging anybody else. I know that if it were not for Your mercy, I would be guilty of the very things for which I have disdained others. Help me not to be hypocritical.

> God sits in the living quarters of the minds of men and beholds their thoughts.

But without faith it is impossible to please Him: for he that cometh to God must believe that He is, and that He is a rewarder of them that diligently seek Him. Hebrews 11:6

There are no manuals that instruct us step by step as to the proper way to seek the Lord. Like lovemaking, the pursuit is spontaneous and individually conceived out of the power of the moment. Some seek Him quietly, with soft tears falling quietly down a weary face. Others seek Him while walking the sandy beaches of a cove, gazing into the swelling currents of an evening tide. Some would raise their hands and praise and adore Him with loving expressions of adoration. There are no rules—just that we seek Him with our whole hearts.

We are like blind people when it comes to spiritual issues; we are limited. However, we should be challenged by our limitations. When there is a strong desire, we overcome our inabilities and press our way into His presence.

My friend, don't be afraid to stretch out your hands to reach after Him. Cry after Him. Whatever you do, do not allow this moment to pass you by!

> *And hath made of one blood all nations of men for to dwell on all the face of the earth, and hath determined the times before appointed, and the bounds of their habitation; that they should seek the Lord, if haply they might feel after Him, and find Him, though He be not far from every one of us (Acts 17:26-27).*

Like groping fingers extended in the night trying to compensate for a darkened vision, we feel after God. We feel after His will and His ways. I'm amazed at all the people who seem to always know everything God is saying about everything. In the hymn "My Faith Looks Up to Thee," Ray Palmer and Lowell Mason wrote, "My faith looks up to thee, Oh lamb of Calvary, savior divine." My faith looks up because my eyes can't always see. On the other hand, there is a healthy reaction that occurs in blindness; our senses become keener as we exercise areas that we wouldn't normally need.

There are no rules—just that we seek Him with our whole hearts.

It is of the Lord's mercies that we are not consumed, because His compassions fail not. They are new every morning: great is Thy faithfulness.
Lamentations 3:22-23

Forgive me for condemning and judging anybody else. I know that if it were not for Your mercy, I would be guilty of the very things for which I have disdained others. Help me not to be hypocritical.

This kind of prayer and confession enhances your relationship with God as you begin to realize that you *were* saved by grace; you *are* saved by grace; and you *will be* saved by grace! Knowing this, how can you not be grateful? You know that He loves you so much that He stays in the house you haven't fully cleaned. He hates the acts; He despises the thoughts; but He loves the thinker.

Neither is there any creature that is not manifest in His sight: but all things are naked and opened unto the eyes of Him with whom we have to do. Seeing then that we have a great high priest, that is passed into the heavens, Jesus the Son of God, let us hold fast our profession. For we have not an high priest which cannot be touched with the feeling of our infirmities; but was in all points tempted like as we are, yet without sin (Hebrews 4:13-15).

Immediately after the writer of the Book of Hebrews tells us that God knows all our business and that all our thoughts parade around naked before His scrutinizing eyes, he mentions the high priest that we have in Christ. He knows we are going to need a high priest for all the garbage and information that the Holy Spirit is privy to, yet others would never know. What greater compassion can be displayed than when the writer goes on to say that God, through Christ, can be *touched by how I feel*. No wonder Jeremiah said His mercies are "new every morning"! (See Lamentations 3:22-23.)

God knows all our business and that all our thoughts parade around naked before His scrutinizing eyes.

But Jesus turned him about, and when he saw her, he said, Daughter, be of good comfort; thy faith hath made thee whole. And the woman was made whole from that hour. Matthew 9:22

One of the greatest deliverances people can ever experience in life is to have their attitude delivered. It doesn't do you any good to be delivered financially if your attitude doesn't change. I can give you five thousand dollars, but if your attitude, your mental perspective, doesn't change, you will be broke in a week because you'll lose it again. The problem is not how much you have, it's what you do with what you have. If you can change your attitude, you might have only 50 dollars, but you'll take that 50 and learn how to get 5 million.

When God comes to heal, He wants to heal your emotions also. Sometimes all we pray about is our situation. We bring God our shopping list of desires. Fixing circumstances is like applying a Band-Aid, though. Healing attitudes set people free to receive wholeness.

The woman who was crippled for 18 years was delivered from her infirmity. (See Luke 13.) The Bible says she was made straight and glorified God. She got a new attitude. However, the enemy still tried to defeat her by using the people around her. He does not want to let you find health and strength. He may send another circumstance that will pull you down in the same way if you don't change your attitude.

When you first read about this woman, you might have thought that the greatest deliverance was her physical deliverance. I want to point out another deliverance that was even greater. The Bible said that when the Lord laid His hand on her, she was made straight. That's physical deliverance. Then her attitude changed. She entered into praise and thanksgiving and worshiped the Lord. This woman began to leap and rejoice and magnify God and shout the victory like anybody who has been delivered from an 18-year infirmity should. While she was glorifying God over here, the enemy was stirring up strife over there. She just kept on glorifying God. She didn't stop praising God to answer the accusers.

> *Healing attitudes set people free to receive wholeness.*

We Are What We Think

For as he thinketh in his heart, so is he. Proverbs 23:7

If no one knows what we think, why shouldn't we allow our minds to collect scum and clutter without any regard to cleaning and renewing the mind? Here is one good reason....

We need to continually purge our thoughts because *we become what we think*. It is not just the lust that we must clean out, but also low self-esteem, pride, arrogance, hidden jealousy, and much, much more. The mind is the "placenta" of the spirit man. It holds and nurtures the seeds it has been impregnated with until their time of delivery. If you don't want the child that that seed of thought produces, your only recourse is to abort before it is carried to full term.

If you don't want depression, why do you continue to regurgitate those same sickening thoughts that lead you down the tunnel of emotional depravity? You don't need a famous minister to lay hands on you to win the battle over your mind! The truth is, generally speaking, those fantastic demonstrations of public power seldom accomplish deliverance from mental images. What you need is the inner discipline required of all disciples to resist evil thoughts before they become evidenced in your life.

Most people who are unsuccessful in their lives do not lack talent. Some of the most talented people I have ever known weren't successful, even in the area of their talent. Why? There always seemed to be some little thought they entertained that affected their tenacity or their commitment to excellence. Some dwarfed self-image, or worse still, some over-inflated ego preempted them from reaching their aspirations and sent them plummeting to the ground of failure and the rocks of frustration. If you can see traces of this in your own life (and most of us can), abort the seeds that are causing you to miss the mark and press on! Don't you realize that anything you stop feeding is sure to die?!

> We need to continually purge our thoughts because *we become what we think.*

Ask, and it shall be given you; seek, and ye shall find; knock, and it shall be opened unto you: For every one that asketh receiveth; and he that seeketh findeth; and to him that knocketh it shall be opened. Matthew 7:7-8

God knows what it will take to bring us to a place of searching. He knows how to stir us from our tranquil and comfortable perching position of supremacy. There are times when even our great sages of this age murmur in the night....In spite of our strong gait and stiff backs, in spite of our rigid posture and swelling speech, behind the scenes we tremble in our hearts at the presence of God whose sovereign will often escapes the realm of our human reasoning.

Searching releases answers....Many things available to us will not be found without an all-out search. Seeking God also takes focus. This search has to be what the police call an A.P.B....an "all points bulletin." All of the department is asked to seek the same thing. Thus our search can't be a distracted, half-hearted curiosity. There must be something to produce a unified effort to seek God. Body, soul, and spirit—all points—seeking the same thing. There is a blessing waiting for us. It will require an A.P.B. to bring it into existence, but it will be worth attaining. Who knows what God will release if we go on an all-out God-hunt....

The crucial times that arise in our lives require more than good advice. We need a word from God. There are moments when we need total seclusion. We come home from work, take the telephone receiver off the hook, close the blinds, and lie before God for a closer connection. In Job's case, he was going through an absolute crisis. His finances were obliterated. His cattle, donkeys, and oxen were destroyed. His crops were gone. In those days it would be comparable to the crash of the stock market. It was as if Job, the richest man, had gone bankrupt. What a shock to his system to realize that all are vulnerable. It is sobering to realize that one incident, or a sequence of events, can radically alter our lifestyles.

> Who knows what God will release if we go on an all-out God-hunt.

They said, "Teacher, we know that You are an honest man and that You teach the truth about God's way. You are not afraid of what other people think about You, because You pay no attention to who they are." Matthew 22:16b (NCV)

(For the weapons of our warfare are not carnal, but mighty through God to the pulling down of strong holds;) casting down imaginations, and every high thing that exalteth itself against the knowledge of God, and bringing into captivity every thought to the obedience of Christ (2 Corinthians 10:4-5).

The mind is continually being reconstructed by the Holy Spirit. He wants to perpetuate a new mentality within you that enables you to soar above your past. He impregnates us with hope and fills us with destiny. The Scriptures challenge us with the exhortation, "Let this mind be in you, which was also in Christ Jesus: who, being in the form of God, thought it not robbery to be equal with God: but made Himself of no reputation…" (Phil. 2:5-7).

Simply stated, Christ has a balanced mind. He doesn't suffer from low self-esteem. He "thought it not robbery" to be equal with God. For Him, being equal with God was and is a reality. That might be a little extreme for you and me, but the point is that He was comfortable with His exaltation. He didn't allow the controversial opinions of other men to determine who He "thought" He was. His inner perception was fixed.

The miracle of His strength is that, unlike most people who are that strong about their inner worth, Christ Jesus did not wrestle with arrogance. He knew who He was, yet He "made Himself of no reputation" (Phil. 2:7a). When you have healthy thoughts about your own identity, it frees you from the need to impress other people. Their opinion ceases to be the shrine where you worship!

> *When you have healthy thoughts about your own identity…[others'] their opinion ceases to be the shrine where you worship!*

If you do not stand firm in your faith, you will not stand at all. Isaiah 7:9b (NIV)

The Lord is your defense. You do not have to defend yourself. When God has delivered you, do not stop what you're doing to answer your accusers. Continue to bless His name, because you do not want your attitude to become defensive. When you have been through difficult times, you cannot afford to play around with moods and attitudes. Depression and defensiveness may make you vulnerable to the devil.

> *And He laid His hands on her: and immediately she was made straight, and glorified God. And the ruler of the synagogue answered with indignation, because that Jesus had healed on the sabbath day (Luke 13:13-14a).*

This woman had to protect herself by entering into defensive praise. This was not just praise of thanksgiving, but defensive praise. Defensive praise is a strategy and a posture of war that says, "We will not allow our attitude to crumble and fall."

When you get to the point that you quit defending yourself or attacking others, you open up a door for the Lord to fight for you.

When this woman began to bless God, she built walls around her own deliverance. She decided to keep the kind of attitude that enabled the deliverance of God to be maintained in her life. When you have been through surgery, you cannot afford to fool around with Band-Aids.

When you're in trouble, God will reach into the mess and pull you out. However, you must be strong enough not to let people drag you back into it. Once God unleashes you, don't let anyone trap you into some religious fight. Keep praising Him. For this woman, the more they criticized her, the more she was justified because she just stood there and kept believing God. God is trying to get you to a place of faith. He is trying to deliver you from an attitude of negatives.

> *God is trying to get you to a place of faith. He is trying to deliver you from an attitude of negatives.*

Know ye not that ye are the temple of God, and that the Spirit of God dwelleth in you? If any man defile the temple of God, him shall God destroy; for the temple of God is holy, which temple ye are. 1 Corinthians 3:16-17

Most of us come to the Lord damaged. We're dead spiritually, damaged emotionally, and decaying physically. When He saved you, He quickened, or made alive, your dead spirit. He also promised you a new body. Then He began the massive renovation necessary to repair your damaged thoughts about life, about others, and about yourself—here come all types of nails, saws, levels, bricks, and blocks.

While we dress and smell nice outwardly, people do not hear the constant hammering and sawing going on inwardly, as the Lord works within us, trying desperately to meet a deadline and present us as a newly constructed masterpiece fit for the Master's use.

> *For we are His workmanship, created in Christ Jesus unto good works, which God hath before ordained that we should walk in them (Ephesians 2:10).*

Beneath our pasted smiles and pleasant greetings, we alone hear the rumblings of the midnight shift. God is constantly excommunicating lethal thoughts that hinder us from grasping the many-faceted callings and giftings buried beneath the rubble of our minds. No matter who we meet, once we get to know them, we begin to realize that they have their own challenges. Have you ever met someone and thought he had it all together? Once you become closely involved with that person, you will begin to notice a twisted board here, a loose nail there, or even a squeaky frame!

Yes, we all need the Lord to help us with ourselves. We came to Him as condemned buildings, and He reopened the places that satan thought would never be inhabited. The Holy Spirit moved in, but He brought His hammers and His saw with Him. He will challenge the thoughts of men.

> He came to Him as condemned buildings, and He reopened the places that satan thought would never be inhabited.

Seek ye the Lord while He may be found, call ye upon Him while He is near: let the wicked forsake his way, and the unrighteous man his thoughts: and let him return unto the Lord, and He will have mercy upon him; and to our God, for He will abundantly pardon. Isaiah 55:6-7

Unfortunately, it generally takes devastation on a business level to make most men commit more of their interest in relationships. Job probably could have reached out to his children for comfort, but he had lost them too. His marriage had deteriorated to the degree that Job said his wife abhorred his breath (see Job 19:17). Then he also became ill. Have you ever gone through a time in your life when you felt you had been jinxed? Everything that could go wrong, did! Frustration turns into alienation. So now what? Will you use this moment to seek God or to brood over your misfortune? With the right answer, you could turn the jail into a church! …

Job said, "Behold, I go forward, but He is not there" (Job 23:8a). It is terrifying when you see no change coming in the future. Comfort comes when you know that the present adversity will soon be over. But what comfort can be found when it seems the problem will never cease? Job said, "I see no help, no sign of God, in the future." It actually is satan's trick to make you think help is not coming. That hopelessness then produces anxiety. On the other hand, sometimes the feeling that you eventually will come to a point of transition can give you the tenacity to persevere the current challenge. But there often seems to be no slackening in distress. Like a rainstorm that will not cease, the waters of discouragement begin to fill the tossing ship with water. Suddenly you experience a sinking feeling. However, there is no way to sink a ship when you do not allow the waters from the outside to get on the inside! If the storms keep coming, the lightning continues to flash, and the thunder thumps on through the night, what matters is keeping the waters out of the inside. Keep that stuff out of your spirit!

Have you ever gone through a time in your life when you felt you had been jinxed?

For My thoughts are not your thoughts, neither are your ways My ways, saith the Lord. For as the heavens are higher than the earth, so are My ways higher than your ways, and My thoughts than your thoughts. Isaiah 55:8-9

We need to renew our minds daily in God's presence, for I believe that *as we hear the thoughts of God, His thinking becomes increasingly contagious.* It is so important that we have a relationship with Him. His Word becomes a lifeline thrown to a man who would otherwise drown in the swirling whirlpool of his own thoughts. Peter was so addicted to hearing Jesus speak that when other men walked away, Peter said, "Lord, to whom shall we go? Thou hast the words of eternal life" (John 6:68).

Peter recognized his need to keep hearing the Word of God. Many years before Peter, Job said that he esteemed God's Word more than his necessary food (see Job 23:12). As for me, God is my counselor. He talks with me about my deepest, darkest issues; He comforts the raging tide of my fears and inhibitions. What would we be if He would wax silent and cease to guide us through this perilous maze of mental mania? It is His soft words that turn away the wrath of our nagging memories. If He speaks to me, His words become symphonies of enlightenment falling like soft rain on a tin roof. They give rest and peace.

For as the rain cometh down, and the snow from heaven, and returneth not thither, but watereth the earth, and maketh it bring forth and bud, that it may give seed to the sower, and bread to the eater: so shall My word be that goeth forth out of My mouth: it shall not return unto Me void, but it shall accomplish that which I please, and it shall prosper in the thing whereto I sent it. For ye shall go out with joy, and be led forth with peace: the mountains and the hills shall break forth before you into singing, and all the trees of the field shall clap their hands. Instead of the thorn shall come up the fir tree, and instead of the brier shall come up the myrtle tree: and it shall be to the Lord for a name, for an everlasting sign that shall not be cut off (Isaiah 55:10-13).

$\mathcal{A}$s we hear the thoughts of God, His thinking becomes increasingly contagious.

I will bless the Lord at all times: His praise shall continually be in my mouth. My soul shall make her boast in the Lord: the humble shall hear thereof, and be glad. Psalm 34:1-2

When you have had problems for many years, you tend to expect problems.

And He laid His hands on her: and immediately she was made straight, and glorified God. And the ruler of the synagogue answered with indignation, because that Jesus had healed on the sabbath day, and said unto the people, There are six days in which men ought to work: in them therefore come and be healed, and not on the sabbath day. The Lord then answered him, and said, Thou hypocrite, doth not each one of you on the sabbath loose his ox or his ass from the stall, and lead him away to watering? And ought not this woman, being a daughter of Abraham, whom Satan hath bound, lo, these eighteen years, be loosed from this bond on the sabbath day? And when He had said these things, all His adversaries were ashamed: and all the people rejoiced for all the glorious things that were done by Him (Luke 13:13-17).

God must have healed this woman's emotions also because she kept praising Him instead of paying attention to the quarrel of the religious folks around her. She could have easily fallen into negative thinking. Instead, she praised God.

Can you imagine what would have happened if she had stopped glorifying God and started arguing? If an argument could have gotten through her doors, this whole scene would have ended in a fight. But she was thankful and determined to express her gratitude.

The Lord wants to speak a word of faith to you. He wants to set you free from every power that has kept you in bondage. In order for that to be received in your spirit, you must allow Him to come in and instill faith. The emotional walls that surround us have to come down.

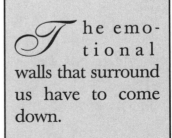

The emotional walls that surround us have to come down.

JUST HOLD ON

DAY 211

For the vision is yet for an appointed time, but at the end it shall speak, and not lie: though it tarry, wait for it; because it will surely come, it will not tarry. Habakkuk 2:3

Like a desperate sailor trying to plug a leaking ship, Job frantically cast back and forth in his mind, looking for some shred, some fragment of hope, to plug his leaking ship. Exasperated, he sullenly sat in the stupor of his condition and sadly confessed, "Behold, I go forward, but He is not there" (Job 23:8a). "I can't find Him where I thought He would be." Have you ever told yourself that the storm would be over soon? And the sun came and the sun left, and still the same rains beat vehemently against the ship. It almost feels as if God missed His appointment. You thought He would move by now! Glancing nervously at your watch you think, "Where is He!" Remember, dear friend, God doesn't synchronize His clock by your little mortal watch. He has a set time to bless you; just hold on.

Someone once said that studying the past prepares us for the future. It is important to look backward and see the patterns that cause us to feel some sense of continuity. But Job said, "Looking back, I could not perceive Him" (see Job 23:8b). "Why did I have to go through all of this? Is there any reason why I had to have this struggle?" Quite honestly, there are moments when life feels like it has all the purpose of gross insanity. Like a small child cutting paper on the floor, there seems to be no real plan, only actions. These are the times that try men's hearts. These are the times when we seek answers! Sometimes, even more than change, we need answers! "God, if You don't fix it, please, please explain it!" We are reasoning people; we need to know why. Isn't that need one of the primary characteristics that separate us from animals and lesser forms of life? We are reasoning, resourceful creatures. We seek answers. Yet there are times that even after thorough evaluation, we cannot find our way out of the maze of happenstance!

God doesn't synchronize His clock by your little mortal watch.

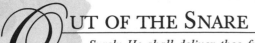
Surely He shall deliver thee from the snare of the fowler, and from the noisome pestilence.
Psalm 91:3

God's Word will accomplish what it is sent out to do. God says, "I won't stop in the middle of the job. I will not give up on you. I will keep hammering until you are balanced in your thinking and whole in your judgments." The greatest part is, no one would ever believe that you were initially in such a deplorable state! He covers you with His precious blood even while His Word works on you. The benefit is that you are simultaneously *privileged with privacy* and *challenged to change....*

If anybody ought to praise the Lord, it ought to be those who have a deep appreciation for His unfailing love. It is to them He has spoken His word and changed their thoughts and directions. He has healed the bitter waters of a turbulent mind!

Human thoughts are healed by the Word of God. By the "foolishness of preaching" (see 1 Cor. 1:21), God filters into the dark places of our diseased or oppressed minds and reconstructs thought patterns by sharing His own mind with us. We must, at all cost, maintain an appetite for preaching. Why? "So then faith [a change of mind] cometh by hearing, and hearing by the word of God" (Rom. 10:17). It boggles the mind of secular scholars to see the power of God's Word transforming dysfunctional members of our society into productive and affluent parts of our community. They are amazed—and that is without knowing our whole stories.

Most of the time God delivers us (or is in the process of delivering us) while we maintain a veil of secrecy to protect our reputations and public perceptions. These secular scholars would be appalled if they knew how many of us were in serious trouble when we came to our wit's end and submitted to the redemptive work of the Lord. It was He who delivered us out from under the stress and the strain of our crises. His power forces open the fowler's snare that entrapped the mind. His Word gives us the grace to seize the opportunity to escape and go on with our lives!

His power forces open the fowler's snare that entrapped the mind.

But now, O Lord, Thou art our father; we are the clay, and Thou our potter; and we all are the work of Thy hand. Isaiah 64:8

Where is the God who sent an earthquake into the valley of dry bones and put them together? (See Ezekiel 37.) Or where is the God of the clay, who remolds the broken places and mends the jagged edge? (See Isaiah 64:8.) If the truth were told, the God we seek is never far away. The issue is not so much His presence as it is my perception. Many times deliverance doesn't cost God one action. Deliverance comes when my mind accepts His timing and purpose in my life.

How many persons needlessly died because they struggled in the water and finally drowned? We say they drowned because they couldn't swim. The real truth is many times they drowned because they couldn't trust! If they would relax, the same current that drummed them down would bear them up so they could float. It isn't always the circumstance that is so damaging to us; it is our reaction to the circumstance. The hysterical flailing and gasping of desperation causes us to become submerged beneath the currents of what will soon pass if we can keep our wits about us.

In my hours of crises, many times I found myself searching for the place of rest rather than for the answer. If I can find God, I don't need to find money. If I can find God, I don't need to find healing! If I can find Him, my needs become insignificant when I wave them in the light of His presence. What is a problem if God is there? Even in the stench of Job's decaying flesh, he knew that his answer wasn't screaming out for the healing. He was screaming out for the Healer! Do you realize the power of God's presence? I hear many people speak about the acts of God, but have you ever considered the mere presence of God? He doesn't have to do anything but be there, and it is over!

If I can find God, I don't need to find healing!

Thou hast proved mine heart; Thou hast visited me in the night; Thou hast tried me, and shalt find nothing; I am purposed that my mouth shall not transgress. Psalm 17:3

He sent forth His word and healed them; He rescued them from the grave. Let them give thanks to the Lord for His unfailing love and His wonderful deeds for men (Psalm 107:20-21 NIV).

As we journey deeper into the dregs of this subject, let us consider the power of thought itself. There is a strong tie between thought and action. Some time ago, when we discovered the power of our words, we began to teach Christians to speak positively. That is good. The only problem is, we were *thinking* one thing while the mouth was *confessing* something else. The results were not rewarding.

The Scriptures tell us that "with the heart man believeth unto righteousness; and with the mouth confession is made unto salvation" (Rom. 10:10). There is a strong tie between what is believed and what is confessed. Your thoughts have to align with your confession—otherwise your house is divided against itself! Even God works out of the reservoir of His own thoughts. He does not consider what others think about you. Some of those people don't even believe in God. Nevertheless, He doesn't work out of their thoughts; He works out of His own! Quit trying to change the minds of other people—change your own. Your works will come out of the healing of your thoughts!

How great are Your works, O Lord, how profound Your thoughts! (Psalm 92:5 NIV)

Yes, our God is reaping the rewards of His own thoughts—and so are you. Whether that is good or bad depends on what you are thinking. Whether you are thinking of a secret lust that will eventually become fornication, or thinking of violent aggression that will become an act of physical domination over another, you are reaping the rewards of your own thoughts. No wonder the Bible warns us, "Where there is no vision, the people perish" (Prov. 29:18a)!

> **Quit trying to change the minds of other people—change your own.**

LOVE IS NOT LIMITED BY TIME

The Lord is good. His love is forever, and His loyalty goes on and on. Psalm 100:5 (NCV)

Love is eternal. It is not limited by time. When you commit yourself to loving someone, you make that commitment to all the person is. You are who you are because of your history. For me, that means I love my wife and who she has become. But in order for me to love her effectively, she must allow me into her history.

Many couples in a relationship argue over relatively insignificant things. Often the reason these things are important is one or the other is reminded of a past event. How can one person love another if he or she doesn't know the other person's history?

The Church has become too narrow in its approach to attitude. We want to keep our attitudes to ourselves and simply take them to God. Although we certainly should take them to Him, we also need to learn to "bear ye one another's burdens" (Gal. 6:2a).

Thousands walk in fear. The Church can give strength to counter that fear. Thousands have built a wall around them because they do not trust anyone else. The Church can help its members learn to trust one another. Thousands are codependent and get their value from a relationship with another person. The Church can point to God's love as the source for self-worth. We are not valuable because we love God; we are valuable because He loves us.

Jesus took away the ability of the infirm woman in Luke 13 to make excuses for herself and gave her the strength to maintain an attitude of gratitude and praise. The Church today is to be the kind of safe haven that does the same thing. Those who are wounded should be able to come and find strength in our praise.

> **You are who you are because of your history.**

No weapon that is formed against thee shall prosper; and every tongue that shall rise against thee in judgment thou shalt condemn. This is the heritage of the servants of the Lord, and their righteousness is of Me, saith the Lord. Isaiah 54:17

If we could talk to the three Hebrews who survived the fiery furnace, perhaps they would describe their experience with the Lord in the midst of the fire in this manner:

"When we were nearing the end of the Babylonian sentencing, we knew that this would be the most trying moment of our lives. We were not sure that the Lord would deliver us, but we were sure that He was able. When they snatched us wildly from the presence of the king, the crowd was screaming hysterically, 'Burn them alive! Burn them alive!' Someone said they turned the furnace up seven times hotter than it should have been. We knew it was true for when they opened the door to throw us in, the men who threw us in were burned alive. We landed in the flames in a fright, terrified and trembling. We didn't even notice that the first miracle was our still being there.

"The fire was all over us. Our ropes were ablaze, but our skin seemed undisturbed. We didn't know what was going on. Then something moved over in the smoke and ashes. We were not alone! Out of the smoke came a shining, gleaming…. We never got His name. He never said it. He never said anything. It was His presence that brought comfort in the fire. It was His presence that created protection in the midst of the crisis. Now, we don't mean that the fire went out because He was there. No, it still burned. It was just that the burning wasn't worthy to be compared to the brilliancy of His presence. We never saw Him again. He only showed up when we needed Him most. But one thing was sure: We were glad they drug us from the presence of the wicked one into the presence of the Righteous One! In His presence we learned that, 'No weapon that is formed against thee shall prosper!'" (See Daniel 3 and Isaiah 54:17.)

> He only showed up when we needed Him most.

And if any man think that he knoweth any thing, he knoweth nothing yet as he ought to know. But if any man love God, the same is known of Him. 1 Corinthians 8:2-3

You need to allow new meditations to dwell in your heart by faith, for your life will ultimately take on the direction of your thinking.

> *My mouth shall speak of wisdom; and the meditation of my heart shall be of understanding (Psalm 49:3).*

> *Let the words of my mouth, and the meditation of my heart, be acceptable in Thy sight, O Lord, my strength, and my redeemer (Psalm 19:14).*

> *O how love I Thy law! it is my meditation all the day. Thou through Thy commandments hast made me wiser than mine enemies: for they are ever with me. I have more understanding than all my teachers: for Thy testimonies are my meditation (Psalm 119:97-99).*

Many weaknesses, such as procrastination and laziness, are just draperies that cover up poor self-esteem and a lack of motivation. They are often symptoms of the subconscious avoiding the risk of failure. Remember that "nothing shall be impossible unto you" if you will only believe! (See Matthew 17:20.)

God creates by speaking, but He speaks out of His own thoughts. Since God's Word says "out of the abundance of the heart the mouth speaketh" (Matt. 12:34b), then we go beyond the mouth to bring correction to the words we speak. We have to begin with the thoughts we think.

I pray that somehow the Spirit will reveal the areas where you need Him to heal your thinking so you can possess what God wants you to have. Then you will be able to fully enjoy what He has given you. Many people have the blessing and still don't enjoy it because they conquered every foe *except the enemy within*!

> *Many people have the blessing and still don't enjoy it because they conquered every foe except the enemy within!*

The Lord of hosts hath sworn, saying, Surely as I have thought, so shall it come to pass; and as I have purposed, so shall it stand (Isaiah 14:24).

Thou wilt show me the path of life: in Thy presence is fulness of joy; at Thy right hand there are pleasures for evermore. Psalm 16:11

Job was sitting in sackcloth and ashes searching through the rubbish of his life, looking for God. He knew that only the presence of the Lord could bring comfort to his pain! Have you begun your search for a closer manifestation of His grace? Your search alone is worship. When you seek Him, it suggests that you value Him and recognize His ability. The staggering, faulty steps of a seeker are far better than the stance of the complacent. He is not far away. He is in the furnace, moving in the ashes. Look closer. He is never far from the seeker who is on a quest to be in His presence. I don't blame the enemy for trying to convince you that you are alone. That old flame-thrower doesn't want you to find the fire-quenching presence of God!

Have you been searching and seeking and yet feel that you are getting no closer? Perhaps you are closer than you think. Here is a clue that may end your search. Job told where to find Him. He told where He works. Now if you were looking for someone and you knew where he worked, you wouldn't have to search for very long. Job said that God works on the left hand! I know you've been looking on the right hand, and I can understand why. The right hand in the Bible symbolizes power and authority. That's why Christ is seated on the right side of God (see Mark 16:19). Whenever you say someone is your right hand, you mean he is next in command or authority. "Right hand" means power. Naturally, then, if you were to search for God, you would look on the right hand. Granted, He is on the right hand. He is full of authority. But you forgot something. His strength is made perfect in weakness (see 2 Cor. 12:9). He displays His glory in the ashes of human frailty. He works on the left hand!

Behold, I go forward, but He is not there; and backward, but I cannot perceive Him: on the left hand, where He doth work, but I cannot behold Him; He hideth Himself on the right hand, that I cannot see Him (Job 23:8-9).

That old flame-thrower doesn't want you to find the fire-quenching presence of God!

For as many as are led by the Spirit of God, they are the sons of God. For ye have not received the spirit of bondage again to fear; but ye have received the Spirit of adoption, whereby we cry, Abba, Father. The Spirit itself beareth witness with our spirit, that we are the children of God. Romans 8:14-16

When at King David's command Ziba returned from Lodebar with Mephibosheth, the crippled son of Jonathan, to David's palace, Mephibosheth couldn't sit at the table without falling to the floor. He struggled with his position because of his condition. His problem wasn't merely his twisted feet or his crippled body. It was his dysfunctional mentality. Even after he had been raised from the deplorable condition he was in, he was still so oppressed in his mind that he described himself as a "dead dog" (see 2 Sam. 9:8). He was a king's kid, but he saw himself as a dead dog!

Perception is everything. Mephibosheth thought of himself as a dead dog, so he lay on the floor like one. I feel a word going out from the Lord to you: *You have been on the floor long enough!* It is time for a resurrection, and it is going to start in your *mind*. Has God blessed you with something you are afraid of losing? Could it be that you think you are going to lose it because you don't feel worthy? I realize that living in the palace can be a real shock to someone who is accustomed to being rejected and ostracized. Without realizing it, you will accept being treated as though you were a dog. Mephibosheth had been through so much that he began to think himself a dead dog.

Understand this one fact: *Just because you've been treated like a dog doesn't make you one!* Get up off the floor and take a seat at the Master's table—you are worthy. You have a right to be in the place and position you are in, not because of your goodness, but by virtue of His invitation. I pray that God will heal your thoughts until you are able to enjoy and rest in what God is doing in your life right now!

You have a right to be in the place and position you are in, not because of your goodness, but by virtue of His invitation.

I thank my God always on your behalf, for the grace of God which is given you by Jesus Christ; that in every thing ye are enriched by Him, in all utterance, and in all knowledge; even as the testimony of Christ was confirmed in you. 1 Corinthians 1:4-6

And when Jesus saw her, He called her to Him, and said unto her, Woman, thou art loosed from thine infirmity. And He laid His hands on her: and immediately she was made straight, and glorified God....And when He had said these things, all His adversaries were ashamed: and all the people rejoiced for all the glorious things that were done by Him (Luke 13:12-13,17).

Gratitude and defensive praise is contagious. Although the Bible doesn't specifically say so, I imagine that those who saw what was going on the day Jesus healed the infirm woman were caught up in praise as well. The Church also must find room to join in praise when the broken are healed. Those who missed the great blessing that day were those who decided to argue about religion.

The Bible describes Heaven as a place where the angels rejoice over one sinner who comes into the faith.

Likewise, I say unto you, there is joy in the presence of the angels of God over one sinner that repenteth (Luke 15:10).

They rejoice because Jesus heals those who are broken. Likewise God's people are to rejoice because the brokenhearted and emotionally wounded come to Him.

The Spirit of the Lord is upon Me, because He hath anointed Me to preach the gospel to the poor; He hath sent Me to heal the brokenhearted, to preach deliverance to the captives, and recovering of sight to the blind, to set at liberty them that are bruised (Luke 4:18).

Christ unleashed power in the infirm woman that day. He healed her body and gave her the strength of character to keep a proper attitude. The woman who is broken and wounded today will find power unleashed within her too when she responds to the call and brings her wounds to the Great Physician.

> *G*od's people are to rejoice because the brokenhearted and emotionally wounded come to Him.

The Lord works out everything for His own ends—even the wicked for a day of disaster.
Proverbs 16:4 (NIV)

Behold, I go forward, but He is not there; and backward, but I cannot perceive Him: on the left hand, where He doth work, but I cannot behold Him; He hideth Himself on the right hand, that I cannot see Him (Job 23:8-9).

Great growth doesn't come into your life through mountaintop experiences. Great growth comes through the valleys and low places where you feel limited and vulnerable. The time God is really moving in your life may seem to be the lowest moment you have ever experienced.…God is working on you, your faith and your character, when the blessing is delayed. The blessing is the reward that comes after you learn obedience through the things you suffered while waiting for it!…

I am not finished with the left hand—nor do I want to be finished. The prerequisite of the mountain is the valley. If there is no valley, there is no mountain. After you've been through this process a few times, you begin to realize that the valley is only a sign that with a few more steps, you'll be at the mountain again! Thus if the left hand is where He works, and it is; if the left hand is where He teaches us, and it is; then at the end of every class is a promotion. So just hold on!…

It is difficult to perceive God's workings on the left hand. God makes definite moves on the right hand, but when He works on the left, you may think He has forgotten you! If you've been living on the left side, you've been through a period that didn't seem to have the slightest stirring. It seemed as if everything you wanted to see God move upon, stayed still. "Has He gone on vacation? Has He forgotten His promise?" you've asked. The answer is no! God hasn't forgotten. You simply need to understand that sometimes He moves openly. I call them right-hand blessings. But sometimes He moves silently, tip-toeing around in the invisible, working in the shadows. You can't see Him, for He is working on the left side!

> *If the left hand is where He teaches us, and it is; then at the end of every class is a promotion.*

But the Lord is faithful, who shall stablish you, and keep you from evil. And we have confidence in the Lord touching you, that ye both do and will do the things which we command you. 2 Thessalonians 3:3-4

Your confession is great. You've fought and defended yourself against attackers, and you have seen some increase; but when you allow God to heal your thoughts, you will explode into another dimension. Sometimes we have been strong because we had great struggles. We fought valiantly in the face of the enemies of life. However, when sunset falls on the battlefield, and after the troops have gone home, we hang up our gear and wish we were as valiant inwardly as we displayed outwardly! Perceive and believe what God is doing in you. If you can get that in your head, you can reap it in your life!

The harvest field that God wants to plant is in your head. Amidst all your troubles, hold onto your field of dreams. If you can water your own field when men are trying to command a drought in your life, God will mightily sustain you....

I recently had the privilege of entertaining my 90-year-old grandmother. I could see that sun burning behind her leathery skin and glazed eyes. My grandmother smiled and gazed out of a window as if she were looking at Heaven itself....

Now I know why my grandmother smiled quietly and looked distantly. She had learned the art of being her own company. She had learned how to irrigate her own mind and entertain her own hours. She was simply self-reliant, not independent (we all need other people). She had learned how to rely on her own thoughts, how to motivate her own smiles, and how to find a place of confidence and serenity within herself as she privately communed with God. There is still much to be accomplished in the person who has maintained thoughts of greatness in the midst of degrading dilemmas. These are the smiles that paint the faces of people who know something greater and deeper, who see beyond their circumstances. They look out of the window, but they see far down the road.

> *P*erceive and *b e l i e v e* what God is doing in you. If you can get that in your head, you can reap it in your life!

Behold, happy is the man whom God correcteth: therefore despise not thou the chastening of the Almighty: for He maketh sore, and bindeth up: He woundeth, and His hands make whole. He shall deliver thee in six troubles: yea, in seven there shall no evil touch thee. Job 5:17-19

When my daughter Cora was born, her mother and I noticed that she learned to hold her bottle in her right hand. We naturally assumed that she was right-handed. However, to our surprise, when she grew a little older she held her cup in her left hand. To this day there are certain things she does with her right hand and certain things she does with her left. Technically, they call it ambidexterity. Cora is what my grandmother would call even-handed. The hand she uses depends on what she is trying to accomplish. Cora is ambidextrous. So is God! He is simply ambidextrous. There are times He will move on the left side.

Listen for God's hammering in the spirit. You can't see Him when He's working on the left side; He is invisible over there. It appears that He is not there, but He is....

Perhaps you have been going through a time of left-side experiences. You've said over and over again, "Where is the move of God that I used to experience? Why am I going through these fiery trials?" Let me minister to you a minute. God is there with you even now. He is operating in a different realm. He is working with a different hand, but He is still working in your life! In order for Him to do this job in your life, He had to change hands. Trust Him to have the same level of dexterity in His left hand as He does when He moves with the right hand.

I know so well how hard it is to trust Him when you can't trace Him! But that's exactly what He wants you to do—He wants you to trust Him with either hand. It may seem that everybody is passing you right now. Avoid measuring yourself against other people. God knows when the time is right. His methods may seem crude and His teachings laborious, but His results will be simply breathtaking. Without scams and games, without trickery or politics, God will accomplish a supernatural miracle because you trusted Him while He worked on the left side.

In order for Him to do this job in your life, He had to change hands.

(...Now he that ministereth seed to the sower both minister bread for your food, and multiply your seed sown, and increase the fruits of your righteousness;) being enriched in every thing to all bountifulness, which causeth through us thanksgiving to God. 2 Corinthians 9:10-11

If in your thoughts you see something beyond where you are, if you see a dream, a goal, or an aspiration that others would think impossible, you may have to *hold it*. Sometimes you may have to *hide it*, and most of the time you will have to *water it* as a farmer waters his crops to sustain the life in them. But always remember they are your fields. You must eat from the garden of your own thoughts, so don't grow anything you don't want to eat. As you ponder and daydream, receive grace for the hard places and healing for the damaged soil. Just know that whenever your children, your friends, or anyone else comes to the table of your wisdom, you can only feed them *what you have grown in your own fields*. Your wisdom is so flavorful and its texture so rich that it can't be "store bought"; it must be *homegrown*.

A whispering prayer lies on my lips: *I pray that this word God has given me be so powerful and personal, so intimate and applicable, that it leaves behind it a barren mind made pregnant. This seed of greatness will explode in your life and harvest in your children, feeding the generations to come and changing the winds of destiny.*

As I move on to other issues and as we face our inner selves, we strip away our facades and see ourselves as we really are. I am not fearful of our nakedness nor discouraged by our flaws....

In my heart I smell the indescribable smell of an approaching rain. Moisture is in the air and the clouds have gathered. Our fields have been chosen for the next rain and the wind has already started to blow. Run swiftly into the field with your precious seeds and plant them in the soft ground of your fertile mind. Whatever you plant in the evening will be reaped in the morning. My friend, I am so excited for you. I just heard a clap of thunder...in just another moment, there'll be rain!

> Whatever you plant in the evening will be reaped in the morning.

But we all, with open face beholding as in a glass the glory of the Lord, are changed into the same image from glory to glory, even as by the Spirit of the Lord. 2 Corinthians 3:18

I've learned to be thankful for the end results. Through every test and trial you must tell yourself what Job said. "I shall come forth as pure gold. I might not come forth today. It might not even be tomorrow. But when God gets through melting out all the impurities and scraping off the dross; when the boiling and the toilings of trouble have receded and the liquified substances in my life have become stable and fixed, then I will shine!" You bubbling, tempestuous saint who is enduring a time of walking through the left side of God, be strong and very courageous. The process always precedes the promise!

Soon you will be reshaped and remade into a gold chalice from which only the King can drink. All dross is discarded; all fear is removed. The spectators will gather to ask how such a wonderful vessel was made out of such poor materials. They will behold the jewels of your testimony and the brilliant glory of that fresh anointing. Some will wonder if you are the same person that they used to know. How do you answer? Simply stated, just say no!

Now you sit on the Master's right side, ready and available to be used, a vessel of honor unto Him. No matter how glorious it is to sit on His right hand and be brought to a position of power, just remember that although you have overcome now, you were boiled down and hollowed out while you lived on the left side of God. Join me in looking back over your life. Review your left-side experiences. Taste the bitter tears and the cold winds of human indifference and never, ever let anyone make you forget. You and I know. It's our secret, whether we tell them or sit quietly and make small talk. You've not always been where you are or shined as you shine. What can I say? You've come a long way, baby!

> Some will wonder if you are the same person that they used to know. How do you answer? Simply stated, just say no!

Jesus did many other miraculous signs in the presence of His disciples, which are not recorded in this book. But these are written that you may believe that Jesus is the Christ, the Son of God, and that by believing you may have life in His name. John 20:30-31 (NIV)

The best parts of school when I was an eight-year-old were recess and the walk home from school. I liked recess because it gave me an opportunity to stretch my legs and play with my friends. I liked the walk home from school because I usually had a quarter buried deep within my pocket, hidden somewhere beneath the bubble gum, the baseball cards, and all the other paraphernalia that eight-year-olds think are valuable.

I would save that quarter until we walked down Troy Road toward "old man Harless' " store…That quarter of mine was saved for the brightly colored books that were stacked in a display for all the children to see. There were all of my old friends…Superman and Captain Marvel, Captain America and Spiderman. I would purchase a copy of the latest issue and hurry a little farther down Troy Road. Once I found the old path that led up the hill behind the house, I would start my ascent to the big rock beneath the apple tree. There, hidden from public scrutiny, I would pull out my prized hero magazine and imagine that I was one of these men, a super hero who could transform as needed into anything necessary to destroy the villain.

I know all of this sounds terribly old-fashioned. Maybe it sounds a little too much like a scene that should include Andy Griffith, Aunt Bea, and the whole Mayberry clan, but that was really how it was in the days before children started carrying guns instead of comic books. I grew up reading about heroes. We believed in possibility, and though we were neither wealthy nor affluent, we could escape like a bird through the window of a full-color magazine and become anybody we wanted to be for at least 30 minutes—before my mother's voice would be heard from the rickety back porch behind the house.

> We could escape like a bird through the window of a full-color magazine and become anybody we wanted to be for at least 30 minutes.

But I would have you without carefulness. He that is unmarried careth for the things that belong to the Lord, how he may please the Lord: but he that is married careth for the things that are of the world, how he may please his wife.... 1 Corinthians 7:32-34

Some of you do not understand the benefits of being single. In reality, while you're not married, you really ought to be involved with God. When you get married, you direct all of the training that you had while you were unmarried toward your spouse. The apostle Paul addressed this issue in his first letter to the church at Corinth.

Single women often forget some very important advantages they have. At five o'clock in the morning you can lie in bed and pray in the Spirit till seven-thirty, and not have to answer to anyone. You can worship the Lord whenever and however you please. You can lie prostrate on the floor in your house and worship and no one will become annoyed about it. "The unmarried woman careth for the things of the Lord."

Often those who minister in churches hear unmarried women complain about their need for a husband, but rarely does a single woman boast about the kind of relationship she is free to build with the Lord. Are you complaining about how you need someone? Take advantage of the time you don't have to worry about cooking meals and caring for a family. While a woman is single she needs to recognize that she has the unique opportunity to build herself up in the Lord without the drains that can occur later.

> $\mathcal{R}$arely does a single woman boast about the kind of relationship she is free to build with the Lord.

And what shall I more say? for the time would fail me to tell of Gedeon, and of Barak, and of Samson, and of Jephthae; of David also, and Samuel, and of the prophets: who through faith subdued kingdoms, wrought righteousness, obtained promises, stopped the mouths of lions, quenched the violence of fire, escaped the edge of the sword.... Hebrews 11:32-34

We need heroes today. We need someone to believe in and look up to. We need someone who has accomplished something to give us the courage to believe in the invisible and feel the intangible. We need role models and men whose shadows we may stand in, men who provide a cool refreshing place of safety away from the despair of our oppressive society. It's just that all the "supermen" in the Church seem to have somehow gotten zapped by "kryptonite." Either they or their reputations have wilted into the abyss of human failure.

What are we going to do as we face this generation? From drug-using political officials to prostitute-purchasing preachers, the stars are falling on the heads of this generation! All of their wonder and dreams have turned into a comic book—a comic book that somehow doesn't seem funny anymore. Where did the heroes go?

This isn't just a church issue. We're suffering from an eroding sense of family, not just of family values. The entire concept of the family, period, has been crumbling because of this society's growing acceptance of non-traditional families. More and more women have chosen to be mothers without choosing fathers, while others have become single parents by necessity, not by choice. The gay community has added to the confusion by establishing "homes" that do not reflect God's original plan for child-rearing. So now we have twisted homes that are producing twisted children.

There is a cry coming up out of the city streets:

Our fathers went out for coffee and came back with cocaine. Their hands will not tuck us in because their feet are shackled to the prison floor.

Mother is out of milk and brother just joined a gang. Even in the neighborhood we used to drive through and dream that we lived in, we see ambulances.

Moving vans just moved Mommy away from Daddy, and now we see them by appointment. The whole country has fallen into the trash can like discarded comic books whose story lines are out-of-date. Where are the heroes?

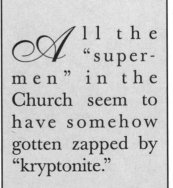

*A*ll the "supermen" in the Church seem to have somehow gotten zapped by "kryptonite."

Whom have I in heaven but Thee? and there is none upon earth that I desire beside Thee. Psalm 73:25

This time is in your life for you to charge up the battery cells. It's time to pamper; a time to take luxurious baths in milk and honey. You can lie there in the bath and worship the Lord. It's a ministry you have. Before you ask God for another man, take care of Him. If you are not ministering to His needs, and yet you are always before Him, asking Him to give you one of His princes to minister to, your prayers are not being heard because you are not being faithful to Him. When you become faithful in your singleness, then you will be better prepared to be faithful with a husband.

If you disregard the perfect husband, Jesus, you will certainly disregard the rest of us. If you ignore the one who provides oxygen, breath, bone tissue, strength, blood corpuscles, and life itself, you will certainly not be able to have regard for any earthly husband. The Lord wants to make sweet love to you. I'm not being carnal, I'm being real. He wants to hold you. He wants you to come in at the end of the day and say, "Oh, Lord, I could hardly make it today. Whew, I went through so much today. I'm so glad I have You in my life. They tried to devour me, but I thank You for this time we have together. I just couldn't wait to get alone and worship You and praise You and magnify You. You're the One who keeps me going. You're the lover of my soul, my mind, my emotions, my attitude and my disposition. Hold me. Touch me, strengthen me. Let me hold You. Let me bless You. I've set the night aside for us. Tonight is our night. I'm not so busy that I don't have time for You. For if I have no time for God, surely I have no time for a husband. My body is Yours. Nobody touches me but You. I am holy in body and in spirit. I am not committing adultery in our relationship. My body is Yours."

> **Before you ask God for another man, take care of Him.**

If we say that we have no sin, we deceive ourselves, and the truth is not in us. If we confess our sins, He is faithful and just to forgive us our sins, and to cleanse us from all unrighteousness. 1 John 1:8-9

Our healing will require more than a processional of religious ideas that are neither potent nor relevant. We need to understand that God is able to repair the broken places, but it requires us to expose where those broken places are. If we don't say to Him, "This is where I am hurting," then how can He pour in the oil and the wine?

We need to lay ourselves before Him and seek His face in the beauty of holiness—the holiness that produces wholeness. This isn't a matter of one denomination arguing with another over who is right; it is a matter of a broken family seeking healing and answers that can only come from the presence of God. *I am convinced He can heal whatever we can confess!*

> *Come, and let us return unto the Lord: for He hath torn, and He will heal us; He hath smitten, and He will bind us up (Hosea 6:1).*

It is in these moments that we are forced to reevaluate our concepts. Have we misaligned ourselves with God, or were our goals "out of kilter" to begin with? I really believe that we have made the unfortunate error of Old Testament Israel, whose attempt to attain righteousness produced a self-righteous mentality in many.

The Old Testament expressed the righteousness of God, a righteousness that the New Testament fully revealed in the gospel of Jesus Christ. Although the Old Testament could not completely reveal the righteousness of God, it certainly introduced a concept of how God defines holiness to humanity and Israel. God knew that the children of Israel would fail in their attempts to achieve the morality contained in the Law. Through their failures, God wanted the Israelites to find the redemption that He had allocated through the blood. Unfortunately, instead of honestly confessing to God the enormity of their failure, they became increasingly hypocritical. The whole purpose of the Law was spoiled because the fleshly egos of men would not repent and seek divine assistance for justification.

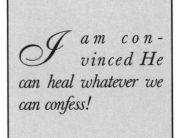

I am convinced He can heal whatever we can confess!

One thing have I desired of the Lord, that will I seek after; that I may dwell in the house of the Lord all the days of my life, to behold the beauty of the Lord, and to inquire in His temple. Psalm 27:4

The Scripture calls unmarried women virgins because God is of the opinion that if you do not belong to a man, you belong strictly to Him. God thinks you are His. God's heart was broken with the ancient nation of Israel. It was broken because Israel came to Him and said, "Make us a king to judge us like all the nations" (1 Sam. 8:5). God had thought He was their King. When they preferred a man over Him, He gave them Saul, and Israel went to the dogs.

There is nothing wrong with wanting to be married. Simply take care of the Lord while you're waiting. Minister to Him. Let Him heal you and loose you, and worship Him. Single women ought to be the most consecrated women in the Church. Instead of singles being envious of married women, the married ought to be jealous of singles. You are the ones whose shadows ought to fall on people and they be healed. You are in a position and posture of prayer. The Lord has become your necessary food. While some married women are dependent on their husbands, single women learn to be dependent on the Lord. God has no limitations. A married woman may have a husband who can do some things, but God can do everything. What a privilege to be married to Him. He told Joel, "And upon the handmaids…will I pour out My spirit" (Joel 2:29). God has a special anointing for the woman who is free to seek Him. Her prayer life should explode in miracles!

> *Single women ought to be the most consecrated women in the Church.*

I exhort therefore, that, first of all, supplications, prayers, intercessions, and giving of thanks, be made for all men; for kings, and for all that are in authority; that we may lead a quiet and peaceable life in all godliness and honesty. 1 Timothy 2:1-2 (Ref. 1 John 1:8-9)

For I am not ashamed of the gospel of Christ: for it is the power of God unto salvation to every one that believeth; to the Jew first, and also to the Greek. For therein is the righteousness of God revealed from faith to faith: as it is written, The just shall live by faith (Romans 1:16-17).

It takes great courage to exemplify total honesty with God. We have not even been totally released to admit our insufficiencies with others, and sometimes even with ourselves. How tragic! *When we discover our own limitations, we become eligible to discover the all-sufficiency of God.* Here we stand, like Israel in tainted armor, before the presence of a God whose brilliancy dims the radiant brightness of the sun. Yet there is a method to the madness of our predicament.

God knew who we were when He called us. Perhaps the sharp contrast between the people God uses and the God who uses them is to provide the worshiper with a clear distinction of who is to be worshiped!

It is undeniable that we face faltering visions and visionaries. Let us seek God for His divine purpose. Could it possibly be that God's intent is to establish *believable heroes*?

We need no glaring, gleaming, high-polished people for this day! We need heroes whose tarnished suits cannot hide their open hearts or their need to touch broken lives. The cry is going out for something *believable*—for something that even if not glorious, is at least fathomable.

The stress of trying to impress others with elitist presentations of spiraling spiritual altitudes has produced isolation and intimidation. No wonder our leaders are dying in the pulpit and suffering from an epidemic of heart attacks and strokes! It is hard to take an ordinary man from an ordinary background, saddle him with responsibility and tremendous visibility, and tell him, "You must be god-like."

> We need heroes whose tarnished suits cannot hide their open hearts or their need to touch broken lives.

Humble yourselves therefore under the mighty hand of God, that He may exalt you in due time. 1 Peter 5:6

Writing in all honesty, the greatest of the apostles—the writer of most of the New Testament epistles—confessed that though he aspired to "apprehend," he hadn't attained (see Phil. 3:12). In what area did this apostle fail? The Holy Spirit has granted him some semblance of diplomatic immunity that at least affords him the right of privacy in spite of imperfections. Yet we continually eat a perfect word from his stained hands, a word that converts the soul and challenges the most godly amongst us. I speak, of course, of the apostle Paul himself!

> Brethren, I count not myself to have apprehended: but this one thing I do, forgetting those things which are behind, and reaching forth unto those things which are before, I press toward the mark for the prize of the high calling of God in Christ Jesus (Philippians 3:13-14).

Alas, the call is a high calling. Yet it has been answered by lowly men who had the discernment to see a God high and lifted up. They stood on their toes like children, but still fell short of reaching His splendor. In short, the heroes in the Bible were not perfect, but they were powerful! They were not superhuman, but they were revelatory. Often chastised and corrected, they were still not discarded, for the Lord was with them.

Jesus was forever having to correct His disciples. Their pettiness, their anger and stinginess—these faults often reaffirmed the fact that they were "men of like passions." I, for one, am glad that they were. Their human frailties encourage the rest of us that we too can be used by God in spite of our feeble, crippled, and fragmented attempts at piety and true devotion.

At the risk of tarnishing a record that no one believes anyway, could we reevaluate what a hero really is? Isn't a hero someone who puts himself at risk to help someone else? Is it someone whose unselfish heart allows him to take dangerous risks to accomplish definite results to help someone else? I wonder if some of the men and women whom we say "failed" actually tarnished their records by having the courage to climb high enough to take the risks that others would not be willing to take...in order to help others.

> The heroes in the Bible were not perfect, but they were powerful!

I beseech you therefore, brethren, by the mercies of God, that ye present your bodies a living sacrifice, holy, acceptable unto God, which is your reasonable service. Romans 12:1

Being single and devoted to God does not mean it is wrong for you to want physical companionship. God ordained that need. While you are waiting, though, understand that God thinks He's your husband. Be careful how you treat Him. He thinks He's your man. That's why He does those special favors for you. It is God who made you into a beautiful woman. He has been taking care of you, even when you didn't notice His provision. He is the source of every good thing. He keeps things running, and provides for your daily care. It is He who opened doors for you. He has been your edge, your friend and your companion.

Those who are married seek to please their spouse. Unmarried people seek to please the Lord. There is a special relationship of power between God and the single believer. Paul wrote, "Let every man abide in the same calling wherein he was called" (1 Cor. 7:20). In other words, the person who is single should be abiding, not wrestling, in singleness. Rather than spend all of our effort trying to change our position, we need to learn to develop the position where He has placed us. Isn't that what this means: "…I have learned, in whatsoever state I am, therewith to be content" (Phil. 4:11). I speak peace to you today.

Maybe you haven't been living like you really should. Maybe your house hasn't been the house of prayer that it really could have been. I want you to take this opportunity and begin to sanctify your house and body. Maybe your body has been mauled and pawed by all sorts of people. I want you to sanctify your body unto the Lord, and give your body as a living sacrifice to God (see Rom. 12:1). If you can't keep your vow to God, you would never be able to keep your vow to a man. Give your body to God and sanctify yourself.

> Give your body to God and sanctify yourself.

"For I know the plans I have for you," declares the Lord, "plans to prosper you and not to harm you, plans to give you hope and a future." Jeremiah 29:11 (NIV)

Let's not glamorize sin. Sin is sin and it stinks in the nostrils of God. But have our noses become more sensitive than God's? Would we, like the others outside the tomb, choose to condemn to an eternal grave the man Lazarus, whose decomposing body had been shut up in a tomb for three days and begun to stink? *Thank God that Jesus didn't let the stink stop Him from saving the man.*

You have to be a hero to even expose yourself to the jealousy and cruelty of being raised up as a leader. Leaders are ostracized by their peers and criticized by their subordinates. They serve valiantly, though they often receive blows from satan and stabs from friends. Through it all, they continue to minister as if all were well.

I pause to lift to the throne every man or woman of God who is under attack by the enemy. Whether it be a financial, spiritual, or moral attack, I pray for you, my silent, alienated, wounded physician. May the medicine you have given to others come to your aid and bless you. May you recover all that satan desires to destroy in your life! In Jesus' name, Amen!

These all died in faith, not having received the promises, but having seen them afar off, and were persuaded of them, and embraced them, and confessed that they were strangers and pilgrims on the earth. For they that say such things declare plainly that they seek a country (Hebrews 11:13-14).

It is imperative that our vision be both progressive and regressive. In the forefront of our minds must be a plan that promises bright hopes for the future. I often say that a man cannot die with a twinkle in his eye! There must be a strong sense of destiny lodged firmly in our minds that dispels the despair of past failures. We must live our lives facing the rising sun.

> A man cannot die with a twinkle in his eye!

Let the husband render unto the wife due benevolence: and likewise also the wife unto the husband. 1 Corinthians 7:3

When God picks a wife for one of His royal sons, He will pick her from those who are faithful and holy unto Him. He may pass over those who didn't keep a vow to Him. If you will marry a king, he will have claimed you to be a queen. Begin to sanctify yourself. Bring your body before God. Bring your nature before God. Bring your passion to Him. Allow God to plug into your need.

Allow God to strengthen you until you can tell the devil, "My body belongs to God; my whole body belongs to God. I'm God's. And from the crown of my head to the soles of my feet, all that I am belongs to God. Early in the morning will I seek His face. I lie upon my bed at night and call on His name. I'll touch Him, embrace Him. He is the God of my salvation."

Marriage is ministry. If you are single, your ministry is directly unto the Lord. If you are married, your ministry is through your spouse. Then you learn how to be devoted to God through the relationship you have with your spouse.

Submitting yourselves one to another in the fear of God. Wives, submit yourselves unto your own husbands, as unto the Lord. For the husband is the head of the wife, even as Christ is the head of the church: and He is the savior of the body. Therefore as the church is subject unto Christ, so let the wives be to their own husbands in every thing. Husbands, love your wives, even as Christ also loved the church, and gave Himself for it; that He might sanctify and cleanse it with the washing of water by the word, that He might present it to Himself a glorious church, not having spot, or wrinkle, or any such thing; but that it should be holy and without blemish. So ought men to love their wives as their own bodies. He that loveth his wife loveth himself. For no man ever yet hated his own flesh; but nourisheth and cherisheth it, even as the Lord the church: for we are members of His body, of His flesh, and of His bones. For this cause shall a man leave his father and mother, and shall be joined unto his wife, and they two shall be one flesh. This is a great mystery: but I speak concerning Christ and the church. Nevertheless let every one of you in particular so love his wife even as himself; and the wife see that she reverence her husband (Ephesians 5:21-33).

> *I*f you are married, your ministry is through your spouse.

SET YOUR MIND FORWARD

Brethren, I count not myself to have apprehended: but this one thing I do, forgetting those things which are behind, and reaching forth unto those things which are before, I press toward the mark for the prize of the high calling of God in Christ Jesus. Philippians 3:13-14

Although heroes don't have to be perfect, I realize they must be people who are resilient enough to survive tragedy and adversity. All of us have experienced the pain of adversity in our warfare, whether it was a physical, emotional, economical, spiritual, or sexual attack. Regardless of which category the attack falls under, they are very personal in nature. Real heroes not only survive the incident, but also overcome the lingering side effects that often come from it.

Why do I say that? If you don't survive, you can't save anyone. No young man in a combat zone can carry his wounded comrade if he himself does not survive. Live long enough to invest the wealth of your experience in the release of some other victim whom satan desires to bind or incapacitate!

And truly, if they had been mindful of that country from whence they came out, they might have had opportunity to have returned (Hebrews 11:15).

The faith of these heroes sets them apart from other men. It is your convictions that cause you to be distinctly different from others whose complacency you can't seem to share. The people referred to in Hebrews 11 were not mindful of where they came from. In other words, their minds were full of where they were going. These valiant heroes were not perfect, but they were convinced that what God had promised He was able to perform. Now if their minds had been full of their origin instead of their destiny, they would have gone back. Be assured that *people always move in the direction of their mind*. Whatever your mind is full of, that is where you eventually move. Thank God for people who can see the invisible, and touch with their faith the intangible promises of God.

People always move in the direction of their mind.

The Scriptures declare that its heroes were made strong out of weakness. In order to be a real success, *you must be able to be strengthened through struggle*. What we need is a hero who can, as these men did, report back to the world that he escaped. He may have felt weak, he may have cried and suffered, but he still made it. Look at these men mentioned in Hebrews 11:32. Examine their lives. They were not glaring examples of flawless character; yet they epitomized faith toward God. Even though most of them experienced failures and flaws, they would have made the front pages of the newspapers in our day for their heroism. We must be careful when judging the weak moments in their lives. Consider the entirety of their lives and you will see that the dent in their armor didn't affect their performance on the battlefield.

Gideon failed the biblical faith test when he sought a sign. Samson shined on the battlefield but had struggles in the bedroom. This anointed judge of Israel wrestled with more than a failed marriage that he could not seem to regain. He had an insatiable appetite for strange flesh, which led to his demise, yet he still made it to the list of the few, the proud, and the brave.

Oh yes, then there is Jephthah, the illegitimate child who was rejected by his siblings and ostracized by his family. He went to the land of Tob where he became what we would call a gang leader. He gathered together the "vain" fellows, a sampling of social rejects, and became their leader. In spite of his adolescent struggles, and his rash tendency to make wild vows (which cost him the destruction of his daughter's future), he still made it to the roll of the renowned. He made it because he believed God. He lifted himself above his circumstances and fought the enemies without and within!

> $\mathscr{T}$he Scriptures declare that heroes were made strong out of weakness.

Behold, I stand at the door, and knock: if any man hear My voice, and open the door, I will come in to him, and will sup with him, and he with Me. Revelation 3:20

Marriage is the place in human society where true love can be expressed in a great way. Marriage partners are to give self-sacrificially to one another. Jesus gave Himself for the Church. So also do husbands and wives give themselves to each other. Marriage is not a place where we seek self-gratification. It is the place where we seek to gratify another.

The sacredness of marriage is found in the relationship between Christ and the Church. Jesus continues to intercede on behalf of the Church, even after He gave His all for us. He is the greatest advocate of believers. He stands before God to defend and proclaim our value. Similarly, husbands and wives are to be bonded together to the extent that they become the greatest advocate of the other. Not demanding one's own way, but always seeking to please the other.

There can be no doubt that God has special plans for each one of us. The woman who is single needs to recognize her position and seek to please God in every way. "Single" means to be "whole." Enjoy being a whole person. The greatest visitation of the Holy Ghost in history happened to an unmarried woman named Mary. Before Joseph could, the Holy Ghost came upon her. That same life-giving anointing wants to come upon you. Stop murmuring and complaining. His presence is in the room! Worship Him! He is waiting on you.

The greatest visitation of the Holy Ghost in history happened to an unmarried woman named Mary.

He is despised and rejected of men; a man of sorrows, and acquainted with grief: and we hid as it were our faces from Him; He was despised, and we esteemed Him not. Isaiah 53:3

To me, Jephthah's gang in Judges 11 reveals the part of ministry that we are missing: *He built an army out of rejects.* There is something powerful about being a "chosen reject"; chosen by God but rejected by men. There is a focus that evolves in the heart of someone who has been rejected by men. Their rejection creates a feeling of misplacement. Have you ever felt misplaced? Have you ever struggled to fit into some network or order in which it seemed you were not welcomed? It is God's design that causes us to experience rejection, even though it is painful.

When we have been ostracized by someone or something that we wanted to belong to, our streaming tears cannot soften the hard truth. Rejection tastes like bile in our gut. However, the experience can make us bitter, or it can make us better. I choose better. What about you?

I believe this kind of pain causes us to achieve a level of consecration that is out of the reach of people who have never been rejected. Why? Once the reality hits us that God purposely chooses to use misplaced and rejected people, then first and foremost, we experience a sense of warm gratitude that flows through our human hearts like hot syrup. It fills every crack and crevice of our minds, which suggested there was no place of meaning for us. It is in the shadows of these moments that we worship behind the veil, wrapped in His Shekinah Glory, enveloped in the love of the sacrificed Lamb of God, the God *who created a place for the misplaced and chose us for Himself.*

I can't help but wonder if we have forsaken some of God's finest people because they were under attack, people whom God wanted to use to make a tremendous statement in the Body of Christ. These vicarious soldiers would have been so glad to receive a second chance to return to active duty. They could bring to us a voice from the grave. They could express the truth that there is life after death.

> *There is something powerful about being a "chosen reject"; chosen by God but rejected by men.*

But God hath chosen the foolish things of the world to confound the wise; and God hath chosen the weak things of the world to confound the things which are mighty; and base things of the world, and things which are despised, hath God chosen, yea, and things which are not, to bring to nought things that are: That no flesh should glory in His presence.... 1 Corinthians 1:27-31

Dead circumstances cannot hold down the body of someone who has been chosen! If no one else embraces these bleeding, purple heart soldiers, perhaps they should rally together and find comfort in the commonality of their mutual experience. Thank God for Jephthah, who reminds us of the deep, abiding reality that even if we were thrown into a refuse receptacle by closed minds who decided that our dry bones couldn't live again, God is still in the business of recycling human lives!

I must confess that more than once I have seen His hand pick up the pieces of this broken heart and restore back to service my crushed emotions and murky confidence, while I stood in awe at the fact that God can do so much with so little....

The greatest place to preach isn't in our great meetings with swelling crowds and lofty recognitions. The greatest place to preach is in the trenches, in the foxholes and the hogpens of life. If you want a grateful audience, take your message to the messy places of life and scrape the hog hairs off the prodigal sons of God, who were locked away in the hog pens by the spiritual elite.

It is here in these abominable situations that you will find true worship being born, springing out of the hearts of men who realize the riches of His grace. No worship seminar is needed for someone whose tearstained face has turned from humiliation to inspiration. Their personal degradation has become a living demonstration of the depths of the unfathomable love of God! My friend, this is Davidic worship! This is the praise of David, whose critical brothers and distracted father helped him become the canvas on which God paints the finest picture of worship these weary eyes have ever witnessed!...

It is time for us to redefine and redirect our gaze to find the heroes of God among us. We must not forget that God purposely chooses to use misplaced and rejected people, and He may be looking in our direction.

> We must not forget that God purposely chooses to use misplaced and rejected people, and He may be looking in our direction.

And the Lord God caused a deep sleep to fall upon Adam, and he slept: and He took one of his ribs, and closed up the flesh instead thereof; and the rib, which the Lord God had taken from man, made He a woman, and brought her unto the man. Genesis 2:21-22

Nearly every home in America is wired for electricity. Walls are covered with receptacles which deliver the electric current. In order to take advantage of the power, something must be plugged into the receptacle. The receptacle is the female and the plug is the male.

Women were made like receptacles. They were made to be receivers. Men were made to be givers, physically, sexually and emotionally, and by providing for others. In every area, women were made to receive.

The woman was made, fashioned out of the man, to be a help meet. Through their union, they find wholeness in each other. She helps him meet and accomplish his task. In other words, if you have a power saw, it has great potential for cutting. However, it is ineffective until it is plugged in. The receptacle helps the power saw meet its purpose. Without that receptacle, the power saw, although mighty, remains limited.

However, there is a vulnerability about the receptacle. The vulnerability exists because they must be careful what kind of plug they are connected with. Receptacles are open. Women are open by nature and design. Men are closed. You must be careful what you allow to plug into you and draw strength from you. The wrong plugs may seek your help and drain your power.

God recognizes your vulnerability; therefore, He has designed that those who plug into a woman sexually will have a covenant with that woman. God never intended for humanity to have casual sex. His design always included the commitment of a covenant. He purposed that a man who has sexual relations with a woman would be committed to that same woman for life. Nothing short of this commitment meets His standard. God wants you covered like an outlet is covered, in order that no one tamper with your intended purpose. The married woman is covered by her husband. The single woman is covered by her chastity and morality. It is dangerous to be uncovered.

> Women were made like receptacles....You must be careful what you allow to plug into you and draw strength from you.

And God said, Let Us make man in Our image, after Our likeness: and let them have dominion over the fish of the sea, and over the fowl of the air, and over the cattle, and over all the earth, and over every creeping thing that creepeth upon the earth. Genesis 1:26

Originally, God created humanity perfect and good. "And God said, Let Us make man in Our image, after Our likeness: and let them have dominion over the fish of the sea, and over the fowl of the air, and over the cattle, and over all the earth, and over every creeping thing that creepeth upon the earth" (Gen. 1:26).

God placed Adam in the garden He had prepared for him. The only rule was man should not eat of the tree of the knowledge of good and evil. God wanted mankind to rely on Him for moral decisions. After the fall, history records the consequences of man trying to make moral decisions for himself.

Although God had made a wonderful place for Adam to live, the man remained less than complete. He needed a woman. Keep in mind, though, that she completed his purpose, not his person. If you're not complete as a person, marriage will not help you.

> *And the Lord God caused a deep sleep to fall upon Adam, and he slept: and He took one of his ribs, and closed up the flesh instead thereof; and the rib, which the Lord God had taken from man, made He a woman, and brought her unto the man (Genesis 2:21-22).*

In Genesis chapter 3, we see that Eve allowed herself to be taken advantage of by satan, who plugged into her desire to see, taste and be wise. The enemy took advantage of her weakness. "And the man said, The woman whom Thou gavest to be with me, she gave me of the tree, and I did eat" (Gen. 3:12).

Eve had given her attention over to someone else. "And the Lord God said unto the woman, What is this that thou hast done? And the woman said, The serpent beguiled me, and I did eat" (Gen. 3:13). Adam's anger is shown by his statement, "You gave her to be with me." The woman answered, "Well, I couldn't help it. He plugged into me, or he beguiled me."

You've got to be careful who you let uncover you, because they can lead you to complete destruction.

> *I*f you're not complete as a person, marriage will not help you.

Wherefore seeing we also are compassed about with so great a cloud of witnesses, let us lay aside every weight, and the sin which doth so easily beset us, and let us run with patience the race that is set before us. Hebrews 12:1

There must be something beyond the acquisition of a goal. If there isn't, then this book is nothing more than a motivational message, something which the secular field is already adept at. Many people spend all their lives trying to attain a goal. When they finally achieve it, they still secretly feel empty and unfulfilled. This will happen even in the pursuit of godly goals and successes if we don't reach beyond the mere accomplishment of an ambitious pursuit. In short, success doesn't save! Why then does God put the desire to attain in the hearts of His men and women if He knows that at the end is, as Solomon so aptly put it, "Vanity of vanities…all is vanity" (Eccles. 12:8)? Could it be that we who have achieved something of effectiveness must then reach a turn in the road and begin to worship God beyond the goal!

A runner trains himself to achieve a goal. That goal ultimately is to break the ribbon, the mark of success. After he has broken the ribbon, if there is no prize beyond the goal, then the race seems in vain. No runner would run a race and then receive the broken ribbon as the symbol of his success. At the end of the race is a prize unrelated to the race itself—a trophy that can be given only to people who have reached the pinnacle of accomplishment. What we must understand in the back of our minds as we ascend toward God's purpose is it blesses God when we attain what we were created to attain. It is His eternal purpose that we pursue. However, we can be blessed only by the God behind the purpose. If we build a great cathedral for the Lord and fail to touch the God whom the cathedral is for, what good is the building aside from God?

A runner trains himself to achieve a goal.

The weapons we fight with are not the weapons of the world. On the contrary, they have divine power to demolish strongholds. 2 Corinthians 10:4 (NIV)

In Genesis chapter 3, we see that Eve allowed herself to be taken advantage of by satan, who plugged into her desire to see, taste and be wise. The enemy took advantage of her weakness....

> *And the Lord God said unto the serpent, Because thou hast done this, thou art cursed above all cattle, and above every beast of the field; upon thy belly shalt thou go, and dust shalt thou eat all the days of thy life: and I will put enmity between thee and the woman, and between thy seed and her seed; it shall bruise thy head, and thou shalt bruise His heel (Genesis 3:14-15).*

There is a special enmity between femininity and the enemy. There is a special conflict between the woman and the enemy. That's why you must do spiritual warfare. You must do spiritual warfare against the enemy because you are vulnerable in certain areas and there is enmity between you and the enemy. You must be on your guard. Women tend to be more prayerful than men, once they are committed. If you are a woman living today, and you're not learning spiritual warfare, you're in trouble. The enemy may be taking advantage of you.

He is attracted to you because he knows that you were designed as a receptacle to help meet someone's vision. If he can get you to help meet his vision, you will have great problems. God said, "And I will put enmity between thee and the woman, and between thy seed and her seed" (Gen. 3:15a).

Now, God didn't say only "her seed and your seed." He said, "Between you and the woman."

> *If you are a woman living today, and you're not learning spiritual warfare, you're in trouble.*

But I fear, lest by any means, as the serpent beguiled Eve through his subtlety, so your minds should be corrupted from the simplicity that is in Christ. 2 Corinthians 11:3

There is a fight between you and the devil.

And the Lord God said unto the serpent, Because thou hast done this, thou art cursed above all cattle, and above every beast of the field; upon thy belly shalt thou go, and dust shalt thou eat all the days of thy life: and I will put enmity between thee and the woman, and between thy seed and her seed; it shall bruise thy head, and thou shalt bruise His heel (Genesis 3:14-15).

Who are the victims of the most rapes in this country? Who are the victims of the most child abuse? Who are the victims of much of the sexual discrimination in the job market? Who has the most trouble getting together, unifying with each other and collaborating? Over and over again, satan is attacking and assaulting your femininity.

Satan is continually attacking femininity. Mass populations of women have increased over the country. The Bible says that the time will come when there will be seven women to every one man (see Isa. 4:1). Statistics indicate that we are living in those times right now. Where you have more need than supply, there is growing enmity between the woman and the enemy.

If godly women do not learn how to start praying and doing effective spiritual warfare, they will not discern what is plugging into them. Perhaps you become completely vulnerable to moods and attitudes and dispositions. Perhaps you are doing things and you don't know why. Something's plugging into you. If you are tempted to rationalize, "I'm just in a bad mood. I don't know just what it is. I'm just evil. I'm tough," don't believe it. Something's plugging into you.

Something's plugging into you.

But if someone obeys God's teaching, then in that person God's love has truly reached its goal. 1 John 2:5 (NCV)

Many of us are constantly in God's presence, praising His name, but we fail to accomplish anything relative to His purpose. Isaiah was in the presence of God to such a degree that the glory of the Lord filled the temple like a train, and the doorpost moved (see Isa. 6:1-4). Nevertheless, there was still a time when God sent him from His presence to accomplish His purpose. As an eagle stirs her nest, so God must challenge us to leave the familiar places and perform the uncertain future of putting into practice the total of all we have learned in the Lord's presence. The priest went into the Holy of Holies to see the glory of the Lord, but the work of the Lord was to be performed outside the veiled place of secret consecration. As Isaiah said, "Here am I; send me" (Isa. 6:8), go from the gluttony of storing up the treasure to being a vessel God can use!

The other extreme is equally, if not more, dangerous. What makes us think we can do the work of the Lord and never spend time with the Lord of the work? We get burned out when we do not keep fresh fire burning within! We need the kind of fire that comes from putting down all the work and saying to the Lord, "I need my time with You." What good is it to break the finish line if you do not go beyond that temporary moment of self-aggrandizement to receive a valued reward? The accomplishment isn't reward enough because once it is attained, it ceases to be alluring.

For example, when my twin boys were toddlers, I helped potty train them. When they learned to use the potty, we had an all-out celebration. I never knew I could be that glad to see a bowel movement in a pot! However ridiculous as it might sound, we all clamorously screamed and laughed and were delighted at this moment of success. They are now 14 years old. We don't quite act that way now when necessity mandates that they visit the toilet. We do not continue to celebrate what we have already accomplished.

> The accomplishment isn't reward enough because once it is attained, it ceases to be alluring.

And Adam called his wife's name Eve; because she was the mother of all living. Genesis 3:20

In Genesis 3, God wasn't finished with His pronouncements addressed to the serpent after the fall. Next He addressed Eve directly.

> *Unto the woman He said, I will greatly multiply thy sorrow and thy conception; in sorrow thou shalt bring forth children; and thy desire shall be to thy husband, and he shall rule over thee (Genesis 3:16).*

God explained that birthing comes through sorrow. Everything you bring forth comes through pain. If it didn't come through pain, it probably wasn't worth much. If you're going to bring forth—and I'm not merely talking about babies, I'm talking about birthing vision and purpose—you will do so with sorrow and pain. If you're going to bring forth anything in your career, your marriage or your life, if you're going to develop anything in your character, if you're going to be a fruitful woman, it's going to come through sorrow. It will come through the things you suffer. You will enter into strength through sorrow.

Sorrow is not the object; it's simply the canal that the object comes through. Many of you are mistaking sorrow for the baby instead of the canal. In that case, all you have is pain. You ought to have a child for every sorrow. For every sorrow, for every intense groaning in your spirit, you ought to have something to show for it. Don't let the devil give you sorrow without seed. Any time you have sorrow, it is a sign that God is trying to get something through you and to you.

Be careful that you don't walk away with the pain and leave the baby in the store. You are the producers. You are the ones through whom life passes. Every child who enters into this world must come through you. Even Jesus Christ had to come through you to get legal entry into the world. He had to come through you. You are a channel and an expression of blessings. If there is to be any virtue, any praise, any victory, any deliverance, it's got to come through you.

*Y*ou are the ones through whom life passes.

YOU WILL GIVE BIRTH

But we were gentle among you, even as a nurse cherisheth her children: so being affectionately desirous of you, we were willing to have imparted unto you, not the gospel of God only, but also our own souls, because ye were dear unto us.
1 Thessalonians 2:7-8

Satan wants to use you as a legal entry into this world or into your family. That's how he destroyed the human race with the first family. He knows that you are the entrance of all things. You are the doors of life. Be careful what you let come through you. Close the doors to the planting of the enemy. Then know that when travail comes into your spirit, it's because you're going to give birth.

You will give birth! That's why you have suffered pain. Your spirit is signaling you that something is trying to get through. Don't become so preoccupied with the pain that you forget to push the baby. Sometimes you're pushing the pain and not the baby, and you're so engrossed with what's hurting you that you're not doing what it takes to produce fruit in your life.

When you see sorrow multiply, it is a sign that God is getting ready to send something to you. Don't settle for the pain and not get the benefit. Hold out. Disregard the pain and get the promise. Understand that God has promised some things to you that He wants you to have, and you've got to stay there on the table until you get to the place where you ought to be in the Lord. After all, the pain is forgotten when the baby is born.

What is the pain when compared with the baby? Some may have dropped the baby. That happens when you become so engrossed with the pain that you leave the reward behind you. Your attention gets focused on the wrong thing. You can be so preoccupied with how bad it hurts that you miss the joy of a vision giving birth.

> *Know that when travail comes into your spirit, it's because you're going to give birth.*

If any man's work abide which he hath built thereupon, he shall receive a reward. 1 Corinthians 3:14

Since the beauty of the moment soon fades and you find yourself again seeking new conquest, there must be something beyond just achieving goals and setting new goals. You would be surprised at the number of pastors all across this country who race wildly from one goal to the other without ever feeling fulfilled by their accomplishments. What is even worse is the fact that other men and women often envy and sometimes hate these ministers because they would love to have what these ministers have attained. Yet the poor chaps themselves can't see their own worth. Little does anyone know that these spiritual celebrities are being widely driven by the need to accomplish without ever being fulfilled. It is the cruelest form of torture to be secretly dying of the success which others envy. If you are in that situation, whether you are a business person or a minister, I speak to your addiction (that's right, addiction) in the name of Jesus Christ. I command that nagging, craving, family-abusing ambition to loose you and let you go!

Release comes so you can enter the presence of God to be restored. To be restored means to be built back up, to be restocked. Only God can put back into you what striving took out. Will you strive for a goal again? Yes! You need to strive, but you don't need the obsession that it can create. There will never be anything that God gives you to do that will replace what God's mere presence will give. You will never build your self-esteem by accomplishing goals because, as in the case of my twins, once you've done it, it's done! No lasting affirmation comes from a mountain that has been climbed. Only Christ can save you, affirm you, and speak to how you feel about yourself. The praises of men will fall into the abyss of a leaky heart. When you have a crack, everything in you will leak out. Let God fix it. Your job can't do it. Sex can't do it. Marriage can't do it. Another graduate degree can't do it, but God can! He is the Doctor who specialized in reconstructive surgery!

> To be restored means to be built back up, to be restocked.

STRUGGLES = CHARACTER

No discipline seems pleasant at the time, but painful. Later on, however, it produces a harvest of righteousness and peace for those who have been trained by it.
Hebrews 12:11 (NIV)

Wouldn't it be a foolish thing for a woman to go into labor, go through all of the pain, stay on the delivery table, stay in labor for hours and hours, and simply get up and walk out of the hospital. It would be foolish for her to concentrate on the pain to the extent that she would leave the baby lying in the hospital. However, that is exactly what happens when you become preoccupied with how bad the past hurts you. Maybe you have walked away and left the baby lying on the floor.

For every struggle in your life, God accomplished something in your character and in your spirit. Why hold the pain and drop the baby when you could hold the baby and drop the pain? You are holding on to the wrong thing if all you do is concentrate on past pain. Release the pain. Pain doesn't fall off on its own. It's got to be released. Release the pain. Allow God to loose you from the pain, separate you from what has afflicted you and be left with the baby and not the problem.

He said, "In sorrow thou shalt bring forth children" (Gen. 3:16b). That includes every area of your life. That's in your character. That's true in your personality. It is true in your spirit as well as in your finances. Bring forth, ladies! If it comes into this world, it has to come through you. If you're in a financial rut, bring forth. If you're in need of healing for your body, bring forth. Understand that it must be brought forth. It doesn't just happen by accident.

For every struggle in your life, God accomplished something in your character and in your spirit.

Beareth all things, believeth all things, hopeth all things, endureth all things. 1 Corinthians 13:7

In the delivery room, the midwife tells a woman, "Push." The baby will not come forth if you don't push him. God will not allow you to become trapped in a situation without escape. But you've got to push while you are in pain if you intend to produce. I'm told that when the pain is at its height, that's when they instruct you to push, not when the pain recedes. When the pain is at its ultimate expression, that is the time you need to push.

As you begin to push in spite of the pain, the pain recedes into the background because you become pre-occupied with the change rather than the problem. Push! You don't have time to cry. Push! You don't have time to be suicidal. Push! This is not the time to give up. Push, because God is about to birth a promise through you. Cry if you must, and groan if you have to, but keep on pushing because God has promised that if it is to come into the world, it's got to pass through you.

There remains a conflict between past pain and future desire. Here is the conflict. He said, "...in sorrow thou shalt bring forth children; and thy *desire* shall be to thy husband, and he shall rule over thee" (Gen. 3:16). In other words, you have so much pain in producing the child that, if you don't have balance between past pain and future desire, you will quit producing. God says, "After the pain, your desire shall be to your husband." Pain is swallowed by desire.

Impregnated with destiny, women of promise must bear down in the spirit. The past hurts; the pain is genuine. However, you must learn to get in touch with something other than your pain. If you do not have desire, you won't have the tenacity to resurrect. Desire will come back. After the pain is over, desire follows, because it takes desire to be productive again.

> *Impregnated with destiny, women of promise must bear down in the spirit.*

LET GO!

The four and twenty elders fall down before Him that sat on the throne, and worship Him that liveth for ever and ever, and cast their crowns before the throne, saying, Thou art worthy, O Lord, to receive glory and honor and power: for Thou hast created all things, and for Thy pleasure they are and were created. Revelation 4:10-11

There is a place in the presence of God where crowns lose their luster. There is a place where the accolades of men sound brash and out of pitch. There is a place where all our memorials of great accomplishments seem like dusty stones gathered by bored children who had nothing better to collect. There are times when we trade success for solace. In Revelation, 24 elders traded their golden, jewel-encrusted crowns for a tear-stained moment in the presence of a blood-stained Lamb. Many wonderful people are suffering with their success because they cannot discern when to throw down their crowns and just worship....

I drove a delivery truck one summer while I was in college. I had never driven a stick shift vehicle before. It was all right at first. I handled it rather well. In fact, I was on my way to that special place of self-enthroned egotism when I had to stop at a traffic light. The only problem was, this light was on a steep hill....I had to keep my left foot on the clutch while easing my right foot from the brake to the gas with the timing and grace of Fred Astaire. My first attempt caused the truck to lurch forward, when the engine died and the whole truck started sliding backwards. I nearly slid into a car that was behind me. I was sick! Traffic was backing up and I could see the person in my rearview mirror saying something that I was glad I couldn't quite hear!...

I finally prayed—which is what I should have done at first. My task was getting the timing. I had to learn when to ease my right foot off the brake and onto the gas and my left foot from the clutch with computerlike precision without killing the engine....When it was all over, my head was spinning, my pulse was weak and, to be blunt, my bladder was full! In spite of all that, I learned something on that hill that many people don't learn about themselves and the things they hold on to. I learned when to let go!

> *Many wonderful people are suffering with their success because they cannot discern when to throw down their crowns and just worship.*

There is surely a future hope for you, and your hope will not be cut off. Proverbs 23:18 (NIV)

I have been in the delivery room with my wife as she was giving birth. I witnessed the pain and suffering she endured. I believe that there were times of such intense pain that she would have shot me if she had had a chance. Her desire made her continue. She didn't simply give up. She endured the pain so new life could be born. Once the child was born, the pain was soon forgotten.

Until the desire to go forward becomes greater than the memories of past pain, you will never hold the power to create again. However, when the desire comes back into your spirit and begins to live in you again, it will release you from the pain.

God wants to give us the strength to overcome past pain and move forward into new life. Solomon wrote, "Where there is no vision, the people perish" (Prov. 29:18a). Vision is the desire to go ahead. Until you have a vision to go ahead, you will always live in yesterday's struggles. God is calling you to today. The devil wants you to live in yesterday. He's always telling you about what you cannot do. His method is to bring up your past. He wants to draw your attention backward.

God wants to put desire in the spirit of broken women. There wouldn't be any desire if there wasn't any relationship. You can't desire something that's not there. The very fact that you have a desire is in itself an indication that better days are coming. David said, "I had fainted, unless I had believed to see the goodness of the Lord in the land of the living" (Ps. 27:13). Expect something wonderful to happen.

> Until you have a vision to go ahead, you will always live in yesterday's struggles.

Because the creature itself also shall be delivered from the bondage of corruption into the glorious liberty of the children of God. Romans 8:21

When I was a boy, we had a dog named Pup. Don't let the name fool you, though. He was a mean and ferocious animal. He would eat anyone who came near him. We had him chained in the back of the house to a four-by-four post. The chain was huge. We never imagined that he could possibly tear himself loose from that post. He would chase something and the chain would snap him back. We often laughed at him, as we stood outside his reach.

One day Pup saw something that he really wanted. It was out of his reach. However, the motivation before him became more important than what was behind him. He pulled that chain to the limit. All at once, instead of drawing him back, the chain snapped, and Pup was loose to chase his prey.

That's what God will do for you. The thing that used to pull you back you will snap, and you will be liberated by a goal because God's put greatness before you. You can't receive what God wants for your life by looking back. He is mighty. He is powerful enough to destroy the yoke of the enemy in your life. He is strong enough to bring you out and loose you, deliver you, and set you free.

What we need is a seed in the womb that we believe is enough to produce an embryo. We must be willing to feed that embryo for it to grow and become visible. When it will not be hidden anymore, it will break forth in life as answered prayer. It will break forth. No matter how hard others try to hold it back, it will break forth.

> He is mighty. He is powerful enough to destroy the yoke of the enemy in your life.

And every creature which is in heaven, and on the earth, and under the earth, and such as are in the sea, and all that are in them, heard I saying, Blessing, and honor, and glory, and power, be unto Him that sitteth upon the throne, and unto the Lamb for ever and ever. And the four beasts said, Amen. And the four and twenty elders fell down and worshipped Him that liveth for ever and ever.
Revelation 5:13-14

When you come into the presence of God and His anointing, cast down your crowns and bend your knees. You can let it go and still not lose it. Like the 24 elders in Revelation who threw their crowns before the throne, you must learn to trade a monument for a moment. The real reward you need to seek can be paid only by the one who hired you—God Himself. You see, the 24 elders knew that they had received results and rewards, but the real credit went to the Lord. They were wise enough not to be too impressed with their own success. They knew that it was God all the time. When you learn the time to take your foot off the clutch and give the glory back to God, you will be fulfilled in His presence and not frustrated by worshiping His presents!

I have a question I would like you to ponder. What makes a connoisseur of fine restaurants leave the elegant, aristocratic atmospheres and the succulent cuisine of gourmet food, only to stop by a hamburger joint for a sandwich and fries? Time's up. Here's the answer. Each of us has within us a need for balance and a sense of normalcy. It is so important that we balance our areas of expertise with plain everyday humanism. I shared in an earlier chapter how I started out preaching in the most adverse of circumstances. I don't think I really knew how adverse they were because I had nothing to compare them to. I went from sleeping in a child's bedroom of somebody's home to penthouse suites. I remember ministering in churches where the finances did not allow for a hotel room or even a real guest room. The evangelist would stay with the pastor, and usually the pastor had a house full of children. One of these bright-eyed children would have to give up his or her room to accommodate the man of God. I still pray for those families who gave what they had to make me as comfortable as they could. I earnestly appreciate it.

> The real reward you need to seek can be paid only by the one who hired you—God Himself.

My substance was not hid from Thee, when I was made in secret, and curiously wrought in the lowest parts of the earth. Psalm 139:15

Put the truth in your spirit and feed, nurture and allow it to grow. Quit telling yourself, "You're too fat, too old, too late, or too ignorant." Quit feeding yourself that garbage. That will not nourish the baby. Too often we starve the embryo of faith that is growing within us. It is unwise to speak against your own body. Women tend to speak against their bodies, opening the door for sickness and disease. Speak life to your own body. Celebrate who you are. You are the image of God.

Scriptures remind us of who we are. "I will praise Thee; for I am fearfully and wonderfully made: marvellous are Thy works; and that my soul knoweth right well" (Ps. 139:14). These are the words that will feed our souls. The truth will allow new life to swell up within us. Feed the embryo within with such words as these.

> *When I consider Thy heavens, the work of Thy fingers, the moon and the stars, which Thou hast ordained; what is man, that Thou art mindful of him? and the son of man, that Thou visitest him? (Psalm 8:3-4)*

"And the Lord shall make thee the head, and not the tail; and thou shalt be above only, and thou shalt not be beneath" (Deut. 28:13a). "I can do all things through Christ which strengtheneth me" (Phil. 4:13). The Word of God will provide the nourishment that will feed the baby inside.

Celebrate who you are. You are the image of God.

Now faith is being sure of what we hope for and certain of what we do not see. This is what the ancients were commended for. By faith we understand that the universe was formed at God's command, so that what is seen was not made out of what was visible. Hebrews 11:1-3 (NIV)

The Book of Hebrews provides us with a tremendous lesson on faith. When we believe God, we are counted as righteous. Righteousness cannot be earned or merited. It comes only through faith. We can have a good report simply on the basis of our faith. Faith becomes the tender, like money is the legal tender in this world that we use for exchange of goods and services. Faith becomes the tender, or the substance, of things hoped for, and the evidence of things not seen. "By it the elders obtained a good report" (Heb. 11:1-2).

"Through faith we understand that the worlds were framed by the word of God, so that things which are seen were not made of things which do appear" (Heb. 11:3). The invisible became visible and was manifested. God wants us to understand that just because we can't see it, doesn't mean that He won't do it. What God wants to do in us begins as a word that gets in the spirit. Everything that is tangible started as an intangible. It was a dream, a thought, a word of God. In the same way, what man has invented began as a concept in someone's mind. So just because we don't see it, doesn't mean we won't get it.

There is a progression in the characters mentioned in this chapter of Hebrews. Abel worshiped God by faith. Enoch walked with God by faith. You can't walk with God until you worship God. The first calling is to learn how to worship God. When you learn how to worship God, then you can develop a walk with God. Stop trying to get people to walk with God who won't worship. If you don't love Him enough to worship, you'll never be able to walk with Him. If you can worship like Abel, then you can walk like Enoch.

Enoch walked and by faith Noah worked with God. You can't work with God until you walk with God. You can't walk with God until you worship God. If you can worship like Abel, then you can walk like Enoch. And if you walk like Enoch, then you can work like Noah.

> *Just because we don't see it, doesn't mean we won't get it.*

Henceforth there is laid up for me a crown of righteousness, which the Lord, the righteous judge, shall give me at that day: and not to me only, but unto all them also that love His appearing. 2 Timothy 4:8

Imagine me, nearly six-foot-three-inches tall and the better part of 280 pounds, sleeping in a canopied bed designed for a ten-year-old girl with ribbons in her hair. I still break out into hysterical laughter as I picture myself sticking one extremity after the other out of the bed, trying to find a place to sleep! Now, I normally have excellent accommodations—though I admit that coming from my background, excellent accommodations can still mean a private room with a bed that can hold all my vital organs!...In spite of all this improvement, on occasion I still seek to leave the well-insulated environment of a first-class establishment. I'll go find a little, "do drop in" kind of a place and then return to my suite with some down-home food and probably more grease than I could jog off in a year!

Balance helps to keep you from falling. It does not guarantee that you won't fall, but it does safeguard against the possibility. Never lose your balance—it will assist you in being a person and not just a personality....Ordinary people who have extraordinary callings are the order of the day in this age. You will see in this age God raising Davids to the forefront, not Sauls. He will raise up men who don't look as if they would be kings. When you get your crown, don't use it to belittle people who need you. Instead cast it at the feet of the Lord who is the Giver of gifts as well as the preferred Prize of all that He gives.

Finally, the disciples asked the Lord to teach them how to pray. They had noticed that prayer was the helm that turned the ship toward the winds of destiny. They had noticed that Jesus periodically would disappear from the crowd. He would steal away and fill His arms with the presence of His Father embracing Him so He could affect the people and us later. They asked Him when they learned that the secret weapon of public success was just plain old prayer. It is not books, tapes, or videos; just groanings and moanings into the incense-filled altars of Heaven. Since Jesus had taught on everything else, they decided to ask Him to teach them how to pray.

> When you get your crown, don't use it to belittle people who need you.

He hath made every thing beautiful in His time: also He hath set the world in their heart, so that no man can find out the work that God maketh from the beginning to the end. Ecclesiastes 3:11

"But without faith it is impossible to please Him: for he that cometh to God must believe that He is, and that He is a rewarder of them that diligently seek Him" (Heb. 11:6). God will reward those who persevere in seeking Him. He may not come when you want Him to, but He will be right on time. If you will wait on the Lord, He will strengthen your heart. He will heal you and deliver you. He will lift you up and break those chains. God's power will loose the bands from around your neck. He will give you "the garment of praise for the spirit of heaviness" (Isa. 61:3).

Abraham was a great man of faith. The writer of Hebrews mentions many areas of Abraham's faith. Abraham looked for a city whose "builder and maker" was God (Heb. 11:10). However, he is not listed in the faith "hall of fame" as the one who produced Isaac. If Abraham was famous for anything, it should have been for producing Isaac. However, he is not applauded for that.

"Through faith also Sarah herself received strength to conceive seed, and was delivered of a child when she was past age, because she judged Him faithful who had promised" (Heb. 11:11). When it comes to bringing forth the baby, the Scriptures do not refer to a man; they refer to a womb-man.

Sarah needed strength to conceive seed when she was past childbearing age. God met her need. She believed that He was capable of giving her a child regardless of what the circumstances looked like. From a natural perspective, it was impossible. The enemy certainly didn't want it to happen. God, however, performed His promise.

> He may not come when you want Him to, but He will be right on time.

Lord, Thou hast heard the desire of the humble: Thou wilt prepare their heart, Thou wilt cause Thine ear to hear. Psalm 10:17

Why would you allow your vision to be incapacitated for the lack of a man? Many women have unbelieving husbands at home. Have faith for yourself. Be a womb-man. It doesn't matter whether someone else believes or not; you cling to the truth that He is doing a good work in you.

> *Being confident of this very thing, that He which hath begun a good work in you will perform it until the day of Jesus Christ (Philippians 1:6).*

Each of us needs our own walk with God. Stand back and thank God. Believe God and know that He is able to do it. Sarah didn't stand on her husband's faith; she stood on her own.

You are God's woman. You are not called to sit by the window waiting on God to send you a husband. You had better have some faith yourself and believe God down in your own spirit. If you would believe God, He would perform His Word in your life. No matter the desire or the blessing that you seek, God has promised to give you the desires of your heart.

> *Delight thyself also in the Lord; and He shall give thee the desires of thine heart (Psalm 37:4).*

Recognize that where life has seemed irrational and out of control, He will turn it around. When trouble was breaking loose in my life, and I thought I couldn't take it anymore, God intervened and broke every chain that held me back. He will do no less for you.

> *No matter the desire or the blessing that you seek, God has promised to give you the desires of your heart.*

After this manner therefore pray ye: Our Father which art in heaven, hallowed be Thy name. Thy kingdom come. Thy will be done in earth, as it is in heaven. Give us this day our daily bread. And forgive us our debts, as we forgive our debtors. And lead us not into temptation, but deliver us from evil: For Thine is the kingdom, and the power, and the glory, for ever. Amen. Matthew 6:9-13

When Jesus taught on prayer, He was teaching us how to steer the ship of life through the boisterous winds of adversity. If we can follow the "manner" of prayer, then we can follow the course of life. In order to pray effectively, we must know the personage of God. Hence He said, "Our Father." This establishes the basis of the relationship that we have with God. He is more than just Creator. He is our Father. We can create something and not be related to it, but if we father it, a part of us will always be in the things we father. So I must know that I am related to God and not just created by Him.

"Which art in heaven" addresses the fact that the God I am related to is the Ruler of the universe. He sits on the circle of the earth. The Bible teaches us that Heaven is God's throne. So when we say, "which art in heaven," we are proclaiming the absolute sovereignty of our Father. We say, in effect, "Not only are You my Father, but You also are uniquely qualified to answer my prayer. You are related to me and empowered to perform." This phrase points directly to God's position. Now knowing the person and the position of Him, let us praise Him.

"I am not ashamed to praise You as I know the extent of Your authority. I take this time to approach You correctly. 'Hallowed be Thy name.' I almost forgot that just because You are my Father, my 'Abba,' that doesn't give me the right to show disrespect for Your position as Ruler in Heaven and earth. So 'hallowed be Thy name' reminds me that I must enter into Your gates with thanksgiving and into Your courts with praise." (See Psalm 100:4.) Praise will turn God's head. It will get His attention. I dare you to learn how to praise His name. When you praise His name, you are praising His character. He is "above board." He is holy!

> *If we can follow the "manner" of prayer, then we can follow the course of life.*

And they that be wise shall shine as the brightness of the firmament; and they that turn many to righteousness as the stars for ever and ever. Daniel 12:3

Abraham had many promises from God regarding his descendants. God told Abraham that his seed would be as the sands of the sea and the stars of Heaven.

That in blessing I will bless thee, and in multiplying I will multiply thy seed as the stars of the heaven, and as the sand which is upon the sea shore; and thy seed shall possess the gate of his enemies (Genesis 22:17).

There were two promises of seed given to Abraham. God said his seed would be as the sands of the earth. That promise represents the natural, physical nation of Israel. These were the people of the Old Covenant. However, God didn't stop there. He also promised that Abraham's seed would be as the stars of Heaven. These are the people of the New Covenant, the exalted people. That's the Church. We are exalted in Christ Jesus. We too are seed of Abraham. We are the stars of Heaven.

God had more plans for Abraham's descendants than to simply start a new nation on earth. He planned a new spiritual Kingdom that will last forever. The plan started as a seed, but it ended up as stars.

The only thing between the seed and the stars was the woman. Can you see why Sarah herself had to receive strength to conceive a seed when she was past childbearing age? Because the old man gave her a seed, she gave him the stars of Heaven. Whatever God gives you, He wants it to be multiplied in the womb of your spirit. When you bring it forth, it shall be greater than the former.

> Whatever God gives you, He wants it to be multiplied in the womb of your spirit.

Not unto us, O Lord, not unto us, but unto Thy name give glory, for Thy mercy, and for Thy truth's sake. Psalm 115:1

"Thy kingdom come" releases the downpour of the power of God. Praise will cause the very power of God to come down in your life. But what good is power without purpose? Thus Jesus taught the disciples, "Thy will be done in earth, as it is in heaven." That is a step up from power to purpose. Now the purpose of God comes down to your life....You can't have success without purpose!

"Give us this day our daily bread" deals with the provisions of Heaven coming down. This is more than a prayer; it is a divine direction. After receiving the power in your life, you come to understand the purpose. Never fear; if you know your purpose, God will release the provisions....

There's nothing like provisions to give you the grace to forgive. It is easier to forgive when you discover that your enemies didn't stop the blessing from coming down. Here Jesus teaches His disciples to pray for the penitence of a forgiving heart. "Forgive us our debts, as we forgive our debtors."...Finally, Jesus taught us to seek deliverance from evil. Pray for the problems that still exist at every stage, and better still, at every success in life!...

There must come in every person's life a turning point....At this stage of life you begin to reevaluate what you call success. God gets the glory when He can give you anything and you can turn from all He gave you and still say from your heart, "Lord, I've found nothing as dear to me as You. My greatest treasure is the assurance of Your divine presence on my life. I am giving it all to You. 'For Thine is the kingdom,'—yes, I know I just prayed it down, but here it is. I am giving it back to You. Wait a minute, Lord. I want to say something else. 'And the power.' You can have that too. Oh, and about all that glory I've been getting—it's Yours as well! What? You want to know how long? Forever and ever and ever. It is so!

> *A*t this stage of life you begin to reevaluate what you call success.

UNAFRAID

Yea, though I walk through the valley of the shadow of death, I will fear no evil: for Thou art with me; Thy rod and Thy staff they comfort me. Psalm 23:4

The enemy wants to multiply fear in your life. He wants you to become so afraid that you won't be able to figure out what you fear. You may be frightened to live in your own home. Some are afraid to correct their children. Some people fear standing up in front of others. Intimidated and afraid, many do not deliver a prophecy. God wants to set you free from fear as you are filled with faith.

In order to move forward, we must be willing to give up yesterday and go on toward tomorrow. We have to trust God enough to allow Him to come in and plow up our lives. Perhaps He needs to root out closet skeletons and replace them with new attitudes.

Sometimes women are so accustomed to being hurt that if anyone comes near them, they become defensive. Some may look tough and angry toward men, but God knows that behind that tough act, you are simply afraid. God deals directly with the issues of the heart and lets you know you do not have to be afraid. The plans of God are good. He is not like the people who have hurt and abused you. He wants only to help you be completely restored.

The enemy chains us to the circumstances of the past to keep us from reaching our potential. Satan has assigned fear to block up your womb. It blocks up your womb and causes you to be less productive than you like. He wants to destroy the spirit of creativity within you. God wants you to know that you have nothing to fear. You can be creative. He will make you into the womb-man that He wants you to be.

> **God wants you to know that you have nothing to fear.**

He that hath an ear, let him hear what the Spirit saith unto the churches. Revelation 2:29

Every aspect of creation that receives anything, gives it back to God....The mineral kingdom gives strength to the vegetable kingdom. The vegetable kingdom is consumed by the animal kingdom. Everything reaches the point of return....

Near my home, crouched in the valley beneath the proud swelling mountains of West Virginia, runs a river whose rushing waters cannot be contained. The Elk River cannot keep receiving the cascading streams of water from the ground in the mountains without finally pushing its blessing on into the Kanawha River. This river, though larger, is no less able to break the laws of the kingdom. It drinks in the waters from its sources and then turns its attention to its destiny and gives back its waters to the system. So the mighty Ohio says Amen. From the Ohio to the Mississippi and on into the Gulf of Mexico, each body of water receives only to give. You see, my friend, success is not success without a successor.

We as Christians reach fulfillment when we come to the point where we bring to the Lord all that we have and worship Him on the other side of accomplishment. This need to return an answer to the Sender is as instinctive as answering a ringing telephone. There is a ringing in the heart of a believer that requires an answer. Why do we answer a phone? We do so because of our insatiable curiosity to know who is calling. He is calling us. His ring has sounded through our triumphs and conquests. A deep sound in the recesses of a heart turned toward God suggests that there is a deeper relationship on the other side of the blessing. As wonderful as it is to be blessed with promises, there is still a faint ringing that suggests the Blesser is better than the blessing. It is a ringing that many people overlook. The noise of the bustling, blaring sound of survival can be deafening. There must be a degree of spirituality in order to hear and respond to the inner ringing of the call of God!

> There is a ringing in the heart of a believer that requires an answer.

The Lord openeth the eyes of the blind: the Lord raiseth them that are bowed down: the Lord loveth the righteous. Psalm 146:8

Maybe you have been tormented and in pain. You have been upset. You have been frustrated. It is hindering your walk. God is releasing you from fear. "For God hath not given us the spirit of fear; but of power, and of love, and of a sound mind" (2 Tim. 1:7). You need to allow Him an opportunity in your life. Then you will start seeing beauty at all different stages of your life. Maybe you have been afraid of aging. God will give you the strength to thank Him for every year.

Although we must be careful not to become trapped by the past, we should look back and thank God for how He has kept us through the struggles. If you're like me, you will want to say, "I would never have made it if You had not brought me through." Celebrate who you have become through His assistance. In every circumstance, rejoice that He was with you in it.

I believe God is bringing health into dry bones, bones that were bowed over, bones that were bent out of shape, bones that made you upset with yourself. All are giving way to the life of the Spirit. Perhaps you responded to your history with low self-esteem. God will heal the inner wound and teach you how important you are to Him. You do make a difference. The world would be a different place if it were not for you. You are a part of His divine plan.

> God is bringing health into dry bones, bones that were bowed over, bones that were bent out of shape, bones that made you upset with yourself.

We are of God. He who knows God hears us; he who is not of God does not hear us. 1 John 4:6 (NKJ)

I can think of no better illustration of this concept than the ten lepers in the Bible (see Luke 17:11-19). These ten distraught, grossly afflicted men were entombed by the prison of their own limitations. No matter who they were before, now they were lepers. Like bad apples, they were separated and cast out from friends and family. They were denied the feeling of warmth, love, and intimacy. Like all alienated groups, their only refuge was in each other's company. Pain brings together strange bedfellows. Ten men huddled together on the side of the road heard that Jesus was passing by. The most frightening thing that could happen in any hurting person's life is for Jesus to just pass by. These men, however, seized the moment. They took a risk…they cried out to Him. Desperate people do desperate things. Have you ever had a moment in your life that pushed you into a radical decision? These lepers cried out!

No one can hear like the Lord does. He can hear your thoughts afar off (see Ps. 139:2), so you know He can hear the desperate cry of someone who has nothing left to lose. When the ten cried, He responded. There were no sparks, no lightning, and no thunder, but the power of His words whisked them off into the realm of miracles. He told them to go show themselves to the priest. Thus they walked toward a goal. Step by step they walked. I don't know which dusty step it was along the way that brought to them a cleansing of their leprous condition. Perhaps, as with most people, it is no one step that brings you to success, but a relentless plowing through of obstacles and insecurities that brings the result of prayers answered and miracles realized.

Nevertheless, somewhere between Jesus' words and their going to the priest, they stepped into the greatest experience of their lives. Where there had been white, oozing, encrusted flesh, there was new skin as clear as a baby's. That is the wonderful thing about knowing Jesus—He takes away the old ugly scars of sin and leaves newness and fresh beginnings.

> *He can hear the desperate cry of someone who has nothing left to lose.*

And such were some of you: but ye are washed, but ye are sanctified, but ye are justified in the name of the Lord Jesus, and by the Spirit of our God. 1 Corinthians 6:11

When the angel came to Mary and told her what God was going to do in her life, Mary questioned how it could be possible (see Luke 1:34). Perhaps God has been telling you things He wants to do in your life, but you have questioned Him. Perhaps your circumstance does not seem to allow you to accomplish much. Maybe you lack the strength to accomplish the task alone. Perhaps, like Mary, you are thinking only in the natural and that you must have a man to do God's will.

And the angel answered and said unto her, The Holy Ghost shall come upon thee, and the power of the Highest shall overshadow thee: therefore also that Holy Thing which shall be born of thee shall be called the Son of God (Luke 1:35).

If you have been wondering how God will make things come to pass in your life, remember that He will accomplish the task. No man will get the credit for your deliverance. He told Mary, "The Holy Ghost shall come upon thee." I believe the same is true of godly women today. The Holy Spirit will fill you. He will impregnate you. He will give life to your spirit. He will put purpose back into you. He will renew you. He will restore you.

God had a special plan for Mary. She brought forth Jesus. He has a special plan for us. We, however, aren't privileged to see the future. We don't know what kind of good things He has in store for us. But, He has a plan. God's women are to be womb-men. They are to be creative and bring forth new life. That is exactly what God wants to do with those who are broken and discouraged.

No man will get the credit for your deliverance.

And one of them, when he saw that he was healed, turned back, and with a loud voice glorified God, and fell down on his face at His feet, giving Him thanks: and he was a Samaritan. And Jesus answering said, Were there not ten cleansed? but where are the nine? There are not found that returned to give glory to God, save this stranger. And He said unto him, Arise, go thy way: thy faith hath made thee whole. Luke 17:15-19

Ten men walked like hikers on the side of the road with nothing but a word from God. They were changed while in the process of obeying the command of a Savior whom they had called out to a few miles back on the dusty road where all miracles are walked out. Peeking beneath their clothes, checking spots that had once been afflicted, they laughed in the wind as the reality of their deliverance became even more real with every step they took. There is no success like the success of a man who had to persevere in order to receive it. People appreciate the victory when they have to walk it out.

Beneath the clutter of their weary footsteps, God performed a miracle. Their healing meant much more than just a physical healing of leprosy. When Jesus healed them, He gave them back their dignity. He restored their potential to marry. He gave them back to their community. Thus success affects every area of life....But one man grew silent as his mind drifted beyond his own personal glee. For him there was something missing. It wasn't that he lacked appreciation for his healing; it was just a nagging feeling that this great moment was somehow incomplete. He had been told to go show himself to the priest. But perhaps the real priest was not in front of him, but behind him.

As his nine friends laughed and celebrated their victory, he began to lag behind. In the shadows of his mind lurked the figure of the Man on the road who spoke that word of healing. Why was he so discontented with what the other men seemed to be satisfied? After all, had not the Man sent them on their way? He pivoted on his heels like a soldier who had heard a command. He had an impulse, a pulling toward something beyond personal allurement. He decided to return to the Sender. The Sender seemed to be satisfied, but it was the former leper who wanted something more. He traveled back to the Sender, Jesus, the Miracle Worker.

> *People appreciate the victory when they have to walk it out.*

For we are His workmanship, created in Christ Jesus unto good works, which God hath before ordained that we should walk in them. Ephesians 2:10

If great things came from those who never suffered, we might think that they accomplished those things of their own accord. When a broken person submits to God, God gets the glory for the wonderful things He accomplishes—no matter how far that person has fallen. The anointing of God will restore you and make you accomplish great and noble things. Believe it!

The hidden Christ that's been locked up behind your fears, your problems and your insecurity, will come forth in your life. You will see the power of the Lord Jesus do a mighty thing.

After the angel told Mary those words, do you know what she said? "And Mary said, Behold the handmaid of the Lord; be it unto me according to thy word. And the angel departed from her" (Luke 1:38). "Be it unto me according to thy word." Not according to my marital status. Not according to my job. Not according to what I deserve. "Be it unto me according to thy word."

Mary knew enough to believe God and to submit to Him. She was taking an extreme risk. To be pregnant and unmarried brought dire consequences in those days. Yet she willingly gave herself over to the Lord.

Mary had a cousin named Elizabeth who was already expecting a child. The child in Elizabeth's womb was to be the forerunner of the Messiah. The two women came together to share their stories. When Elizabeth found a woman who would build her up, the Bible says that the baby leaped in her womb and she was "filled with the Holy Ghost" (Luke 1:41).

> The anointing of God will restore you and make you accomplish great and noble things.

If ye then, being evil, know how to give good gifts unto your children, how much more shall your Father which is in heaven give good things to them that ask Him? Matthew 7:11

Jesus healed ten lepers and only one returned to Him (see Luke 17:11-19). When he came to Jesus, he fell down at His feet and worshiped Him. Then Jesus asked a question. It's seldom that Jesus, the omniscient One, would ask anything-but this time He had a question. I shall never forget the pointedness of His question. He asked the one who returned, "Where are the nine?"

Every good gift and every perfect gift is from above, and cometh down from the Father of lights, with whom is no variableness, neither shadow of turning (James 1:17).

Perhaps you are the one in ten who has the discernment to know that this blessing is nothing without the One who caused it all to happen. Most people are so concerned about their immediate needs that they fail to take the powerful experience that comes from a continued relationship with God! This is for the person who goes back to the Sender of gifts with the power of praise. Ten men were healed, but to the one who returned Jesus added the privilege of being whole. Many will climb the corporate ladder. Some will claim the accolades of this world. But soon all will realize that success, even with all its glamour, cannot heal a parched soul that needs the refreshment of a change of peace. Nothing can bring wholeness like the presence of a God who lingers on the road where He first blessed you to see if there is anything in you that would return you from the temporal to embrace the eternal.

Remember, healing can be found anywhere, but wholeness is achieved only when you go back to the Sender with all of your heart and thank Him for the miracle of a second chance. Whatever you do, don't forget your roots. When you can't go anywhere else, my friend, remember you can go home!

> Healing can be found anywhere, but wholeness is achieved only when you go back to the Sender.

Therefore if any man be in Christ, he is a new creature: old things are passed away; behold, all things are become new. 2 Corinthians 5:17

The anointing of God will restore you and make you accomplish great and noble things. The hidden Christ that's been locked up behind your fears, your problems and your insecurity, will come forth in your life. You will see the power of the Lord Jesus do a mighty thing....

The things you had stopped believing God for will start leaping in your spirit again. God will renew you. Often women have been working against each other, but God will bring you together. You will come together like Mary and Elizabeth. You will cause your babies to leap in your womb, and the power of the Lord Jesus will do a new thing in your life. The Holy Ghost will come upon you and restore you.

If you are a woman who has had a dream, and sensed a promise, reach out to Him. Every woman who knows that they have another woman inside them who hasn't come forth can reach their hearts toward God and He will meet those inner needs and cause them to live at their potential. He will restore what was stolen by your suffering and abuse. He will take back from the enemy what was swallowed up in your history.

He wants to bring you together, sisters. Every Mary needs an Elizabeth. He needs to bring you together. Stop your wars and fighting. Drop your guns. Throw down your swords. Put away your shields. God put something in your sister that you need. When you come together, powerful things will happen.

Satan attempts to keep us from our potential. He allows and causes horrible things to happen in lives so those lives will take on a different outlook. The fear of abuse can be removed only by the power of the Holy Spirit. There is great potential in women who believe. That potential may be locked up at times because of ruined histories. God will wipe the slate clean. He will likely use others to help in the process, but it is His anointing that will bring forth new life from deep within.

God will wipe the slate clean.

So the man gave names to all the livestock, the birds of the air and all the beasts of the field. But for Adam no suitable helper was found. Genesis 2:20 (NIV)

Attractions are allurements that can be based on memories, past experiences, and early associations. It is therefore very difficult to explain the extremely sensitive and fragile feelings that cause us to be attracted. Suffice it to say that we are instinctively attracted to inner needs. That attraction may be based upon a need to be with someone whom we think is attractive, which creates within us a certain validation of our own worth, or the attraction may be based on a deeper, less physical value. Either way, need is the fuel that spawns attraction. Opinions on what characteristics are attractive vary from person to person.

Most of us have had the unfortunate experience of being the victim of some matchmaking friend who inappropriately sets us up with someone who doesn't quite fit the bill. The blind date can be a terribly embarrassing situation. It is very difficult for even our close friends to predict who will attract us. I can remember contemplating the decision to marry. I sought the counsel of a very close friend. My friend told me, "I can't choose who will make you a good wife. Choosing a wife is one of the most personal decisions you will ever have to make—far too personal to accept the advice of people who will not have to live with the decision." Our friendship is still intact, and so is my marriage. Thank God for wise counsel.

Attractions, for many people, can be as deadly as a net to a fish. Seemingly, they can't see that the net is a trap until it is too late. They struggle, trying to get away, but the more they struggle, the more entangled they become....The key is not to struggle with the thing or the person. The deliverance comes from within and not from without. God is far too wise to put your deliverance into the hands of someone or something that may not have any compassion for you. The victory is won within the battleground of your mind, and its memories and needs.

> Choosing a wife is one of the most personal decisions you will ever have to make—far too personal to accept the advice of people who will not have to live with the decision.

O Pain No Gain

To whom also He showed Himself alive after His passion by many infallible proofs, being seen of them forty days, and speaking of the things pertaining to the kingdom of God. Acts 1:3

Perhaps it is no coincidence that the Greek word *pathos*, usually translated as "suffer" or "to feel," is used here to describe Christ's crucifixion. What a strange choice of expression for such a hideous occurrence. Yet it alludes to a deeper truth that each of us must face. Although the inference is toward His suffering, look a little deeper beneath the sufferings that He experienced and understand that there was an underlying ecstasy beneath the pain of the cross. The writer of Hebrews alludes to it as he lifts the veil and peeks behind the crisis of the cross and reports the purpose of the cross.

> *Looking unto Jesus the author and finisher of our faith; who for the joy that was set before Him endured the cross, despising the shame, and is set down at the right hand of the throne of God (Hebrews 12:2).*

The cliché, "No pain no gain," suggests that gain validates the pain we incur. That is only true for the person who has opened up and allowed himself to want or need something bad enough to endure the unpleasantness attached to attaining his goal. The problem with most people is that they stand around like dreamers, gazing into the night at distant stars instead of working in the day to build a ship to reach the stars. Regardless of how far away the goal may seem, if there is a real passion for it, we can accomplish much in His name.

Here lies the reality of fulfillment. There can be no fulfillment where there is no passion. The passion that causes us to achieve has to be strong enough to make us uncomfortable. The discomfort that comes from the desire must be intense enough to keep the obstacles between you and the thing you desire from aborting the intensity of your desire! Simply stated, you must want it bad enough to survive the process required to attain it.

*S*imply stated, you must want it bad enough to survive the process required to attain it.

She shall be called Woman, because she was taken out of Man. Genesis 2:23b

So the Lord God caused the man to fall into a deep sleep; and while he was sleeping, He took one of the man's ribs and closed up the place with flesh. Then the Lord God made a woman from the rib he had taken out of the man, and He brought her to the man (Genesis 2:21-22 NIV).

The first female mentioned in the Bible was created mature, without a childhood or an example to define her role and relationship to her husband. The first female was created a woman while Adam was asleep. That the Lord "brought her to the man" is the first hint of marriage. I believe it would be better if we still allowed God to bring to us what He has for us. The only biblical evolution I can find is the woman, who evolved out of man. She is God's gift to man. When God wanted to be praised, He created man in His own likeness and in His image. Likewise, God gave man someone like himself. Adam said that she is "bone of my bones, and flesh of my flesh" (Gen. 2:23). His attraction to her was her likeness to him. He called her "womb man" or woman. Like the Church of Christ, Eve was his body and his bride.

For no man ever yet hated his own flesh; but nourisheth and cherisheth it, even as the Lord the church: for we are members of His body, of His flesh, and of His bones. For this cause shall a man leave his father and mother, and shall be joined unto his wife, and they two shall be one flesh. This is a great mystery: but I speak concerning Christ and the church (Ephesians 5:29-32).

The only biblical evolution I can find is the woman, who evolved out of man.

And God said, "Let the land produce living creatures according to their kinds: livestock, creatures that move along the ground, and wild animals, each according to its kind." And it was so. God made the wild animals according to their kinds, the livestock according to their kinds, and all the creatures that move along the ground according to their kinds. And God saw that it was good. Genesis 1:24-25 (NIV)

My children have a remote control toy car. The remote is designed so the car can be controlled even from a distance. The reason we can manipulate the car by an external item is the small apparatus inside the car that is affected by the remote control. If we remove the inner apparatus, the remote will not work. It is the same way with attractions. They evolve and manipulate us only because there is some inner apparatus that makes us vulnerable to them. If the wrong person, place, or thing controls our remote, we are in trouble. We may not be able to stop the person from playing with the buttons, but we can remove the inner apparatus.

We are communal by nature; we have a strong need for community and relationships. However, whatever we are in relationship with, we also are related to. It is important that we do not covenant with someone or something with which we are not really related. Every living being was created to pursue and cohabit with its own kind. I emphasize *kind*. There should be an agreement in species to achieve maximum compatibility. For instance, most men are incompatible with ducks. Right? ...

Hence, we are forbidden from seeking intimacy, which is a legitimate need, from an inappropriate source. This is a biological law that governs biological order. If we break this law, we produce grossly disfigured, badly deranged, terribly mutated species that would give the normal mind nightmares. Whether or not a man is Christian, this law is still in effect. He can break it, but its penalties would be incomprehensible. What was introduced in the shadow of Old Testament theology as a biological law is magnified in the New Testament as a spiritual reality. In the Old Testament, each creature was mandated to bond with its own species. In the New Testament, the believer is commanded not to seek companionship outside the sanctity of the Church. Why? The Church is a species separate from any other, a species of which Christ is the firstborn.

> *Every living being was created to pursue and cohabit with its own kind. I emphasize kind.*

But now they desire a better country, that is, an heavenly: wherefore God is not ashamed to be called their God: for He hath prepared for them a city. Hebrews 11:16

There can be no fulfillment where there is no passion. The passion that causes us to achieve has to be strong enough to make us uncomfortable. The discomfort that comes from the desire must be intense enough to keep the obstacles between you and the thing you desire from aborting the intensity of your desire! Simply stated, you must want it bad enough to survive the process required to attain it. It doesn't matter whether it is a good marriage, a ministry, a business, or whatever. There will always be hindrances to overcome. It is the force of your personal passion to achieve that gives you the force to break down the wall between you and the thing you desire.

Jesus, our prime example of success, had a cross between Him and His goal. The cross was not the end; it was the means. He didn't enjoy the means, but He endured it—His passion was for the end. What gave Him the power to endure His means to achieve the end? It was His passion.

The desire that burns and inflames your heart, the desire that is forever in your thoughts, becomes the fuel that enables you to withstand whatever life sends against you. His suffering was for the sins of this world. It was more than groping in the gross darkness of a feverish death. It was the suffering of the passionate!

There is an intense discomfort associated with passion and desire. It is not pleasant; it is, in fact, *suffering*. It is an intense, unquenched desire that gnaws at the fibers of our minds, motivating us to actions of fulfillment. Have you ever noticed that God mightily uses some of the most wretched sinners whom He converted into great ministers? It is because these characters were people who were accustomed to passion and acquisition. They were people who dared to desire. They were people who, although misdirected at one time, possessed such a burning passion that, if bridled and directed, could make them people of great accomplishment.

> The desire that burns and inflames your heart...becomes the fuel that enables you to withstand whatever life sends against you.

But from the beginning of the creation God made them male and female. For this cause shall a man leave his father and mother, and cleave to his wife. Mark 10:6-7

Man and woman were made of the same material. Adam says, "She is bone of my bone." He says nothing of her size, body build or hair color. These superficial components are like placing a product in an attractive container. The container may get the consumer to try it. But only the product will keep the consumer coming back. His attraction goes much deeper than externals. These outward attractions are certainly an advantage, but be assured that when it comes to marriage, no one ever stayed together simply because they were attractive. I don't know whether I agree with those who say there is only one person in the world for you. I would be afraid that, out of the billions of people on this planet, I wouldn't be able to find them. However, I do know that when you find a person with whom you are compatible, there is a bonding that consummates marriage and that has nothing to do with sex. I also understand how you could feel this person to be the only choice in the world. Let's face it, everyone you meet isn't bone of your bone! It is so important that you do not allow anyone to manipulate you into choosing someone with whom you have no bond. When Ezekiel speaks about the dry bones in the valley, he says, "The bones came together, bone to his bone" (Ezek. 37:7). Every person must pray and discern if the other is someone they could cleave to the rest of their life.

The term *cleave* is translated from the Hebrew word *debaq*. It means "to impinge, cling or adhere to; figuratively, to catch by pursuit or follow close after." There is a great need in most of our lives to cleave, to feel that this is where we belong. It is sad to realize our society has become so promiscuous that many have mistaken the thrill of a weekend fling for a knitting together of two thirsty hearts at the oasis of a loving commitment.

There is a great need in most of our lives to cleave, to feel that this is where we belong.

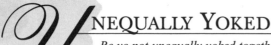
Be ye not unequally yoked together with unbelievers: for what fellowship hath righteousness with unrighteousness? and what communion hath light with darkness? 2 Corinthians 6:14

Therefore, if anyone is in Christ, he is a new creation; the old has gone, the new has come! (2 Corinthians 5:17 NIV)

We believers also are told in Second Corinthians 6:14 not to be unequally yoked with unbelievers. We are twice-born people; we are born and then born again. Now, it is not biologically illegal for us to bond with unbelievers; it is spiritually illegal. In the sight of God, yoking ourselves with unbelievers is spiritual necrophilia—having intimate relationships with the dead! To be a sinner is to be dead in sin!

And you hath He quickened, who were dead in trespasses and sins (Ephesians 2:1).

As physical death is separation of the spirit and the body, so spiritual death, the state sinners are in, is the spirit of man separated from relationship with his Creator. Like Adam, he is hiding in the bushes of sin and covering himself with the fig leaves of excuses. This verse in Ephesians refers to the fact that sin is in itself a type of deadness of spirit. In the Scriptures, death doesn't mean the cessation of life. It clearly means separation. When a person dies physically, it is not the end of life; it is merely the separation of the body from the spirit. That's why James wrote, "Even so faith, if it hath not works, is dead, being alone" (James 2:17). The Book of Revelation also refers to eternal damnation as the second death! (See Revelation 21:8.) It is called the second death not because existence or consciousness ends, but because it pronounces eternal separation from God. Without debating your concepts of hell, I am sure you would agree that eternity without God is a type of hell in itself. That is what the Book of Revelation calls the second death. It is eternal separation from the presence of God. It is the final step of sin. Sin is separation of relationship with God, but the second death is separation from the presence of God!

*N*ow, it is not biologically illegal for us to bond with unbelievers; it is spiritually illegal.

Delight thyself also in the Lord; and He shall give thee the desires of thine heart.
Commit thy way unto the Lord; trust also in Him; and He shall bring it to pass.
Psalm 37:4-5

Oh, thou man or woman of great passion, driven by intense feelings and desire, you often wrestle with your ambitious nature. Hear me and hear me well: You don't want to kill your passion; you just need to redirect it toward a godly vision. That is why satan has desired to have you. He knows that if you ever line up your passion with God's purpose, you will become a spiritual dynamo. Then there will be no stopping you until the flames of your passion are quenched in the streams of your eternal destiny!

Do not resent your passion. Control it, yes, but please don't kill it. Without it, you would be as limp as an overcooked noodle, your life as bland as hospital food. God created you to be zesty and alive! Even though you may have often misdirected your passions, allow God to recycle your feelings. Retrieve your passions from your dusty religious receptacle and place them in God's recycling program!

I realize that passions create suffering. Many people *cease to desire* just to relieve themselves of the pain and struggle of trying to attain their dreams. They become zombies trapped in an intermediate, lukewarm state of existence that is neither hot nor cold! Their lukewarm, placid philosophy causes them to sink into the abyss of mediocrity. They live, marry, buy cars, accumulate stocks, have children, and do everything that their living counterpart does—but without passion, they just basically *go through the motions*!

How sad it is to see them rise out of bed every morning, arms extended, humming a monotone melody of melancholy undertones. They grunt incoherent answers at others as though they are deeply medicated. These mummies may be mommies or daddies; they may even be preachers or teachers. *They are corpses who aren't quite dead.* Their nebulous state of affairs exempts them from pain, but denies them pleasure. Now they are safe from failure, but threatened by depression.

> *Do not resent your passion. Control it, yes, but please don't kill it.*

And they twain shall be one flesh: so then they are no more twain, but one flesh. Mark 10:8

If you are reading this book and are not married, as you pray and seek God for companionship, consider these issues carefully. Find ten couples who have been married 12 years or more. Look at their wedding album. You will see that many of them have drastically changed. Realize that if those initial impressions were all that held a marriage together, these would already be over. Certainly, you owe it to your spouse and yourself to be all that you can. Still, there is much more involved in marriage than the superficial.

Marriage is so personal that no one will be able to stand outside your relationship and see why you bond with that person. If you are married, understand that your spouse isn't running for office. He shouldn't have to meet the approval of all your family and friends. Do not expect everyone to see what you see in each other; to cleave is to stick together. Have you made the commitment to stay together? The secret to cleaving is leaving. "For this cause shall a man *leave* his father and mother…" (Mark 10:7). If you enter into marriage and still keep other options open, whether mental, emotional or physical, it will never work. When the tugging of adversity tries the bonds of your matrimony, you will fall apart. You must leave and cleave to your spouse. It is so unhealthy to cleave to someone other than your spouse for support. Now we all need wholesome friendships. However, none should have more influence over you than your spouse (after God). Some of you could save your marriages if you would leave some of these extra-marital ties and cleave to your companion!

> *Marriage is so personal that no one will be able to stand outside your relationship and see why you bond with that person.*

The thief cometh not, but for to steal, and to kill, and to destroy: I am come that they might have life, and that they might have it more abundantly. John 10:10

Let me make one final note about the spiritually dead, the sinners. They remind me of the bone-chilling horror movies we used to watch as children. Remember the sound of the wind sweeping through the trees? Then would come the shrill screeching of an old owl perched on a withered branch overlooking a poorly attended cemetery. Pushing through the soft, freshly turned soil, a hand emerged. By self-inflicted torturous tenacity, the corpse would exhume himself from the grave and stand up. I remember how in the sound track an old reedy organ would play a high note as on the screen appeared the bloody letters, "The Living Dead."

These zombies would walk the earth with their hands extended, always searching for but never attaining rest, leaving a trail of victims behind them. That's pretty ghoulish, but it is an accurate description of what sin is: "The Living Dead"! If you are an empty, brokenhearted person walking around always searching for things, for mere tokens of success, then I have a word from God for you. He says, "I am come that [you] might have life…" (John 10:10b). Accept Him today! Wake up from the nightmare of "The Living Dead" and become a living, loving testimony to the authenticity of the power of God!

When you are in sin, you reach after anything that will numb the pain and help you forget for a few minutes that something is missing. That doesn't work. It's God that's missing—a real relationship with Him. If you are missing Him, you can be reconciled to God at this very moment! The Bible makes the statement that you were dead in the trespass of sin (see Eph. 2:1). It teaches that you, as well as all of us, were separated from God because of sin. *But God* has reconciled His people to Himself. Being reunited with Him means I have life, and have it more abundantly (see John 10:10)….

This brings me to the fact that to be willfully disobedient and choose a companion who you know is dead in the trespasses of sin, is to be involved in spiritual necrophilia.…I am not referring to those who, while still a sinner, married another sinner, and then were converted.…No, I am concerned for the precious hearts who find themselves attracted to others who haven't had this born-again experience. The person who willingly chooses to ignore God's stop signs is bound to experience adversity.…It's not His will for the living to marry the dead!

> $\mathcal{B}$ecome a living, loving testimony to the authenticity of the power of God!

THE WINNING WAY

Day 284

Who can find a virtuous woman? for her price is far above rubies. Proverbs 31:10

Cleaving to your spouse is not always a matter of feelings. We use the following verse about other things, so why not about marriage? Romans 1:17 says, "For therein is the righteousness of God revealed from faith to faith: as it is written, The just shall live by faith." Believe God for your marriage! It will not be your feelings that heal your relationship; it will be your faith. Did you know that you cannot trust your own feelings? I counsel people all the time who sit with tears streaming down their weary faces and say, "I just can't trust him." I've got news for you. You can't trust yourself either! Your feelings will swing in and out. But your faith will not move. Cleaving implies that you don't want to get away. A marriage erodes like the banks of a river do—a little each day. There is a certain way a woman treats a man when she is fulfilled. It takes faith to treat a marriage that is frustrating with the same respect you would treat the prosperous relationship. I am simply saying many times you feel yourself holding back who you would like to be so you can maintain this strong exterior. Listen, do not allow another person to cause you to play a role that isn't really who you are. I realize that many of you may be in the middle of an awful relationship, but I can't counsel what I can't see. For specific needs, I recommend pastoral care and counseling. Nevertheless, I do want to warn you that suppressing the gentle side of you as a defense will not stop you from being hurt! If you suppress who you are, you will fall into depression! It is terrible to arrest who you are in an attempt to "fight fire with fire." The best way to fight fire is with water! The winning way of a woman is not in her words, it is in her character.

> The winning way of a woman is not in her words, it is in her character.

And that, knowing the time, that now it is high time to awake out of sleep: for now is our salvation nearer than when we believed. Romans 13:11

What good is life without living? *Taste it, live it*—even at the risk of occasional failure and adversity! If you are going to stand at the plate, then take a swing at the ball! "Suppose I miss?" you say. Well, I say, "Suppose you miss out, and you haven't even taken a swing?" Have you any passion to triumph? Your desire to protect yourself from further disappointment has placed you in a comatose state. Wake up and play! You are not dead! There may be many things about you that are dead, but you are not dead!

I feel like God is speaking to someone who has quit. No one knows you have quit, but inside, you have thrown in the towel and said, "I give." You wanted to make a difference, but since you ran into some obstacle, some cross, you decided to adjust your expectations to your limitations and just keep smiling!

You are wrong! I am blowing a trumpet loudly into your *rigor mortis*-ridden ear! *God has too much for you to do!* Arise, breathe deeply of this moment. There will never be another moment in your life like this one! I can't spare you tears, fears, or traumas; each passion has its "cross of validation." In fact, it is the cross that validates the enormity of the passion. *It is what you endure that expresses how deeply you desire.*

> *And unto the angel of the church in Sardis write; These things saith He that hath the seven Spirits of God, and the seven stars; I know thy works, that thou hast a name that thou livest, and art dead. Be watchful, and strengthen the things which remain, that are ready to die: for I have not found thy works perfect before God (Revelation 3:1-2).*

*Y*our desire to protect yourself from further disappointment has placed you in a comatose state.

The heart of her husband doth safely trust in her, so that he shall have no need of spoil.
Proverbs 31:11

Wives, in the same way be submissive to your husbands so that, if any of them do not believe the word, they may be won over without words by the behavior of their wives, when they see the purity and reverence of your lives (1 Peter 3:1-2 NIV).

For this is the way the holy women of the past who put their hope in God used to make themselves beautiful. They were submissive to their own husbands, like Sarah, who obeyed Abraham and called him her master. You are her daughters if you do what is right and do not give way to fear (1 Peter 3:5-6 NIV).

Recently, while teaching a seminar, a lady raised her hand and said, "I am a widow. I lost my husband and he died unsaved." She was obviously wrestling with grief as she spoke. She continued, "I claimed First Peter 3:1 and at the end of his life he still was not saved." I responded, "That scripture doesn't mean that the responsibility of getting the husband saved rests on the wife. It just says that a submissive, quiet woman creates an atmosphere so he may be won." I rebuked the condemning spirit of guilt and she worshiped God under the anointing of the Holy Spirit. This passage of Peter's is not given to abuse women; it is given to instruct them about what works well in the home. Faith is not loud and fleshly; it is quiet and spiritual. Believe me when I say it is effective. No one can do anything to make another person be saved. You can't make them come home. You can't make someone love you. But you can create an atmosphere where your conduct is not undermining your prayers!

> *You can't make someone love you. But you can create an atmosphere where your conduct is not undermining your prayers!*

Remember that at that time you were separate from Christ, excluded from citizenship in Israel and foreigners to the covenants of the promise, without hope and without God in the world. But now in Christ Jesus you who once were far away have been brought near through the blood of Christ. Ephesians 2:12-13 (NIV)

Consider someone who has lost a loved one. This person has lost someone whom he or she had once been connected to and involved with. Now the beloved has expired. Grief-ridden and upset, the one left behind wishes with all of his or her might to be with that person again. The acidic taste of despair fills his or her mouth and wrenches his or her face into a pain-filled expression....

How unthinkable it would be, for instance, for a grief-stricken widow to stay behind to spend one final night in trying to move those icy arms into an embrace. It would be difficult to excuse her actions just because she was in love with someone who had died. The real disgust is in thinking that she could be attracted to something so morbid. How could she find arousal in the crisp touch of a cold clay doll? Regardless of what the relationship was at one time, surely she would recognize that death changes the reality—not the memory, but certainly the reality.

Who would walk past a casket in a funeral home and wink at a corpse? The very idea wavers between being disgusting and hilarious! What type of mind could not grasp the fact that this is inappropriate behavior for intelligent human beings? No widower would take his deceased wife out for a final weekend of romance. Romancing a stone? I should think not!

If this whole idea is so terrible, and it is, then why would born-again Christians who have been made alive by the power of God, go back into their own past and rummage through the graveyard of circumstances that God says are dead and over with? Why continue to embrace what ought to be buried? Regardless of how alive the event was at the time, when God says it is dead, then it is dead! How strange it must be in the spirit world for you, a living soul, to be wrapped up with a dead issue you have not yet relinquished.

> **Why would born-again Christians who have been made alive by the power of God...rummage through the graveyard of circumstances that God says are dead and over with?**

...but by love serve one another. Galatians 5:13b

Women tend to be vocal while men tend to be physical. Women feel that everything needs to be discussed. Communication is crucial to a healthy relationship, it is just that men don't always talk with words. Men communicate through touch even in male to male relationships. A pat on the back, a two-handed handshake, means "I like you." Some think that men always communicate through sex. That isn't always the case. A coach playfully slaps a basketball player on the rump. He is not being sexual. He is saying, "Good job!" We must learn each other's method of communication. Instead of always feeling like you are neglected, ask your husband to share with you why he does what he does. Or better still, observe his method of communication and teach him yours. In all your getting, get understanding! It is terrible to be misunderstood! I am a giver. Whenever I feel affection, the first thing I want to do is buy a gift for my wife. I was shocked to find that although my wife will acknowledge the gifts, she will go into orbit over cards! To me this is insane! She keeps cards that are so old they've turned yellow. I read cards and enjoy them, but I seldom keep them. We spent the first few years of our marriage teaching each other our language.

Your spouse may really think he's telling you something that you keep complaining about not getting. He feels like "What more does she want? I told her that I married her. I did this and that and the other." You may be living in the Tower of Babel. That was the place where families divided because they could not understand each other's language. Sit down and learn each other's language before frustration turns your house into the Tower of Babel. At Babel all work ceased and arguing began. If you are arguing, it is because frustration exists between you. People who don't care don't argue. No one argues over what they would rather leave!

> $\mathcal{S}$it down and learn each other's language....

And it came to pass, when the time was come that He should be received up, He sted-fastly set His face to go to Jerusalem, Luke 9:51

Jesus suffered the loss of His disciples, His earthly ministry, His friends, and even His clothes. They cast lots at His bleeding feet for His seamless robe (see John 19:23-24), but they could not strip away His passion. Even while He was dying He continued to minister His message. He went through hell to reach the joy set before Him, but when He had finished (after His passion), He got up with the keys to death and hell! His trophies were the stinger snatched from death itself and victory yanked from the grave. His prize was a Church purchased by the blood He shed. But what is ultimately important is that He accomplished it with His passion.

For God so loved the world, that He gave His only begotten Son, that whosoever believeth in Him should not perish, but have everlasting life (John 3:16).

He "so loved" us. That's what He did on the cross; He "so loved" us. This passionate lover, whose Kingdom was not of this world, came to our world and, with unfeigned love, reached into the jaws of damnation and caught my falling soul. His love is exemplified in His coming, but it is consummated in His dying. In His living He betrothed us, but in His dying He procured us.

Jesus Christ, the greatest lover the world has ever known, gives Himself openly and unashamedly. He has found in the cross a mode of expression that becomes a picture of the magnitude of His love. His suffering was a by-product of His passion. His intense love for His ungodly creations led Him to three nails and one tree.

Where there is no passion, there simply is no power. I fear greatly that the enemy will attempt to either steal the passion or smother it beneath the fear of failure and rejection. If we exist without passion, we slump into a state of stagnation that hinders us from achieving the purpose of God in our lives.

> *H*is intense love for His ungodly creations led Him to three nails and one tree.

Likewise, ye wives, be in subjection to your own husbands; that, if any obey not the word, they also may without the word be won by the conversation of the wives. 1 Peter 3:1

Married women—when you approach your husband, do not corner him. Catch him at a time when he won't feel interrogated. You would be surprised at how men tend to avoid open confrontation. I have seen big burly macho men intimidated about telling their 100-hundred pound wives they are going to do something they fear she will not like. Even men who are physically abusive still have moments when they feel anxiety about facing their wives.

It is better to dwell in the corner of the housetop, than with a brawling woman and in a wide house (Proverbs 25:24).

It is better to dwell in the wilderness, than with a contentious and an angry woman (Proverbs 21:19).

Unless you are trying to drive him away, remember you could win the argument and still lose the man. Men's communication is different. I am not suggesting that men can't learn the communication method of their wives. I am merely saying that spouses must learn to appreciate each other's language. Remember, I briefly discussed faith for your marriage. Faith calls those things that are not as though they were.

(As it is written, I have made thee a father of many nations,) before him whom he believed, even God, who quickeneth the dead, and calleth those things which be not as though they were (Romans 4:17).

Everything you were going to do for him when he changes, do it now and do it by faith. Then God will turn your Tower of Babel into a Pentecost! At Pentecost each person heard the message in their own language (see Acts 2:6). I pray that God would interpret the language of your spouse and that your love be fruitful and productive.

> You could win the argument and still lose the man.

UNHOLY ALLIANCES

Day 291

And what concord hath Christ with Belial? or what part hath he that believeth with an infidel? And what agreement hath the temple of God with idols? for ye are the temple of the living God; as God hath said, I will dwell in them, and walk in them; and I will be their God, and they shall be My people. 2 Corinthians 6:15-16

To be willfully disobedient and choose a companion who you know is dead in the trespasses of sin, is to be involved in spiritual necrophilia....There is a spirit of necrophilia eating at the hearts of many Christians. It is not so much the literal act of having intercourse with the dead. No, satan is far too subtle for that. Nor is it just a matter of people filled with the life of God purposely disobeying His Word and entering into covenant with the dead, sinful lives of unbelievers and calling it holy matrimony. Whether we admit it or not, we know that an unholy alliance cannot produce holy matrimony. No, the subtle serpent has gone deeper than that! He has many wonderful, well-meaning Christians praising, worshiping, and going to church, but in the stillness of the night, when no one is around, they lie in bed in the privacy of their homes, pull out guilt, scars, and memories, and play with the dead. If it's dead—and it is—then bury it!

Brethren, I count not myself to have apprehended: but this one thing I do, forgetting those things which are behind, and reaching forth unto those things which are before (Philippians 3:13).

I once preached a message with a powerful title that I had heard years earlier. It was this: "Admit It! Quit It, and Forget It!" That's all you can do with the past, regardless of what it was or even who was at fault. When I say "forget it," that doesn't mean you actually lose awareness of the event. You don't have to be senile to be delivered! Rather, it means that you release the pain from the memory. The link that keeps you tied to what is past must be broken. In fact, I agree with you right now in the name of Jesus that those unsettled and unsettling issues that keep holding you in the night and affecting you in the light are broken by the power of God!

An unholy alliance cannot produce holy matrimony.

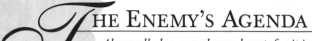

Above all else, guard your heart, for it is the wellspring of life. Proverbs 4:23 (NIV)

It is the burning effect of a vision that causes us to escape destruction. I repeat, I believe with all my heart that a man never dies with a twinkle in his eye. A gleam of expectation found in the faces of visionaries creates a tenacity that is not easily vanquished. If satan could steal nothing from you but your passion, he would have stolen much of your potency and power in one fell swoop!

The thing you must be aware of, my friend, is that the enemy is trying to steal something from you *that is not visible*. Any time the invisible is stolen, its absence is not readily detected. On what day does passion leave a marriage? On which morning did the worker lose interest in his job? At what point does the customer decide, "I am not going to buy the product"?

Depletion comes when enthusiasm leaks out of a person like air seeping silently out of a tire. Stealthily, the thief siphons life from you like a minute cut saps the strength of the tire. Suddenly, what was meant to roll and bear much weight can now only wobble. There has been such a loss of pressure that what was once inflated has now become deflated....

The only solution lies in the absolute, committed guarding of the heart. Your greatest treasure isn't your certificate of deposit. It isn't your retirement, or your stocks and bonds. Your greatest treasure is in the strength of the passion that is locked in the recesses of your heart. Out of the heart flow the issues of life.

You must keep a firm sobriety about you, warming your heart with it like it was a warm coat on a wintry night. Keep a sobriety that refuses to become drunken with fear, discontentment, or insecurity. Wrap your godly attitude closely around your heart, for it is the wellspring or the resource from which comes the strength to keep on living and giving!

> *Stealthily, the thief siphons life from you like a minute cut saps the strength of the tire.*

And the eyes of them both were opened, and they knew that they were naked; and they sewed fig leaves together, and made themselves aprons. Genesis 3:7

And the Lord God called unto Adam, and said unto him, Where art thou? And he said, I heard Thy voice in the garden, and I was afraid, because I was naked; and I hid myself (Genesis 3:9-10).

Take it off—take it all off! No, not your clothes! It's the fig leaves that must go. Marriage is at its best when both parties can be naked and not be ashamed. It is important that your husband be able to take it off, to take it all off. There is no resting place for the man who hides in his own house. The Lord asked Adam, "Where art thou?" When men are restored to their rightful place in the home, the family will come out of chaos. Listen as Adam exposes the tendency of most men to avoid open confrontation. These are the four points of his confession: (a) I heard Thy voice. (b) I was afraid. (c) I was naked. (d) I hid myself. When you become confrontational, it's not that men don't hear you. But when men become afraid or exposed (naked), they have a tendency to hide. Marriage needs to be transparent. Fear will not heal, it will only hide. Both you and your spouse need to be able to expose your vulnerabilities without fear or condemnation. Woe to the man who has no place to lay his head.

And they were both naked, the man and his wife, and were not ashamed (Genesis 2:25).

Marriage is at its best when both parties can be naked and not be ashamed.

How shall we, that are dead to sin, live any longer therein? Know ye not, that so many of us as were baptized into Jesus Christ were baptized into His death? Therefore we are buried with Him by baptism into death: that like as Christ was raised up from the dead by the glory of the Father, even so we also should walk in newness of life. Romans 6:2b-4

Intercourse brings two into oneness. Be careful what you allow to become one with you. You cannot continue to live in or be filled with the past. It is dead and over; break away from the intimate contact it would have on your life. Some things might never get resolved. They are like zombies walking around inside you all your life. Enough is enough! Everything that will not be healed must be forsaken. Really, to forsake it is to forget it. You cannot live in an intertwining embrace with something that God says you are to reckon as dead! Do not yield your body, your time, or your strength to this phantom lover! Tell that old corpse, "You can't touch this!"

> *Likewise reckon ye also yourselves to be dead indeed unto sin, but alive unto God through Jesus Christ our Lord. Let not sin therefore reign in your mortal body, that ye should obey it in the lusts thereof. Neither yield ye your members as instruments of unrighteousness unto sin: but yield yourselves unto God, as those that are alive from the dead, and your members as instruments of righteousness unto God (Romans 6:11-13).*

Thank God for the transparent testimony of the apostle Paul when he confided that all of his old issues were not yet laid to rest. Here he explains that there were moments when he was torn between who he wanted to become and who he used to be. Thank God for an honest testimony. Thank God for someone who tells the truth. We can hardly find a real witness anymore. We always tell how we came out, but we say nothing at all about how we went through! Paul, however, wasn't afraid of that pharisaical spirit that causes guilty men to be judgmental. He just said it plainly: "I am struggling with an old ghost that I want to be free from." Thank you, Paul, from all the rest of us would-be great men who thought there would be no struggle. Thanks for warning us—no, comforting us —with the honesty of your human aggravations.

> *You cannot continue to live in or be filled with the past.*

Healing, Blessings, and Freedom

But by the grace of God I am what I am, and His grace toward me was not in vain; but I labored more abundantly than they all, yet not I, but the grace of God which was with me. 1 Corinthians 15:10 (NKJ)

I must be careful to say that you can't spend the rest of your life trying to protect yourself from the struggles of life. They are unavoidable. All men face struggles and the seasons of life, irregardless of their economical, spiritual, or sociological persuasion! If you become intimidated by that fact, it will cause you to live your life in an emotional incubator, insulated but isolated. Having declared that, we must no longer focus on what can be protected. It is not *what we go through* that must be closely monitored. It isn't the pain that we are adamantly resisting—it is *the loss of passion!* We can no more stop pain than we can stop labor pains from coming upon a woman who is in travail!

Look at the birthing table of the expectant mother. It is designed to hold her in the birth position in spite of the pain. Can you maintain your position—even when it means that you will be exposed to a harsh level of pain? That is what good ministry does in our lives. It holds us in place, even when we would have stepped out of the will of God to save ourselves from the stress of the process. Jesus was tied to the birthing table in the garden of Gethsemane. The Church was in Him "from the foundation of the world," and it was to be brought out of His bleeding side on the cross. He was laid in the stirrups in the garden. As the pains became greater, He prayed to change position. He didn't want to be in the vulnerable position of delivery!

Saying, Father, if Thou be willing, remove this cup from Me: nevertheless not My will, but Thine, be done (Luke 22:42).

*G*ood ministry...holds us in place, even when we would have stepped out of the will of God to save ourselves from the stress of the process.

For the lips of a strange woman drop as an honeycomb, and her mouth is smoother than oil: but her end is bitter as wormwood, sharp as a two-edged sword. Proverbs 5:3-4

I want to share something with you that may sound unorthodox. I pray it will bless someone. I want to stop by Delilah's house (see Judg. 16:4-20). Most women would not want to stop at her house; most men would! Most men are not afraid of Delilah; most women do not like her. Her morals are inexcusable, but her methods are worth discussing. There are some things that every wife could learn, must learn, from Delilah. With all the colorful exegesis of our preachers who have described her as some voluptuous love goddess, they say she walked like a swinging pendulum, smelled like the richest incense and smiled like the glow of an exquisite candelabra. But, in actuality the Bible says nothing about her appearance. Her clothing, makeup or hairdo are not mentioned. What was it about this woman that was so powerful? What was it that attracted and captivated the attention of this mighty man, Samson? What was it about this woman that kept drawing him back to her arms? What was it about this woman that, when none of the warriors could get to Samson, the Philistine government put her on the payroll because of what she knew about men? What was it that made Samson keep going back to her bed even when he knew she was trying to kill him? He could not leave her alone—he desperately needed her. It is a "fatal attraction" in the Old Testament!

And it came to pass, when she pressed him daily with her words, and urged him, so that his soul was vexed unto death; that he told her all his heart (Judges 16:16-17a).

> What was it that made Samson keep going back to her bed even when he knew she was trying to kill him?

What a wretched man I am! Who will rescue me from this body of death?
Romans 7:24 (NIV)

Paul uses these terms to declare his struggles because he is wrestling with a corpse. One of the punishments decreed in Paul's day for certain types of criminals was capital punishment. But how they administered this death was quite bizarre. They would take the body of the murdered victim and tie it on the murderer. Thus everywhere the murderer went, the corpse did too, for it was attached to him. Worse still, the murdered victim was ever upon him—he could not forget his victim. He was weighted down by him. He could not avoid the putrid, rancid flesh to which he was attached. This kind of intimate contact would be unpleasant even if the man were alive, but because the man was dead, it was unbearable. The mere odor of the soft, decomposing, deteriorating flesh would reek with the stench of rot, contaminating all of life's moments with the ever-present aroma of decadence. What could we enjoy in life with this flesh hanging on as a sentinel from the past?

This nauseating level of intimacy with mushy flesh would turn the strongest stomach. That is exactly how Paul felt about the old nature that continued to press in so closely to his existence—rubbing him, touching him, always reminding him of things he could neither change nor eradicate. Eventually, for the punished murderer, this bacteria-filled, murky, mushy flesh would pass its fungus and disease to him until he died from this association with the dead. What an agonizing, disgusting way to die. When the apostle realized that his association with his past was affecting his present, he cried out, "O wretched man that I am! Who shall deliver me from so great a death?" That "who" rang throughout the heavenlies, searched the angels, and found no one worthy to answer the call. That "who" searched the underworld and found no one able to answer. It searched the earth—past, present, and future—and found a bleeding Lamb and an empty tomb. Then the angels cried, "Worthy is the Lamb! He is so worthy. Let Him untie you from this curse and be healed!"

> **What could we enjoy in life with this flesh hanging on as a sentinel from the past?**

Confess your faults one to another, and pray one for another, that ye may be healed. The effectual fervent prayer of a righteous man availeth much. James 5:16

We are tied to our destiny like a little trembling lamb is tied to the altar for sacrifice. Like a woman lifted to the birthing bed, trembling in pain, forehead drenched with perspiration—we who are on the verge of miracles are always kept in a perpetual state of vulnerability! If it were not for our passion for an expected end, we would have just fainted away entirely, declaring that the process is too great and the reward too insignificant.

There has to be a certain intensity of desire to empower a person to persevere. Even when we pray, God isn't moved by our vocabulary. He has answered the broken, fragmented prayers of the illiterate mind, whose limited intellect could not abort the childlike faith that produces miracles. He is, as the Scriptures declare, "touched with the feeling of our infirmities" (Heb. 4:15). The passionate God is, in fact, touched by the passions of the prayers of the infirm.

> *For we have not an high priest which cannot be touched with the feeling of our infirmities; but was in all points tempted like as we are, yet without sin (Hebrews 4:15).*

The term rendered as "infirmities" is, first of all, mentioned in its plural form to indicate that there is generally more than one. How tragic that most of us will not even admit to the presence of one infirmity, much less the multiplicity of our infirmities. When God is "touched" by them, that means He is *sympathetic* to the feeling of our infirmities.

Strong's Exhaustive Concordance of the Bible tells us that the Greek word *astheneia* means "feebleness (of mind or body); by implication, malady; morally, frailty." This is the word that the Authorized Version translates as "infirmities." Somewhere in the most gifted heart, mind, or body, exists some malady or frailty—whether moral, mental, or physical—that incapacitates us to the degree that we need God's mercies newly bestowed upon us every morning.

Most of us will not even admit to the presence of one infirmity, much less the multiplicity of our infirmities.

And beheld among the simple ones, I discerned among the youths, a young man void of understanding…behold, there met him a woman with the attire of an harlot, and subtle of heart.…With her much fair speech she caused him to yield, with the flattering of her lips she forced him. He goeth after her straightway, as an ox goeth to the slaughter, or as a fool to the correction of the stocks. Proverbs 7:7,10,21-22

This discussion is for women married to men working in high-stress positions—men who are powerful and full of purpose; men who are the envy of everyone around them. Samson was that kind of man. Jesus described well the problem of highly motivated men. Jesus said, "Foxes have holes, and birds of the air have nests; but the Son of man hath not where to lay His head" (Luke 9:58). Where can the mighty man lay his head? Where can he become vulnerable? Where can he take off his armor and rest for a few hours? He doesn't want to quit; he merely needs to rest. Is your home a restful place to be? Is it clean and neat? Is it warm and inviting? Delilah's place is ready. I am sure she has problems, but he doesn't have to solve them as soon as he comes home from fighting the enemy. She knows he is tired, so she says, "Come, lay your head in my lap."

I know we have pictured Delilah as being as lust-ridden as a porno star. But remember that the Bible doesn't even mention their sex life. I am sure that it was a factor. But Samson has had sex before. He had gotten up from the bed of the prostitute in Gaza and drove back the Philistines. He is not a high school boy whose mind is blown away by a new sexual idea. No, he is a mighty man. Wasn't it David who questioned at the demise of Saul, "How are the mighty fallen"? Well, tell David to ask Delilah, or if she is not at home, to ask Bathsheba! Delilah knew that all men are little boys somewhere deep inside. They are little boys who started their lives being touched by women. You sang their first song. You gave their first bath and when they were tired, they laid their weary heads against your warm breast and lapsed into sleep. They listened at your silky voice calling them, "Momma's little man." You talked to them. You touched them and they felt safe in your arms—not criticized, not ostracized, just safe. Delilah stroked Samson. She talked to him. She gave him a place to lay his head. Even God inhabits the room of a praiser and allows the murmurer to wander. Men, created in the likeness of God, respond to praise. Praise will make a weary man perform. A woman who knows what to say to a man is difficult to withstand. For all men's tears and all their fears, they need your arms, your words, your song.

> *All men are little boys… who started their lives being touched by women.*

It is a faithful saying: for if we be dead with Him, we shall also live with Him: if we suffer, we shall also reign with Him: if we deny Him, He also will deny us: if we believe not, yet He abideth faithful: He cannot deny Himself. 2 Timothy 2:11-13

Likewise reckon ye also yourselves to be dead indeed unto sin, but alive unto God through Jesus Christ our Lord. Let not sin therefore reign in your mortal body, that ye should obey it in the lusts thereof. Neither yield ye your members as instruments of unrighteousness unto sin: but yield yourselves unto God, as those that are alive from the dead, and your members as instruments of righteousness unto God (Romans 6:11-13).

You can live with those dead things hanging and clinging to you no better than Paul could. Allow the transforming power of God to rush through your life and cut the cord between you and your past. Whatever you do, remember to get rid of the old body. If the past is over, there is no need for you to walk around with mummies on your back—or should I say, on your mind! Get rid of that body and do it now! Those old memories will try to negotiate a deal, but you don't need a twin hanging on you. You don't need a secret affair with a corpse. You don't even need it as a roommate.

This is the time for an epitaph, not a revival. There are some things in life you will want to revive, but not this one. The past is something you want to die. It is always challenging for me as a pastor to assume the task of an eulogist at funerals. In order to effectively administer comfort and final services, you must know something of the relationship of the deceased to the family. It has been said that funerals are for the living, and I must totally agree with that thought. The funeral affords the remaining friends and loved ones an opportunity to resolve in their minds that the deceased is gone and that the relationship, as they had known it, is no more. Death doesn't seem to have the finality to a family that burial does. For some reason, until they officially put the deceased away, they seem to struggle with continuing their lives. Everything is placed on hold until the funeral is concluded.

> There are some things in life you will want to revive, but not this one.

Healing, Blessings, and Freedom

WE ARE OF LIKE PASSION

Now therefore ye are no more strangers and foreigners, but fellowcitizens with the saints, and of the household of God; and are built upon the foundation of the apostles and prophets, Jesus Christ Himself being the chief corner stone. Ephesians 2:19-20

By God's design, left splayed before us on the pages of the Scriptures, are the intricate details of the life of David, whose passions were both an asset and a liability. We openly filter through his secret thoughts as casually as if we were reading the evening *Times*. His inner struggles and childhood dysfunctions are openly aired on the pages of the text like the center foldout in a tabloid.

God didn't display David's failures in a divine attempt to expose the secret prayers of His struggling king. Rather, His purpose is to give us a point of reference that exhibits the manifold grace of God. How marvelous is the message that instructs us that if God could use a David, He also can use us, as we are all men of *like passions*.

I do not dispute the passions. In fact, without them I can never migrate from the obscure hills and shepherd fields of yesteryear to the victorious acquisition of the palace to which I have been called. Yet I want to issue a point of warning in the midst of this dissertation *to the one who dares to lay bare his innermost passions and desires* before God—He who has examined the inner workings of every heart. In reality, in Acts 14:15 the phrase "like passions" comes from the Greek word *homiopathas* which literally translated means "to be similarly affected."

Did you know that God used men who were similarly affected (as you are) by certain stimuli and struggles? What a joy to know that treasure can be surrounded by trash and still not lose its value! Is a diamond less valuable if it is found in a clogged drain? Of course not!

And saying, Sirs, why do ye these things? We also are men of like passions with you, and preach unto you that ye should turn from these vanities unto the living God, which made heaven, and earth, and the sea, and all things that are therein (Acts 14:15).

> If God could use a David, He also can use us, as we are all men of *like passions*.

But he that is married careth for the things that are of the world, how he may please his wife. There is difference also between a wife and a virgin. The unmarried woman careth for the things of the Lord, that she may be holy both in body and in spirit: but she that is married careth for the things of the world, how she may please her husband. 1 Corinthians 7:33-34

Marriage is a ministry. There is much more involved in it than selfish fulfillment. Love is centered around giving, not taking. When you marry someone, you marry everything he is and everything he has been. You inherit his strengths, fears and weaknesses. It is impossible to pick the parts you want and to leave the parts you don't. It is a package deal. God grants you the grace of ministering to your spouse, to the child in him. Don't be discouraged if you don't see immediate change. I want to remind you that it takes time even for a small cut to heal. Healing is a process and it takes time! God will give you the oil of compassion and the sweet wind of a sincere love to pour into the wounds of your husband....

Marriage is so much a ministry that the apostle Paul teaches the married woman she cannot afford to become so spiritual that she is unavailable for the ministry of marriage. The Greek word used there for "careth" means to be anxious about or to have intense concern. God says, "I want the married woman to be concerned about pleasing her husband and vice versa." Many married women who spend a great deal of time fellowshiping with single women do not realize that their perspective and availability should be different. Your ministry, as a wife, begins not in the mall, not in the nursing home, but in your own home and to your own spouse. Now, I am certainly not implying that a woman should be locked in the kitchen and chained to the bed! I am sharing that priorities need to start in the home and then spread to careers, vocations and ministerial pursuits. For the woman who "careth for," God will anoint you to be successful in the ministry of marriage.

*G*od will anoint you to be successful in the ministry of marriage.

GET RID OF THE GHOSTS

And you hath He quickened, who were dead in trespasses and sins; wherein in time past ye walked according to the course of this world, according to the prince of the power of the air, the spirit that now worketh in the children of disobedience. Ephesians 2:1-2

I can still remember being a young man of 16 when they lowered my father into the cold Mississippi clay. I stood just over top of the grave looking down, face twisted in pain, confused and distraught. "This is it!" I thought. "He is absolutely gone!" I was devastated! But I also was aware that there is only one step between time and eternity, and that step was a lot shorter than I had thought. There is no hammer that presses the finality of death into the head of the onlooker like committing the body to the ground. Now the deceased loved one exists in brief shadows and glimpses, in memories that appear like dew on a pathway, wisps of moments envisioned, often as shadows. Philosophically, I know that my father exists in the very stroking of the computer as I write, and in the successes and failures of his children. Theologically, he exists somewhere in the great beyond where all Christians await the reunion that death has separated. But physically, there is no question about it; he is gone. Still, I have looked for him more often than I would ever confess!

There are some things you would like to have removed extremely far away. There are things I would like to lay to rest in such a definite way that they become merely fleeting wisps of fog faintly touching the recesses of the mind— gone, over, finished! It is those dearly departed, ghostly, painful issues of which I wrote....These phantom assassins are not to be trifled with; they must be laid to rest! This funeral, my friend, is not for them—it is you who must know it's over. Mark down this day as a record that it was this day you put away your nighttime playmates and moved into abundant life. Gather together all those villainous ghosts that desecrate the sanctity of what God would do in your life. Examine them. Cry if need be; scream if necessary—but when the service is over, bury every incident in the freshly turned soil of this word from God. Know that God has delivered you from playing with *dead* things.

> **Gather together all those villainous ghosts that desecrate the sanctity of what God would do in your life.**

Keep back thy servant also from presumptuous sins; let them not have dominion over me: then shall I be upright, and I shall be innocent from the great transgression. Psalm 19:13

The same passion that makes us very good could potentially make us very bad. Undirected passion becomes a spawning bed for perversity and dankness. It is *what we do with what we feel* that controls the direction of our lives. The same sail that causes a ship to run before an eastward wind through fog and rain can also push it headlong in another direction.

Hear me, O passionate dreamer, whose passion is to walk after God: *The same drive that has become a sword wielded against the enemy, can become a billboard of disgrace if not carefully attended!*

The same John who preached in the desert with power and conviction about the coming of the King and His Kingdom, one day lay trembling on the cold, damp floor of a jail cell, haunted by one question. *Was the Christ he baptized and called "the Lamb of God" really authentic?* Under growing pressure, he finally sent a messenger to ask the infamous question, "Art Thou He that should come, or do we look for another?" (Matt. 11:3)

What a wailing in prayer this truth should elicit from the hearts of men and women! …Now they must watch carefully, lest the same serum that made them who they are now perpetuate a downfall! Our defense is naked, honest, fervent prayer. It is the mediatory power of God that so often catches our falling souls and sets us back in the nest with the tenderness of a mother sparrow.

Passions are to be submitted to the Father, just as our Lord submitted His all on the cross. That is the place where He wielded all of His passion and all of His force—His passion was aimed at the joy set before Him, the target of being a submitted Son. God tested the power of committed passion at Calvary. If it had not been effective, Christ would have had to buy Joseph's tomb instead of borrow it. This is frightening if you read this with the mummylike mentality that preempts most people from accomplishing anything. They *neutralize their passion* with an apathy and unconcern that renders them flaccid and ineffective.

> The same drive that has become a sword wielded against the enemy, can become a billboard of disgrace if not carefully attended!

Marriage is honorable in all, and the bed undefiled: but whoremongers and adulterers God will judge. Hebrews 13:4

There will be no marriages in Heaven (see Matt. 22:30). Marriage is for this world. Inasmuch as it is a worldly institution, married people cannot divorce themselves from the "things of the world." Notice this definition of the Greek word *kosmos* translated as "world" in our text:

> Adorn, Adorning *kosmos* #2889 in *Strong's*, "a harmonious arrangement or order, then, adornment, decoration, hence came to denote the world, or the universe, as that which is Divinely arranged. The meaning 'adorning' is found in 1 Pet. 3:3. Elsewhere it signifies the world. Cp. *kosmios*, decent, modest, 1 Tim. 2:9; 3:2. See (World)" (*Vine's Expository Dictionary of Biblical Words*, Thomas Nelson Publishers, 1985).

It implies that there should be a concern for a harmonious order in the house. God gives the gift of marriage, but you must do your own decorating. Decorate your relationship or it will become bland for you and for your spouse. Decoration does not come where there is no concern. So God says, in effect, "I release the married woman from the level of consecration I expect from the single woman so she will be able to spend some time decorating her relationship." You have a ministry to your companion. I can hear someone saying, "That is good, but I need to spend time with the Lord." That is true. The Scripture didn't say married women were to be carnal. It just sets some priorities. Where there are no priorities, there is a sense of being overwhelmed by responsibility. You can still consecrate yourself as long as you understand you are called to be a companion to your spouse. God has ascribed honor to marriage. Your bed is undefiled. (See Hebrews 13:4.) However you choose to decorate your relationship is holy. Do not neglect each other in the name of being spiritual. God wants you to be together!

> **G**od gives the gift of marriage, but you must do your own decorating.

So we fix our eyes not on what is seen, but on what is unseen. For what is seen is temporary, but what is unseen is eternal. 2 Corinthians 4:18 (NIV)

Wherefore come out from among them, and be ye separate, saith the Lord, and touch not the unclean thing; and I will receive you (2 Corinthians 6:17).

I am told that Mozart, one of the great composers of all time, sat late at night writing what was to be a masterpiece of symphonic excellence....He decided to stop and go to bed. Stumbling upstairs to his room, he changed with all the agility of a sluggish child who merely wants to go immediately to bed.

Strangely, once he was in bed, he found sleep evasive and he tossed and turned into the night. His work continued churning around in the chambers of his mind. You see, he had ended the symphony with an augmented chord. An augmented chord gives the feeling of waiting on something else to be heard. It is a feeling of being suspended over a cliff. Finally, when this composer could stand it no longer, he rose, tossed his wool plaid robe across his willowy shoulders, and stumbled down the steps. He went through all that to write one note. Yet how important that note was. It gave a sense of ending to the piece, and so was worth getting out of bed to write. People can never rest while living in a suspended mode. This composer then placed the quill back on his desk, blew out the lantern once more, and triumphantly retraced his way up the stairs and back to bed.

Now this great patriarch of symphonic excellence slipped into the bed with a feeling of satisfaction. He fluffed beneath his head the pillow that had once felt like a rock and just before the whistling wind outside his window ushered him into the sleep that only the peaceful can enjoy, he sighed faintly. Then his body gave way to the gentle caress of fatigue and he entered through the portal of tranquility with the slightest hint of a smile hanging around the corners of his mouth. For him, the struggle was over.

> People can never rest while living in a suspended mode.

The husband should fulfill his marital duty to his wife, and likewise the wife to her husband. The wife's body does not belong to her alone but also to her husband. In the same way, the husband's body does not belong to him alone but also to his wife. Do not deprive each other except by mutual consent and for a time, so that you may devote yourselves to prayer.... 1 Corinthians 7:3-5 (NIV)

If you are looking for someone to be your everything, don't look around, look up! God is the only One who can be everything. By expecting perfection from the flesh, you ask more out of someone else than what you can provide yourself. To be married is to have a partner: someone who is not always there or always on target or always anything! On the other hand, should you ever get in trouble and you don't know who to look to for help, you can count on your partner! It is to have someone to curl up against when the world seems cold and life uncertain. It is having someone who is as concerned as you are when your children are ill. It is having a hand that keeps checking your forehead when you aren't well. To be married is to have someone's shoulder to cry on as they lower your parent's body into the ground. It is wrapping wrinkled knees in warm blankets and giggling without teeth! To the person you marry you are saying, "When my time comes to leave this world and the chill of eternity blows away my birthdays and my future stands still in the night; it's your face I want to kiss good-bye. It is your hand I want to squeeze as I slip from time into eternity. As the curtain closes on all I have attempted to do and be; I want to look into your eyes and see that I mattered. Not what I looked like. Not what I did or how much money I made. Not even how talented I was. I want to look into the teary eyes of someone who loved me and see; I mattered!"

If you are looking for someone to be your everything, don't look around, look up!

Unto the woman He said, I will greatly multiply thy sorrow and thy conception; in sorrow thou shalt bring forth children; and thy desire shall be to thy husband, and he shall rule over thee.
Genesis 3:16

Have you faced some tragedies that almost left you in a state of shock? I can really relate to that feeling. I remember going through a time of complete emptiness in my ministry….Normally I am a stickler for details. However, during my time of depression, I became indifferent about whether or not things were done—I simply was "disconnected." It seemed safe to be disconnected because *as long as I didn't care, it didn't hurt.* I had lost the passion to continue. I was completely disenchanted….

When God spoke to the first woman about childbirth, He spoke of sorrow and travail. He spoke of the violent, tempestuous pain of labor. He forewarned her about the billowing progression of contractions she would experience at the end of the third trimester of pregnancy. As her pelvic bones are literally moved apart, as if separated by the effects of an earthquake, she is opened as the gates of her femininity prepare for the birth of a child.

The near-deathlike pains come faster and harder as she gets closer to delivery. The soft feminine flesh of the woman whose petals are crushed beneath the weight of an oncoming child is engulfed in a traumatic rush to deliver life. Afterwards, you would expect her to vow never to know another man again!

However, God says that at the end of all this labor and pain, He would recycle the relationship between the woman and the man by the return of desire! He says, "And thy desire shall be to thy husband…" (Gen. 3:16b). God knows that *there is no cure for past pain like present desire.* If the desire is strong enough, the pain of the past will dissipate like bubbles in a glass of water. The wounded and the weary will rise victoriously with new desire, and the cycle continues.

Listen, my friend: Perhaps you have gone through some earthshaking experience that affected and traumatized you. I understand the fear of being hurt again. Once a child has been burned, he will dread fire. But you can't live the rest of your life in fear and dread; *God wants to renew your passion and revive your desire!*

> *God knows that there is no cure for past pain like present desire.*

TABLE FOR TWO

He brought me to the banqueting house, and his banner over me was love. Song of Solomon 2:4

I hope you can relate to what a blessing it is to be alive, to be able to feel, to be able to taste life. Lift the glass to your mouth and drink deeply of life; it is a privilege to experience every drop of a human relationship. It is not perfect; like a suede jacket, the imperfection adds to its uniqueness. I am sure yours, like mine, is a mixing of good days, sad days and all the challenges of life. I hope you have learned that a truly good relationship is a spicy meal served on a shaky table, filled with dreams and pains and tender moments. Moments that, in those split-second flashbacks, make you smile secret smiles in the middle of the day. Moments so strong that they never die, but yet are so fragile they disappear like bubbles in a glass. It does not matter whether you have something to be envied or something to be developed; if you can look back and catch a few moments, or trace a smile back to a memory, you are blessed! You could have been anywhere doing anything but instead the maitre d' has seated you at a TABLE FOR TWO!

Two are better than one; because they have a good reward for their labor. For if they fall, the one will lift up his fellow: but woe to him that is alone when he falleth; for he hath not another to help him up. Again, if two lie together, then they have heat: but how can one be warm alone? And if one prevail against him, two shall withstand him; and a threefold cord is not quickly broken (Ecclesiastes 4:9-12).

> You could have been anywhere doing anything but instead the maitre d' has seated you at a TABLE FOR TWO!

And wisdom and knowledge shall be the stability of thy times, and strength of salvation: the fear of the Lord is His treasure. Isaiah 33:6

What a celebration ought to be going on inside you at this moment. There ought to be a threefold celebration going on in your heart right now. First, you ought to look back over your times of obscurity, when He was plowing and fertilizing you, and thank God that you are still here to attest to His sustaining power. A lesser vessel would not have survived your testimony. Second, look around you at the blessings that you have right now. With a twinkle in your eye and a melody in your heart, thank God for what He is doing even at this moment. Your freshly cultivated ground is full of seeds and unborn potential. Who knows all that God has planted in you. He has begun a work—a good work—in you. Celebrate that every time you wake up in the morning. Look over your straw-covered fields, fan back the birds of doubt and fear, and thank God. Breathe the fresh air into grateful lungs, being glad just to be here.

Third, you should celebrate what God is about to do in your life. Your heart ought to be thumping in your chest; your blood ought to be racing like a car engine about to peel rubber! You are about to step into the greatest harvest of your life. The enemy knows you are about to be harvested. That's why he fought you like he did. He realizes that this is your time. Don't you? A powerful prophetic move is about to explode over your life. Are you ready for the word of the Lord that was spoken over you to come to pass? Get ready! Hurry, get your mind ready, change your clothes! Put on your shouting shoes! When the news that's in your spirit gets in your mind, tears of joy will wet the runway for your take-off. Don't ever read about anyone else and wish you were him. Don't ever wish you had lived at any other time. You were created for this moment—and this moment was created for you! Stop reading and look at the clock. Laugh to yourself and praise your God. Do you know what time it is? *It's your time!*

> **A**re you ready for the word of the Lord that was spoken over you to come to pass?

A SHOCKING GUEST LIST

And supper being ended, the devil having now put into the heart of Judas Iscariot, Simon's son, to betray Him; Jesus knowing that the Father had given all things into His hands, and that He was come from God, and went to God; He riseth from supper, and laid aside His garments; and took a towel and girded Himself. After that He poureth water into a basin, and began to wash the disciples' feet.... John 13:2-5

Supper is over and the dishes are cleared away. Supper is also over for those of us who have had a "reality check" through the unveiling of Judas. We now realize that our ultimate purpose for gathering isn't really for fellowship. He gathers us to sharpen and prune us through our attempts at fellowship. He often uses the people with whom we worship to prune us. They become the utensils the Lord uses to perfect those whom He has called. As lavishly garnished as the table is, and as decorative as it may appear to the youthful gaze of the new Christian, it is only a matter of time before they begin the stage-by-stage unmasking and realize that the guests around the table of the Lord are bleeding.

Imagine how shocked you would be to find yourself invited to a prestigious dinner party like this one. You have been so careful to respond appropriately. Now shaven and manicured, clean and perfumed, you carefully begin the laborious task of attiring yourself in an elegant, yet tasteful manner. You desperately want to make a positive impression on the Host, as well as on the guests. After arriving on time, you hasten toward the door where you are announced and then ushered into the banqueting room of your dreams....

As your eyes begin to warily make the rounds across the table, a bitter taste of bile begins to rise and lodge in your throat. Each guest has some sort of gross deformity beneath their gracious smile. Neither rubies nor diamonds, neither tuxedos nor tails can camouflage the scars and gaping wounds represented around the table. You are shocked that you spent all evening trying to prepare yourself to meet people who have more flaws than you have ever imagined! The only spotless splendor for the human eye to gaze upon is the Host Himself—all others are merely patients; just mutilated, torn, dilapidated, disfigured caricatures of social grace and ambiance.

> It is only a matter of time before they begin the stage-by-stage unmasking and realize that the guests around the table of the Lord are bleeding.

Are not two sparrows sold for a farthing? and one of them shall not fall on the ground without your Father. But the very hairs of your head are all numbered. Fear ye not therefore, ye are of more value than many sparrows. Matthew 10:29-31

We are fascinated with beauty. There are contests of all kinds to determine who is the most beautiful of all. Advertisers spend millions of dollars to promote beauty pageants. The beauty industry is one of the largest in America. Women spend huge amounts of money on makeup, fashionable clothing, and jewelry. Plastic surgeons are kept busy cutting and tucking extra flesh and reshaping features to make people more attractive.

In spite of all this attention, what is the true beauty of a woman? What is it that makes her genuinely attractive? Many feel unattractive because they don't meet a certain image to which they have aspired. Others are constantly frustrated in trying to get someone to notice their attractiveness.

No scientist has ever been able to make a woman. No doctor has been able to create a woman. No engineer has been able to build a woman. However, God has made fine women. You don't have to look like a TV commercial to be beautiful. No one stays 21 forever.

We must learn to thank God for who we are. Don't be a silly woman watching television and crying because she doesn't look like the girl who opened up the window in the game show. You are not supposed to look like that. If God had wanted you to look like that, He would have made you like that. God will send somebody along who will appreciate you the way you are.

While waiting on that person, start appreciating yourself. Remind yourself, "I am valuable to God. I am somebody. And I won't let another use me and abuse me and treat me like I'm nothing. Yes, I've been through some bad times. I've been hurt and I've been bent out of shape, but the Lord touched me and loosed me and now I am glorifying God and I'm not going back to where I came from."

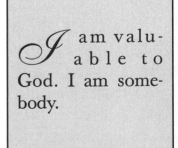

I am valuable to God. I am somebody.

Then said He also to him that bade Him, When thou makest a dinner or a supper, call not thy friends, nor thy brethren, neither thy kinsmen, nor thy rich neighbors; lest they also bid thee again, and a recompence be made thee. But when thou makest a feast, call the poor, the maimed, the lame, the blind: and thou shalt be blessed; for they cannot recompense thee: for thou shalt be recompensed at the resurrection of the just. Luke 14:12-14

Then said He unto him, A certain man made a great supper, and bade many: and sent his servant at supper time to say to them that were bidden, Come; for all things are now ready. And they all with one consent began to make excuse. The first said unto him, I have bought a piece of ground, and I must needs go and see it: I pray thee have me excused. And another said, I have bought five yoke of oxen, and I go to prove them: I pray thee have me excused. And another said, I have married a wife, and therefore I cannot come. So that servant came, and showed his lord these things. Then the master of the house being angry said to his servant, Go out quickly into the streets and lanes of the city, and bring in hither the poor, and the maimed, and the halt, and the blind. And the servant said, Lord, it is done as thou hast commanded, and yet there is room. And the lord said unto the servant, Go out into the highways and hedges, and compel them to come in, that my house may be filled. For I say unto you, That none of those men which were bidden shall taste of my supper (Luke 14:16-24).

These harsh realities are merely a semblance of what we gradually encounter as we face the rude awakenings of ministry. We learn to understand Peter's anger and his occasional tendency to lie. We feel the constant insecurities of Thomas, whose doubtful warnings seem to come against every attempt we would make toward progress. We encounter the painful betrayal of our old friend, Judas Iscariot, whose twisted way of loving us never seems to stop him from killing us....

When we see Jesus, we can only sit in splendor and thank God that He is gracious enough to invite the impaired and the impoverished—lest the very seat in which we sit be emptied as well!

> **T**hank God that He is gracious enough to invite the impaired and the impoverished—lest the very seat in which we sit be emptied as well!

If thou put the brethren in remembrance of these things, thou shalt be a good minister of Jesus Christ, nourished up in the words of faith and of good doctrine, whereunto thou hast attained. 1 Timothy 4:6

No one prepares a meal to last forever. There is a time when we must move beyond suppertime. We must move beyond the stage in our development where we come to a ministry just to be fed, where our whole focus for coming to the table is always to receive. We must make the transition that every believer must make—some call it the transition from believership to discipleship, but I just call it the transition *from suppertime to service time....*

God only opens your eyes so you can get up from the table and give someone else a turn in the seat. It is time for you to learn the art of service and move beyond the gluttony of supper.

"And supper being ended..." the Scripture says in John 13:2. ...First, you must understand that suppertime is coming to an end....When you want to stay where you are, but you've got to go where He calls, supper is over....

Jesus then rises from supper. I am afraid that most of us have never risen from supper. We are still trying to "get all we can, and can all we get." We have never risen from supper; instead, we are resting on the laurels of indifference and contentment. It reminds me of people who go to a restaurant and fellowship throughout the meal. Then, though the evening wanes, the candles collapse, and the flames flicker out, the crowd still sits around a cluttered table, oblivious to the need to move on.

I wonder if we have chattered away the age and jested away a generation. Are we still sitting around the cluttered dishes of dead programs whose crushed crumbs are not enough to feed the impoverished age in which we have been called? Shouldn't we have quit shouting long enough to rise from the table? Hold the music and turn up the lights! Even the waiter is gone home, and here we sit in the same spot, rehearsing the same excuses! We need men and women who will rise from supper.

Healing, Blessings, and Freedom

> *𝒲e are still trying to "get all we can, and can all we get."*

LIFE IS NOT A FAIRY TALE

Whose adorning let it not be that outward adorning of plaiting the hair, and of wearing of gold, or of putting on of apparel; but let it be the hidden man of the heart, in that which is not corruptible, even the ornament of a meek and quiet spirit, which is in the sight of God of great price. 1 Peter 3:3-4

As I mentioned earlier, there is an important lesson to learn from the account of Samson and Delilah in the Old Testament (see Judg. 16). The Philistines were enemies and they could not kill Samson with swords or bows, but they found a door. The Bible says that Samson loved Delilah. He became so infatuated with her that he was vulnerable.

> *And she said unto him, How canst thou say, I love thee, when thine heart is not with me? thou hast mocked me these three times, and hast not told me wherein thy great strength lieth. And it came to pass, when she pressed him daily with her words, and urged him, so that his soul was vexed unto death (Judges 16:15-16).*

It was not Delilah's beauty that captivated. It was not even her sexuality that destroyed Samson. Samson had known beautiful women before. He had slept with prostitutes. It was not just sexual exercise that caused her to get a grip on this man. I'll call it the Delilah syndrome.

Beauty and sex appeal are not the areas to concentrate on. When you focus on the wrong areas, you don't get the right results. Society teaches you today that if you have the right hair, the right face, the right shape, the right clothes, and the right car, then you will get the right man. Then you expect that you will buy the right house, have the right children, live the right life and live happily ever after. That is simply not true. Life is not a fairy tale.

God put some things into the feminine spirit that a man needs more than anything God put on the feminine body. If a woman knows who she is on the inside, no matter what she looks like, she will have no problem being attractive to a man. If she knows her own self-worth, then when she comes before that man, he will receive her.

> Today if you have the right hair, the right face, the right shape, the right clothes, and the right car, then you will...live the right life and live happily ever after.

But if ye have respect to persons, ye commit sin, and are convinced of the law as transgressors. For whosoever shall keep the whole law, and yet offend in one point, he is guilty of all. James 2:9-10

He riseth from supper, and laid aside His garments; and took a towel and girded Himself. After that He poureth water into a basin, and began to wash the disciples' feet, and to wipe them with the towel wherewith He was girded (John 13:4-5).

The Master now rises from the table in the presence of these, His guests, and begins the unnerving process of disrobing in a room where all others are clothed. I must tell you—after playing football in school and spending many hours in musty locker rooms with strangers—it is much easier to undress when others are undressing than it is to walk into an executive boardroom and unbuckle your belt and disrobe! This would be true even if that room was filled with the same men whom you work out with in the health spa. It is not who they are that matters. It is that your comfort zone is destroyed when you feel as though you are the only one who is naked.

Jesus taught a powerful lesson about ministry as He rose from supper and began to disrobe in front of men who were still clothed. Isn't our problem the fact that we don't want to be seen as the only one? The fear of being different can lock you in a vault. It can close you in a prison of disobedience because you are afraid of being alone.

We will never have real ministry until someone changes the atmosphere in our boring little conferences and conventions. Real ministry will start the moment we stop trying to impress each other and say, "Look! This is how I really look beneath my name, my reputation, or my success. This is who I really am!"

Jesus paid the price. He took the leap that few would ever dare to take. He laid aside His garments before those whom He had labored to inspire. Yet we have not followed His example. The closer we get to leaders, the more they hide! They are afraid, and understandably so. We have asked them to be God! We have asked them to be flawless! We have asked them to be more than what we could ever be, and we have imprisoned them in their callings and chained them to their giftings.

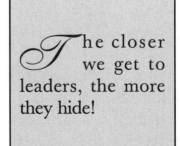

$\mathcal{T}$he closer we get to leaders, the more they hide!

But it shall not be so among you: but whosoever will be great among you, let him be your minister; and whosoever will be chief among you, let him be your servant: even as the Son of man came not to be ministered unto, but to minister, and to give His life a ransom for many. Matthew 20:26-28

Wailing, shrieks of broken hearts, and screams of terror echo behind our stiffly starched shirts and satiny smooth dresses. The words have increased; the technology has improved; but the power of ministry will never be unleashed until those who are called to deliver it find the grace, or perhaps the mercy, that will allow them to *lay aside their garments*!

"Is He mad? Has He lost His mind?" Can you imagine what the disciples thought as Jesus changed the atmosphere of the feast by disrobing before them? How could a person of His stature stoop so low? I tell you, He never stood as tall as He did when He stooped so low to bless the men whom He had taught. Even Peter said, "Lord, not my feet only, but also my hands and my head" (John 13:9).

We are still squirming and fuming over exposing, forgiving, and washing one another's feet! We need the whole of us cleansed! We have never accepted people in the Church. We take in numbers and we teach them to project an image, but we have never allowed people—real people—to find a place at our table!

Jesus was running out of time. He had no more time for fun and games. He ended the supper and laid aside His garments. Hear me, my friend; we too are running out of time! We have a generation before us that has not been moved by our lavish banquets or by the glamorous buildings we have built.

Someone, quick! Call the supper to an end and tell us who you really are beneath your churchy look and your pious posture. Tell us something that makes us comfortable with our own nudity. We have carefully hidden our struggles and paraded only our victories, but the whole country is falling asleep at the parade!

> *Call the supper to an end and tell us who you really are beneath your churchy look and your pious posture.*

Favor is deceitful, and beauty is vain: but a woman that feareth the Lord, she shall be praised.
Proverbs 31:30

The enemy wants you to be so focused on your outer appearance that you won't recognize your inner beauty, your inner strength, your inner glory. Your real value cannot be bought, applied, added on, hung from your ears, or laid on your neck. Your real strength is more than outward apparel and adornment for men. This real thing that causes a man to need you so desperately he can't leave you is not what is on you, but what is in you.

You need to recognize what God has put in you. God, when He made the woman, didn't just decorate the outside. He decorated the inside of the woman. He put beauty in her spirit.

The Scriptures talk about not having the outward adornment of gold, silver, and costly array. The Church took that passage and made a legal doctrine out of it. It was declared that there could be no jewelry, no makeup and no clothing of certain types. We are so negative at times. We were so busy dealing with the negative that we didn't hear the positive of what God said. God said that He had adorned the woman inwardly.

"Likewise, ye wives, be in subjection to your own husbands" (1 Pet. 3:1a). Notice that it didn't say women are to be subject to all men, just to her own husband. God did not make you a servant to all men. You have the right to choose who you will be in subjection to—and please choose very carefully.

Healing, Blessings, and Freedom

> *You need to recognize what God has put in you.*

LAY ASIDE YOUR GARMENTS

When the priests enter therein, then shall they not go out of the holy place into the utter court, but there they shall lay their garments wherein they minister; for they are holy; and shall put on other garments, and shall approach to those things which are for the people. Ezekiel 42:14

After the Last Supper, Jesus laid aside His garments. That is what ministry is all about. It requires you to lay aside your garments. Lay aside your personal ambitions and visions of grandeur....Ministry is birthed when you are stripped down to your heart's desire, when beneath every other thread of whimsical grandeur, something in your heart says more than anything else, *I want my life to have counted for something. I want to accomplish something for God.*

Have you ever prayed the kind of prayer that pleads, "Oh God, don't let me impress anyone else but the One to whom I gave my life"?

Have we given our lives to the Lord? I am absolutely serious....If we have, then why are we still standing around the table arguing over who is going to sit on the left and who is going to sit on the right?! *Why have we not laid aside our garments?*

The garment represents different things to different people. It is whatever camouflages our realness, whatever hinders us from really affecting our environment. Our garments are the personal agendas that we have set for ourselves (many of which God was never consulted about). Like the fig leaves sewn together in the garden, we have contrived our own coverings. The terrible tragedy of it all is that, sooner or later, whatever we have sown together will ultimately be stripped away.

The Lord often uses trials to realign us. The strong winds of adversity will attack everything in us that can be shaken. Weaned by the wind, we release every idol in His presence. Every person who finds real purpose will, sooner or later, go through some series of adversities that will cause them to let go of the temporal and cleave to the eternal. Some awaken in hospital rooms with respirators and monitors beeping in their ears. There, beneath the quiet canopy of painted ceilings and with the soft smell of disinfectant, they realize that many of the things that seemed important mean nothing at all.

> *Our garments are the personal agendas that we have set for ourselves (many of which God was never consulted about).*

She girdeth her loins with strength, and strengtheneth her arms. Proverbs 31:17

> *That, if any obey not the word, they also may without the word be won by the conversation of the wives (1 Peter 3:1b).*

Understand that the word *conversation* there refers to life style. You will not win him through lip-service; you will win him through your life style. He will see how you are, not what you say. He will watch how you act. He will watch your attitude. He will watch your disposition. A real problem for women believers today is that with the same mouth they use to witness to their husbands, they often curse others. You cannot witness to and win a man while he sits up and listens to you gossip about others.

"While they behold your chaste conversation [lifestyle] coupled with fear" (1 Pet. 3:2). It didn't say anything about your ruby red lips or your long 25-dollar eyelashes. He should behold your life style, your chaste life style. *Chaste* is a word that means pure. Wives can win a husband by reverencing him.

> *Whose adorning let it not be that outward adorning of plaiting the hair, and of wearing of gold, or of **putting on of apparel** (1 Peter 3:3).*

If that verse meant you could not wear these things, then it means you must be naked. Woman's beauty and strength are not on the outside. There is more to you than clothes. There's more to you than gold. There's more to you than hairdos.

Society promotes the notion that beauty is found in these outer things. However, if you keep working only on these outer things, you will find yourself looking in the mirror to find your value.

> *If you keep working only on these outer things, you will find yourself looking in the mirror to find your value.*

Then Job arose, and rent his mantle, and shaved his head, and fell down upon the ground, and worshipped, and said, Naked came I out of my mother's womb, and naked shall I return thither: the Lord gave, and the Lord hath taken away; blessed be the name of the Lord. In all this Job sinned not, nor charged God foolishly. Job 1:20-22

Left with nothing of importance but the simplicity of a second chance, they lie there. Their certificates of deposit in the bank, their cars in the garage, and their clothes somewhere in a closet, have all lost their importance. Beneath those thin, frail hospital sheets, they discover they are really no different from "Joe Poor" down the hall, who is there on his Medicaid card. They are stripped beneath the sheets and, for the first time, they don't care to read the paper, check the stocks, or catch the news. At least for a while, they are *naked and not ashamed*!

Others discover in the heated battle of a divorce court that the person they thought was everything can walk away and leave them for anything. With hot tears and strong angry words, they are stripped down to what they had before. Job discusses this terrible stripping that seems to be characteristic of the call. He goes through a brief but painful period that yanks away everything that appeared to be important in his life. He used to be very successful, but now he is naked and sick. His home is in shambles, his marriage is a joke, and his children—his precious children—are dead.

What word of wisdom falls from his encrusted lips? What grain of comfort does he afford himself in the vanity of his own thoughts? His only shade beneath the blistering sun of adverse circumstances is found in the fact that he can only be stripped down to what he started with before. He can be stripped of the temporal, but not the eternal.

Some things you never have to lose. I'm not talking about friends, wealth, or fame. We often forget that all of these things are mere threads and imitations of life, just shallow images of status. Character, class, and Christianity are at least three things that can survive the strippings of life!

> He can be stripped of the temporal, but not the eternal.

But the Lord said unto Samuel, Look not on his countenance, or on the height of his stature; because I have refused him: for the Lord seeth not as man seeth; for man looketh on the outward appearance, but the Lord looketh on the heart. 1 Samuel 16:7

You could go broke fixing up the outside and still be lonely and alone. You need to understand that what brought Samson to Delilah so much he couldn't get up, was she became a place where he could rest. He lay on her and slept. The man was tired. She gave him rest. He needed it so desperately that even though he knew she was trying to kill him, he couldn't stay away.

If satan can work Delilah's strengths against men, then God can use them for men. If you are married, you can enrich your marriage through inner beauty. If you're not married, when you do get married, you'll understand it's not the necklaces you wear that make you attractive. It's not the twists you put in your hair. It's something that God puts in your heart that actually affects the man.

"But let it be the hidden man of the heart, in that which is not corruptible, even the ornament of a meek and quiet spirit, which is in the sight of God of great price" (1 Pet. 3:4). God gave you the ornament of a meek and quiet spirit that is more valuable than any other outer form of jewelry. It is worth more than gold. It is more powerful than sexual ability.

When Samson hit Delilah's lap, she calmed him. Can you see what made Adam partake of the forbidden fruit, knowing it was evil? The Bible says Eve was deceived, but he knew. Do you see how powerful your influence is? The enemy wants to capitalize on what God put in you. That is why you must watch what goes through your doors.

> *G*od gave you the ornament of a meek and quiet spirit that is more valuable than any other outer form of jewelry.

WORSHIP COMES FROM SACRIFICE

WORSHIP COMES FROM SACRIFICE

By Him therefore let us offer the sacrifice of praise to God continually, that is, the fruit of our lips giving thanks to His name. But to do good and to communicate forget not: for with such sacrifices God is well pleased. Hebrews 13:15-16

DAY **323**

True worship is born when true sacrifice occurs. When we lay upon the altar some bleeding object that we thought we would keep for ourselves (but realized it was God's all the while), that's worship. You can never be really anointed until you personally experience a situation that calls you to lay aside your garments. It is from this river that the tears of worship are born....

People who see you worship will never be able to determine why you worship by looking at things you have. It is *what you left behind* and *laid aside* that seasons you into the real aroma of worship. How much does it cost to be the "real" you? What did you lay aside to follow Him? Whatever you have laid aside, or will lay aside, determines the effectiveness of your ability to touch the world at its feet and speak to its heart!

Jesus, in one final blaze of teaching excellence, did an illustrated sermon in the nude. By washing their feet, He showed the disciples that they can never change the atmosphere or wash the feet of anybody until they had gone through sacrifice and endured risk and rejection. Do you have great ambitions or plans? Lay them aside—the Lord has need of you.

Laying aside your garment requires you to say:

"Here are my grudges and my unforgiveness. Here is my need to impress and be acknowledged. Here's my time, and here is my overtime. Here's my second job. Here is anything that I may be wrapped up in that hinders me from receiving new glory.

"You will never have to take these things, Lord. You will not have to snatch them from my clenched fist as I wrestle in rebellion with Your tender whispers in the night. I have heard the soft brush of Your voice like wind across my face. I will give You what it takes to be who You want me to be. Even if I have to be *the only one* who stands in crowds of religious indifference, I will lay aside my garments!"

> *You can never be really anointed until you personally experience a situation that calls you to lay aside your garments.*

For after this manner in the old time the holy women also, who trusted in God, adorned themselves...even as Sarah obeyed Abraham, calling him lord; whose daughters ye are, as long as ye do well, and are not afraid with any amazement. 1 Peter 3:5-6

In the times of the patriarchs, they decorated themselves through their trust in God. Sarah was beautiful because she exhibited inner beauty and lived in obedience to Abraham.

You are Sarah's daughters when you are not afraid with any amazement. When you resist the temptation to react to circumstances and maintain a peaceful, meek and quiet spirit in times of frustration, then you are Sarah's daughters.

Jesus called the infirm woman. He unleashed a daughter of Abraham. If you can stay calm in a storm, if you can praise God under pressure, if you can worship in the midst of critics and criticism, God says you are Sarah's daughter.

If you can keep a calm head when the bills are more than the income, and not lose control when satan says you won't make it, if you can stand in the midst of the storm, you are Sarah's daughter.

If you can rebuke the fear that is knocking at the door of your heart, and tell that low self-esteem it cannot come in, and rebuke all the spirits that are waiting to attack you and make you captive, you are Sarah's daughter.

If you can stand calm in the midst of the storm and say, "I know God will deliver me," you are Sarah's daughter. If you can walk with God in the midst of the storm and trust Him to bring you through dry places, you are Sarah's daughter.

If you can judge God faithful, and know that God cannot lie, understanding that satan is the father of lies, you are Sarah's daughter.

If you can stand there when fear is trying to get you to overreact and fall apart, you are Sarah's daughter. If you can stand there and push a tear from off the side of your face and smile in the middle of the rain, you are Sarah's daughter.

> You are Sarah's daughters when you are not afraid with any amazement.

THE GREAT LEVELER

For I say, through the grace given unto me, to every man that is among you, not to think of himself more highly than he ought to think; but to think soberly, according as God hath dealt to every man the measure of faith. For as we have many members in one body, and all members have not the same office. Romans 12:3-4

Thank God for all the Kathryn Kuhlmans, the Oral Roberts, and the Benny Hinns whose lives have touched the world. The hot blaze of camera lights never caught the true basis of their ministry. It was the things they *laid aside* that made them who they were. Thank God they laid them aside. Thousands are healed because they did. Thousands were saved because they did.

What about "Pastor Littlechurch" and "Evangelist Nobody" who never sold a tape or wrote a book? They paid the price nonetheless, and for the souls they touched they are unsung heroes. Like Noah, their membership roll never exceeded eight souls, but they faithfully led them nonetheless. They wanted to do more. They thought they would go farther than they did, but they had *laid aside their garments*. They said, "If I am not called to help everybody, then please, God, *let me help somebody*!" This is the cost of Christianity stripped down to one desire, stripped to the simplicity of bareness.

The truth of the matter is that when men are stripped bare, there is no difference between the executive and the janitor. When they are stripped bare, there is no difference between the usher and the pastor. Is that why we are afraid to let anyone see who we really are? Have we become so addicted to our distinctions that we have lost our commonality?...

There are no differences in the feet of the washed and the feet of the one who washes them....Your ministry truly becomes effective when you know that there is precious little difference between the people you serve and yourself. Then and only then have you laid aside your garments!...

Marriages are failing all over the country because couples are reciting vows before an overworked preacher, and an overspent family, promising to do what they will never be able to do! Why? You can't love anybody like that until you *lay aside your garments* and allow their needs to supercede your needs....They can never be one until they have laid aside their garments. Then and only then can they come together as one.

> When they are stripped bare, there is no difference between the usher and the pastor.

Many daughters have done virtuously, but thou excellest them all. Proverbs 31:29

And, behold, there was a woman which had a spirit of infirmity eighteen years, and was bowed together, and could in no wise lift up herself. And when Jesus saw her, He called her to Him, and said unto her, Woman, thou art loosed from thine infirmity (Luke 13:11-12).

God is adorning you with glory, power and majesty. He will send people into your life to appreciate your real beauty, your real essence. It is the kind of beauty that lasts in a face full of wrinkles, gray hair, falling arches, crow's feet, and all the pitfalls that may come your way. There's a beauty that you can see in a 90-year-old woman's face that causes an old man to smile. God is decorating you on the inside. He is putting a glory in you that will shine through your eyes. A man will come along and look in your eyes. He will not talk about whether they were blue or whether your eye-shadow was right or not. He will look in your eyes and see trust, peace, love and life.

Appreciate the ornaments of God. Let God give you a new attitude. Let Him wash everything out of your spirit that is against Him. Let go of anger, hate, frustration and bitterness. God wants you unleashed. He repeats today, just as He did two thousand years ago, "Woman, thou art loosed."

Beauty comes in many ways. However, true beauty is always on the inside. A faithful wife is more precious than words can express. The inner beauty that makes you valuable to God will also make you valuable to others. Some may take just longer to notice it. Regardless of how long it takes, know the attractiveness and beauty that is within.

Perhaps you feel scarred by the past. Maybe you think you are unattractive and unworthy. Nothing could be more untrue. God painted a wonderful piece of artwork one day. That painting is you.

> *Beauty comes in many ways. However, true beauty is always on the inside.*

No Distinction

For ye know the grace of our Lord Jesus Christ, that, though He was rich, yet for your sakes He became poor, that ye through His poverty might be rich. 2 Corinthians 8:9

He riseth from supper, and laid aside His garments; and took a towel and girded Himself. After that He poureth water into a basin, and began to wash the disciples' feet, and to wipe them with the towel wherewith He was girded (John 13:4-5).

Jesus so loved those men that He didn't wait on them to make the first move. He taught them by going first. He rose up! He laid aside His garments and He washed their feet! He didn't respond to their actions—He initiated their actions. Are you always going to be a responder who only reacts to what others dictate, or are you going to initiate change in the Body? If you are going to change it, then you must be willing to be a trendsetter! You must be *naked and not ashamed.*

Now I know some wise theologian is thinking, "Jesus served with a towel gird about Himself." Yes, you are right. No one can work without covering! But please remember that somewhere between His evening dinner wear and the servant's towel with which He was to be girded—somewhere in the process—Jesus stood before them naked. They witnessed the scene as their Master stepped down to become a servant. He laid aside His garments—not only for them, but for us all. He came to earth and stripped Himself of the glory He had with the Father before the foundations of the world!

Jesus normally dressed with distinction. He was such a fashion statement that even while He was dying on the cross, affluent Roman soldiers were gambling to win the prize of Jesus' seamless robe. But this was not a time for form. Neither was it a time for fashion, for real ministry is done with a complete loss of distinction. If He were to leave a lasting impact on these men in the upper room, He must cover Himself only in a plain towel!

Real ministry is done with a complete loss of distinction.

Let this mind be in you, which was also in Christ Jesus: who, being in the form of God, thought it not robbery to be equal with God: but made Himself of no reputation, and took upon Him the form of a servant, and was made in the likeness of men: and being found in fashion as a man, He humbled Himself, and became obedient unto death, even the death of the cross. Wherefore God also hath highly exalted Him, and given Him a name which is above every name. Philippians 2:5-9

After Jesus ate His last supper with the disciples, He laid aside His garments and washed their feet. (See John 13:2-5.) The glamorous Prince of Peace stripped Himself to appear before them in only a common towel. As He knelt down on the floor and began to wash the disciples' feet, He looked so lowly that it was embarrassing. Peter almost refused to allow Him to be seen in that light! To think that the One he called Master would appear in a towel! One moment He was as stately as a prince, and the next moment He knelt naked before them as just a man!

The final touch of God was delivered through a Man who had humbled Himself and wrapped His vulnerabilities up in His ministry. He was covered like a servant, ready to help the hurting. His suit, His clerical attire, was neither His seamless robe nor His nakedness. His ministry was best seen when He wrapped Himself in a towel!

If you believe that God would exalt you, if you believe that you have the ability to wash the dusty sands of life from the feet of this world, then please don't join the spiritual elitists who are impressed with their own speech!

Lay aside every distraction. Lay aside your garments, wrap every naked human flaw in the warm towel of servanthood as you help others, and draw the water! With joy we draw water from the wells of salvation! (See Isaiah 12:3.) But what good is that water if we fail to use it to wash away the weariness of someone's journey? I can almost hear the cascading sound of the cooling waters. They fall like mountains of water plummeting from the Rock. God has enough water. He just needs someone who will take the risk of being the first one. He is searching for someone to end the long supper and lay aside his garments. You may be the only one at your table who knows that the hour has come and the supper is ended. Wait no longer—we are losing our generation! *Lay aside your garments!* The waters are drawn, my friend; we are waiting...on you!

> The glamorous Prince of Peace stripped Himself to appear before them in only a common towel.

And let us not be weary in well doing: for in due season we shall reap, if we faint not.
Galatians 6:9

Do you remember how in winter icicles hang from the roofs of old houses, pointing toward the ground like stalactites in a cave? As the cold blitz of winter was challenged by budding trees and warmer days, the icicles began to drip and diminish. Slowly the earth changed its clothes for a new season....

Winter is just the prelude God plays to introduce the concerto of summer. In spite of its cold, frostbitten hand seizing our forest, lawns, and streams, its grip can still be broken through the patient perseverance of the season that is sensitive to timing and divine purpose. There is nothing like a sense of time. It cannot be faked. It is like seeing a choir sway to the beat of a gospel ballad. Someone invariably will be moving spastically, trying desperately to simulate a sense of timing. Moving his feet with all the grace of the Tin Man in *The Wizard of Oz*, he can't quite learn what the body has to sense. The lack of timing is as detrimental as planting corn in the bitter winds of an Alaskan winter. There may be absolutely nothing wrong with the seed or the ground, just the time in which the farmer chose to expect the process to occur.

Assuming that you understand the necessity of small beginnings, and assuming that you realize whatever you have will not replace the One who gave it and that success only creates a platform for responsibility to be enlarged—then you can begin to ascertain where you are on the calendar, the divine almanac of God. Did you know that God has an almanac? Perhaps you do not know what an almanac is. My mother always consulted the almanac to determine the best time to plant the crop she intended to harvest. It is a calendar that presents the seasons and cycles of a year. You see, the principle of seed time and harvest will not override the understanding of time and purpose. God does everything according to His eternal almanac of time and purpose!

> God does everything according to His eternal almanac of time and purpose!

There remaineth therefore a rest to the people of God. Hebrews 4:9

We have dealt with many aspects of the story of Jesus healing the infirm woman in Luke 13. However, I would like to look at an issue underlying the miracle. It does not really concern either the woman or Christ. It is the time of healing: the Sabbath day.

The Sabbath is a day of rest. It is a day of restoration. Following creation, on the seventh day, God rested (see Gen. 2:2). Rest is for the purpose of restoration. It is not just because you're tired. It is during a time of rest that you replenish or receive back those things that were expended or put out. It is during the time of restoration that the enemy wants to break off your fellowship with the Lord.

I don't want you to think of rest just in terms of sleep. Please understand that rest and restoration are related concepts. The enemy does not want you to have rest. You need calmness or Sabbath rest because it is through the resting of your spirit that the restoration of your life begins to occur.

It is not a mere coincidence that this woman was healed on the Sabbath day. The Bible goes to great pains to make us aware that it was during the Sabbath that this woman experienced her healing. The Sabbath was meant not only for God to rest, but also for God to enjoy His creation with man. The issues are rest and communion.

In the nation of Israel, God used the Sabbath day as a sign of the covenant. It proved that they were His people. They spent time in worship and fellowship with the Lord. That is the Sabbath. It is real communion between the heart of man and heart of God.

When Jesus began to minister in a restful situation, needs began to be manifested. The infirm woman's need was revealed in the midst of the Sabbath. You can never get your needs met by losing your head. When you calm down, God speaks.

> You can never get your needs met by losing your head.

For if thou altogether holdest thy peace at this time, then shall there enlargement and deliverance arise to the Jews from another place; but thou and thy father's house shall be destroyed: and who knoweth whether thou art come to the kingdom for such a time as this? Esther 4:14

In autumn, you turn over the ground so last year's stalks and stems can become next year's harvest. Broken clods freshly turned, filled with crushed cornstalks and covered with manure, form the mulch you need to prepare the ground and replenish the starving soil after the previous yield. Like the ground that has given much and received little, you too need to be broken and turned over, allowed to rest for a time, and prepared for the next season of yield. Perhaps you have just completed a time of being turned over and undergoing manure-filled experiences. That period was just a prerequisite for a miracle! Thank God for the seasons of rest He gives to His children. If the ground produced without ever resting, it would soon be stripped of all the precious minerals it needs to be productive....

Mordecai taught Queen Esther an essential lesson when he spoke those words in Esther 4:14. He wanted her to realize that God had given her an opportunity to be a blessing. Now, it wasn't given to her so she could brag about the nobility of which she became a part. God isn't interested in human grandeur. When He allows us to ascend into the clouds, it is only so we can stop the rain with the enlightenment we gained from the laborious progression of our own experiences. Mordecai showed Esther that God had been grooming her all her life for this moment. In spite of the tremendous challenge set before her, she was the woman for the job. She was God's choice, a handmaiden fitly chosen and wonderfully endowed for the acquisition of a victorious report.

Go, gather together all the Jews that are present in Shushan, and fast ye for me, and neither eat nor drink three days, night or day: I also and my maidens will fast likewise; and so will I go in unto the king, which is not according to the law: and if I perish, I perish (Esther 4:16).

> God had been grooming her all her life for this moment.

Create in me a clean heart, O God; and renew a right spirit within me. Cast me not away from Thy presence; and take not Thy holy spirit from me. Restore unto me the joy of Thy salvation; and uphold me with Thy free spirit. Psalm 51:10-12

When you start murmuring and complaining, the only thing God can focus on is your unbelief. When you start resting in Him, He can focus on your problems and on the areas of your life that need to be touched.

When you begin to enter into real worship with God, that's the best time to have Him minister to your needs. That's the time God does restoration in your life. Satan, therefore, wants to break up your Sabbath rest.

And when Jesus saw her, He called her to Him, and said unto her, Woman, thou art loosed from thine infirmity. And He laid His hands on her: and immediately she was made straight, and glorified God. And the ruler of the synagogue answered with indignation, because that Jesus had healed on the sabbath day, and said unto the people, There are six days in which men ought to work: in them therefore come and be healed, and not on the sabbath day. The Lord then answered him, and said, Thou hypocrite, doth not each one of you on the sabbath loose his ox or his ass from the stall, and lead him away to watering? And ought not this woman, being a daughter of Abraham, whom Satan hath bound, lo, these eighteen years, be loosed from this bond on the sabbath day? (Luke 13:12-16)

Jesus healed this woman on the Sabbath. One thing you can't seem to deliver religious people from is their being religious. Sometimes I would rather deal with rank sinners than with religious people. They esteem religiosity above God's creation. They are more concerned about keeping doctrine than about helping people. Man is God's concern above everything else.

The infirm woman was not sitting around complaining. She was not murmuring. She was not hysterical. She had a problem, but she was calm. She was just sitting there listening to the words of the Master. She brought her problem with her, but her problem had not dominated her worship.

> When you begin to enter into real worship with God, that's the best time to have Him minister to your needs.

Then Esther bade them return Mordecai this answer, Go, gather together all the Jews that are present in Shushan, and fast ye for me, and neither eat nor drink three days, night or day: I also and my maidens will fast likewise; and so will I go in unto the king, which is not according to the law: and if I perish, I perish. So Mordecai went his way, and did according to all that Esther had commanded him. Esther 4:15-17

Mordecai's counsel prepared Esther's mind for the purpose God had from the beginning for elevating her position. Counsel may prepare your mind, but only fervent prayer can prepare your spirit for the vast undertakings that come with it being your time. No one counsel will prepare your heart like prayer.

I once met an evangelist at a retreat in Chicago. He woke every morning while the rest of the ministers were still asleep and went jogging for hours in the early morning dew. When I awoke, he was coming down the hall with a flushed face and glistening with perspiration. He was smiling like he knew a secret. I asked him later, "Why don't you try to rest instead of racing around the grounds like you are preparing for a fight with Muhammad Ali?" He laughed, and I will never forget his answer. He said, "Every day I read for my mind. I pray for my spirit. And I run for my body." He explained, "If I touch all three areas, all parts of my being have been exercised to perform well." I looked down at my bountiful waist and thought, "Two out of three isn't bad."

Esther was a wise woman; she called a fast. Once Mordecai had exercised her mind through wise counsel, she called a time of fasting and prayer to prepare her spirit. She knew that prayer undergirds the spirit and keeps a person from sagging beneath the weight of opposition. Not only did she pray, but she also taught everyone under her authority to pray as well. I have learned that it is difficult to work with people who do not pray. Even our children pray. Now, I'm not suggesting that we are perfect. We don't pray because we are perfect—we pray because we are not! Prayer is a strong defense against satanic attack. If Esther had not prayed, she would have fallen prey to the cunning devices of Haman, her wicked enemy!

> *Prayer undergirds the spirit and keeps a person from sagging beneath the weight of opposition.*

Who being the brightness of His glory, and the express image of His person, and upholding all things by the word of His power, when He had by Himself purged our sins, sat down on the right hand of the Majesty on high. Hebrews 1:3

I want to zoom in on the Sabbath day because what the Sabbath was physically, Christ is spiritually. Christ is our Sabbath rest. He is the end of our labors. We are saved by grace through faith and not by works, lest any man should be able to boast (see Eph. 2:8-9). Jesus said:

> *Come unto Me, all ye that labor and are heavy laden, and I will give you rest. Take My yoke upon you, and learn of Me; for I am meek and lowly in heart: and ye shall find rest unto your souls. For My yoke is easy, and My burden is light (Matthew 11:28-30).*

The rest of the Lord is so complete that when Jesus was dying on the cross, He said, "It is finished" (John 19:30). It was so powerful. For the first time in history, a high priest sat down in the presence of God without having to run in and out bringing blood to atone the sins of man. When Christ entered in once and for all, He offered up Himself for us that we might be delivered from sin.

If you really want to be healed, you've got to be in Him. If you really want to be set free, and experience restoration, you've got to be in Him, because your healing comes in the Sabbath rest. Your healing comes in Christ Jesus. As you rest in Him, every infirmity, every area bent out of place will be restored.

The devil knows this truth, so he does not want you to rest in the Lord. Satan wants you to be anxious. He wants you to be upset. He wants you to be hysterical. He wants you to be suicidal, doubtful, fearful and neurotic.

Christ is our Sabbath rest. He is the end of our labors.

EMPOWERED TO PERFORM

Now it came to pass on the third day, that Esther put on her royal apparel, and stood in the inner court of the king's house, over against the king's house: and the king sat upon his royal throne in the royal house, over against the gate of the house. And it was so, when the king saw Esther the queen standing in the court, that she obtained favor in his sight: and the king held out to Esther the golden sceptre that was in his hand.... Esther 5:1-2

Esther's changing her apparel signifies our need to alter our circumstances to facilitate the success of the vision that is before us. Everything must be committed to the goal—body, soul, and spirit. When the king beheld a prepared person, he granted an expected end. He drew her into his presence because she had prepared herself for her time. Please hear me; there is a blessing on the horizon for the person of purpose. Only the prepared will be eligible to receive this endowment from the Lord, so be ready!

Like sands cascading down in an hourglass, time silently slips away, without the chance of retrieval, from almost everyone everyday. The misuse of anything as precious as time should be a crime. If someone steals your car, it would be an inconvenience but not a tragedy because you can easily acquire another. If someone snatches your wallet, it would be an annoyance but a few phone calls would salvage the majority of your concerns. But who can you call if you suffer the loss of time—and not just time, but *your time*? Who can afford to miss their time? I can't, can you?

Ask God to give you the patience you need to become empowered to perform. You may feel like a child waiting in line at a carnival. There will always be times when other people receive their dues and you are forced to wait your turn. This is not injustice; it is order. There is nothing unjust about order. But after I have waited my turn and paid my dues, there comes a time when it is all mine. The most frightening thing I can think of is the possibility of missing my time. Generally, somewhere on the other side of a tremendous test is the harvest of your dream. If you have planted the seeds of a promise and watered them thoroughly with the tears of struggle, then this is your time. Woe unto the person who has seeds without water. The tears of struggle become the irrigation of the Holy Spirit. It is through your own tear-filled struggles that God directs the waters of life to the field of your dreams.

Ask God to give you the patience you need to become empowered to perform.

Rest in the Lord, and wait patiently for Him: fret not thyself because of him who prospereth in his way, because of the man who bringeth wicked devices to pass. Psalm 37:7

…he also hath ceased from his own works, as God did from His. Let us labor therefore to enter into that rest, lest any man fall after the same example of unbelief (Hebrews 4:10-11).

Sometimes it takes work to find the place of rest and calm. Our hectic world does not lend itself to quiet and peace. It creates noise and uneasiness. Even though the infirm woman of Luke 13 was bowed over and could not lift herself, she rested in the fact that she was in the presence of a mighty God. He is able to do exceedingly and abundantly above all that we may ask or think (see Eph. 3:20).

Jesus also confronted the woman at the well with some exciting truths.

Then cometh He to a city of Samaria, which is called Sychar, near to the parcel of ground that Jacob gave to his son Joseph. Now Jacob's well was there. Jesus therefore, being wearied with His journey, sat thus on the well: and it was about the sixth hour. There cometh a woman of Samaria to draw water: Jesus saith unto her, Give Me to drink. (For His disciples were gone away unto the city to buy meat.) Then saith the woman of Samaria unto Him, How is it that Thou, being a Jew, askest drink of me, which am a woman of Samaria? for the Jews have no dealings with the Samaritans. Jesus answered and said unto her, If thou knewest the gift of God, and who it is that saith to thee, Give Me to drink; thou wouldest have asked of Him, and He would have given thee living water. The woman saith unto Him, Sir, Thou hast nothing to draw with, and the well is deep: from whence then hast Thou that living water? Art Thou greater than our father Jacob, which gave us the well, and drank thereof himself, and his children, and his cattle? Jesus answered and said unto her, Whosoever drinketh of this water shall thirst again: but whosoever drinketh of the water that I shall give him shall never thirst; but the water that I shall give him shall be in him a well of water springing up into everlasting life (John 4:5-14).

Jesus was sitting at the well waiting for someone to return. He was relaxed. He was calm and resting. He knew who He was. God doesn't get excited about circumstances.

> *Sometimes it takes work to find the place of rest and calm.*

They that sow in tears shall reap in joy. Psalm 126:5

Greatness has a tremendous thirst. This thirst is quenched in the tear-stained struggle toward destiny. One thing I learned about life is neither fellowship nor friendship can lower the price of personal sacrifice. What I mean is, no one can water your dreams but you. No matter how many people hold your hand, you still must shed your own tears. Others can cry with you, but they can't cry for you! That's the bad news. The good news is there will be a harvest at the end of your tears!

On the other hand, you must know when you have shed enough tears. It is important that you don't get stuck in a state of lamentation. In short, don't overwater the promise! A certain amount of tears is necessary during the time of sowing. But when you have come into harvest, don't let the devil keep you weeping. Tears are for the sower, but joy is for the harvester. Harvest your field with joy. You've paid your dues and shed your tears—now reap your benefits. It's your turn. Reap in knee-slapping, teeth-baring, hand-clapping, foot-stomping joy!

> *He that goeth forth and weepeth, bearing precious seed, shall doubtless come again with rejoicing, bringing his sheaves with him (Psalm 126:6).*

Everything has a season and a purpose (see Eccles. 3:1). You need to understand that God is just and that He appropriates opportunities to advance according to His purpose. I don't know whether this is true for everyone, but usually obscurity precedes notoriety. The first Psalm teaches that the blessed man meditates on the Word while he waits. It says that you bring forth fruit in your own season. It is good to recognize your season and prepare for it before it comes. But the fruit will not grow prior to its right season. Don't demand fruit when it is not in season. Even restaurant menus have a notation that says certain items can be served only when their fruit is in season.

Ask God to give you the patience you need to become empowered to perform.

I have set the Lord always before me: because He is at my right hand, I shall not be moved. Therefore my heart is glad, and my glory rejoiceth: my flesh also shall rest in hope. Psalm 16:8-9

One time the disciples and Jesus were on a ship. The storm arose and appeared to be about to sink the ship. However, Jesus didn't become concerned about circumstances. In fact, He was sleeping, resting in the middle of a crisis. Everyone else was running all over the boat trying to figure out how they would get into life jackets and into the lifeboats. Was Jesus resting because He was lazy? No, He was resting because He knew He was greater than the storm. Jesus rose up and spoke to the winds and waves and said, "Peace, be still" (Mark 4:39).

When you know who you are, you don't have to struggle. You don't have to work Him up.

That was Christ's attitude when the woman at the well met Him. (See John 4.) When this woman came down with her waterpot on her shoulder, she was all upset and worried about the water she needed to draw. Jesus was sitting by the well. He began to demonstrate calmness. He told her, "If you drink of the water that you have, you will thirst again, but if you drink of the water that I have, you will never thirst."

The woman saith unto Him, Sir, give me this water, that I thirst not, neither come hither to draw. Jesus saith unto her, Go, call thy husband, and come hither (John 4:15-16).

Jesus shifted the focus of the conversation to the real need.

The woman answered and said, I have no husband. Jesus said unto her, Thou hast well said, I have no husband: for thou hast had five husbands; and he whom thou now hast is not thy husband: in that saidst thou truly (John 4:17-18).

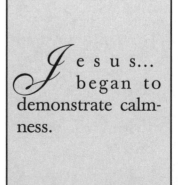

Jesus... began to demonstrate calmness.

And he shall be like a tree planted by the rivers of water, that bringeth forth his fruit in his season; his leaf also shall not wither; and whatsoever he doeth shall prosper.
Psalm 1:3

You feel as though you have been waiting without seeing any results, almost like a car waiting at an intersection. Then the light suddenly changes from red to green and you are free to move. When God changes the light in your life from red to green, you can accomplish things that you tried to do at other times but could not perform….I call those seasons "green light" time….What an exciting time it is to suddenly find your engine kicking into gear and your turbines turning in harmonious production. Your tires screech from a dead stop to jet speed in seconds and bang! You are on the road again.

This is an exciting time for the prepared believer. I believe with all my heart that soon people whom God had waiting their turn will burst to the forefront and pull into the fast lane. Trained by patience and humbled by personal challenges, they will usher in a new season in the cycle of the Kingdom. Are you a part of what God is doing, or are you still looking back at what God has done? I want to see you burn some spiritual rubber for Jesus!

There may be some degree of reservation in the mind of the thinking person. "What if I enter my season and experience the rich blessings God has been promising for a long time, and then the season ends? How can I stand to go back into seclusion and be content? Isn't it difficult, once a person has been a main player, to become subdued and lethargic after being exposed to the racing, titillating feeling of a green light time in life?" All of these are excellent questions, ones that must be addressed. After all, what good is having your season if over your head gather the gloomy clouds of warning that keep thundering a nagging threat in your ears? They threaten that all you are doing now will not last.

I want to see you burn some spiritual rubber for Jesus!

And have put on the new man, which is renewed in knowledge after the image of Him that created him. Colossians 3:10

When the woman at the well met Jesus, He calmly addressed her real need.

> *The woman answered and said, I have no husband. Jesus said unto her, Thou hast well said, I have no husband: for thou hast had five husbands; and he whom thou now hast is not thy husband: in that saidst thou truly (John 4:17-18).*

Like this woman, you can get yourself into situations that wound and upset your spirit. These kinds of wounds can't be healed through human effort. You must get in the presence of God and let Him fill those voids in your life. You will not settle it up by going from friend to friend. This woman had already tried that. She had already gone through five men. The answer is not getting another man. It's getting in touch with *the Man—Jesus.*

The woman at the well threw down her waterpot and ran to tell others about the man she had met at the well. We too need to get rid of the old, carnal man. Some of those old attachments and old ways of living need to be replaced with the calmness of the Spirit.

This woman could never have rid herself of the old man until she met the new man. When you meet the new, you get the power to say good-bye to the old. You will never be able to break the grip on your life that those old ways have until you know Jesus Christ is the real way. You will never get it straight without Jesus. You must come to Him just as you are. Knowing Him will give you the power to break away from the old self and the ties that bind.

If you have something that has attached itself to you that is not of God, you won't be able to break it through your own strength.

> *Submit yourselves therefore to God. Resist the devil, and he will flee from you (James 4:7).*

As you submit to God, you receive the power to resist the enemy.

When you meet the new, you get the power to say good-bye to the old.

Loving From Faith to Faith

For therein is the righteousness of God revealed from faith to faith: as it is written, The just shall live by faith. Romans 1:17

What good is having your season if over your head gather the gloomy clouds of warning that keep thundering a nagging threat in your ears?…

First, let me rebuke the spirit of fear. Fear will hide in the closet as we are blessed and make strange noises when no one else is around. We need to declare God to this fear. We dare not fall in love with what God is doing, but we must always be in love with who God is. God does not change. That's why we must set our affections on things that are eternal. He said, "For I am the Lord, I change not" (Mal. 3:6a). It is such a comfort, when the chilly voice of fear speaks, to know that God doesn't change. His purpose doesn't change. His methods may change, but His ultimate purpose doesn't. People have a need to know what comes next. God doesn't always make us privy to such information, but He has promised that if we walk uprightly, He will not withhold any good thing from us (see Ps. 84:11). I therefore conclude that if God withheld it, then it was no longer working for my good. I am then ready for the next assignment—it will be good for me.

The thing we must always remember is God can bless us in many different areas. Even while we were in the waiting periods of our lives, some other area was being blessed. There are really no "down" times in God. We only feel down when, like spoiled children, we demand that He continue to give us what He did at one stage without appreciating the fact that we are moving from one stage to another. It is what the Word calls going from faith to faith (see Rom. 1:17).

God has put too much training into you to leave you without any area of productivity. He has been grooming you in the furnace of affliction. When He begins to move you into your season, don't allow even well-meaning people to intimidate you with the fear of change.

> There are really no "down" times in God.

Blessed be the God and Father of our Lord Jesus Christ, who hath blessed us with all spiritual blessings in heavenly places in Christ. Ephesians 1:3

The woman then left her waterpot, and went her way into the city, and saith to the men, Come, see a man, which told me all things that ever I did: is not this the Christ? Then they went out of the city, and came unto Him. And many of the Samaritans of that city believed on Him for the saying of the woman, which testified, He told me all that ever I did. So when the Samaritans were come unto Him, they besought Him that He would tarry with them: and He abode there two days. And many more believed because of His own word; and said unto the woman, Now we believe, not because of thy saying: for we have heard Him ourselves, and know that this is indeed the Christ, the Savior of the world (John 4:28-30; 39-42).

This woman didn't even go back home. She ran into the city telling everyone to come and see the Man who had told her about her life. You do yourself a disservice until you really come to know Jesus. He satisfies. Everyone else, well, they pacify, but Jesus satisfies. He can satisfy every need and every yearning. He heals every pain and every affliction. Then He lifts every burden and every trouble in your life.

You have had enough tragedy. You have been bent over long enough. God will do something good in you. God kept you living through all those years of infirmity because He had something greater for you than what you've experienced earlier. God kept you because He has something better for you.

You may have been abused and misused. Perhaps all those you trusted in turned on you and broke your heart. Still God has sustained you. You didn't make it because you were strong. You didn't make it because you were smart. You didn't make it because you were wise. You made it because God's amazing grace kept you and sustained you. God has more for you today than what you went through yesterday. Don't give up. Don't give in. Hold on. The blessing is on the way.

> **God has more for you today than what you went through yesterday.**

For this cause have I sent unto you Timotheus, who is my beloved son, and faithful in the Lord, who shall bring you into remembrance of my ways which be in Christ, as I teach every where in every church. 1 Corinthians 4:17

There is a peace that Christians must have in order to enjoy life. I believe one of Saul's greatest mistakes was to fall in love with the kingdom and not the King! He was so intimidated when God decided to move someone into his position that he tried to kill his successor. You would be surprised how many good people try to kill their successors. Mothers are jealous of their own daughters. Fathers belittle their own sons. If your time as a good boxer is up, then why can't you learn the art of being an excellent coach? You see, there always is an area where you can be fruitful; it simply may not be the same area all the time.

Speaking of coaches, the apostle Paul, who was an excellent minister of the gospel, began in the winter of his ministry to pour his knowledge into his successor. He wasn't jealous....He counsels Timothy to develop the ability to be prepared in season and out of season....I could never quite understand this verse until another preacher began to share with me some farming techniques that I had not applied to this pursuit of excellence in ministry or in any other area.

The farmer who continuously produces crops can do so because he produces more than one type of crop. He has several different fields and he rotates a certain crop from one field to another. He plants corn in one field and it grows and produces ears of yellow corn on tall green stalks that sway in the wind and gleam in the sun. Eventually the corn goes out of season. The farmer takes the old stalks that turned brown and withered and plows them under. Now, a farmer always thinks in terms of tomorrow. He plows and fertilizes the field and allows it to rest from growing corn. Meanwhile in the other field the alfalfa is cut for the last crop of hay and it too is plowed. In the spring the farmer rotates his crops; the field that once grew corn now produces alfalfa, and the field that previously was planted in alfalfa now sprouts cornstalks. This coverall-clad soldier will always be productive because he understands the importance of being multi-faceted.

> There always is an area where you can be fruitful; it simply may not be the same area all the time.

There be many that say, Who will show us any good? Lord, lift Thou up the light of Thy countenance upon us. Thou hast put gladness in my heart, more than in the time that their corn and their wine increased. I will both lay me down in peace, and sleep: for thou, Lord, only makest me dwell in safety. Psalm 4:6-8

I dare you to realize that you can do all things through Christ who strengthens you (see Phil. 4:13). Once the infirm woman knew that she didn't have to be bent over, she stood straight up. Jesus told the woman at the well to get rid of the old. He wanted her to step away from that old pattern of selfishness. Suddenly, she recognized that she didn't have what she thought she had. The sinful things that you have fought to maintain are not worth what you thought they were.

I'm referring to some of those things that have attached themselves to your life in which you find comfort. Some of those habits you have come to enjoy, some of those relationships you thought you found security in, were not profitable. Often we settle for less because we didn't meet the best. When you get the best, it gives you the power to let go of the rest.

The infirm woman that Jesus healed in Luke 13 didn't panic because of her crippling disease. She had been in torment and pain for 18 years. When she came into the presence of Jesus, she relaxed in Him. She expected that He would take care of her. The result was a wonderful healing. The woman at the well from John 4 expected water, but left the well having found the Savior. She sought temporal satisfaction, but found eternal satisfaction.

That's what rest and Sabbath is. It is the ability to find eternal satisfaction in Jesus. The world will never give us peace and satisfaction. Jesus offers both freely.

The woman who has struggled can find satisfaction. You can find hope for your soul. It is found in the Master of the universe. He will not deny you because of your past. He will not scrutinize your every action. He will take you as you are and give you rest. He will provide a peace that will satisfy the very yearning of your soul.

> The world will never give us peace and satisfaction. Jesus offers both freely.

So God created man in His own image, in the image of God created He him; male and female created He them. Genesis 1:27

Paul tells Timothy to be instant in season and out of season (see 2 Tim. 4:2). He then tells him to be diverse. According to his instructions, we must reprove and rebuke. We also must be able to let things rest and encourage others. I believe many people lose their sense of self-worth because they fail to diversify themselves. Then, when the season of one gift is over, they are unprepared for any other area. If we listen carefully to the voice of God, we can be productive at every stage of life. It doesn't matter whether we are respected as players or as coaches. What matters is ultimately we contribute on some level to the game. We need to stay in the game. In short, diversity is a key to longevity.

Psalm 1 says that the blessed man doesn't just grow; he is also planted. Do you realize that God plants the feet of the blessed man? Never does he "just happen." He is not a weed. He is planted at a specific time in a specific place to accomplish a divine purpose. I have noticed that people who always move from place to place do not grow very well. The blessed man is planted! If you have been planted, you grow down before you grow up. I simply mean that God isn't concerned about how high your trunk grows. He is concerned about how deep your roots go. He knows that the real challenge is to produce quality, not quantity.

The Master has created a masterpiece in you. He has taken every struggle and test, every mishap and neglect, to cultivate in you the soil needed to make you reproductive. Contrary winds were sent to blow you away from people and cliques that would not create a climate conducive for what God wants to do in your life. In the light of His own divine "Sonshine," He has enlightened and established you. He is about to unveil a new realm of glory in your life.

> The Master has created a masterpiece in you.

Not that I have already obtained all this, or have already been made perfect, but I press on to take hold of that for which Christ Jesus took hold of me. Philippians 3:12 (NIV)

The obscure side of a struggle is the awesome wrestling match many people have with success. First success is given only at the end of great struggle. If it were easy, anybody could do it. Success is success only because it relates to struggle. How can you have victory without conflict? To receive something without struggle lessens its personal value. Success is the reward that God gives to the diligent who, through perseverance, obtain the promise. There is no way to receive what God has for your life without fighting the obstacles and challenges that block your way to conquest. In fact, people who procrastinate do so because they are desperately trying to find a way to reach the goal without going through the struggle.

When I was a youngster, we kids used to go into the stores and change the price tags on the items we could not afford. We weren't stealing, we thought, because we did pay something. It just wasn't nearly what the vendor wanted us to pay. I guess we thought we would put the product on sale without the permission of the store manager. I believe many people are trying to do the same thing today in their spiritual life. They are attempting to get a discount on the promises of God. That doesn't work in the Kingdom. Whatever it costs, it costs; there is no swapping the price tags.

You must pay your own way. Your payment helps you to appreciate the blessings when they come because you know the expense. You will not easily jeopardize the welfare of something not easily attained.

The zeal it takes to be effective at accomplishing a goal ushers you up the steps of life. As you journey up the steps, it becomes increasingly difficult to be successful without others finding you offensive. Some people will find your success offensive, whether or not you are arrogant. They are offended at what God does for you.

> The zeal it takes to be effective at accomplishing a goal ushers you up the steps of life.

And the Lord said unto Cain, Why art thou wroth? and why is thy countenance fallen? If thou doest well, shalt thou not be accepted? and if thou doest not well, sin lieth at the door....Genesis 4:6-7

Some people...are offended at what God does for you. I call those people "Cain's children." Cain's children, like their father, will murder you because you have God's favor. Watch out for them. They will not rejoice with you. They can't be glad for you because somehow they feel your success came at their expense. They foolishly believe that you have their blessing. No diplomacy can calm a jealous heart. They don't want to pay what you paid, but they want to have what you have.

It is amazing the relationships that can be lost as you travel upward. As long as you're in the day of small beginnings, you are acceptable. If you accelerate into new dimensions, however, cynicism eats at the fibers of their conversations and in their hearts....Your enemy will not wound you because he is too far way. In order to be a good Judas, he must be at the table with the victim of his betrayal! Who sits at your table?

Imagine Jesus, at the height of His ministerial career, sitting at the table with John, the beloved, on one side and Judas, the betrayer, on the other. The problem is in discerning which one is which. One of them is close enough to lay his head on your breast. The other has enough access to you to betray you with a kiss. They are both intimate, but one is lethal....Keep your affections on the Giver and not the gifts. "Lord, help us to keep our eyes on the things that will not change."...

How many times have you prayed for a blessing? Then, when you received it, you realized there were strings attached that you didn't originally consider? To be honest, being blessed is hard work. Everything God gives you requires maintenance. God gave man the Garden, but the man still had to dress it. There is a "down" side to every blessing. That is why Jesus said, "No man builds without counting the cost" (see Luke 14:28-30). You must ask yourself if you are willing to pay the price to get the blessing.

> Being blessed is hard work. Everything God gives you requires maintenance.

For the Lord loves the just and will not forsake His faithful ones. They will be protected forever, but the offspring of the wicked will be cut off. Psalm 37:28 (NIV)

There is awesome power in women. God has chosen that women serve as the vehicles through which entry is made into this world. He has shared His creativity with women. Women are strong and willing to nurture others.

In spite of this, millions of women continually suffer emotional, physical, and spiritual strain. The enemy has attempted to destroy God's vehicle of creativity.

You may be one of those who suffer. Perhaps you sit and wonder whether life will ever be normal for you. Maybe you feel like your circumstance has made you different from other women. You feel like you are alone, with no one to help you find healing.

It could be that your emotional strain comes from having been abused. Others have taken advantage of you and used you in the most horrible and depraved ways. You are left feeling used and dirty. How could anyone want someone who has been abused? Nevertheless, you are wanted. God wants you, and God's people want you.

Mistakes made early in life impact the rest of our lives. Some become involved sexually without the commitment of marriage. Maybe you believed him when he told you that he loved you. Perhaps you really did think that yielding would show your true love. Or, maybe, you simply wanted to have a good time without thinking about the consequences. You too feel less than normal.

> You are wanted. God wants you, and God's people want you.

His lord said unto him, Well done, good and faithful servant; thou hast been faithful over a few things, I will make thee ruler over many things: enter thou into the joy of thy lord. Matthew 25:23

You must ask yourself if you are willing to pay the price to get the blessing. Another question people seldom ask themselves is whether they are willing to endure the criticism and the ridicule that come with success.

With these questions we have already weeded out half the people who say they want something from the Lord. We have weeded out all the women who say they want a husband and children but don't want to cook, care, or clean. We have weeded out all the men who say they want a wife but don't want to love, provide, and nourish! Most people are in love with the image of success, but they haven't contemplated the reality of possessing the blessing. It is a good thing God doesn't give us everything we ask for because we want some things simply because they look good in someone else's life. The truth is, we are not ready for those things and it would probably kill us to receive what we are not prepared to maintain....

So you're whimsically toying with the idea of exercising your ability to receive a blessing? This is a good place to start. I believe that God starts His children out with what they have to teach consistency on the level they are on. There must be an inner growth in your ability to withstand the struggles that accompany the things you have. I am so glad that God allowed me to go through the pain-ridden days of stress and rejection early in my life. I found out that if you really want to pursue your dream, there is a place in God whereby you build up an immunity to the adversity of success. It is simply a matter of survival. Either you become immune to the criticism and confusing pressures and isolation, or you go absolutely stark raving, mouth-foaming mad!

> There is a place in God whereby you build up an immunity to the adversity of success.

All things are yours...the world or life or death or the present or the future—all are yours, and you are of Christ, and Christ is of God. 1 Corinthians 3:21b-23 (NIV)

God has determined your need. He looked down from Heaven and saw your pain and guilt. He evaluated the situation and decided that you needed a Redeemer. You need Someone to reach down and lift you. He saw that you needed to recognize how important you are. It is impossible to know all that was in the mind of God when He looked down on broken humanity, but we know He looked past our broken hearts, wounded histories, and our tendency to sin, and saw our need.

He met that need through Jesus Christ. Jesus took your abuse on Himself on the cross of Calvary. He paid for your shame. He made a way for you to be clean again. He took your indiscretions and sins upon Himself and died in your place. He saw your desire to please others and feel good. Thus, He took all your sinful desires and crucified them on the cross.

When you accept Him, you become clean and holy. You are made pure. Don't think you were alone, though; everyone struggles with the same kinds of sins as you, whether they show it on the outside or not.

The abused little girl with all her wounds was healed by the stripes of Jesus (see Isa. 53:5). The sins of the woman who wanted to fulfill her lusts were crucified on the cross with Him (see Gal. 2:20). The past is paid for. The wounds may leave scars, but the scars are only there to remind us that we are human. Everyone has scars.

God recognizes the possibility of what you can become. He has a plan. He sees your potential. He also knows that your potential has been bound by your history. Your suffering made you into a different woman from the one He originally intended you to be. The circumstances of life shaped your way of thinking. The responses you made to those circumstances often kept you from living up to your potential.

You need Someone to reach down and lift you.

For in the time of trouble He shall hide me in His pavilion: in the secret of His tabernacle shall He hide me; He shall set me up upon a rock. Psalm 27:5

If you are always weeping over rejection and misunderstanding, if you're always upset over who doesn't accept you into their circles anymore, you may be suffering from an immunity deficiency syndrome. You waste precious time of communion when you ask God to change the minds of people. It is not the people or the pressure that must change, it is you. In order to survive the stresses of success, you must build up an immunity to those things that won't change. Thank God that He provides elasticity for us. Remember, you can't switch price tags just because you don't like the price. My constant prayer is, "Lord, change me until this doesn't hurt anymore." I am like David—I am forever praying my way into the secret place. The secret place in the king's court was called a pavilion. There you are insulated from the enemy. If you could make it to the secret place, all hell could break loose outside, but it would not matter to you, for in the secret place is peace. If you want to accomplish much, if you intend to survive Cain's hateful children, then you need to get in the secret place and stay there! …

What a place of solace God has for the weary heart who is bombarded with the criticism of cynical people and the pressures to perform. I often think of how many times I allowed to overwhelm me things that really didn't make any difference. In retrospect, half of the things I was praying about should have been dismissed as trivialities. Maturity is sweet relief for the person who hasn't yet learned how to survive the blessings God has given them. I know that sounds strange, but many people don't survive their own success. Notoriety comes and goes, but when it is over you want to still be around. Many people lose their own identities in the excitement of the moment. When the excitement ebbs, as it always does, they have lost sight of the more important issues of self, home, and family!

> ℐn order to survive the stresses of success, you must build up an immunity to those things that won't change.

...but the people that do know their God shall be strong, and do exploits. Daniel 11:32b

God knows that there is a Sarah, a Rahab, a woman at the well, a Ruth, or even a Mary in you. Hidden inside of you is a great woman who can do great exploits in His name. He wants that woman to be set free. He wants the potential within you to be unleashed so you can become the person you were created to be.

There is only one way to reach that potential. He is calling you. He will spiritually stir your heart and let you know that He is moving in your life, if you will only respond to His call.

The power to unleash you is in your faith. Dare to believe that He will do what He said He would do. Shift your confidence from your own weaknesses to His power. Trust in Him rather than in yourself. Anyone who comes to Christ will find deliverance and healing. He will soothe your wounds. He will comfort you in your desperate moments. He will raise you up.

Believe that He paid the price for your sin and guilt. Believe that He has washed you and made you clean. Believe that He will satisfy every need created by your history. Have faith that He will reward you when you call on Him and it shall be done.

You have nothing to lose, and everything to gain. Jesus will straighten the crooked places in your heart and make you completely whole. When you allow Him access to every area of your life, you will never be the same broken person again.

Therefore, if anyone is in Christ [s]he is a new creation; the old has gone, the new has come! (2 Corinthians 5:17 NIV)

Hidden inside of you is a great woman who can do great exploits in His name.

For where you have envy and selfish ambition, there you find disorder and every evil practice. James 3:16 (NIV)

Many people lose their own identities in the excitement of the moment. When the excitement ebbs, as it always does, they have lost sight of the more important issues of self, home, and family!

Another issue is your change in values as you progress. Hopefully your morality does not change, but your sense of what is and is not acceptable should. For example, consider how differently you feel now as opposed to how you felt when you were younger. When I was younger, something six or eight blocks away was right around the corner. Today I can still walk as far as I did then, I am just not sure that I want to. In the same way, luxuries become necessities once you become accustomed to them. Once you are exposed to certain things, it is difficult to go back to what other people might consider normal. If that's not true, then why don't you stir cake batter with a spoon like my mother did when I was small? I can still see her arm beating and beating the butter into the sugar. Who wants to do that now?

Why don't people wash their clothes on a washboard like my grandmother did? She used to boil the white clothes in a pot and then hang them in the sun. As for bleach, what was that? When the microwave was first introduced, consumers were afraid of it. Now you can't imagine not having one. My point should be obvious. Once you become accustomed to any life style, it is hard to go back to what you once thought was sufficient. To add to the complexity of this issue, when you move into a different place in your life, you are still surrounded by people in the other stage. Now you must deal with envy and criticism. Many people suffer inside because they are surrounded by others who live where they were and not where they are. These are the same types of people who called Christ the carpenter's son (see Matt. 13:55).

> *Many people suffer inside because they are surrounded by others who live where they were and not where they are.*

Yet the Lord will command His lovingkindness in the daytime, and in the night His song shall be with me, and my prayer unto the God of my life. Psalm 42:8

While others sleep, there are those of us who walk the floor as a mother with a suckling child. While others enter into the bliss of calmness and lie in the warmth of peaceful beds, there are those who have a conversation where there are no ears to hear. There are those who find no solace in ordinary things in the middle of the night. They have a restlessness, almost an anticipation, that something is about to happen.

Rising like smoke from a chimney, thoughts float and ascend into the conscious mind with all the grace of a ballerina. Who can log the moment when thought becomes prayer? Sometimes it changes in the middle of a sentence. In the stillness of the night, these nightwalkers move across their rooms and stare blankly out of their windows into the dark nothingness of night. They look at something beyond vision. They speak the inaudible to the Intangible, birthing a prayer—fleeting vaporous thoughts whose pattern defies grammar. Oratorical nightmares, they are just the feeble cries of a heart whose conflict has pushed the head to bow in humble submission to One greater than itself.

Understand that real prayer was not made for human ears. If you have a problem that can be easily prayed through in public, then it is not a problem. When we earnestly pray, we are surprised at how inner feelings we didn't even know we had come to the surface. In that regard, prayer is a nausea of the mind. It brings up the unresolved past that swirls around and around inside us.

Who of us would want others to hear us as we release our inner groanings before the throne? Religion and its images do not relieve the heart of its brokenness. There is much more involved here than the pious sputterings of religious refinement. This is a midnight cry for divine assistance! Often what we convey around others is more like a plastic-covered superficial replica of what real prayer is all about. It is a dressed-up, Sunday-go-to-meeting counterfeit that is impressive, but completely inconsequential!

> *Understand that real prayer was not made for human ears.*

For jealousy is the rage of a man: therefore he will not spare in the day of vengeance. He will not regard any ransom; neither will he rest content, though thou givest many gifts. Proverbs 6:34-35

Dear friend, as painful as it is to be criticized by those you are in covenant with, it is far worse to give up the course that God has for you just for their acceptance. In short, as much as you need to be affirmed and understood, at some point you must ask yourself, "How much am I willing to lose in order to be accepted?" If the truth were told, people do not always want to see you move on—especially if they perceive you as moving more rapidly than they are. Can you endure the pressure they will put on you to come down? Or will you be like Nehemiah, who said, "I am doing a great work, so that I cannot come down" (Neh. 6:3b). Exaltation may cost you a degree of acceptance and reward you with isolation. In fact, God may be grooming you right now for a new level by exposing you to opposition and criticism. He may be building up your immunity so when the greater blessing comes, you won't break.

Successful people tend to be passionate people. These are people who have intense desire. I admit there are many passionate people who are not successful. But I didn't say that passionate people are successful; I said that successful people tend to be passionate. You can be passionate and not be successful. Passion, basically, is raw power. If it is not harnessed and focused for a goal, it becomes an animalistic force. But if you can focus passion for a divine purpose, you will be successful. Some people never use their desire in a positive way. Instead of harnessing it and allowing it to become the force they use to overcome hindrances, it becomes a source of frustration and cynicism. Success only comes to a person who is committed to a cause or has a passion to achieve. The crux of the matter basically is this: "How bad do you want to be blessed?"

> *Success only comes to a person who is committed to a cause or has a passion to achieve.*

Yet the Lord will command His lovingkindness in the daytime, and in the night His song shall be with me, and my prayer unto the God of my life. Psalm 42:8

Heaven sees the hands that tightly clasp their nice gleaming Bibles in leather cases. Heaven sees the 14-karat gold necklaces draped carefully across the napes of necks held high in the glistening sunlight on Sunday morning. Only Heaven can see the liturgical order of pious hearts whose heads have contrived a method that seems spiritually edifying. The grandstands of Heaven behold the attempts of the righteous at piety and honor. How impressive are our sanctuaries—each more glamorous than the other. How stately are the auditoriums and how distinguished are the people who rush in to fill them for a punctual hour of spiritual rhetoric!

There is nothing quite comparable to the pomp and circumstance of a well-orchestrated service. Never before in the history of the New Testament Church has there been such an emphasis placed on facilities and sanctuaries. As glamorous as the old Catholic churches were in earlier years, they can't even compare to these space age monuments, these brass and glass superstructures as picturesque as the rocky crest of mountain ridges. Our jet-set, microwave age has produced some elaborate and intricately designed places of worship. We have manned them with people displaying the finest of administrative, musical, and oratorical abilities. Our cabinets are filled with resumés, statistics, and ledgers. We have arrived!

Please don't misunderstand me. I am neither commending nor criticizing these advances. My purpose is to point out the inconsistency that blares in my heart like a trumpet. I have heard the swelling tones of well-orchestrated, carefully implemented musical and theatrical presentations. However, I am often distracted by the bleating of the sheep.

Can you hear the hollow moans of sheep who bleed behind the stained glass and upon the padded pew? I do not blame our success as the cause for their pain; neither do I suggest that the absence of ornateness would cure the ills of our society. I can't help but wonder, though, if we have majored on the minor and consequently minored on the major!

> *Can you hear the hollow moans of sheep who bleed behind the stained glass and upon the padded pew?*

Hope deferred maketh the heart sick: but when the desire cometh, it is a tree of life.
Proverbs 13:12

How strong is your desire for accomplishment in your life? It takes more than a mere whimsical musing over a speculative end. It takes floor-walking, devil-stomping, anointed tenacity to overcome the limitations that are always surrounding what you want to do for your God, yourself, and your family!...Desire is kindled in the furnace of need—an unfulfilled need. It is a need that refuses to be placated and a need that will not be silent. Any man will tell you that where there is no desire, there is no passion. Where there is no passion, there is no potency. Without desire, you are basically impotent!

Desire gives you the drive you need to produce. Even natural reproduction is an impossibility to a person who is devoid of passion and desire. Many people who set out to accomplish goals are so easily discouraged or intimidated by their own anxieties that they relinquish their right to fight for their dreams. However, if there is a tenacious burning desire in the pit of your stomach, you become very difficult to discourage. How many cold nights I have warmed my cold feet by the fires of my innermost desire to complete a goal for my life. No one knows how hot the embers glow beneath the ashes of adversity.

Having pastored in the coal fields of West Virginia, I know about wood and coal stoves. You can bank the fire by placing ashes all around it. Then it will not burn out as rapidly and will last through the night. In the frosty chill of the morning you do not need to rebuild the fire, for beneath the ashes lie crimson embers waiting to be stirred. These embers explode into a fire when they are stirred correctly. Many people have gone through situations that banked their fire. The fire isn't dead, but its burning is not as brilliant as it once was. I am glad that if you have an inner desire to survive or succeed, then you only need a stirring for the embers of passion to ignite in your life.

> *Desire gives you the drive you need to produce.*

Hear my prayer, O Lord, and give ear unto my cry; hold not Thy peace at my tears: for I am a stranger with Thee, and a sojourner, as all my fathers were. Psalm 39:12

Now understand, *nothing fuels prayer like need*. Neither the tranquil mood of a calming organ nor a dimly lit room with hallowed walls can promote the power of prayer like the aching of a heart that says, "I need Thee every hour." The presence of need will produce the power of prayer. Even the agnostic will make a feeble attempt at prayer in the crisis of a moment. The alcoholic who staggers toward a car he knows he shouldn't drive will, before the night is over, find himself attempting to dial the number of Heaven and sputter in slurred speech a fleeting prayer in the presence of near-mishap and malady.

Prayer is man's confession, "I do not have it all." Prayer is man admitting to himself that, in spite of his architectural designs and his scientific accomplishments, he needs a higher power. Prayer is the humbling experience of the most arrogant mind confessing, "There are still some things I cannot resolve."

The presence of prayer is, in itself, the birthplace of praise. Prayer is man acknowledging the sovereign authority of a God "who can!" You ask, "Can what?" God can do whatever He wants to do, whenever He wants to do it. What a subliminal solace to know the sovereignty of God!…

Each of us must have the curiosity and the inner thirst to move beyond our images into our realities. It is difficult, sometimes even painful, to face the truth about our circumstances and then possess the courage to ask for *God's best* for our lives. If prayer is to be meaningful, it cannot be fictitious. It must be born out of the pantings of a heart that can admit its need. If we refrain from airing our particular dilemmas with anyone else, at least we must be honest enough to come before God with an open heart and a willing mind to receive the "whatsoevers" that He promised to the "whosoevers" in His Word!

> Prayer is man's confession, "I do not have it all."

But made Himself of no reputation, and took upon Him the form of a servant, and was made in the likeness of men. Philippians 2:7

And the angel said unto her, Fear not, Mary: for thou hast found favor with God. And, behold, thou shalt conceive in thy womb, and bring forth a son, and shalt call His name JESUS (Luke 1:30-31).

Mary, the mother of Jesus, had the baby, but the angel was sent from the Father to give the name. She couldn't name Him because she didn't fully understand His destiny. Don't allow people who don't understand your destiny to name you. They also probably whispered that Jesus was the illegitimate child of Joseph. Maybe there has been some nasty little rumor out on you too. Rumors smear the reputation and defame the character of many innocent people. However, none lived with any better moral character than Jesus—and they still assaulted His reputation. Just be sure the rumors are false or in the past and keep on living. I often say, "You can't help where you've been, but you can help where you're going."

And it came to pass in those days, that Jesus came from Nazareth of Galilee, and was baptized of John in Jordan. And straightway coming up out of the water, He saw the heavens opened, and the Spirit like a dove descending upon Him: and there came a voice from heaven, saying, Thou art My beloved Son, in whom I am well pleased (Mark 1:9-11).

In the chilly river of Jordan, with mud between His toes, it was the voice of the Father that declared the identity of Christ. His ministry could not begin until the Father laid hands upon Him by endorsing Him in the midst of the crowd. It is so important that we as sons receive the blessing of our spiritual fathers. I know countless preachers who ran away from their spiritual homes without their fathers' blessings and, even after many years, are still in a turmoil. If Jesus needed His Father's blessing, how much more do you and I? We should not seek to endorse ourselves.

> *Y*e should not seek to endorse ourselves.

And He was there in the wilderness forty days, tempted of Satan; and was with the wild beasts; and the angels ministered unto Him. Mark 1:13

I remember reading in the Gospels how Jesus needed ministry after being savagely attacked by the enemy at a very vulnerable moment. After 40 days of fasting, He was hungry (see Matt. 4:2; Luke 4:2). Satan makes his attack when you are hungry. Hunger is a *legitimate need* that satan offers to satisfy in a perverted way. The extreme test of faith is to stand fast when you have a legitimate need you could satisfy in an illegitimate way.

Christ seemed to have no problem rebuking the enemy who came against Him. It was after the victory was won that He needed the ministry of angels to continue His vision. There are some people who have not been released from old trials yet because they will not allow God to heal them through the angels of ministry He has chosen to use. Some have been through so much that they simply don't trust anymore. They need *someone*, but they don't trust *anyone*.

What impresses me the most is that in order for Christ to receive the ministry of angels, He had to allow the lesser (the angels) to minister to the greater (the Christ). He allowed the angels whom He created, the same angels He commanded as Captain of the host, to minister to Him. My friend, when pain peaks, you don't care who God uses! You just want to be healed and blessed. If you were in an automobile accident and you needed help, you wouldn't care who the paramedics were. Their education, denomination, or ethnic background would mean nothing to you because of the enormity of your need.

Whenever we seek His will, we must be prepared to receive His way! Many times it is not the will of God that causes us to struggle as much as it is the *way* in which He accomplishes His will. However, if the winds beat fiercely enough and if the rains plummet down with enough thunderous force, then we are stripped by the struggle and brought to a place of open, naked prayer.

> Whenever we seek His will, we must be prepared to receive His way!

I know thy works, that thou art neither cold nor hot: I would thou wert cold or hot. So then because thou art lukewarm, and neither cold nor hot, I will spue thee out of My mouth. Revelation 3:15-16

I love to surround myself with people who can stir up the fire in me. Some people in the Body of Christ know just what to say to ignite the very fire in you. However, no one can ignite in you what you do not possess! If the cold winds of opposition have banked the fire and your dream is dying down, I challenge you to rekindle your desire to achieve whatever God has called you to do. Don't lose your fire. You need that continued spark for excellence to overcome all the blight of being ostracized.

Fire manifests itself in two ways. First, it gives light....Second, fire gives heat....Every man and woman of God must also remember that fire needs fuel. Feed the fire. Feed it with the words of people who motivate you. Feed it with vision and purpose. When stress comes, fan the flames. Gather the wood. Pour gasoline if you have to, but don't let it die!

Sometimes just seeing God bless someone else gives you the fortitude to put a demand on the promise that God has given you. I don't mean envy, but a strong provocation to receive. Look at the situation of Hannah, Elkanah's wife, in First Samuel 1. She wanted to have a child. In order to stir up Hannah, God used a girl named Peninnah who was married to the same man but able to bear children. The more Hannah saw Peninnah have children, the more she desired her own. Peninnah provoked Hannah; she stirred Hannah's embers. She made Hannah pray. It wasn't that Hannah got jealous and didn't want to see Peninnah be blessed. She didn't begrudge the other woman her blessing. She just wanted her own. If seeing others blessed makes you want to sabotage their success, then you will not be fruitful. I have learned how to rejoice over the blessings of my brother and realize that the same God who blessed him can bless me also. Other people's blessings ought to challenge you to see that it can be done.

> **Rekindle your desire to achieve whatever God has called you to do.**

There is a level of sickness where a suffering victim's hospital gown rides up on her body. Her hair has fallen down, and her body emits an odor. This patient knows there is someone in the room, but she just doesn't care anymore.

We need to get to the point where we lose our self-consciousness because we are sick and tired of allowing the enemy to subdue what God has given to us. We need to get to the point where *all we want is to get well*, the point where "getting well" is the only thing that really matters. Why? Stripped down somewhere below our image and our name, even beyond the opinions of others, there is a power that boggles the mind. It may just be that you can't get what you need from the Lord because you are too cognizant of people and too oblivious to the presence of God.

There is a place of *naked prayer* that we occasionally read about in the Word of God. Hannah came to the Lord in the temple and poured out her bitterness before the Lord (see 1 Sam. 1:12-18). There was so much locked up in her that when she began to empty herself out, she appeared drunk—even to the aristocracy of the church. God is raising up some people who will even blow the minds of religious people!

Radical Christians are coming to the forefront. These people have nothing to lose. Like Christ, they have been stripped on the cross and are speaking the truth under the threat of nails and spears…"Let anyone gamble for my clothes who wants them! I have learned the power of transparency and the strength of being backed in a corner."

Besides all this, we learn faith when our options diminish.…Who needs faith for the parting of the sea when there are bridges standing strong and erect? Faith is reserved for those times when there are no options, when "push" has collided with "shove"! There is nothing we can do but be crushed by the inevitable—or look unto the Invisible to do the impossible! Your crisis is a privilege because God has given you an opportunity to experience a deeper realm of miracle-working power!

> *T*here is nothing we can do but be crushed by the inevitable—or look unto the Invisible to do the impossible!

...For unto whomsoever much is given, of him shall be much required: and to whom men have committed much, of him they will ask the more. Luke 12:48

$\mathcal{S}$uccess cannot be defined in generalities; it can be defined only according to individual purpose and divine direction. If you don't understand this concept, you can have great riches or fame and still be unsuccessful. You would be surprised at how many highly anointed people are tormented by a need to evaluate themselves in the light of another's calling. Your assignment is to dig for your own gold. Just cultivate what the Lord has given to you. It's simple: Find out what you have to work with, and then work it, work it, work it!

I am always concerned that Christians not manipulate each other by trying to get people to worship their talents rather than God's purpose for their lives. How can any person know you well enough to discern whether you are successful, other than the God who created you? In short, there is no way to define success without examining purpose. What did the inventor have in mind when he made the machine? That is the first question. The second question asks, "Did it accomplish the purpose it was created to perform?" It doesn't matter what else it did; if it didn't satisfy the mandate of its creator, it is unsuccessful. When people other than the Creator define success, it becomes idolatry.

There are no ifs, ands, or buts; the greater the blessing, the more the responsibility. It is expensive to be blessed. Everyone can't handle the success. Some may choose tranquility over notoriety. They don't like criticism and they abhor pressure. But if you are the kind of person who desperately needs to attain the hope of his calling, then go for it. Some people will never be satisfied with sitting on the bench cheering for others who paid the price to play the game. Locked within them is an inner ambitious intrigue not predicated on jealousy or intimidation. It is built upon an inner need to unlock a predestined purpose. For them, it does not matter. Inflationary times may escalate the price of their dreams, but whatever the price, they are compelled, drawn, and almost driven toward a hope.

> $\mathcal{T}$here are no ifs, ands, or buts; the greater the blessing, the more the responsibility.

Is any among you afflicted? let him pray. Is any merry? let him sing psalms. Is any sick among you? let him call for the elders of the church; and let them pray over him, anointing him with oil in the name of the Lord: and the prayer of faith shall save the sick, and the Lord shall raise him up; and if he have committed sins, they shall be forgiven him. Confess your faults one to another, and pray one for another, that ye may be healed.... James 5:13-16

If you are going through a test and all your options are closing in without any way out, then you should get up and start shouting! *You have been chosen for a miracle.* Faith must have the incubator of impossibility to exhibit its illustrious ability....There is a certain tightness needed to cause faith to be secreted....There is something good in you, and God knows how to get it out.

Now the pressure is mounting. The devil wants you to cry "Uncle!" He is squeezing you every way he can, but he is a liar. Let's discard what we don't need so we can activate what we do need.

Let us lay aside every sin that would so easily beset us. Now that we took that off, let's forgive everyone who ever hurt us or disappointed us. Let's just dismiss it. That's right— *throw the case out of court*. There is to be no more deliberating over the acts of men. We are about to see an act of God!

Slip the spirit of heaviness off your shoulders. That old depression is weighing you down! But don't put on the garment of praise just yet. That is what is wrong today—we have more shouters than we do prayers. Save the garment of praise, though; you're going to need it soon. Now that you are stripped to nothing but prayer, let your request be made known unto God....

Let the cool waters of His Word rinse the residue from your past. The Word is cascading down upon you in torrents. Spread before Him every issue. He can't cleanse what you will not expose. Bathe your mind in the streams of His mercy....

This kind of renewal can only occur in the heart of someone who has been through enough to open his heart, to close up his past, to stand in the rain of His grace, and to tell the next generation the truth. Tell them that the only way you can dress up for God is to lie before Him as a naked offering, a living sacrifice offered up at the altar in *naked prayer*!

> Tell them that the only way you can dress up for God is to lie before Him as a naked offering, a living sacrifice offered up at the altar in *naked prayer*!

GIVE THE RACE YOUR ALL

Know ye not that they which run in a race run all, but one receiveth the prize? So run, that ye may obtain. 1 Corinthians 9:24

Long distance runners make long, steady strides and their emphasis is on endurance, not speed. They take their laps and stretch their limitations, giving themselves over to committing their strength to a goal....As they near the finish line, there is a final burst of energy that kicks in like the final cylinders in an engine. It is the last lap; there are no excuses; it's now or never. Now they go for broke! At least once, before they roll you in on a slab and put a name tag on your cold stiff toe, you owe it to your God and to yourself to experience in some area in your life that last-lap feeling of giving your all....

There are some truths I would like to underscore. First, huge stress comes with success in any area. Before you ask for the house, be sure you have counted up the cost. If, after you calculate the rejection, controversy, criticism, and isolation, you still want it, then realize that you cannot stand the pain of a cross unless you have before you something more important than the pain you endure in the process.

For many of us there is no option....In spite of bruises, cuts, and scrapes, there is a racing pulse and a pounding heart that exist in the chest of someone who has made up his mind, "I will go!"

The question is universal but the answer is totally individual. Can *you* stand to be blessed? If you answer yes, then I want to tell you this: The only way to be blessed is to stand! When you can't seem to put one foot in front of the other, stand. When days come that challenge your destiny, just stand. Realize that there has never been a day that lasted forever. You can't afford to crumple onto your knees like a weak, whimpering lily blown over by a windstorm. Bite your lip, taste your tears, but stand on what God showed you in the night until it happens in the light.

> There is a racing pulse and a pounding heart that exist in the chest of someone who has made up his mind, "I will go!"

$\mathcal{N}$OTES

NOTES

Notes

Notes

$\mathcal{N}$OTES

Healing, Blessings, and Freedom

NOTES

NOTES

Notes

Healing, Blessings, and Freedom

Notes

Notes

NOTES

Notes

Notes

NOTES

Additional copies of this book and other
book titles from DESTINY IMAGE are
available at your local bookstore.

For a bookstore near you, call 1-800-722-6774.

Send a request for a catalog to:

Destiny Image® Publishers, Inc.
P.O. Box 310
Shippensburg, PA 17257-0310

*"Speaking to the Purposes of God for This
Generation and for the Generations to Come"*

**For a complete list of our titles,
visit us at www.destinyimage.com**